ELEUSIS

AND THE ELEUSINIAN MYSTERIES

ELEUSIS

AND THE
ELEUSINIAN MYSTERIES

BY GEORGE E. MYLONAS

PRINCETON, NEW JERSEY

PRINCETON UNIVERSITY PRESS

TO

ALEX

THE excavations conducted at Eleusis under the auspices of the Archaeological Society of Athens, Greece, in the last thirty years were so fruitful that the accounts of the Sanctuary published thus far have to be drastically revised. With the complete clearing of the Sanctuary area, the publication of the Temenos of Demeter is now possible. This long and complicated task has already been started by the scholars who collaborated in the excavation, but completion is still far off. In the belief that in the meanwhile there is urgent need of a general account of the Sanctuary and the Eleusinian cult for the student and the interested nonspecialist, scholar and layman alike, I have attempted the publication of the present volume. Years ago Konstantinos Kourouniotes and I planned the publication of such a book in English. I am happy to have been able to fulfill his wish, although I have greatly missed his generous advice and wise direction. It is strange indeed that the protagonists in the excavations of Eleusis were not destined to undertake the final publication and to enjoy the benefit of their labors and discoveries. The reader, I hope, in the pages that follow will be able to find out the greatness of their work and will appreciate their immense contribution to the uncovering and study of one of the most difficult, as well as one of the most renowned, sites of the pagan Hellenic world.

To the Archaeological Society of Athens, its Council, and its General Secretary Professor A. K. Orlandos I am deeply grateful for the privilege of working at Eleusis and for their unfailing support of that work. I am especially grateful to the late George P. Oikonomos, the unforgettable friend and mentor of all archaeological endeavor in Greece, for his interest, help, and advice in the early years of my efforts. Heartfelt thanks are due to my collaborators at Eleusis, Dr. John N. Travlos and John Threpsiades, for their collaboration and understanding. To Dr. Travlos I am especially grateful for preparing the plans for this volume, for reading my manuscript, for our frequent discussions and valuable suggestions. I want to acknowledge my deep gratitude to Ethan A. H. Shepley, Chancellor of Washington University, to Vice Chancellor

Carl Tolman, to Dean Thomas S. Hall, and Dean Lewis E. Hahn for their interest in my work, their encouragement, and the leaves of absence from the University which enabled me to pursue my research. That research was made possible by the Institute for Advanced Study, the John Simon Guggenheim Foundation, and the American Philosophical Society, whose grants enabled me to go to Greece, to collect, check, and record my material and to spend a term in the hospitable and inspiring atmosphere of the Institute in 1959. To these Foundations and Institutions I want to express my deep appreciation and especially to Dr. Robert Oppenheimer, Dr. Benjamin D. Meritt, and Dr. Homer A. Thompson.

To the many St. Louisans who helped financially the work of excavation, I am grateful. To name them all would result in a long list of wonderful friends who unhesitatingly come to my help whenever needed. I must, however, express my gratitude to Mr. and Mrs. Eugene C. McCarthy, Mrs. Mark C. Steinberg, and to Mr. and Mrs. Richard Weil for their continued support and interest. It will be impossible to pass in silence the moving tribute of my former students and present friends on my sixtieth birthday. It contributed much to the strengthening of my faith in the mission of the teacher and in the future of the humanities in our country. Through their chairmen, Mrs. Elliott D. O'Reilly and Dr. Betty Grossman, I extend to them my thanks and wish them Τύχην Ἀγαθὴν in their own endeavors.

I cannot express adequately my gratitude and admiration to my wife, Lella, whose devotion, faith, and dedicated help in times of happiness and in times of deep sorrow prove a pillar of strength and a light of hope that lift and brighten the dark moods of mind and soul. To my fellow-workers in the field, Spyridon Iakovides, T. Leslie Shear, Jr., Nike Mylonas, Ione Mylonas Shear, Alexander Cambitoglu, and Angelike Andreiomenou, I am indebted for faithful collaboration and cheerful help. My heartfelt thanks are extended to my laborers and especially to my foreman John Karametros, whose sincere efforts made possible exciting periods of discovery and successful achievement of an intricate task. Thanks are due to my colleague Dr. Lucy T. Shoe for reading the manuscript and for valuable corrections and suggestions. I am indebted, likewise, to Miss Elly Travlou, Miss Tina Karayianni, and Miss

Elizabeth Milburn for their help, and to Mr. and Mrs. N. Tombazis for many of the photographs published in this volume; to Mr. Al. Papaeliopoulos for the vignette on the title-page and to my colleague Professor A. K. Orlandos for his permission to publish again his drawing of the temple of Artemis Propylaia.

To the Princeton University Press, its Director, Herbert S. Bailey, Jr., and especially its Fine Arts Editor, Harriet Anderson, I am grateful for their patience, advice, corrections and care expended in the preparation and publication of this volume. I am thankful, likewise, to the Meriden Gravure Company and its Manager, Harold Hugo, for excellent reproduction of my photographs and drawings.

The task of transliteration is a difficult one, and for the inconsistencies that derive from our attempt to adhere as closely as possible to the Greek forms we ask the reader's indulgence.

The volume is lovingly dedicated to the memory of a beloved son, whose untimely death has deprived the humanities of a faithful believer and the community of mortals of a dedicated worker. We would like to believe with Menander that ὅν οἱ θεοὶ φιλοῦσιν ἀποθνῄσκει νέος.

G. E. M.

Washington University
Saint Louis, Missouri

CONTENTS

Destruction of the Telesterion by the Persians, 88.
Altars of the Goddesses, 90. The Peisistratean Peribolos
and its Gates, 91.

City and Sanctuary, 96: The "Kallichoron" Well, 97.
The Temple of Plouton, 99. The Inner Gate and the
Hollow Road, 100. The Successor to the Sacred House,
101. Orientation of the Sanctuary toward Athens, 103

AA	*Archäologischer Anzeiger*
ArchRW	*Archiv für Religionswissenschaft*
AJA	*American Journal of Archaeology*
AM	*Athenische Mitteilungen*
Athens Yearbook	Ἐπιστημονικὴ Ἐπετηρὶς τῆς Φιλοσοφικῆς Σχολῆς τοῦ Πανεπιστημίου Ἀθηνῶν
BCH	*Bulletin de correspondance hellénique*
BSA	*Annual of the British School of Archaeology at Athens*
CIA	*Corpus Inscriptionum Atticarum*
CIG	*Corpus Inscriptionum Graecarum*
CIL	*Corpus Inscriptionum Latinarum*
Deltion	Ἀρχαιολογικὸν Δελτίον
Ephem	Ἀρχαιολογικὴ Ἐφημερίς and Ἐφημερὶς Ἀρχαιολογική
FHG	Müller, *Fragmenta Historicorum Graecorum*
Foucart, *Les Mystères*	Paul Foucart, *Les mystères d'Éleusis,* 1914
Hesperia	*Hesperia,* Journal of the American School of Classical Studies at Athens
Hymn	*Homeric Hymn to Demeter* (Loeb edition, translation H. G. Evelyn-White)
IG	*Inscriptiones Graecae*
Jahrbuch	*Jahrbuch des k. deutschen archäologischen Instituts*
JHS	*Journal of Hellenic Studies*
JIAN	*Journal international d'archéologie numismatique*
JOAI	*Jahreshefte des oesterreichischen archäologischen Instituts*
Kourouniotes, *Guide*	Κ. Κουρουνιώτης, Ἐλευσίς. Ὁδηγὸς τῶν Ἀνασκαφῶν καὶ τοῦ Μουσείου, 1934
Kourouniotes-Travlos, *Telesterion*	Κ. Κουρουνιώτης καὶ Ι. Τραυλός, "Τελεστήριον καὶ ναὸς τῆς Δήμητρος," *Deltion,* 15 (1933-1935), pp. 54-114
Kourouniotes-Travlos, *History of the Eleusinian Telesterion*	Κ. Κουρουνιώτης καὶ Ι. Τραυλός, "Συμβολὴ εἰς τὴν οἰκοδομικὴν ἱστορίαν τοῦ Ἐλευσινιακοῦ Τελεστηρίου," *Deltion,* 16 (1935-36), pp. 1-42

Magnien, *Les mystères*	Magnien, V., *Les mystères d'Éleusis*, 2nd ed., 1938
Mylonas, *Eleusis*	Γ. Μυλωνᾶς, Προϊστορικὴ Ἐλευσίς, 1932
Mylonas, *Hymn*	*The Hymn to Demeter and Her Sanctuary at Eleusis*, 1942
Nilsson, *Religion*	M. P. Nilsson, *Geschichte der Griechischen Religion*, 1955
Noack, *Eleusis*	F. Noack, *Eleusis, die Baugeschichtliche Entwicklung des Heiligtumes*, 1927
Praktika	Πρακτικὰ τῆς ἐν Ἀθήναις Ἀρχαιολογικῆς Ἑταιρείας
Proceedings	*Proceedings of the American Philosophical Society*
RE	Pauly-Wissowa, *Real Encyclopädie der class. Altertumswissenschaft*
REG	*Revue des études Grecques*
RHist	*Revue historique*
RHR	*Revue de l'histoire des religions*
Rev Phil	*Revue de philologie*
RFC	*Rivista di Filologia e d'Istruzione Classica*
RM	*Römische Mitteilungen*
Sylloge[4]	W. F. K. Dittenberger, *Sylloge inscriptionum graecorum*, 4th ed., 1960
Sylloge[2]	W. K. F. Dittenberger, *Sylloge inscriptionum graecorum*, 2nd ed., 1915
Travlos, *Anaktoron*	Ἰ. Ν. Τραυλός, "Τὸ ἀνάκτορον τῆς Ἐλευσῖνος," *Ephem*, 1950-1951, pp. 1-16
Travlos, *Athens*	Ἰ. Ν. Τραυλός, Πολεοδομικὴ ἐξέλιξις τῶν Ἀθηνῶν, 1960

ELEUSIS

AND THE ELEUSINIAN MYSTERIES

CHAPTER I

INTRODUCTION: LEGENDS
AND HISTORY

ELEUSIS lies some fourteen miles west of Athens, by the blue waters of the Aegean and at the extreme end of a pleasant, verdant valley known from time immemorial as the Thriasian Plain (Fig. 1). Today Eleusis is a small industrial town; in antiquity it was one of the most important religious centers of the pagan world. Legends tell us how in the mythological past, some four thousand years ago, a family drama came to a happy end around its craggy hill. To that mythological event Eleusis owes its fame and prosperity. Repeated by bards and playwrights, it gradually became one of the favorite stories of the ancient world.[1]

The story was told in detail for the first time in a long epic poem that has come down to us under the title of the Homeric Hymn to Demeter. Neither the author of this hymn nor the time of its composition is known, but scholars have come more and more to consider it the official story of the Eleusinian traditions, recorded in verse about the end of the seventh century B.C., perhaps around 600 B.C.[2]

---

[1] The story was mentioned for the first time by Hesiod in his *Theogony*, vv. 913-914. Its popularity with Hellenistic and Roman writers is attested by the many poems in which the story was told. For example, Kallimachos uses it in his sixth ode, Nikander in his *Theriaka*, vv. 483-487, Nonnus in his sixth poem. In Ovid we find two complete narratives: *Metamorphoses* V, 341-642, and *Fasti*, IV, vv. 419-619. Cf. Malten in *Hermes*, 1910, 506ff, and R. Foerster, *Der Raub und die Rueckkehr der Persephone*, 1874. English poetry is full of allusions to the story; see for example, Spenser, *Faerie Queene*, I, 1, 37; I, 2, 2; Milton, *Paradise Lost*, IV, 269; Shelley, "Song of Proserpine"; Swinburne, "Hymn to Proserpine," "At Eleusis"; Tennyson, "Demeter and Persephone," etc.

[2] T. W. Allen, W. R. Halliday, and E. E. Sikes, *The Homeric Hymns*, 1936, pp. 111-114. J. Humbert, *Collection des Universités de France*, edition of Hymns, 1936, pp. 38ff. Wilamowitz Moellendorff suggested that the Hymn antedated the sixth century (*Der Glaube der Hellenen*, 1931-1932, II, p. 47). Picard holds that it was written about the middle of the sixth century, *REG*, 40 (1927), p. 350, and *Rev Phil*, 4 (1930), p. 265.

Cf. G. E. Mylonas, *The Hymn to Demeter and Her Sanctuary at Eleusis*, 1942, p. 10, nn. 3-8. Also Noack, *Eleusis*, pp. 45ff. The passages in quotation marks are excerpts from the Hymn.

THE LEGENDARY ARRIVAL OF THE GODDESS

The poem begins with a brief statement of its scope in true epic style: "I begin to sing the fair-haired Demeter, august Goddess—of her and her trim-ankled daughter whom Aidoneus abducted." This Aidoneus is, of course, Plouton, the God and master of the nether world, and the brother of Zeus with whose consent the deed was done. Long ago, when gods and heroes walked in the vales of Greece, Persephone, daughter of Demeter and Zeus, was playing and gathering flowers, "roses and crocuses and beautiful violets, irises also and hyacinths and narcissi," in a "soft meadow," accompanied by the daughters of the Ocean. When she reached out to pick a most marvelous flower, with a hundred blooms and a delicious fragrance, the "wide-pathed earth yawned" and out of it sprang Plouton with his immortal horses. "He caught her up reluctant in his golden car and bore her away lamenting." Her mother, Demeter, heard Persephone's desperate cries; "bitter pain seized her heart, and she rent the covering upon her divine hair with her dear hands; her dark cloak she cast down from both her shoulders and sped, like a wild-bird, over the firm land and yielding sea, seeking her child. . . . For nine days, queenly Deo wandered over the earth with flaming torches in her hands, so grieved that she never tasted ambrosia and the sweet draught of nectar, nor sprinkled her body with water." On the tenth day she learned the truth from Helios. Angered against Zeus, who had consented to this monstrous deed, "she avoided the gathering of the gods and high Olympos, and went to the towns and rich fields of men" in the guise of an old woman. So disguised, she came to Eleusis and sat "near the wayside by the Maiden well, from which the women of the city were accustomed to draw water, in a shady place over which grew an olive shrub." There she was found by the daughters of Keleos, the ruler of Eleusis, who invited her to accept the hospitality of their home.

In the palace, Demeter was received with all honor by Metaneira, the queen of Eleusis, and was made to forget her grief, even though momentarily, and to smile at the quips and jests of Iambe, the old and trusted servant of the queen. Refusing to drink wine, since "it was not lawful for her to drink red wine, she bade them mix meal and water with soft mint," to make a special potion, a kykeon, with which she broke her fast. To her care was entrusted the upbringing of the baby, Demophon, "whom the gods gave" Metaneira in her old age and beyond her hope, "a son much prayed for and most welcome." The child, nursed by the Goddess, grew like some immortal being; "by day fair-crowned Demeter would anoint him with ambrosia . . . and breathe sweetly upon him as she held him in her bosom. . . . But at night she would hide him like a brand in the heart of the fire, unknown to his dear parents." Surprised by Metaneira, who wondered at the marvelous growth of her child and wanted to find out the secret, Demeter disclosed her identity: "Lo! I am much-honored Demeter, the greatest help and cause of joy to the undying Gods and mortal men." Her disclosure was followed by a specific command: "But now, let all the people build me a great temple and an altar below it beneath the citadel and its sheer wall upon a rising hillock above the Kallichoron. And I myself will teach my rites, that thereafter you may reverently perform them and so win the favor of my heart." (vv. 270-274) Straightway, Keleos, the king of Eleusis, "called the countless people to an assembly and bade them build a goodly temple for fair-haired Demeter and an altar upon the rising hillock. And they obeyed him right speedily."

When the temple was completed, Demeter closed herself up in it "apart from all the blessed gods," and caused a "most dreadful and cruel year for mankind over the all-nourishing earth: the ground would not make the seed sprout, for rich-crowned Demeter kept it hid. In the fields the oxen drew many a curved plough in vain, and much white barley was cast upon the land without avail. So she would have destroyed the whole race of men with cruel famine and have robbed them who dwell on Olympos of their glorious right of gifts and sacrifices." The entreaties of the Gods, who came to her temple "one after another" were in vain for "she vowed that she would never set foot on fragrant Olympos nor let fruit spring out of the ground, until she beheld with her eyes her own sweet-faced daughter."

Zeus was forced to compromise and to recall Persephone from the lower world, and Aidoneus, ruler of the dead, had to obey the behest of Zeus and send Persephone to her dark-robed mother. But, while she joyously was preparing for her journey to earth, Plouton "secretly gave her sweet pomegranate seed to eat, taking care for himself that she might not remain continually with august, dark Demeter." Mounted upon the golden chariot of Plouton, drawn by deathless horses and guided by Hermes, Persephone left the dark domain of the shades and once more beheld the glorious light of the Sun. Before her mother's fragrant temple at Eleusis, Hermes at last stopped his fiery horses. "When Demeter saw them, she rushed forth as does a Maenad down some thick-wooded mountain, while Persephone on the other side, when she saw her mother's sweet eyes, left the chariot and horses, and leaped down and ran to her, and falling upon her neck, embraced her." But when her immortal mother asked with anxiety: "My child, tell me, surely you have not tasted any food while you were below . . . for if you have tasted food, you must go back again," Persephone had to confess that she had eaten a few pomegranate seeds. Plouton's precaution gave assurance that Demeter's daughter would spend "a third part of the seasons" every year in the lower world with her husband although she was free to spend the rest of the year in the upper world with her mother and the other Olympian Gods. Their reunion, however, brought them greater joy than the sorrow that was to be experienced at parting, and to that joy they gave themselves and "their hearts had relief from their griefs, while each took and gave back joyousness."

At the invitation of Zeus, the Goddesses returned to Olympos, where they were to spend part of the year together. Before leaving Eleusis, her town, Demeter "straightway made fruit to spring from the rich land, so that the whole wide earth was filled with leaves and flowers. Then, to the kings of Eleusis who deal justice, Triptolemos and Diokles, the horse-driver, and the valiant Eumolpos and Keleos, leader of the people, she showed the conduct of her rites and taught them all her mysteries . . . awful mysteries which no one may in any way transgress or pry into or utter, for deep awe of the Gods checks the voice." And when the bright Goddess had taught them all, she went to Olympos, there to dwell with Zeus.

THE HISTORY OF THE CULT OF DEMETER

In this way the Eleusinian tradition attributed to Demeter herself the introduction of her cult to Eleusis, at the end of a sorrowful experience. Unlike other pagan religious rites, the cult of Demeter and Persephone was not open to the general public, as were the rites of what we may call the state religion, but only to those who were properly initiated through a ritual prescribed by tradition and who had solemnly promised not to divulge the secret rites, which "no one may in any way transgress or pry into or utter." Consequently, the cult came to be known as the Mysteries of Demeter, and since it was held at Eleusis, the Eleusinian Mysteries. A local cult originally, perhaps even a family cult limited to the members of the family or clan, it gradually spread beyond the narrow confines of Eleusis and the Thriasian Plain, and in historic times, when the town became part of the Athenian State, it developed into a Panhellenic institution. When at a later time the cult was adopted by the Romans, it acquired universal status.

The Panhellenic character of the cult is indicated by the establishment, perhaps in the fifth Olympiad (760 B.C.) of a festival and sacrifice at Eleusis known as the *Proerosia*. About the time of that Olympiad a great famine desolated Greece. The oracle of Delphi ordered the Athenians to offer a sacrifice to Demeter in the name of all the Greeks before the beginning of the ploughing season. The sacrifice was held at Eleusis and the famine came to an end. Under the leadership of the Athenians, the Greek states voluntarily sent to Eleusis annual offerings of the first fruits, known as ἀπαρχαί, as a token of gratitude.[3]

The ever-increasing popularity of the cult of Eleusis was followed, of course, by the continuous expansion of the precinct area and of the facilities for the initiation of the constantly increasing numbers of pilgrims. As time passed, the smaller temples were replaced by greater ones built over the same area on which the original temple to Demeter had stood. The enceinte walls, known as the peribolos walls, which from the beginning became necessary for the privacy of the cult, were gradually extended to enclose more

---

[3] Suidas, *s.v.* εἰρεσιώνη, p. 1615A and προηροσίαι. Isokrates, *Paneg.*, 4. 31. Cf. Aristides, I, p. 168 (Dindorf); Euripides, *Suppliants*, 28ff; *Ephem*, 1895, p. 44. *Sylloge*[4], No. 83, p. 105.

and more territory to the north, to the south, and to the east. Heavy retaining walls were constructed to support the terraces on which the Temple of Demeter stood, magnificent propylaia were built, and the courts of the Sanctuary were filled with votive monuments. Practically all the leaders of Athens who are associated with the architectural greatness of the Athenian State—Solon, Peisistratos, Kimon, Perikles, Iktinos, Lykourgos, Philon—shared in these changes and additions. In Roman Imperial times, with the contribution of the Emperors Hadrian, Antoninus Pius, and Marcus Aurelius, the sanctuary of Demeter at Eleusis reached the zenith of its development. It was then that destruction and decay set in.

Apparently some of the buildings, certainly the great Temple of Demeter, were destroyed in the late summer of the year 170 of our era during an incursion of the wild Sarmatian tribe of the Kostovoks.[4] But the damage was repaired and the Sanctuary was restored to its ancient glory when the barbarians were expelled from Attika. With the coming of Christianity and its establishment in Greece, the importance and prosperity of the Sanctuary began to wane. Some sparks of life and activity were rekindled in the days of Julian the Apostate (361-363), but Theodosios, towards the end of the fourth century (379-395), issued strict laws against secret cults, and these must have affected the fortunes of the Sanctuary. Evidently even the administrative arrangements of the cult were interfered with, since the last high priest of Eleusis, the last Hierophant, was not from the family of the Eumolpids as prescribed by tradition, nor was he even an Athenian or an Eleusinian, but a citizen of Thespiai, a follower and priest of Mithras.[5] A great part of the Sanctuary was perhaps destroyed by the hordes of Alaric, when in the year 395 they invaded and devastated Attika. By the end of the fifth century of our era, however, the Sanctuary seems to have been completely destroyed by the Early Christians, who built their church near the ruined temple of the Mysteries and buried their dead in the sacred area. Crosses, scratched especially upon the marble pavement of the Greater Propylaea, mark this transformation of the "temenos of the world" into a wasteland and serve as the funeral symbols of a glorious cult which served humanity for almost

[4] Cf. A. Von Premerstein, *Klio*, 12 (1912), pp. 145-164.
[5] Eunapios, Βίοι σοφιστῶν (Μάξιμος), pp. 52ff, ed. Boissonade, 1822.

two thousand years and which was buried under its own debris when a new hope and a new religion came into being in the Hellenic and Hellenized world. Almost a thousand years later, when the Ottoman Turks imposed their rule and their Dark Age on the territory, even the memory of the Sanctuary seems to have been buried.

REPORTS OF EARLY TRAVELERS ON THE SITE

The village that sprang up on the ruins of the Sanctuary had a tenuous existence for centuries, and the number of inhabitants was increased, perhaps in the fourteenth century, by the importation from Albania of farmers. But even the village was abandoned for a while under the threat of pirates shortly before 1676. We get our first glimpse of the ruins of the Sanctuary in the writings of the early travelers to Greece, especially in the account of George Wheler, who visited the site on February 5, 1675/6 when Greece was still under the rule of the Ottoman Turks. A more complete destruction than he describes can hardly be imagined. "Eleusis is now crushed down under their hard Fortune; having been so ill treated by the Christian Pirates, more inhuman than the very Turks that all its Inhabitants have left it; there being nothing remaining, but Ruins. . . . The whole Hill seems to have been built upon; but chiefly towards the Sea: Whether the first thing we came unto was the stately Temple of *Ceres*, now laid prostrate on the Ground: I cannot say, not having one Stone upon another; for it lieth all in a confused heap together: The beautiful Pillars buried in the Rubbish of its dejected Roof and Walls; and its goodly carved and polished Cornishes, used with no more respect, than the worst Stone of the Pavement. . . . It lies in such a rude and disorderly manner, that it is not possible to judge of its antient Form; only it appeared to have been built of the most beautiful white Marble, and no less admirable Work."[6] Apparently, the building described by Wheler was the Lesser Propylaea, because the Ionic capitals he mentions agree with those found later by the expedition of the Dilettanti in their excavation of that building.

"Hard by," Wheler continues, "a little more South-West, among the Ruins of old Walls, we found the Remains of Goddess herself;

---

[6] *Journey to Greece*, pp. 428-429.

viz. a part of her Statue from the Head to below the Waste [*sic*], made of very white Marble, of admirable Work, and perhaps of no less a Master, than *Praxiteles* himself. . . . It is a colossus at least three times bigger than nature. . . . I designed the Statue perhaps well enough, to give some rough imperfect Idea of it; but not to express the exquisite Beauties of the Work. . . . A little higher on the Brow of the Hill we found a large Basis for a Statue. . . . Here we found other Inscriptions also; some upon Stones above Ground, and in the Walls of Old Churches; others we found almost buried in the Ground, and digged them out; For we carried a Mattock and a Spade usually from *Athens* with us. . . . Some are dedications to the Goddesses, *Ceres* and *Proserpine*; some to the Emperors, as *Marcus Aurelius*; which, for Brevities sake, I shall omit."

About one hundred years later (August 31, 1765 to June 11, 1766), the site was visited by Richard Chandler, a member of the first expedition to Asia Minor sent by the Society of the Dilettanti. By then apparently the inhabitants of the village had returned and had re-established themselves in their old homes. "Eleusis," writes Chandler, "is now a small village at the eastern extremity of the rocky brow, on which was once a castle; and is inhabited by a few Albanian families, employed in the culture of the plain, and super-intended by a Turk, who resides in an old square tower. The proprietor was Achmet Aga, the primate or principal person of Athens. . . . About three fourths of the cottages are within the precinct of the mystic temple, and the square tower stands on the ruined wall of the inclosure. . . . At a small distance from the north end of the inclosure is a heap of marble consisting of fragments of the Doric and Ionic orders . . . near it is the bust of a colossal statue of excellent workmanship, maimed, and the face disfigured. . . . It probably represented Proserpine. In the heap are two or three inscribed pedestals; and on one are a couple of torches, crossed. We saw another fixed in the stone stairs, which lead up to the square tower on the outside. It belonged to the statue of a lady who was hierophant or priestess of Proserpine and had covered the altar of the goddess with silver. . . . A tradition prevails that if the broken statue be removed, the fertility of the land will cease. Achmet Aga was fully possessed with this superstition, and declined permitting us to dig or measure there, until I had overcome his scruples by a present of a handsome snuff-box containing several Zechins or pieces of gold."[7] Thus again the ground of Eleusis was tested by those who could afford to pay its rulers.

The ruins and the so-called statue of Proserpine were also seen and described by Ed. Dodwell in his first journey to Greece (1804). "This protecting deity," he wrote, "in its full glory, [is] situated in the centre of a threshing-floor ἀλώνη, among the ruins of her temple."[8] It was seen in 1801 by E. D. Clarke "on the side of the road, immediately before entering the village, and in the midst of a heap of dung, buried as high as the neck, a little beyond the farther extremity of the pavement of the Temple. Yet even this degrading situation had not been assigned to it wholly independent of its ancient history. The inhabitants of the small village which is now situated among the ruins of *Eleusis* still regard this *Statue* with a very high degree of superstitious veneration. They attributed to its presence the fertility of their land; and it was for this reason that they heaped around it the manure intended for their fields. They believed that the loss of it would be followed by no less a calamity than the failure of their annual harvest; and they pointed to the ears of bearded wheat, among the sculptured ornaments upon the head of the figure, as never-failing indication of the produce of the soil."[9] Elsewhere, Clarke states that the villagers of Eleusis "believed that the arm of any person who offered to touch it with violence, would drop off; and said, that once being taken from her station by the French she returned back in the night to her former station."[10] Yet, Clarke succeeded in carrying it away and later presented it to the University of Cambridge where it is now exhibited in the Fitzwilliam Museum.[11] It should perhaps be noted that curiously enough the boat that conveyed it to England, the Princess, was wrecked and lost near Beachy Head, although the

---

[7] Richard Chandler, *Travels in Greece*, 1776, pp. 181-191. The other members of the mission were: N. Revett, an architect, and W. Pars, a painter. It is interesting to note how all visitors were equipped with picks, tools useful for the new sport of digging the earth of Greece.

[8] Ed. Dodwell, *A Classical and Topographical Tour through Greece*, 1819, I, pp. 581-585.

[9] E. D. Clarke, *Travels in Various Countries of Europe, Asia, and Africa*, 1818, VI, p. 601.

[10] *Idem, Greek Marbles Brought from the Shores of the Euxine, Archipelago and Mediterranean*, 1809, pp. 32ff.

[11] Cf. A. Michaelis, *Ancient Marbles in Great Britain*, 1882, p. 242. Cf. *infra* p. 159 and Fig. 56.

statue was saved. The early travelers who saw the statue at Eleusis do not record a name for it. But Lenormant states that his laborers called it St. Demetra. That the story of Demeter and Persephone was not completely wiped out of the memory of the inhabitants of the village but, modified, had become part of their folklore is indicated by the story of the charitable woman Demetra and her beautiful daughter who was abducted by a Turk, told to Lenormant by an aged priest.[12] The story was repeated to me by an octogenarian inhabitant of Eleusis when I started working there in 1929.

While the Ottoman Turks were still in control of Greece, the Society of the Dilettanti sent another mission to the Eastern Mediterranean led by Sir William Gell and the architects, John Peter Grandy and Francis Redford. The members of the expedition reached Eleusis in 1812 and carried out important excavations that resulted in the clearing of the Propylaea and the temple of Artemis of the Portals. They were able also to locate the temple of the Goddess, although their hypothesis of its form proved incorrect. After the liberation of Greece additional investigations of the area around the Propylaea were carried out by Lenormant in 1860.

THE EXCAVATION OF THE SITE

To the Greek Archaeological Society of Athens belongs the honor of the systematic and complete excavation of the site, started in 1882 and, with few interruptions, continued to the present day. For the excavation of Eleusis we are especially indebted to three great Greek scholars whose devoted and inspired work revealed the broken remains of the great Sanctuary. In 1882, Demetrios Philios began the exploration and cleared the great Temple of Demeter almost completely. In his work he had from the very beginning the collaboration of Wilhelm Dörpfeld, to whose expert skill we owe the architectural plans that accompany the reports of Philios. These reports, appearing almost annually from 1882 to 1890, give us a step-by-step account of the work and discovery, and in a dramatic way raise in instalments the heavy mantle of forgetfulness

[12] F. Lenormant, *Monographie de la voie sacrée éleusinienne*, 1864, I, 398, repeated in translation by A. B. Cook in his *Zeus*, 1914, I, 173-175, note, where one can also find the pertinent bibliography.

under which the ruins were buried. Philios worked from 1882 to 1892. My late Professor Andreas Skias continued Philios' work from 1894 to 1907, investigating particularly the court of the Sanctuary, its southern section, the Geometric cemetery, and the prehistoric remains to the south of the precinct. In 1917 Konstantinos Kourouniotes undertook the direction of the work and for years continued the exploration of the ruins in small excavations. Beginning in 1930, and assisted by a generous contribution of the Rockefeller Foundation obtained through the efforts of Edward Capps, then chairman of the Managing Committee of the American School of Classical Studies in Athens, he was able to carry out excavations on a large scale and almost to complete the exploration of the Sanctuary. I had the rare privilege of working with him in this extensive investigation, and for this privilege I am deeply grateful to the "Master." His other collaborators in this work were the architect, Dr. John N. Travlos, the ephor of antiquities John Threpsiades, and, for a short period, George Bakalakis, now professor of Archaeology at the University of Thessaloniki. After the death of Kourouniotes in 1945, the Archaeological Society of Athens entrusted the further excavations of Eleusis to Professor Anastasios K. Orlandos of the University of Athens, to Dr. John N. Travlos, and to me.[13]

Over a period of a century and a half, gradually and painstakingly, the entire Sanctuary area has been cleared and, relieved of its accumulated soil, it was made by the spade of the excavator to yield its remains. Where once the pilgrim found beautiful temples and imposing marble monuments, the visitor of today will find a maze of foundations and broken stones that bring to mind the picture of the fallen giants of mythology. Even the brilliant light of Greece is incapable of imparting life to the broken shrine of Demeter. The spring has dried up; its mission has ended, and only the ruins, piled by the hand of man, remain to testify to its past greatness.

[13] The results of the excavations have been partially published in a number of articles and books the most important of which are marked with an asterisk in our Selected Bibliography. The study of the celebrated Mysteries of Eleusis kept pace with the excavations and a rich bibliography has accumulated since the days of the early travelers of Greece. Some of the articles and books published will be found in our Selected Bibliography.

DERIVATION OF THE CULT OF DEMETER

The almost complete absence of descriptive references to the sacred buildings of Eleusis in the writings of ancient authors makes apparent the importance of the topographic and historic details to be found in the Hymn, especially in the passages we have already quoted. The Hymn can well be considered as a guide to the intricate life of the Sanctuary. Its attribution of the beginnings of the Mysteries to the Goddess herself indicates the great antiquity of that cult. Furthermore, the legend that Demeter, who arrived at Eleusis as a stranger and from other lands, taught her rites to Keleos and his princes, the lack of any tradition indicating the existence at that village of an earlier shrine that was usurped by the Goddess, and the further lack of any rumors of a contest over the site with another divinity or power that once held sway over it, prove definitely that the cult of Demeter was introduced to Eleusis from some other part of the Hellenic or Mediterranean world.[14]

One may well wonder whence the cult was introduced to Eleusis, and when. As to the date, Greek tradition offers some information. We learn from Apollodoros that "when Erichthonios died and was buried in the sanctuary of Athena, Pandion became king, in whose time Demeter and Dionysos came to Attika. However, Demeter was received by Keleos at Eleusis, and Dionysos by Ikarios." The reign of Pandion, the son of Erichthonios, is placed by the Parian Chronicle ca. 1462-1423 B.C. According to the same Chronicle, Demeter came to Athens in the reign of Erechtheus or ca. 1409/8 B.C. To the reign of Erechtheus the Parian Chronicle refers not only the advent of Demeter, but also the first sowing of wheat in the Rharian plain of Eleusis, a section of the Thriasian Plain adjacent to the township, and the first celebration of the Mysteries at Eleusis by Eumolpos.[15] In spite of the evident discrepancy in the two sources, we may assume that tradition, in general, places the introduction of the cult of Demeter in the second half of the fifteenth century, B.C.

[14] Notable examples of such usurpation is the story of the Delphic oracle taken over by Apollo from its earlier owners—Earth, Themis, Poseidon (Pausanias, x, 5, 5). Apollo gave Poseidon in exchange the island of Kalauria off Troizen. The famous contest of Athena and Poseidon, immortalized by Pheidias on the West Pediment of the Parthenon, is another example.

[15] Apollodoros, *Bibliotheke*, III, 14, 7. F. Jacoby, *Das Marmor Parium*, 1904, pp. 6-7.

The Hymn, of course, narrates events which occurred long before its composition. From the description of the palace of Keleos as well as from the indications of the political system described we can deduce that the events are reputed to have taken place in the Mycenaean age. Keleos is the "κοίρανος," the lord of Eleusis, who calls his "countless people to an assembly" to order them to build a temple to Demeter. He is surrounded by vassal princes, by "βασιλεῖς" who have great power and honor and are chief among the people, guarding the city's coif of towers by their wisdom and true judgements. Keleos is the "leader of people"; the princes are "θεμιστοπόλοι βασιλῆες," kings who deal justice. This political system fits well the Mycenaean age.[16] And so it was in that age, in the course of the fifteenth century B.C., that according to the popular tradition the cult of Demeter was introduced to Eleusis.

From where? The origin and provenience of the cult remain uncertain. Thus far, four main sections of the Mediterranean world—Egypt, Thessaly, Thrace, and Krete—have been proposed one after the other as possible districts from which the Mysteries of Demeter may have been imported into Eleusis. As early as the fifth century B.C., Herodotos, the father of History, equated Demeter with Isis and looked to Egypt for the provenience of the Mysteries. In modern times, P. Foucart, noticing the similarities existing between the Eleusinian myth and the Egyptian story of Isis and Osiris and recalling the story of Danaos and his daughters, taught that the Mysteries were introduced to Eleusis from Egypt in the XVIII Dynasty.[17] The great popularity this theory enjoyed for almost a quarter of a century has declined considerably. In 1927, Charles Picard proved that the theory was untenable and pointed out that not a single object of Egyptian origin, or indicating Egyptian influence, and dating from the second millennium was found in the Sanctuary of Eleusis.[18] That observation becomes more striking now that one of the cemeteries of Eleusis is completely ex-

[16] In the tablets of Linear Script B, we have *wanax* instead of κοίρανος as a title for the king and βασιλεύς as a title for less important, though lordly personalities. Cf. M. Ventris and J. Chadwick, *Documents in Mycenaean Greek*, 1956, pp. 120-122; and T. B. L. Webster, *From Mycenae to Homer*, 1958, p. 11.

[17] Herodotos, II, 123. P. Foucart, *Les Mystères d'Eleusis*, 1914, pp. 20-40. Cf. V. Magnien, *Les Mystères d'Éleusis*, 2nd ed., 1938, pp. 44ff and especially p. 46, where the followers of this theory are cited.

[18] Ch. Picard, "Sur la patrie et les pérégrinations de Demeter," *REG*, 40 (1927), pp. 321-330.

plored. In that cemetery we found and cleared graves belonging to the second millennium B.C., and the evidence from them proves a normal cultural development, but no Egyptian influence whatsoever. The myths also exhibit a good many differences, as Picard pointed out, and they cannot be equated in spite of Herodotos and Foucart.

Picard proposed a Kretan, instead of an Egyptian origin for the Mysteries and ably defended his thesis in his book on the prehellenic religions of Greece.[19] Before Picard, Axel Persson had maintained that the cult of Demeter at Eleusis went back to prehistoric times, as indicated by the tradition, and accepted a Kretan or Minoan origin for the Mysteries.[20] These scholars still have a good following, and the Kretan or Minoan origin of the Mysteries of Eleusis enjoys great popularity even now. However, the assumptions on which they based their conclusions no longer correspond to the facts as revealed by the latest excavations. The Hall of Initiation, the famous Telesterion at Eleusis, was used by both scholars as evidence proving its Kretan derivation. Persson compared that hall to the theatral areas of Krete and found that the Anaktoron, or the Holy of Holies of Eleusis, was identical with the Kretan Repositories. Picard, denying this, asserts that the Telesterion of Eleusis, from its beginnings to its end, had the plan of a closed hypostyle hall that contrasts with the plan of the megaron-temple and suggests a prehellenic prototype which he finds in Krete.[21]

In their discussions, these eminent scholars have in mind the Hall of Initiation, or Telesterion of the Archaic and Classical periods. The excavations of 1931 and 1932, however, have proved that the oldest temple to Demeter, which goes back to Mycenaean times, is in the form of a megaron and has no relation to Kretan buildings.[22] Besides, the Telesterion of the Early Archaic period does not exhibit an almost square plan, as it was believed until recently, but an oblong that finds parallels in the form of the temples of the Historic era.[23] It can be asserted with certainty that the square plan was introduced by the builders of the Peisistratean

[19] *Idem, Les Religions Préhélleniques*, 1948.
[20] A. Persson, "Der Ursprung der eleusinischen Mysterien," *ArchRW*, 21 (1922), pp. 287-309.
[21] *REG*, 40 (1927), pp. 359-360, and *Religions préhélleniques*, p. 65 n. 2.
[22] *Infra*, p. 49.   [23] *Infra*, p. 68

times, long after the cult was established at Eleusis. The Anaktoron, which was compared to the repositories of Krete or to the hypostyle crypts of the Minoan Palaces, has been proved to occupy a small central section of the Telesterion and not to be an underground structure.[24] As far as the remains that have been revealed to date are concerned—and we must bear in mind that the area of the Telesterion has been cleared completely—there is no evidence indicating even a remote influence of Kretan or Minoan structures on the Eleusinian. Furthermore, not a single object has been found indicating Kretan origin or even influence. The sanctuaries of Demeter have yielded a special type of a vase known as the Kernos (Fig. 87). It is very characteristic of our site and of the Eleusinian cult, and it was taken as evidence of Kretan or Minoan influence. In spite of differences, the Kernoi can be compared to Minoan multiple pots and as Nilsson remarks "nobody denies the connexion, although about a thousand years intervene between the Minoan and the Greek (Eleusinian) specimens."[25] This chronological difference, we believe, excludes Minoan influence; if it existed, we would expect to find such vessels in the early strata of the Sanctuary of Eleusis. To date not a single fragment has been found in the prehistoric strata of the site, and we can conclude that, in later years, this peculiar vessel was developed at Eleusis independently to fill a need that arose from the evolution and crystallization of the ritual of the Eleusinian cult. In exactly the same manner, the Kernos of the Christian worship was developed independently to fill a need of the ritual, long after the secret pagan cults and their utensils were forgotten.[26]

Nor does tradition indicate Minoan relations. It is important to note that a good many legends link Krete with Athens and Megara, the two neighboring cities to the east and the west of Eleusis. The story of Theseus and the Labyrinth, the Minotaur and the Athenian tribute, was one of the most popular myths of the ancient world. The incursions of Minos against Megara were remembered by the inhabitants of that city even in the days of Pausanias.[27] Eleusis is never mentioned in any of these traditional events. In the *Odyssey*

[24] J. N. Travlos, *Anaktoron*, pp. 1-16.
[25] M. P. Nilsson, *Minoan-Mycenaean Religion*, 1950, 2nd ed., p. 452.
[26] St. Xanthoudides, *BSA*, 12 (1905-1906), pp. 20ff.
[27] Pausanias, I, 19, 4; 41, 6; 44, 3.

we find that Demeter had intimate relations with Iasion, and in the *Theogony* of Hesiod we read that the locale was Krete.[28] However, the birth of their offspring, Ploutos, or Wealth, reflects an allegorical and poetic interpretation of the rewards of successful soil cultivation that has nothing to do with the cult of Demeter at Eleusis. Besides, before we can utilize this story we must first prove that its tradition in reality is Kretan and that it existed in Minoan times. We believe that the myth is of a later date, later than the Minoan days, and that from Thessaly it was introduced elsewhere, even to Krete, as the name of the hero Iasion (Iason) seems to indicate. Such an infiltration of traditions and cults from Thessaly to Krete was projected by O. Kern years ago.[29] That it had nothing to do with the cult is indicated by the fact that it is not mentioned in the Hymn, which gives us the official version of the story of the introduction of the rites.

It is true that in the Hymn, the Goddess tells the daughters of Keleos that she came to Eleusis from Krete.[30] We must remember, however, that in the Hymn the Goddess is telling a "story" to conceal her identity and to explain her presence. The use of Krete to hide the real provenience of a traveler or a guest is not unusual in epic poetry. In the stories he creates, Odysseus repeatedly mentions Krete as his birthplace,[31] and it seems that the rhapsodists of that period used that island whenever they wanted to indicate an indefinite, faraway place and provenience that would make possible the introduction of pirates into whose hands a divine or heroic personage had fallen. Hence, we cannot find a proof in that statement of the Goddess.

The name Eleusis too has tempted many scholars. Lately, Nilsson has proved that it is "prehellenic."[32] But this does not strengthen the hypothesis of the Kretan origin. In Attika we have a number of sites bearing "prehellenic" names: Probalinthos, Lykabettos, Hymettos, etc. This proves only that the names were given to the sites in the Early Bronze Age, during which Attika presumably was occupied by tribes akin to those inhabiting the Kyklades and Krete.

---

[28] *Odyssey*, 5, 125-126. *Theogony*, 969-971.
[29] O. Kern, *Religion der Griechen*, I, 1926, pp. 210ff.
[30] Hymn, 123ff.
[31] *Odyssey*, 14, 199ff; 16, 62.
[32] M. P. Nilsson, *op.cit.*, pp. 520ff.

Eleusis too may owe its name to those pre-Indo-European tribes, since we have some evidence indicating that it was inhabited in Early Helladic times. The cult of Demeter seems to have been introduced to Eleusis in Mycenaean, or Late Helladic times, and, consequently, it could have nothing to do with the name of the site. On the other hand, the name Demeter is a Greek name and has no relation to Kretan prehellenic names. It should also be noted that Demeter and Persephone are not to be found among the Gods that are the recipients of offerings recorded on the tablets from Knossos.[33] This would strongly suggest that their cult was not current in Krete in Minoan days. We can, therefore, conclude that we have no evidence, archaeological, traditional, or linguistic, that would indicate a Kretan or Minoan origin of the cult.

There are stronger traditional indications pointing to the north, to Thessaly and to Thrace, as to the place of origin of the cult. Eumolpos, the first celebrant of the Mysteries at Eleusis, whose mother was Chione, is reputed to have come from Thrace.[34] Tradition brings Thracians to the help of the Eleusinians in their war against Athens.[35] In the Historic era, one of the early temples of Demeter was to be seen at Anthele near Thermopylai; the great antiquity of the temple and the reverence in which it was held are indicated by its use as the meeting place of the North Amphiktyony, or Federation of Greek tribes, before it acquired its Delphic character.[36] There are few references to temples and shrines in the poems of Homer, but one of the few examples mentioned is the "temenos" or sanctuary of Demeter at Pyrasos in Thessaly.[37] The name of the site, Pyrasos, indicates a prehellenic origin; that the cult of Demeter at Pyrasos was believed to go back to pre-Homeric days and perhaps to a hoary antiquity is indicated by its association

[33] *Infra*, p. 50.

[34] Pausanias, I, 38, 2 and 3. The passages of Pausanias quoted in this work are in the main taken from the translation of J. G. Frazer.

[35] Apollodoros, III, 15, 4-5.

[36] Herodotos, VII, 200. Cf. Strabo, 429, and the amphiktyonic inscription published first in *BCH*, 24 (1900), p. 142. Farnell, *The Cults of the Greek States*, III, pp. 72-73, aptly remarks that "the first object of the union was no doubt religious; its political influence was a later and secondary result." And he adds, "we are arrested by a fact of primary political and religious importance, that a number of tribes, not all closely related within the Hellenic stock, should have been able to organize a common worship at a time certainly earlier than the Dorian invasion," i.e. earlier than 1100 B.C. at least.

[37] *Iliad*, II, 695.

with the Pelasgians by Kallimachos.[38] The rites held in honor of Demeter, springing from primitive agricultural practices, could naturally have originated in the broad plains of Thessaly and Thrace. However, the evidence is too legendary and tenuous to sustain definite conclusions. Thus far, while we can prove from which sections of the Mediterranean world the cult did not come, we cannot prove decisively where it did originate. That it was imported to Eleusis seems to be a fact; but its place of origin remains uncertain. It is obvious that we favor a North Greek origin.

THE MISSION OF TRIPTOLEMOS

Closely connected with Eleusis and Demeter is the story of Triptolemos and the spreading of the knowledge of the cultivation of the soil or perhaps the spreading of improved methods of agriculture. Triptolemos seems to have been one of those legendary figures that fascinated the minds of men. He is first mentioned in the Hymn as one of the chieftains of the people, "a king who deals justice." He is among the "kings to whom the Goddess showed the conduct of her rites and taught all her mysteries."[39] Pausanias and Apollodoros give us the Athenian version, according to which he was the son of Keleos and Metaneira; but there were other traditions of his lineage, including a mythological origin.[40] Early in the sixth century, the Athenians seem to have maintained that Triptolemos was commissioned by Demeter to go all over the world and teach humanity how to raise cereals. That mission of Triptolemos apparently was the theme of a lost tragedy composed by Sophokles and entitled *Triptolemos*. From a fragment, preserved by Dionysios of Halikarnassos, we learn how Demeter "informed Triptolemos how large a tract of land he would have to travel over while sowing it with the seeds she had given him," and for that task she gave him a car drawn by dragons.[41] We have a hint of the mission of Triptolemos, although he is not mentioned by name, in

[38] Kallimachos, *Hymn to Demeter*, v. 25.

[39] Hymn, vv. 150-153; 475-476.

[40] Pausanias, I, 14, 2; Apollodoros, I, 5, 2. Hyginus, *Fab.*, CXLVII, equates him with Demophon.

[41] Dionysios, *R. A.*, I, 12, 2, and Nauck, *Frag. Tragic. Graec.*, 2nd ed., p. 262 fragm. 539. *The Fragments of Sophocles*, ed. by A. C. Pearson, II, p. 243 fragm. 596.

Plato.[42] There, we find that Attika "was the first to produce human nourishment, namely the grain and barley and that this she did not begrudge to the rest of men, but dispensed it to them also," a very delicate bit of propaganda. The claim of Attika as the original home of civilization, law, and agriculture was upheld by the Amphiktyons and was recorded in a second century B.C. decree found at Delphi.[43] According to the tradition preserved by Pausanias, the "Rharian plain was the first to be sown and the first to bear crops."[44] In that plain we have not only a temple of the hero but also a "threshing floor of Triptolemos." Finally, we may recall the story of Apollodoros, according to which "to Triptolemos, the elder of the children of Metaneira, the Goddess having made a chariot of winged dragons, she gave him wheat with which, wafted through the sky, he sowed the whole inhabited earth."[45]

It took little time for the story of the mission of Triptolemos to become popular, and we find it represented frequently on the vase paintings of the Attik workshops, both of the black- and of the red-figure style.[46] In the Classical era we have representations even in sculpture.[47] Gradually, Triptolemos became a panhellenic hero, and his mission encompassed the universe. Many cities and villages, large and small, maintained that they were the stopping places of the hero, and local cults in his honor sprang up in good number. The place of the mission of Triptolemos in the Mysteries of Eleusis has never been considered with the proper care. Scholars sometimes accept that it formed part of the "Mysteries," without taking the trouble to indicate their reasons. The fact that the story is Eleusinian and that a good many representations of it were found at Eleusis, seems to have been considered sufficient reason to accept it as part of the Mysteries. However, we shall see later that the mission of Triptolemos could not have formed part of the secret rites of Demeter.

[42] *Menexenos*, 7.   [43] *BCH*, 24 (1900), p. 96.
[44] Pausanias, I, 38, 6.   [45] Apollodoros, I, 5, 2.
[46] In Greek vase painting Triptolemos is often seated in a car drawn by dragons. One of the most beautiful examples is on the Kotyle of Hieron in the British Museum. Betty Grossman of St. Louis in a doctoral dissertation entitled *The Eleusinian Gods and Heroes in Greek Art*, has classified some 470 such representations.
[47] Figs. 69, 71, 74.

Legends and traditions portray the beginnings and the life story of the cult held at Eleusis and indicate its splendor and importance to mankind. The excavations conducted in our days not only brought to light the remains of the Sanctuary within which the cult was celebrated, but seem to prove that the cult was a most popular one and blessed humanity for generations. Legends and archaeology agree that at Eleusis for centuries the human mind and soul were sustained by a doctrine and a belief of which the details and the meaning were lost when the lips of the last Hierophant were sealed by death sometime in the fifth century of our era. We cannot know the meaning of the cult today, but we can learn a great many things about it and about the behavior of men over centuries from the ruins that have survived.[48]

[48] The letters used in excavation reports were taken from the Greek alphabet. Here we transliterate the Greek letters with the exception of Θ which is substituted by the Latin letter F to facilitate printing. Letters A to D were used to indicate the various periods of the prehistoric era; E-L consecutively to indicate the periods in sequence of the Historic era. At the end of the book we attach a *Glossary* where the terms employed in the text will be defined.

CHAPTER II

EARLY HISTORY AND REMAINS

THE early history of our site, like that of many other prehistoric settlements, was influenced by its geographic position. Eleusis was advantageously situated on the eastern end of a long and rather low rocky ridge which runs parallel and close to the seashore in the southwestern corner of the Thriasian Plain (Fig. 1). That plain, verdant and almost entirely under cultivation until the recent industrialization of the territory and the creation of a large airfield for military planes, is surrounded on three sides by mountains and low hills, and bordered on the south by the sea. A narrow passage between Mount Aigaleos and Mount Poikilon, outcroppings of massive Mount Parnes, connected the Thriasian with the Attik Plain to the east. The western end of that passage was made more difficult to negotiate by a pair of small lakes known as the Rheitoi. This narrow, easily defended passage, formed the borderline between the territory of the Athenians and of the Eleusinians in the prehistoric era. Between the sea and a low-lying mountain, known as Kerata because of its two peaks that from a distance look like the horns of an animal, an equally narrow and rocky passage separates the Thriasian Plain at its southwesternmost extremity from the Megarian Plain. The impressive masses of Mount Kithairon and Mount Parnes close the plain from the north and the northeast, while the sea, blocked by the island of Salamis, forms a watery barrier on its south side. The Bay of Eleusis and Salamis, a beautiful stretch of blue water that reminds one of the lakes of North Italy, communicates by two passages with the open waters of the Aegean. At the eastern end, lie the straits of Pseitalia, where the famous naval battle of Salamis was fought between the Greeks and the Persians in 480 B.C., while at the west is the passage to the bay of Megara, known today as the Perama.

The crucial factor in this location is that the roads connecting Athens with the Peloponnesos to the west and south and with Thebes and the rest of central and northern Greece to the north pass by Eleusis. If powerful enough, the people of Eleusis could menace the Attik Plain to the east and the Megarian Plain to the west whenever they felt so inclined, or could cut the land communications of their neighbors. This situation determined the relations of Eleusis to Athens, especially in the early years of its history when the village had an independent political existence. Its position, almost in the innermost recess of the Bay of Eleusis, sheltered the site from sudden attack by a hostile fleet and provided a safe anchorage for maritime activities. Perhaps to that position of safety the city owes its beginnings, now lost in mythological conjecture. Pausanias has recorded the legend that the city was named after the hero Eleusis, who, according to some, was the "son of Hermes and Daira, daughter of Okeanos" and according to others the son of Ogygos.[1] The second attribution may possess in it a kernel of truth, for we hear that Ogygos, or Ogygis, was an aboriginal king of Thebes, who lived before the days of Kadmos.[2] The story of the legendary Eleusis, the son of Ogygos, may indicate the expansion of the people of Thebes to the south and the establishment of a port town at Eleusis to serve the inland capital of the mythical king.[3] Since Kadmos is supposed to have ruled Thebes in the fifteenth or the late sixteenth century B.C.,[4] and the legendary Ogygos antedated him, the establishment of Eleusis, as far as legends go, could be assigned to a period before the fifteenth century B.C. Again from legends we learn of the arrival of the cult of Demeter at Eleusis in the fifteenth century[5]—an event that must of course have had a profound influence on the life and activities of the site.

WARS AGAINST ATHENS

We get a glimpse of a militant Eleusis in the days when Erechtheus ruled Athens. It was then that a series of wars began between the two neighboring cities, the first of which was well remembered even in the days of Pausanias. The traveler states that "when the Eleusinians were at war with Erechtheus they were joined by

[1] Pausanias, I, 38, 7.

[2] Pausanias, IX, 5, 1. Hence Thebes is often called by the poets "Ogygian."

[3] Cf. the excellent study of Ch. Picard, "Les luttes primitives d'Athènes et d'Éleusis," *RHist*, 166 (1931), p. 12.

[4] The Parian Chronicle places the arrival of Kadmos in the reign of Amphiktyon, or ca. 1518/7 B.C. (cf. Jacoby, *Marmor Parium*, p. 4). G. E. Mylonas, Τὰ Φοινίκεια γράμματα τοῦ Κάδμου, *Academy of Athens Studies*, 23 (1959), pp. 3-4.

[5] *Supra*, p. 14.

Skiros, a soothsayer from Dodona," who was killed in the war and was buried in a torrent situated in the neighborhood of Athens before one reached the Athenian Kephisos; that "in a battle between the Eleusinians and the Athenians, there fell Erechtheus, king of Athens, and Immarados, son of Eumolpos, and peace was made on these terms: the Eleusinians were to perform the Mysteries by themselves, but were in all other respects to be subjects to the Athenians."[6] Apollodoros furnishes additional information. "War having broken out between the Athenians and the Eleusinians," Eumolpos, ruling in Thrace, "was called in by the Eleusinians and fought on their side with a large force of Thracians. The oracle decreed to Erechtheus that he would be victorious if he sacrificed one of his daughters; and when he sacrificed his youngest, the others also killed themselves. . . . In the battle Erechtheus killed Eumolpos. Since Poseidon destroyed Erechtheus and his house, Kekrops, the eldest of the sons of Erechtheus, succeeded to the throne."[7] Thoukydides too recalls how some of the cities in the days before Theseus fought against Athens, "as, for example, the Eleusinians with Eumolpos did against Erechtheus."[8] The war was commemorated in art in the Historic era, for Pausanias saw on the Akropolis itself a group "of large bronze figures of men confronting each other in combat; they call one of them Erechtheus and the other Eumolpos. And yet Athenian antiquaries themselves are aware that it was Eumolpos' son Immarados who was killed by Erechtheus."[9]

There can be no doubt that these traditions refer to real warfare between the Athenians and the Eleusinians. The question that remains unanswered is whether these traditions refer to one or two wars. Perhaps there were two wars: one fought in the days of Erechtheus and Eumolpos, who was the reputed first celebrant of the Mysteries; the other when a large contingent of Thracians participated at the invitation of the Eleusinians.[10] The proper se-

[6] Pausanias, I, 36, 4 and I, 38, 3.

[7] Apollodoros, III, 15, 4-5. Apollodoros states that in the battle Eumolpos was killed, while Pausanias states that Immarados, son of Eumolpos, was killed.

[8] Thoukydides, II, 15.

[9] Pausanias, I, 27, 4.

[10] Wars waged in a remote past tend to be differently reported in the writings of ancient authors. The war of Eumolpos against the Athenians is mentioned by Plato (*Menexenos*, 239B) by Isokrates (IV, 68; XII, 193) by Demosthenes (LX,

quence of these wars cannot be determined now, but apparently the Athenians, although victorious at the end, were hard pressed in the course of these wars. The sacrifice of a princess of Athens and the graves of Skiros and of Immarados in the neighborhood of that city, the burial of Immarados in fact under the northwestern corner of the Akropolis itself, indicate that the Athenian territory was invaded and Athens itself was seriously threatened. In this connection, we may recall Oscar Broneer's important excavations on the north slope of the Akropolis of Athens. Immediately in front of the abandoned north gate to the Akropolis, Broneer uncovered the foundations of Mycenaean houses which were suddenly abandoned under the threat of enemy attacks and were never again reinhabited.[11] Can we see in these hastily abandoned houses a confirmation of the Eleusinian threat against Athens in the prehistoric era? Broneer says that the inhabitants fled from their houses in the last quarter of the thirteenth century B.C. Can we ascribe to that quarter the later of the two wars? In any case, the end of the first war or wars of Eleusis and Athens came when the Eleusinians were forced to become the subjects of the Athenians but reserved to themselves the right to perform the Mysteries.

The history of Athens after the death of Erechtheus is rather confused, and in that confusion Eleusis too is immersed. We hear

---

8, p. 1391) and others. As a matter of fact, Isokrates states that the war of Eumolpos against Erechtheus was due to the claims of the former to the kingdom of Athens on the grounds that he was the son of Poseidon, who ruled Athens before Athena. The sacrifice of the daughter of Erechtheus is mentioned by a number of ancient writers. Euripides in his *Ion*, vv. 277-280, projects the view that Kreousa, the youngest daughter of Erechtheus, was spared because she was an infant. She later became the wife of Xouthos and the mother of Ion. In his tragedy *Erechtheus*, Euripides immortalized the heroic sacrifice of the daughters of Erechtheus (cf. Nauck, *Fragmenta Trag. Graec.*, 2nd ed., pp. 464ff). Hyginus, *Fabulae*, XLVI, states that Erechtheus was killed by the thunderbolt and so became "Diobletos." A. B. Cook, *Zeus*, II, pp. 22-23. According to the scholiast of Sophokles' *Oidipous Kolonos*, 1053, Eumolpos, who instituted the Mysteries, was the fifth after the one who led the Thracians, the genealogy being: Eumolpos (who led the Thracians), Keryx, Eumolpos, Antiphemos, Mouseos the poet, Eumolpos (who instituted the Mysteries). This genealogy certainly proves that even the ancients had no clear picture of the prehistoric wars and that the differences in their authors puzzled them.

[11] Oscar Broneer, *Hesperia*, 2 (1933), pp. 329ff; 4 (1935), pp. 109ff; *Antiquity*, 30 (1956), p. 12. The abandonment could be attributed to hostile incursions of the Herakleidai, the so-called Dorians, and this view seems to be favored by Broneer; but the only known hostile attack of the Dorians against Athens occurred much later, in the days of Kodros.

that the oldest son of Erechtheus, Kekrops II, reigned for a while, and that he was succeeded by his son Pandion II, who was expelled from Athens by the sons of Metion. He fled to Megara, married the daughter of the king and finally became the king of Megara.[12] After his death, his four sons marched against Athens, expelled the Metionids, and divided the country into four shares. "Aegeus, being the oldest, obtained the kingdom of Athens. . . . Nisos . . . was invested with the kingdom of Megara and of all the country as far as Corinth."[13] According to Strabo,[14] who quotes Philochoros and Andron on the matter, the rule of Nisos extended from the Isthmos to the Pythion, or only as far as Eleusis and the Thriasian Plain. Where this Pythion is located is a matter of conjecture; but whether it is the area of the temple of Apollo, at the Byzantine monastery of Daphni, or in the deme of Oenoe some twelve miles to the northeast of our site, it seems safe to assume that Eleusis was included in the territory of Nisos.

The assumption of the rule of Athens by Aigeus did not bring peace to that city. It continued to face hostile forces, now led by the expelled Metionids, now by the sons of Pallas, the brother of Aigeus. Megara's fate, on the other hand, was even worse. During the reign of Nisos the city was attacked and was captured by the mythical Minos of Krete and the king was killed by treachery.[15] It is reasonable to assume that during those stormy years of the life of Attika the Eleusinians had the chance to revolt against Athens and to assume their independence. At any rate, we hear of a new war in the days of the legendary Ion, shortly before the reign of Theseus. "In the reign of Ion," says Pausanias, "the Eleusinians made war on the Athenians, and the latter having invited Ion to take command of the war, he met his end in Attika and his tomb is in the township of Potamos."[16] Again in his description of Keleai Pausanias states: "Dysaules . . . came [to that city] . . . after he had been expelled from Eleusis by Ion, son of Xouthos, at the time when Ion was chosen commander-in-chief of the Athenians in the war against Eleusis."[17] Strabo too mentions this victorious effort of Ion on behalf of the Athenians, but he assigned to this war the

---

[12] Apollodoros, III, 15, 5.
[13] Pausanias, I, 5, 4; and I, 39, 4.
[14] Strabo, IX, 1, 6 (c. 392).
[15] Pausanias, I, 19, 4.
[16] Pausanias, VII, 1, 5; also I, 31, 3.
[17] Pausanias, II, 14, 2.

Thracians of Eumolpos who were called to the help of the Eleusinians.[18] Of course, Xouthos' and Ion's intervention in the life of
Athens may be completely fictitious. Yet one can see how the
troubled conditions that followed Erechtheus' death may have en-
couraged the Eleusinians to reopen the war. The honors piled on
Ion and the expulsion of Dysaules from Eleusis seem to indicate
that the Athenians were again victorious.

The early wars were followed by Theseus and his efforts to
consolidate the power and existence of Athens. The appearance of
this semi-legendary king of Athens presents further problems.
Apparently in the days of Peisistratos, in the second half of the
sixth century, he was raised from comparative obscurity to the status
of a hero worthy of the greatness of the Athenian state as envisioned
by that benevolent tyrant. Perhaps it was then that to his real
exploits were added others, traditional or imaginary, so that it is
difficult to distinguish among fiction, older tradition, and fact. To
him, of course, was attributed the clearing of the road from Athens
to the Isthmos from its dangerous highwaymen by a series of exploits that may reflect the conquest of the territory by the Athenians
under the reputed leadership of Theseus. We recall that one of the
subdued highwaymen was Skiron, who, according to the Athenian
version of the story recorded by Pausanias, dwelt beside the Ski-
ronian rocks on the way from Megara to the Isthmos and "hurled
every stranger he met into the sea. A tortoise swam at the foot of
the cliffs to pounce on the people who were thrown in. . . . But justice
overtook Skiron; for he was hurled by Theseus into the same sea."[19]
But the Megarians maintained that this Skiron was a man of
exemplary life, the foe of robbers, the friend of men; that he was
the "war minister of Megara" who built the road from Megara to
the Isthmos along the precipitous slopes of the mountains; that he
was the grandfather of Peleus and Telamon and one of the first
settlers of Salamis, who fell at the hand of Theseus in warfare
when the Athenian hero wrested Eleusis from their state.[20] It is
not difficult to believe that the exploits attributed to Theseus along

[18] Strabo, VIII, 7, 1 (c. 383).

[19] Pausanias, I, 44, 8. The tortoise turned into stone by Zeus, can still be seen
(!) off the coast at the area known today as Kaki Skala.

[20] Plutarch, *Theseus*, X. Harpokration, *s.v.* Skiron. The Athenian version that
eclipsed the story of the Megarians is a good example of successful propaganda.

the road from Athens to the Isthmos reflect the conquest of the territory by the Athenians, especially if we assume the order of these exploits to have occurred in a sequence moving from east to west. Professor Picard has pointed out that the sequence, as we have it, from west to east, dates only from the sixth century B.C.,[21] and Plutarch indicates that even in antiquity there was some skepticism regarding the accepted sequence: "It was not, they say, when Theseus first journeyed to Athens, but afterwards, that he captured Eleusis from the Megarians, having circumvented Diokles its ruler and slain Skiron."[22] Whatever the actual sequence of the exploits of Theseus may be, Eleusis apparently was again brought into the domain of Athens during his lifetime. It also seems clear that the ritual of the Mysteries was left in the hands of the Eleusinians.

A generation after Theseus, according to tradition, the Trojan war was fought. The absence of any mention of Eleusis in the *Iliad* and the *Odyssey* would indicate that its people did not participate in that epic struggle, while the Athenians, under the leadership of Menestheus their King, played but a small and inglorious role. Some eighty years after the fall of Troy, the "return of the Herakleidai," the so-called Dorian invasion occurred,[23] and that event marks the end of the Mycenaean age as well as of the early history of our site. In general, we may suggest that the "return" occurred towards the end of the twelfth century B.C.

REMAINS OF THE MIDDLE HELLADIC PERIOD

When from tradition and legend gleaned from literary sources we turn to the actual remains of Eleusis, brought to light by excavators over a period of a century and a half, we find that the stories we have narrated find partial corroboration. The most ancient remains found in some abundance thus far at the site belong to the Middle Bronze age, known as the Middle Helladic period.[24] The

---

[21] Picard, *op.cit.*, p. 51 and n. 5.   [22] Plutarch, *Theseus*, x, 3.

[23] Thoukydides, 1, 2, 6, voicing the current opinion of his time, states that the Dorian invasion occurred eighty years after the fall of Troy. Its date, therefore, would depend upon that of the capture of Priam's city by the Achaeans. Unfortunately the date of the fall of Troy cannot be established with accuracy either from the writings of the ancient authors or from the available archaeological evidence. For a complete discussion of the problem, cf. G. E. Mylonas, "The Date of the Fall of Troy and of the Descent of the Herakleids," *Athens Yearbook*, 1960, pp. 408-469. Also C. W. Blegen, and others, *Troy*, IV, p. 12.

[24] For a fuller discussion of the prehistoric remains of Eleusis, see Mylonas,

discovery on the southern slope of the hill, of a few sherds belonging to the Early Bronze age, or Early Helladic period, indicate that perhaps the site was occupied in that remote age.

A regular settlement of the Middle Helladic period was uncovered on the southern slope of the Eleusinian hill by Skias (1895-1902) and by me (1930-1931). Skias, in an effort to explain the layer of ashes that covered the Middle Helladic remains, maintained that they were the remnants of funeral pyres and thus assumed cremation to be characteristic of that remote period. His theory was accepted by a good many authorities including Wace and Thompson.[25] Our excavations, however, proved that the ashes were due to the conflagration that destroyed the village at the end of the period. Owing to the fact that the settlement was built on the slope of the hill, not a single house has entirely survived, and we have only fragments of foundations to indicate the existence of such structures (Fig. 5). However, these fragments proved sufficient to suggest that the village extended over the entire area on which at a later period the Telesterion was constructed, reaching as far to the north as the Greater Propylaea and as far east as the outer peribolos wall of the Sanctuary. It contained houses separately built, long and narrow in plan, often provided with an open portico on one of the short sides, while the opposite side was closed by an apsidal wall. The most important of the houses were divided by cross-walls into at least a main room and a very small rear chamber, apsidal in shape. Between the walls of adjacent houses and under the floors the bones of infants and small children were found buried either in small square trenches, the sides of which were lined with slabs, or in pots covered with earth. Occasionally, even adults were buried within the confines of the village.[26]

The adults, as a rule, were buried in a cemetery to be found some nine hundred meters beyond the walls of Eleusis to the west on the way to Megara.[27] The graves were arranged in groups and

---

Eleusis, 1932; "Eleusiniaka," *AJA*, 40 (1936), pp. 415-431; Kourouniotes and Mylonas, *AJA*, 37 (1933), pp. 271-286.

[25] *Ephem*, 1912, pp. 22ff; A. J. B. Wace and M. S. Thompson, *Prehistoric Thessaly*, p. 222.

[26] Two adult graves, made of slabs, were found in the area of the settlement (Mylonas, *Eleusis*, figs. 29-33).

[27] This cemetery, used over a period of some twenty-three centuries, will be

each grave contained two to four burials. The earliest examples are cists of small size (averaging 0.95m. x 0.55m. x 0.50m.), built of slabs set vertically in the ground and covered with a single slab. Often the floors were covered with pebbles. Because of the small size of the graves the bodies were laid in a contracted position. When a second body was to be laid in the grave, the bones of the first were swept to the corners. The earliest of these graves contain no gifts (*kterismata*) but as time went on, the custom of placing gifts in the grave is evidenced by the appearance of vases. In one of the latest sepulchers we found indications that the site was becoming more prosperous—gold ornaments, bronze circles covered with gold leaf used for keeping the curls of the hair in position.[28] With the passing of time the cist graves made of slabs gradually developed into built graves of large dimensions with a side door through which the bodies were introduced into the sepulcher; as a rule the door was found blocked with a slab (Fig. 7, a). Both in the graves and in the houses of the settlement vases are the most characteristic finds. They belong to the well-known Middle Helladic varieties: Minyan and matt-painted.

The majority of the graves and of the houses uncovered belong to the second half of the Middle Helladic period, seemingly to the eighteenth and seventeenth centuries B.C. No evidence was found to indicate that the cult of Demeter was celebrated during those centuries in the village. One wonders whether this settlement could be associated with the village established by the legendary Eleusis the son of Ogygos. Chronologically, the settlement belongs to the general period to which the mythological event could be placed and, interestingly enough, the Minyan pottery discovered in it is more closely related to that found at Orchomenos and the rest of Boeotia than to the pottery from the Peloponnesos.

REMAINS OF THE LATE HELLADIC PERIOD

The Middle Helladic village was succeeded by one belonging to the Late Helladic I period, a period that is also known as Early

---

referred to as the west cemetery. Mylonas, *Praktika*, 1952, pp. 58-72; 1953, pp. 77-87; 1954, pp. 50-65; 1955, pp. 67-77; 1956, pp. 57-62; *Proceedings*, 99 (1955), pp. 57-64.

[28] They are the Homeric σφηκωτῆρες. *Praktika*, 1955, pp. 67-68.

Mycenaean and covers approximately the years from 1580 to 1500 B.C. Remains of this village were found not only on the south slope of the hill, but also on the top. Strangely enough, no remains were found in the area of the Telesterion and apparently the area on which in later years the Temple of Demeter was constructed was left uninhabited in Late Helladic I times. The remains of the village are scanty and again we have to base our conclusions on fragmentary walls and pottery. The latter is typical of what came to be known as Early Mycenaean ware and is characterized by geometric patterns, especially spiral and floral, painted on the smoothed and slipped surface of the pots in a brilliant black-brown color. The remains uncovered prove that the culture they represent developed gradually from the preceding one, that no break in continuity exists which could be taken to indicate the arrival of new people with different ideas and cultural traits. The same conclusion was reached in excavating the west cemetery; for there too the earlier graves gradually developed into more advanced types and the burial customs that they exhibit are identical with those current in the earlier period. Now, however, more gifts are placed in the graves and along with the pots bronze weapons occasionally appear. There is no evidence that the cult of Demeter existed at Eleusis during this period.

Beginning with the fifteenth century we have what is known as the Late Helladic II, or Middle Mycenaean period, which along with the Late Helladic III, or Late Mycenaean era, covers the years from about 1500 B.C. to about 1110 B.C. Remains of both these periods were unearthed in the course of the excavations, some on top of the hill, others along its southeastern and eastern slopes and even in the area immediately to the north of the base of the hill. With the exception of the walls belonging to one structure, Megaron B, these remains are fragmentary and give us little information. They prove, however, that especially in the course of the Late Helladic III period the village was enlarged considerably and occupied an area much larger than that of the preceding eras. They also prove that the culture developed at Eleusis in the Late Helladic periods is similar to that discovered in contemporary sites elsewhere and that it did evolve in a normal fashion from what preceded it on the site.

The same evidence was obtained at the west cemetery. The area used for burial was extended during the Late Helladic periods and graves became more varied. The types diverge from those employed in other Mycenaean sites, but for a good reason. The chamber tomb hewn in the rock and in the hillside is the characteristic grave of the Late Helladic II and III times in the Mycenaean territory. As a rule, the people of Eleusis did not make chamber tombs because the rock of their hills is very hard. They continued, therefore, to develop the type of grave used by their ancestors. Yielding, however, to the trend of the times they made a few chamber tombs, but they dug them in the solid earth of the cemetery (Fig. 8).

Tradition points to the Late Helladic II and III periods as the eras in which the cult of Demeter was introduced and established at Eleusis.[29] We may well wonder whether among the ruins found we can recognize the temple reputed to have been erected for the purpose at the command of the Goddess herself. The Hymn not only mentions that temple but also indicates the general locality. In vv. 270-272 we read: "Let all the people build me a great temple and an altar below it and beneath the citadel and its sheer fortification wall upon a rising hillock above the Kallichoron (well)."

THE TEMPLE OF THE HOMERIC HYMN

One of the landmarks mentioned in this description is the fortification wall of the citadel. Our excavations have failed to disclose such a fortification wall, but there can be little doubt that it existed in Mycenaean times. Remains indicate the existence of Late Helladic II and III houses on top of the hill and on its northeastern end; it is probable that others existed, including what served as the palace of the ruling family. According to the building customs of the times, the top of the hill would have been surrounded by a fortification wall following its brow. It is possible to assume that part of this wall was still standing when the Hymn was composed and that it then served as a diateichisma or a cross-wall that separated the Sanctuary area, and more specifically the area of the Telesterion, from the inhabited area of the hill. Perhaps it was destroyed when the expansion of the Telesterion to the west was

[29] *Supra*, p. 14.

{ 33 }

undertaken, an expansion that necessitated the removal of a large area of the slope. The line of the fortification wall along the north-eastern spur of the hill, left in its natural state, is indicated by the surviving remains of Mycenaean or Late Helladic houses. It must have been placed over the edge of that spur and its course must have followed the brow of the hill beyond it to the south. Surviving remains of houses higher up prove that it could not have existed here and, if it had been farther down the slope, then there could not have been a hillock beyond it, as the Hymn indicates. The line of the fortification wall along the edge and a little to the east and south of the small chapel of Panaghitsa, which still stands on the projecting northeastern spur of the hill (Fig. 44, p), is thus indicated both by the technique followed in the construction of fortification walls in Mycenaean times, and by the established fact that remains of houses and traces of occupancy, that presumably would have been within the walled area, were found in the area around the chapel. If we place the wall on this line, then we have to conclude that there is no room on the hill for the Temple of Demeter, that of necessity we have to look to the slope for the location of the temple. We must also remember that it was not to be incorporated in the palace of the ruling family, as was customary in the Mycenaean age, that it was to be a separate and special temple to be constructed below the fortification wall of the citadel.

We believe that the Temple of Demeter mentioned by the Hymn was found in the excavations of 1931 and 1932 by Kourouniotes and his collaborators on the east slope of the citadel of Eleusis where, in a later period, the great Telesteria were constructed (Figs. 6, building B indicated by solid black lines, and 20). The terracing and the artificial fill, which were later required for the construction of large buildings on the slope, were instrumental in preserving the foundations of the earlier buildings, including the remains of this earliest temple.[30]

Below the area on which it was erected, the ground dips rather abruptly to the plain so that it could be said that the structure was standing on a rising hillock. It is oriented from southeast to northwest, or roughly from east to west, with entrance on the southeast.

[30] K. Kourouniotes, "Das eleusinische Heiligtum von den Anfängen bis zur vorperikleischen Zeit," *ArchRW*, 32 (1935), pp. 52-78.

In shape it is a regular megaron, composed of one long and narrow room fronted by a portico (Fig. 11a). The greater part of the structure was excavated in the early days of the exploration of the site and almost no evidence, which would indicate its purpose or its interior arrangements, was left for us to find. The base of a column left in its original position, however, survived. Furthermore, the remains of the Megaron were damaged in antiquity by the construction over it of later buildings.

What survived of the Megaron is illustrated in Figs. 13 and 11a. Its long north wall is preserved to a length of almost 7m., while its south wall to only 4.50m. But at the eastern end we find the original termination of both walls in a well-built anta (Figs. 13, a and 11a). The rear wall of the building is not preserved, but from traces of its line left on the rock, we can restore its course rather accurately. The walls average 0.60m. in width and are built of small unworked stones laid in mortar in two rows as indicated in the ground plan (Fig. 11a). The antae are constructed of rather flat stones laid on a large block that forms the base of the anta (Fig. 13a). Just one course survives of the cross-wall that separates the main room from the portico. On the longitudinal axis of the main room, a column base was found *in situ* and another could be restored about two meters further to the south (Fig. 11a). The inner room, therefore, appears to have had two columns on its longitudinal axis to help support its roof. Two columns perhaps stood in the portico to serve a similar purpose.[31] The floor, made of well-pressed earth and lime mixed with small pebbles, survived in small sections both in the inner chamber and in the portico. Because of the slope of the hill, the floor of the chamber is about 0.30m. above that of the portico and must have required a step. The cross-wall between the two must have acted also as a retaining wall for the artificial fill needed to level off the floor of the chamber.

The portico (*aithousa*) suffered considerably from the foundations of two columns—one of the Kimonian era and of another of Roman Imperial times—which were lowered right through it. Its

[31] The existence of a single row of columns on the longitudinal axis of the main room does not necessitate the placing of one column in the portico on the same axis. At Aghios Kosmas we have megara with two columns in the portico and a single row on the longitudinal axis of the main room. Mylonas, *Aghios Kosmas*, plan 15, House T.

side walls, however, are preserved and its width, amounting to ca. 5.70m., is certain. Its depth of two meters also is certain, since a part of the cross-wall is preserved. The central part of the portico projects about two meters beyond the end of the antae, thus forming a large platform, ca. 3.40m. in width, symmetrically placed so as to leave between it and the antae of the portico on either side a passage averaging 1.40m. in width. In these passages originally were located stairways, which led from the portico to the court below (Fig. 11a). A few of the steps of the south stairway were found *in situ* (Fig. 13, st). The steps of the north stairway were apparently removed when, at a later period, an addition was built on the north side of the Megaron; at least three of the flat stones used in the construction of the north stairway were found built into the walls of the addition.

The building, to be called hereafter Megaron B, stood in a court surrounded by a thick peribolos wall, sections of which survived along the south and north sides of the enclosed court (Figs. 13, B4 and 11, B4, B5, B6). It is built of small unworked stones laid in mortar and averages 0.85m. in width. The south section of the wall is preserved to a length of 19m. while the north measures some 14m. The distance between the two, giving us the width of the court, averages 16m. The length of the court cannot be determined since neither the east nor the west sides of the peribolos have been preserved. The east side is probably covered by the foundations of the portico of the Peisistratean Telesterion, while its west side must have been destroyed when the Telesteria of the Historic period were constructed. The court seems to have had a gate on the north side, indicated by a paved road that leads to it (Fig. 11, B6); but of course we cannot exclude the possibility of the existence of other gates on the sides that are not preserved. At about the middle of its preserved length, the south wall of the peribolos widens (Fig. 11, B4). The function of this bastion-like construction is not certain; perhaps it was built to withstand the rapid flow of rain water at the steepening of the slope. Some 2.50m. east of the bastion a drain was found built through the wall; in that drain terminated a channel that started from the south stairway of the portico (Fig. 11, B5). Apparently the channel and the drain served the portico and the court and they tie together the Megaron, its court, and the peribolos wall. At places the peribolos wall is preserved to a height of 1.20m. and certainly its superstructure, like that of the Megaron itself, was of sun-dried mud brick. Along the walls of the Megaron and of the peribolos a good many sherds were found which help date the structures. The sherds belong to the category known as Late Helladic II, and to that period, accepted as encompassing the fifteenth century B.C.,[32] the Megaron and its peribolos wall should be assigned.

Within the enclosed area and to the northeast of Megaron B, remains of later walls were found, which belong to the closing period of the Mycenaean Age, to Late Helladic III times. The pattern formed by these walls (Fig. 11b) proves that the original Megaron was augmented by the addition of three rooms, a main and two side rooms. The main room, Room B1 (7m. x 4.40m.), was so constructed as to have its front wall rest partially upon the platform of Megaron B. Its entrance (1.60m. wide), almost at the center of the south side, opens onto the platform. A second door opening (1.45m. wide) at its western corner gave access to the street, which separated the addition from the north wall of the peribolos. A very small portion of the floor of this main room was preserved at the time of our excavation and it, like the floor of the room of the Megaron, is made of well-pressed earth mixed with lime and small pebbles.

The side room to the northwest, Room B2, was completely excavated in the early days of the clearing of the Telesterion area and we found only small fragments of its side walls. The northeast room, Room B3, stretches under the foundations of the Peisistratean "prostoon" and it was possible to excavate only a section of it by tunneling. The work, however, enabled us to determine that its width amounts to 5.75m. Its doorway measures ca. one meter in width. Its floor is well preserved and was found to consist of well-packed earth mixed with small pebbles. In the fill of this room a good many sherds were found, indicating that it was in use to the very end of the Late Helladic III period and that its construction must have taken place in the course of what is known as Late Helladic III B era. These sherds and the fact that the walls of Rooms B1 and B2 are built upon parts of Megaron B and its

[32] In dating the prehistoric periods and in terminology we follow the schemes developed by A. J. B. Wace, Carl W. Blegen, and Arne Furumark.

platform, prove that they are later than the Megaron, that they were an addition to the Megaron and not a separate architectural unit. At the southeast corner of the main room B1, and about 0.05m. above the latest Mycenaean floor level were discovered two characteristic handles of Geometric pots, one of which is in the form of a bird, perhaps a dove. These small finds may indicate that perhaps the building was still in use in Geometric times.

In conclusion we may note that the addition did not interfere with the entrance to Megaron B; that the platform of that Megaron could continue to be in use after the additional rooms were built, although then it had the form of a triangular projection placed in the corner of Megaron B and Room B1. This arrangement removed the need of the north stairway which was then demolished. The south stairway, however, was maintained and apparently continued in use as long as the building itself. The construction of the addition made a little more difficult the access to the portico of the original Megaron. A person entering the court through the north entrance would follow the passage around Room B3 to reach the court in front of the platform. It also reduced the space of that court. But it indicates that the need served by the Megaron was so increased that more space was required.

IDENTIFICATION OF MEGARON B WITH
THE TEMPLE OF DEMETER

The excavators of the Megaron believe that it is the Temple of Demeter mentioned by the Hymn. Before we present their reasoning we must consider briefly Noack's ingenious hypothesis regarding the beginning of the Eleusinian cult which has been adopted by many scholars. In his monumental work on Eleusis, he maintained that the beginnings of the Sanctuary of Demeter did not antedate the eighth century B.C.; that then on the eastern slope of the hill, where later the Telesterion was built, was constructed for the first time an artificial terrace supported by a well-built retaining wall. On that terrace originally stood only an altar before which Demeter was worshiped by sacrifices and other rites. At the beginning of the seventh century B.C. a Temple to Demeter was constructed for the first time as specified by the Hymn; it was erected on top of the hill near the area on which stands today the Chapel of Panaghitsa.

That temple was used for whatever part of the cult required temple worship, while the Mysteries proper were held in the open air by the side of the altar which stood on the terrace of the slope below. At a later time in the Archaic period, where the altar stood, was erected a building (der *Alt-Bau* as he calls it) in which the Mysteries for the first time were celebrated in a closed area. Accordingly Noack reached the conclusion, which was advanced before him by Blavette, Svoronos, and Rubensohn, that the Temple of Demeter was different and distinct from the Telesterion. Since remnants of such a temple distinct from the Telesterion were not found in the excavations, Noack, adopting Rubensohn's suggestions, maintained that the original temple to Demeter which stood on the edge of the hill was destroyed when the rock was hewn away to form the terrace on which what he called Temple F was constructed in pre-Persian days; that Temple F took the place of the original temple.[33]

Noack's hypothesis of the existence of two sacred buildings dedicated to the cult of Demeter was formulated before the latest excavations of Kourouniotes and his collaborators, which brought to light Mycenaean remains on the hill and a megaron below the floors of the later Telesteria. With the discovery of Mycenaean houses on top of the hill, which would necessitate the placing of the fortification wall at the very edge of its eastern side, it became clear that no space remained on the hill itself for the erection of a temple. The area on which Noack maintains that the first temple to Demeter once stood would be within the fortified area of the hill and not without. And yet the Hymn specifically states that the first temple to Demeter was erected below the walls of the citadel. Noack's later temple, Temple F as he calls it, does not fare any better. For Kourouniotes and Travlos proved definitely, as we are going to see in Chapter VII, that Temple F, which according to Noack was built in pre-Persian times to take the place of the first and oldest temple to Demeter, dates from Roman times.[34] Consequently the assumptions on which Noack based his hypothesis are proved wrong.

The Hymn speaks of one temple only; it does not mention a temple where the Goddess was to be worshiped and another area or structure where her Mysteries were to be performed. In the

[33] Noack, *Eleusis*, pp. 48, 85, and 218.
[34] Kourouniotes and Travlos, *Telesterion*, pp. 54-114.

clearing of the Sanctuary area one temple to Demeter was found dating from the time of the Hymn or earlier; and that temple is the Telesterion. Noack argues at some length that the Telesterion has a plan totally different from that of the regular Greek temple, that it has a square plan with many columns, and, consequently, it could not have been the temple of the Goddess, which must have had the normal plan of a Greek temple. Yet the ancient Athenians, who well knew what their temples were like, called the Telesterion of Peisistratean times, in spite of its square plan and columns, a neos, a temple.[35] Furthermore, the latest excavations have proved that the square plan with many columns was not the original form of the Telesterion but an innovation introduced apparently in Peisistratean days. The plan of the Archaic Telesterion, that preceded the Peisistratean, was not square but oblong similar to that of the normal Greek temple; and certainly the plan of Megaron B cannot be distinguished from that of a typical temple. The argument of the square columned form is no longer valid. There can be no doubt that one and only one Temple of Demeter existed at Eleusis as the Hymn specified; the same temple where her Mysteries were celebrated. That temple is the Telesterion.

Could the beginnings of the cult of Demeter at Eleusis, which required a temple, be placed early in the eighth century B.C. as prescribed by Noack? It seems to us that not only the archaeological but the traditional evidence as well indicates the existence of the cult at Eleusis long before that century. We have already noted that the Parian Chronicle dates in the fifteenth century B.C. the advent of Demeter to Eleusis, that is, the introduction of her cult to our site. The Hymn, which, as we have seen, seems to represent the official local tradition, places the introduction of the cult in the lifetime of Eumolpos or even earlier; and Eumolpos is a contemporary of Erechtheus, who is placed in the second half of the fifteenth century. The tradition of the early wars of Eleusis and Athens would indicate that date for the people connected with the cult. Herodotos tells us that the Ionians transplanted the cult of Demeter Eleusinia to the southwestern coast of Asia Minor when they colonized that district; that colonization began long before the eighth century. He states more specifically that Phillistos, one of the fol-

---

[35] Cf. *IG* I², 81, ll. 5-9; and *IG* I², 313, col. II, l. 103.

lowers of Neleus, the founder of Miletos, built a temple to Demeter Eleusinia on Mount Mykale.[36] Miletos was colonized by the Ionians about the middle of the eleventh century B.C. Androklos, the son of the last king of Athens, Kodros, who founded Ephesos, apparently introduced into Ionia the Hiera of the Eleusinian Demeter, since his descendants by right presided over the sacrifices held in honor of the Goddess;[37] in a similar manner the descendants of Eumolpos, the reputed instigator of the cult at Eleusis, presided over the Mysteries held there. Aristotle tells us that the Eleusinia, the most ancient of all the ceremonies of Greece, were founded when Pandion governed Athens, and this takes us back at least to about 1300 B.C.[38]

To these traditions we must add those that refer to the widespread dispersal of the cult of Demeter Eleusinia in the Peloponnesos. Most of the reputed founders of the Peloponnesian centers of worship belong to the Heroic age. The cult of Pheneos was established by Naos, a grandson of Eumolpos;[39] that at Keleai by Dysaules, brother of Keleos, who went to that city after he had been expelled from Eleusis by Ion the leader of the Athenians in one of the wars between the Athenians and the Eleusinians that seems to have taken place before the days of Theseus.[40] The cult of the Eleusinian Demeter was taken to Messinia (Andania) by Kaukon and later was emphasized by Lykos, the son of Pandion, one of the mythical Kings of Athens.[41] Of course we must remember the warning of Pausanias that "old legends, being unencumbered by genealogies, left free scope for fiction, especially in the pedigrees of heroes."[42] There is a tendency to attribute to a very remote past the beginnings of a cult or of a custom. Yet the body of evidence is such that these traditions cannot be completely disregarded; taken as a whole they seem to indicate the existence of the cult at Eleusis in prehistoric or Late Mycenaean times. Regarding the Hymn we may note that it is of course a late creation; perhaps it was composed around 600 B.C. However, as we have already seen,

---

[36] Herodotos, IX, 97.

[37] Strabo, XIV, 1, 3 (c. 633).

[38] Aristotle in *FHG*, II, *Fragm.* 282: "πρῶτα μὲν τὰ Ἐλευσίνια διὰ τὸν καρπὸν τῆς Δήμητρος."

[39] Pausanias, VIII, 15, 1.   [40] Pausanias, II, 14, 1.

[41] Pausanias, IV, 1, 5 and 7.   [42] Pausanias, I, 38, 7.

the tradition it contains certainly belongs to the Mycenaean age.[43] We may, therefore, conclude that tradition indicates the existence of a cult at Eleusis in Mycenaean times long before the beginning of the eighth century B.C.

The cult indicated by the body of tradition required a temple. The construction and existence of that temple is specifically indicated by the Hymn. For that temple we have to go beyond the date suggested by Noack. We have noted already that the temple could not have been built on top of the rocky spur of Panaghitsa as Noack, Rubenshon, Blavette, and Svoronos assert.[44] It had to be built on the slope.[45] Megaron B, which we have described in such detail, fits the topographic specifications of the Hymn. One may well ask what other purpose a building like the Megaron could have served.

It could not for two reasons have served as the palace of any of the Eleusinian leaders whose names are to be found in the Hymn. First, it is located beyond the protecting wall of the citadel within which such buildings were usually built. Of course the Megaron had its own peribolos wall, but the value of that wall as a defensive measure is minimal since it could not be defended if attacked from higher points of the hill which were still outside the citadel. Again, the width and construction of the wall do not justify the assumption that it was a fortification wall. It must have been built to insure privacy, to enclose a space. Second, the Megaron is too small to be considered as the dwelling place of a somewhat well-to-do member of the community. We now have from other sites Mycenaean examples of houses and these are composed of more rooms than one and often present a complicated plan. One could recall the foundations of the House of Columns, of the Oil Merchant, of the Shields, of the Sphinxes at Mycenae, excavated by the late Professor Wace and by the Ephor of the district, Dr. N. Verdelis.[46]

---

[43] Mylonas, *Hymn*, pp. 15-22. For the office of the King in Mycenaean times see also Webster's recent book, *From Mycenae to Homer*, 1958, p. 11.

[44] V. Blavette, "Fouilles d'Eleusis," *BCH*, 8 (1884), pp. 254-264; *idem*, 9 (1885), pp. 65-67 and pl. 1; J. N. Svoronos, "Μνημεῖα τοῦ Ἐλευσινιακοῦ κύκλου," and "Ἐλευσινιακά," *JIAN*, 4 (1901), pp. 272-513; 8 (1905), pp. 131-160; O. Rubensohn, *Die Mysterienheiligtümer*, pp. 44ff.

[45] D. Philios, "Ἐλευσινιακὰ μελετήματα," *JIAN*, 7 (1904), 11-60. Mylonas, *Hymn*, pp. 31ff; *Eleusiniaka, AJA*, 40 (1936), pp. 415-431. *Supra*, p. 34.

[46] A. J. B. Wace, *JHS*, 71 (1951), pp. 255ff; 74 (1954), pp. 170-171; *BSA*, 48 (1953), pp. 9-15. *Mycenae*, pp. 91-97; 104-105. N. M. Verdelis, *Archaeology*, 14 (1961), pp. 12-17. G. E. Mylonas, *Ancient Mycenae*, pp. 71-72.

At Eleusis itself foundations have been found indicating that the houses of the period contained a number of rooms.[47] Our Megaron in its initial stage had but a single room. Could it have been the house of a poor citizen who could not afford the construction of a large dwelling? This suggestion also is untenable in view of its peribolos wall and its platform, features that are unique in Mycenaean construction, and by the discovery of a small fragment of lime-plaster bearing the representation of a human eye painted in the fresco technique. This small fragment seems to indicate the existence of murals in the room of the Megaron where it was found. Such frescoes are known from the palaces and the houses of important citizens. If we are to believe that the Megaron was a dwelling, we have to believe that it was the house of a prominent and wealthy member of the community and this conclusion seems untenable in view of the small size of the edifice and its location.

The size of the building and its privacy bear out its function as a temple. Of course, compared to the monumental and often large structures of the Historic era, ours is very small and poor. However, we must remember that in the Mycenaean age temple construction, as far as we know, was limited. Usually, a part of the palace itself, a comparatively small room, served the religious needs of the community. House sanctuaries were common; but they were small and unimpressive and usually consisted of a small room or section of it.[48] The only other temple that seems not to have had any relation to the dwelling of the ruling family or to any other dwelling, is the shrine of Gournia in Krete;[49] and that is a small room (some 4m. x 3m.). Our Megaron in comparison is very elaborate and even sumptuous.

The location of Megaron B, just below the floor of the later Telesteria provides us with another important piece of evidence. It is essential to note that the east slope of the citadel was not an ideal place for the construction of large buildings. Just a little to the north of the base of the Panaghitsa spur were even, flat spaces where large buildings could have been erected with little difficulty.

[47] *Idem, "Eleusiniaka," AJA*, 40 (1936), pp. 419ff.

[48] M. P. Nilsson, *The Minoan-Mycenaean Religion and its Survival in Greek Religion*, 2nd ed., pp. 77-116. With reason he disagrees with Banti (*Culti di H. Triada*, p. 40), who thinks that "after Middle Minoan III times the sanctuaries began to be independent of a palace or house."

[49] *Gournia*, pp. 47ff, and pl. 1.

And yet the Telesteria of the Historic era were erected on a slope badly suited for the placing of large buildings, over an area that required artificial terracing and the construction of heavy retaining walls. Even the outdoor celebration of the Mysteries, assumed by Noack, needed an artificially constructed terrace, fragments of the retaining walls of which have survived. That terrace, dating from the latter part of the Geometric period, from the beginning of the eighth century B.C., was built for cult purposes as is proved by the remnants of sacrificial pyres disclosed by the side of its ascent.[50] One is justified in asking: why in Late Geometric times was the slope chosen, which necessitated costly and laborious construction of retaining walls, when the entire plain was at the disposal of the people of Eleusis? The answer seems obvious: that slope was chosen because its area was already sanctified by previous religious use, by a cult that was celebrated there long before the need arose to build the Late Geometric terrace. In a similar manner, when in later years the need arose to construct larger buildings to accommodate the increased number of initiates, the people of Eleusis constructed those buildings not in the plain but over the same area and slope because it was already sacred. Continuity in cult places, as Nilsson pointed out some time ago, from Mycenaean to Historic times is rather common in the religious history of Greece; examples of such continuity exist at Delos, Delphi, Thebes, etc.[51]

In the Hymn another landmark is mentioned that bears on our quest. The temple to be built for Demeter was not only below the fortification wall of the citadel on a projecting hillock, but also Καλλιχόρου καθύπερθεν, "above the Kallichoron." Scholars agree in believing that the Kallichoron was a well, the Well of the Fair Dances. It was mentioned by Pausanias along with the temple of Artemis and Poseidon; it evidently was found by Philios in the outer court of the Sanctuary (Figs. 4, No. 10, and 33).[52] The Hymn, however, specifies that the temple was to be built καθύπερθεν of the Kallichoron, and that specification has caused a good deal of trouble. Καθύπερθεν, according to Liddell and Scott, can mean either 1) from above, down from above, or 2) atop, above; for a topo-

[50] *Infra*, p. 56-57.

[51] Nilsson, *op.cit.*, pp. 457ff. A. Keramopoullos, *Praktika of Academy*, 2 (1927), pp. 427ff.

[52] D. Philios, *Praktika*, 1892, pp. 33ff; Pausanias, I, 38, 6.

graphical position it can indicate north of, or an upper country farther inland, especially when in the plural, and 3) above, having the upper hand. Of these the meaning "above" seems indicated. The Temple of Demeter therefore was to be constructed, and was actually constructed, above the Kallichoron well. At the most we could assume that the temple was to the north of the well. However, the well which has been identified as the Kallichoron is quite removed from any of the sacred buildings of the Sanctuary (Fig. 4, No. 10). The Telesteria (Fig. 4, No. 50) are located some 100m. to the southwest of it, while some 80m. separate it from the Panaghitsa spur where Noack presumed an early temple. None of the buildings is to the north of that well. This discrepancy, which has given rise to all kinds of hypotheses, could be eliminated if we could locate a well that would agree more fully with the specification of the Hymn. Such a well does exist.

Kourouniotes, in his excavations of 1930, revealed a well cut in the rock at the foot of the northeast corner of the retaining wall of the stoa of Philon (marked W in our Figs. 6 and 18). That well we cleared in 1952; but unfortunately its contents had been emptied before, perhaps by Philios. However, there can be no doubt that it is a very old well. It is associated, by means of a paved road, with the foundations of a structure of some religious significance we uncovered immediately to the east of it, belonging to the closing years of the Mycenaean age and to the Geometric period. Apparently the well was a landmark of respect because when a retaining wall was constructed in the Archaic period to support the terrace of the Telesterion of that period, that retaining wall was made to go around the well enshrining it in a carefully constructed niche (Fig. 18). If it had been a common well, one without significance, this mark of respect would not have been shown. We believe this well, (Fig. 6,W) to be the Kallichoron of the Hymn.

After the Persian destruction of the Sanctuary and in the course of the Kimonian reconstruction, the well was filled in because the entire area was transformed into a large court, raised by some six to seven meters, and because the rites held by it had been transferred presumably by Peisistratos (see below, p. 72). It was then that the name Kallichoron was given to the well in the court. The well in the court we have equated in our study of the Homeric

Hymn with the Parthenion, or Well of the Maidens,[53] at the side of which, according to the Hymn, the Goddess sat to rest. There we pointed out the strange fact that the Parthenion was never mentioned again in literature after its initial appearance in the verses of the Hymn. It seems to us that the name was dropped after the new name, Kallichoron, was given to it. The Kallichoron was a definite landmark of Eleusinian topography; it was mentioned by the Goddess, and its role in the story of Demeter remained the same throughout the ages; hence its existence was essential and its name survived. The transference of the name to another well was not difficult after the original Kallichoron was filled in; and the filling in was not prohibited by reverence or religious scruples since the Kallichoron was only a landmark, not sanctified by a specific act of the Goddess. The importance of the Parthenion was due to the fact that the Goddess sat to rest in its neighborhood. However, that importance was lost when, in the course of time, the "Agelastos Petra," the "Mirthless Stone" was devised as the place where the Goddess sat to rest. That stone was pointed out to the visitors as a sacred landmark and it must have been within the enclosed area since Pausanias does not mention it. It is interesting to note that when Apollodoros tells the story of the coming of Demeter to Eleusis he states that the Goddess "first sat down on the rock which has been named Mirthless after her, beside what is called the Kallichoron well (the Well of the Fair Dances)." This detail, which is contrary to what the Hymn states, is repeated by Kallimachos and Nikander.[54] Scholars have assumed that Apollodoros confused his traditions. We doubt that this is the case. Apollodoros certainly must have known the Hymn, but he also knew the Eleusis of his time, since most probably he was an Athenian.[55] When he came to actual topographic details, he used the landmarks that were pointed out to him when he visited Eleusis. He must have seen the "Mirthless Stone," which by this time had become the

[53] Mylonas, *Hymn*, p. 74; a more detailed discussion of the problem of the wells of Eleusis in pp. 64-81. *Praktika*, 1952, pp. 55-56.

[54] Apollodoros, I, 5, 1. Kallimachos, *Hymn to Demeter*, VI, 15. Nikander, *Theriaka*, vv. 484-487.

[55] Photios identifies the author as Apollodoros, the Athenian grammarian (*Bibliotheka*, ed. Bekker, p. 142a, 37). This identification has been challenged, but C. Robert, *De Apollodori Bibliotheca*, p. 34, has shown that Apollodoros was indeed an Athenian.

traditional resting-place of the Goddess by the roadside, and this was near the well which was then called Kallichoron and not Parthenion. And so he recorded what he actually saw. It is, therefore, possible to maintain that at the time of Apollodoros the old name of the well, Parthenion, was entirely forgotten, and its later name, Kallichoron, was in common use. The same reasoning could apply to the case of Kallimachos who was older than Apollodoros and whose activity is more definitely placed in the reign of Ptolemy Philadelphos (285-247 B.C.). The references in these authors so interpreted strengthen considerably, if they do not prove definitely, the identification proposed.

Our general conclusion regarding the wells, therefore, can only be that the one below the northeast corner of the foundations of the Stoa of Philon is the Kallichoron of the Hymn. Megaron B is exactly καθύπερθεν, above that well, thus satisfying the last of the specifications mentioned in the Hymn. Located below and near the fortification wall of the citadel the Megaron could have been pointed out from the palace; built on a slope at the time unoccupied and steeply inclined, it could be considered as standing on a hillock; it stands above a well, which may have been the Kallichoron of the Hymn; a platform fronts its portico on which the altar of the Goddesses could have been placed and from which the Hiera could have been shown to the initiates standing in the court; the privacy of the court and the secrecy required from the very beginning for the cult were assured by a well-built peribolos wall; it was constructed in the course of a period corresponding in time with the traditional introduction of the cult to Eleusis; the fact that it stands in an area which continued to be used in the Historic era only because it was already sacred in Late Geometric times would indicate its religious function. In general we have every reason to believe that the Megaron is the first temple of Demeter built on the slope of the citadel of Eleusis at the time of the introduction of the cult as specified by the Hymn.

In our excavations we found no evidence that would prove the religious nature of the Megaron. It should be recalled, however, 1) that it was excavated before our day and that very few and very small undisturbed sections of it were left for us to investigate; 2) that prehistoric sanctuaries do not possess monumental works that would indicate their character and function; 3) that, since the Sanctuary remained in use from prehistoric times, any objects of religious nature, any ritualistic vessels and images, the famous sacra of the Eleusinian cult, handed down from generation to generation, must have been taken from the older and deposited in the newer sanctuaries which replaced them. Consequently, such objects, which would have served to prove the sacred use of the building, would not have remained for us to find, even if we had been the first to explore the area. In the absence of relics that could establish the use of the Megaron, we have to use the traditional, the circumstantial evidence, all of which proves that the Megaron is our first temple, the temple of the Hymn.

Perhaps it is legitimate to recall that the corner of a building (Fig. 12, Z), dating from the very end of the seventh century and standing in the area of the Telesteria, has been identified and universally accepted as a temple. We agree fully with the identification, but we would like to point out that nothing was found within that building to prove its sacred character. Its identification as a Telesterion rests on grounds precisely similar to those on which we base the identification of Megaron B as a temple.

Two points remain to which we must turn our attention now. The Megaron has the typical oblong form of a Greek temple, unlike the square halls that were developed in later years. Its parts were adequate to serve all the needs of the Goddess and her ritual. Consequently from the very beginning of the cult we have but one building serving as the Temple of the Goddess and as the area where the Mysteries were celebrated. The assumption, therefore, of the existence of a separate temple for the Goddess and of another structure for the holding of the Mysteries seems unfounded.

Again we may note that the first temple to Demeter is a true megaron in the Homeric sense of the word, the most important unit of a habitation. It was constructed so that the Goddess could dwell in it far from the immortal Gods. The Goddess had no need of the many rooms that were attached to the megaron unit in the Mycenaean palaces and homes. She could close herself up in the room behind the portico and dwell there until the return of her daughter. The simple structure was her temple, her Megaron.

Hence her temple could be called the Megaron of Demeter; and the inner room of that Megaron became the most sacred part of the sanctuary, because it was believed that the Goddess had lived in it for some time. In that part the sacred objects would naturally be kept after the departure of the Goddess; and even when the temples of Demeter at Eleusis were increased in size, it is natural to believe that the original room, or its approximate area, would have formed the most sacred area within the enlarged sanctuaries, the Holy of Holies.[56]

The second point deals with the place of origin of the cult of the Eleusinian Demeter. The Megaron-temple of Demeter, the first Temple of the Goddess *on* our site, is of the normal Greek type and has nothing to do with the shrines of either the Egyptians or the Minoan Kretans. It is a native form developed locally, belonging to the mainland of Greece. This fact will invalidate the argument of the Egyptian or Minoan origin of the cult based upon the square plan of the later Telesteria.

MYCENAEAN SCRIPT

In the last few years there has become available to scholars a new source of information regarding the latest period of the Mycenaean age, the period during which the cult of Demeter was introduced to Eleusis. Clay tablets and vases bearing on them incised and painted inscriptions in a script known as Linear B are now easily accessible to scholars. Thanks to the magnificent achievement of the late Michael Ventris a most significant and decisive advance has been made toward the decipherment of that script.[57] We have no inscribed tablets from Eleusis, but under the Lesser Propylaea, in a Late Helladic III C house, Kourouniotes and Threpsiades found a false-necked amphora bearing a painted inscription in Linear B.[58] It seems that writing was not unknown at Eleusis in Mycenaean times. A good number of inscribed tablets were discovered by Evans at Knossos, by Blegen in the Palace of Nestor at Pylos, and

[56] Cf. *infra*, p. 87, where the suggestion is made of the derivation of the temples of Demeter known as Megara.

[57] Ventris and Chadwick, "Evidence for Greek dialect in the Mycenaean Archives," *JHS*, 73 (1953), pp. 84-103; and *Documents in Mycenaean Greek*, 1956.

[58] G. E. Mylonas, "Eleusiniaka," *AJA*, 40 (1936), pp. 415-431; *Ephem*, 1936, pp. 61-100.

by Wace and Verdelis at Mycenae.[59] In some of these tablets names of Gods have been identified.[60] Are the names of Demeter and Persephone among them? Unfortunately the answer is no.

In the first line of one of the larger tablets from Pylos, Ventris and Chadwick read the words "da-ma-te DA 40." Although in their first publication they suggested that the da-ma-te could be Demeter, they later apparently abandoned this view and pointed out only that Webster and Furumark accepted it as meaning *Damater* (Cornland).[61] This interpretation was challenged by Carratelli, who suggested the reading *dam-dom*, interpreting it as perhaps "family units."[62] Palmer, on the other hand interprets "da-ma-te" as *damartes*, meaning homesteads; and he has been followed in this by Bennett and Ruiperez, who takes it to mean "families."[63] In a special, and provocative study, Webster maintains that it is "still permissible to find Demeter in the thirteenth century Pylos and to suppose that an abbreviation of her name signified an amount of land under corn."[64] It seems to us that the evidence on which the identification rests is too tenuous and it does not allow the conclusion that Demeter is named positively on the tablets thus far discovered.

The evidence of the inscription on the false-necked amphora from Eleusis is equally inconclusive. When I published the vase for the first time, I interpreted the inscription as a dedication to "Pais-Kore" of the potion (kykeon) contained in the vase.[65] The interpretation was based on the equation of the signs to the syllabic

[59] Cf. Bibliography in Ventris and Chadwick, *op.cit.*, 428-433, to which add C. W. Blegen and M. Lang, *AJA*, 62 (1958), pp. 175-191 and pls. 43-49.

[60] Ventris and Chadwick, *op.cit.*, pp. 125-129. The names of Hera, Hermes, Artemis, and perhaps Dionysos are read on tablets from Pylos; of Zeus and Poseidon on tablets both from Pylos and Knossos; of Athena, Eileithyia, Paieon (Apollo?), Enyalios, and possibly Ares from Knossos only.

[61] *JHS*, 73 (1953), p. 97. *Documents in Mycenaean Greek*, pp. 241-242. T. B. L. Webster, *Bull. Inst. Class. Studies*, 1 (1954), p. 13; *Antiquity*, 29 (1955), p. 11. A. Furumark, *Eranos*, 52 (1954), pp. 39ff.

[62] G. P. Carratelli, *La Parola del Passato*, 36 (1954), p. 225.

[63] *TransPhilAs*, 1954, p. 34 n. 1. E. L. Bennett, *AJA*, 60 (1956), pp. 118ff. M. S. Ruiperez, *Minos*, 4 (1956), p. 162.

[64] T. B. L. Webster, *Hommages à Waldemar Déonna, Latomus*, 28 (1957), pp. 531-536. Before we admit for consideration the inscription, presumably in Linear Script A, on the gold votive axe of the Museum of Fine Arts in Boston, we have to prove its provenience and establish its pedigree. Even if proved genuine, still its four signs do not give us the assumed name of Demeter.

[65] Cf. *supra* note 58.

values previously suggested by Persson and to those of the Kypriot script. If that reading had found corroboration, then the existence of the cult at Eleusis in Mycenaean times would have been proved epigraphically. Unfortunately, the syllabic values attributed to the signs by the Ventris system do not admit the interpretation. Those values will give no clear meaning to the inscription since at best they yield a place name and a personal name both known from Knossos.[66] Rubensohn's imaginative recognition of the word "wa-na-ka-te-ro," or Anaktoron, the dwelling place of a king and in our case of queen-Demeter, is based on the assumption that the first sign from the right of the second line, whose syllabic value is *wa*, is an abbreviation of the word.[67] Naturally *"wa"* could be the abbreviation of any number of words that had no connection with the dwelling place of a Goddess. Thus, the inscribed vase from Eleusis does not give us definite proof of the existence of the cult at Eleusis in Late Helladic times.

ART OBJECTS ASSUMED TO REPRESENT DEMETER

The examination of the known Mycenaean works of art that may have a bearing on our quest leads us to a similar negative conclusion. Perhaps the most interesting work of art that has been equated with our Goddesses is the ivory group of two seated women with a boy standing by the knee of one of them, found by Wace in the citadel of Mycenae.[68] The excavator suggested that perhaps the women were Demeter and Persephone and that the boy was Iacchos. Unfortunately, we can prove neither the religious character of the group nor that it was originally placed in a shrine as a cult object or as a votive offering. Nilsson has pointed out that the boy could not be Iacchos, since that divine youth became associated with the Goddesses long after the cult was established at Eleusis. Wace compared them with a terracotta group of two women connected like Siamese twins and bearing a child on their shoulders which was found by Tsountas in a grave at Mycenae. I have maintained that the ivory group has nothing to do with Demeter and Persephone; the two Goddesses together never in

[66] T. B. L. Webster, *From Mycenae to Homer*, p. 125.
[67] O. Rubensohn, *Jahrbuch*, 70 (1955), pp. 47-48.
[68] A. J. B. Wace, *Mycenae*, pp. 83-84 and figs. 101-103; *JHS*, 59 (1939), pp. 210ff.

literature or tradition or art are associated in the tending of a child; I suggested that the ivory group represented divine nurses with a child placed in their care.[69] This suggestion agrees with the function conjectured for Mycenaean figurines found especially in the graves of children. We believe that if a religious significance can be assumed for the ivory group of Mycenae, at the most we should see two divine nurses tending the young male God who seems to appear in Minoan-Mycenaean religion in Late Helladic and Late Minoan times.

Demeter has been seen in the Goddess seated under a tree receiving the adoration of approaching women, carved on the bezel of a gold ring found in the citadel of Mycenae.[70] The identification is attractive but unfortunately not convincing. It is natural that in agricultural communities, like those of Prehistoric Greece, "a mother Goddess or a Goddess of nature and of agriculture" should be worshiped. The difficulty lies in equating these agricultural Goddesses with those of the Historic era. On the ring from Mycenae we have perhaps the representation of the worship of an agricultural Goddess, but is she Demeter? The fact that the votaries are offering to her what has been identified commonly as poppy-heads is not conclusive since poppy-heads could be considered as symbolic of agriculture and consequently of any of the agricultural Goddesses. Furthermore, Marinatos in discussing the similar flower on the head of the idol from Ghazi, Krete, has ingeniously proved that it is neither the common wild poppy which is associated with Demeter, nor a pomegranate, but the cultivated *papaver somniferum* known even to Dioskourides. The plant had medicinal value and is used as a medicinal emblem. The divinity, therefore, associated with it on the ring is not a Goddess of agriculture but of healing.[71] On the other hand, the most conspicuous religious emblem carved on the ring is the double axe, and Demeter was never associated with that emblem. Webster has with reason suggested that the figure hovering in the air and holding the eight-shaped

---

[69] Nilsson, *op.cit.*, p. xxiv and p. 314 n. 20. G. E. Mylonas, "Seated and Multiple Mycenaean Figurines," *The Aegean and the Near East, Studies Presented to Hetty Goldman*, p. 120.

[70] Cf. lately Webster, *op.cit.*, p. 43, and S. Marinatos–M. Hirmer, *Crete and Mycenae*, p. 173 and Fig. 207.

[71] *Ephem*, 1937, pp. 287-288.

shield may be Athena;[72] but Athena is not connected with the worship of Demeter, and the wars of Eleusis against Athens in times shortly removed from the date of the ring have been interpreted as wars of the worshipers of Poseidon (Eleusis) against those of Athena (Athens).[73] One would try in vain to find Kore-Persephone in the representation. The small female figure to be seen behind the tree can hardly be interpreted as the maiden Goddess Persephone, when even the mortal women are represented on a larger scale. It seems to us clear that on the ring from Mycenae we cannot see the Goddess of Eleusis; at least she cannot be proved to be represented on it. Nor can the Ghazi idol with the poppy-heads over its forehead, found by Marinatos, be conclusively equated with Demeter on the basis of the flower alone;[74] indeed its discoverer identifies the idol as a goddess of healing. From the very beginning Demeter is associated with her daughter, Kore-Persephone, and her cult was a combined cult. In art we ought to find them together.

This rapid survey of the written documents and of art objects which could confirm the existence of the cult of Demeter and Persephone in the Mycenaean age has indicated, we believe, if it has not proved, that no artistic or epigraphical evidence has come to light which could be associated definitely with our Goddesses. Therefore, Webster's enthusiastic conclusion that "we have seen also that the story of Demeter and Kore may well have been represented on Mycenaean frescoes" and that "Demeter was worshiped at Pylos and the king was 'initiated' there"[75] is not substantiated by concrete objects and definite evidence. Even as an assumption it should be received with skepticism. No, neither the inscribed documents nor the works of art of the Mycenaean age can prove or even suggest the existence of the cult of Demeter in Greece in the Late Helladic period. We wish they could. Only the remains at Eleusis and the Greek tradition prove the existence of the cult in that remote age and on our site.

[72] Sometimes it is taken as a young male God who accompanies the Goddess in Late Minoan times. That identification, too, is not appropriate for Demeter, who should be associated with a maiden, her daughter Persephone.

[73] Ch. Picard, "Les luttes primitives d'Athènes et d'Éleusis," *RHist*, 166 (1931), pp. 23-42. *Supra*, p. 26 n. 10.

[74] Sp. Marinatos, "Αἱ μινωϊκαὶ Θεαὶ τοῦ Γάζι," *Ephem*, 1937, pp. 287-288.

[75] Webster, *op.cit.*, pp. 124-125.

In closing we should emphasize the fact that Demeter and Kore-Persephone are not to be found among the Gods who are the recipients of various offerings mentioned in the tablets of Knossos. Could one suggest that this perhaps was due to a very old and very strong cult of an agricultural Goddess in Krete, whose prestige prevented the adoption of another Goddess coming from the mainland? And could the omission of the name from the lists of Pylos indicate the localization of the cult to a few traditional places, among which Pylos is not to be found? Could this silence perhaps be attributed to the possibility that already in Mycenaean times the worship of Demeter and Persephone was a secret cult practiced at Eleusis only? Of course, new discoveries lying ahead may add the names of the Eleusinian Goddesses to the lists we now have. Meanwhile, we believe that it is legitimate to have in mind the questions and the possibilities.

CHAPTER III

ELEUSIS IN THE EARLY CENTURIES
OF THE HISTORIC ERA

THE Mycenaean age was brought to an end by the descent into the Peloponnesos of the last wave of the Indo-Europeans who settled in the Greek peninsula, by the iron-bearing Dorian tribes that established themselves in the fertile plains of Corinthia, of Argolis, of the Eurotas river, and of Messinia. Mycenae was destroyed and its role of leadership was taken over by Argos and Sparta. The date of the invasion and the consequent rise of the new centers of power cannot be determined with any degree of accuracy, but it is commonly assumed to have taken place towards the end of the twelfth century.[1] Attika, and Eleusis with it, seem to have been bypassed by the invaders in their southward movement and to have escaped devastation. Some years later, in the days when Kodros was the King of Athens (ca. 1050 B.C.), the "Dorians" tried to conquer Attika, but their efforts were frustrated by the heroic action of Kodros, who allowed himself to be killed in the hope of securing victory for his city as the oracle had promised.

The four centuries that followed the Dorian invasion are known as the proto-Geometric and the Geometric periods,[2] since their most representative relics are vases covered with a painted decoration mostly composed of geometric designs.[3] We place the end of this period around 700 B.C. There can be little doubt that Eleusis was inhabited during this time and that consequently the cult of Demeter continued to be celebrated at the site. Perhaps the Megaron, as augmented, was used well into the Geometric period, but towards its end a number of structures of religious nature were built at the site. Remains of these were uncovered by Philios in the early days of the excavations. Most important are sections of retain-

---

[1] It depends upon the date of the Fall of Troy, which has still to be determined. Cf. *supra* Ch. II n. 23.

[2] Often these periods are called the "dark age" of Greece. However, scholars are now beginning to think that the "age is 'dark' only because we have little or no evidence for it, archaeological, historical, linguistic." (Wace, *Viking*, 1954, p. 222.)

[3] Cf. Fig. 86.

ing walls that supported a terrace constructed over the area on which the Mycenaean Megaron-temple had stood.

REMAINS OF THE PROTO-GEOMETRIC AND GEOMETRIC PERIODS, CA. 1110-700 B.C.

Retaining Terrace Walls. The surviving segment of the north retaining wall (Fig. 4, No. 51), to the point where it turned to the west, can be seen to the left of the ascending Sacred Way (Fig. 4, No. 25) as it approaches the later Telesteria. It is preserved to a height of some 2.50m. above the rock at its eastern extremity, and it is built of rather small and flat stones laid in clay mortar. The corner is carefully constructed of flat stones well fitted together. (Figs. 6, E5 and 14,a). In the period that followed, it was extended to the east in a different style of masonry (Fig. 14,b). The east side of the terrace supported by this wall is buried under the floor of a later structure, but its course, as well as the form and extent of the terrace, is well pictured by Noack in his plate 13. The south retaining wall of the terrace surviving to a length of some 6 meters, was again revealed and studied by Kourouniotes (Figs. 4, No. 53; 6, E1; and 12, E1). It is built of fairly large flat stones laid in mortar and averages 1.25m. in thickness. Perhaps it carried a super-structure of sun-dried brick that rose above the level of the terrace and served as a peribolos wall. We must note that this portion of the wall stands on a fill of earth (Fig. 15) the uppermost layer of which contained pottery of the closing years of the Mycenaean period and some of the proto-Geometric. The wall ends towards the southwest in a well-formed anta, beyond which, and at an angle to which, is still preserved a flight of three steps. (Figs. 6, E2; and 15, E2). Kourouniotes proved that they are part of a stairway of seven steps, which formed the main ascent to the terrace. The steps are made of flat stones, have a width of 0.25-0.30m., and a rise of only 0.13-0.15m. The lowest step is preserved to a length of ca. 4.80m. Thus on the southwestern side of the terrace we have an ascent which, for the period, could be considered as monumental.

Sacrificial pyre. In front of this portion of the retaining wall and between it and Periklean column base III 6 (cf. Fig. 12,p), Philios in 1884 explored a substantial fill (between 0.80-1.00m. deep) in which were found piles of terracotta figurines and broken pottery mixed with ashes and remnants of fire. Noack maintained that this layer was made up of the refuse of the altar on the terrace thrown beyond the retaining wall when that altar was being cleared.[4] However, the reinvestigation of the area and the strong traces of fire and smoke still to be seen on the outer face of the retaining wall prove definitely that in this area, near the stairway and by the wall, sacrifices were held over a long period of time, certainly in honor of Demeter and Kore. That period is indicated by the pottery found, which includes examples of the well-developed Geometric style and of the variety known as proto-Corinthian. We may now recall that the fill under the wall yielded examples of the latest Mycenaean pottery and of the proto-Geometric style. Consequently, the retaining wall, and of course the terrace supported by it, must have been built after the Mycenaean and proto-Geometric period and in the course of the advanced period of the Geometric style. We can, then, with some certainty place the retaining wall and its terrace towards the middle of the eighth century B.C.

Apsidal (?) temple. What purpose did this early terrace serve? Noack maintained that this was the first artificially constructed terrace on which cult acts were held, where the Mysteries were celebrated for the first time in open air, and where later the Telesteria were constructed for the purpose. He further maintained that only an altar was constructed on it and that in front of that altar the Mysteries were celebrated. However, if we accept as a fact that Megaron B of Mycenaean times was the Temple of Demeter, we have to accept that a building must have replaced it in the Geometric period, and not a mere altar. That such a building existed seems to be indicated by the fragment of a wall found by Philios and included by Noack in his plans; it was revealed again and studied more thoroughly by Kourouniotes.[5]

---

[4] Philios, *Praktika*, 1884, p. 76. Noack, *Eleusis*, p. 11. K. Kourouniotes, *Deltion*, 13 (1930-31), Parartema, p. 26. The grave discovered below this fill and called Geometric most probably belonged to the Middle Helladic period. The few sherds found bearing a geometric decoration most probably were matt-painted. In the days of Philios and for a long time afterwards the matt-painted pots, characteristic of the Middle Helladic period, were considered Geometric, and Dörpfeld, who was Philios' constant adviser, refused to admit them to the Middle Bronze Age.

[5] Noack, *Eleusis*, p. 10. K. Kourouniotes, *Deltion*, 13 (1930-31), Parartema, p. 24.

This fragment, apparently forming only the outer face of a wall, stands on top and across the Mycenaean peribolos wall. It has an elliptical form and has survived to a length of 5.50m. (Figs. 23, E3 and 13, E3). It rests on Prehistoric fill and remains, and consequently dates from a period later than the Mycenaean. That fill, the sherds found with it, and the way in which it was built, prove that it is contemporary with the Late Geometric retaining walls.[6] The structure to which it belonged must have stood on the terrace supported by these retaining walls.

What purpose could this fragment have served? It could be assumed that it was part of a building, or, as has been suggested, that it served as a retaining wall. The latter, however, is very doubtful because the wall stands on a contemporary terrace supported already by comparatively strong retaining walls. Another retaining wall on top of the terrace would be meaningless. Could it be part of the altar suggested by Noack? Its radius indicates a size that is incompatible with this interpretation. The structure to which this segment belongs must have been of considerable size and it must have served a religious purpose, since the terrace is proved, by the remains of sacrifices in front of its retaining wall, to have had a sacred character. What religious purpose could be imagined for it, other than that served by a temple for which the terrace was constructed? Thus we can only accept it as belonging to a temple that stood on the terrace. The form of the temple could have been apsidal or elliptical, or, as Kourouniotes believed, circular. The terrace, of a more or less polygonal form would be suitable for a temple of that shape; and apsidal temples were rather characteristic of the Late Geometric period. The temple of Apollo at Thermos is an outstanding example.[7] The narrow width of this fragment may perhaps indicate a superstructure of light material, and Kourouniotes suggested wood. The apsidal temple would have covered all the area previously occupied by the augmented Mycenaean temple and its floor level would have been at the level on

[6] Noack, *Eleusis*, p. 10, would like to consider it earlier than the Geometric period and would place it in Mycenaean times. This, of course, is impossible due to its construction and the fill on which it rests.

[7] K. Kourouniotes, *Deltion*, 13 (1930-31), Parartema, p. 24. For Thermos see *Ephem*, 1900, pp. 171ff and plate opposite page 176.

which stood the Peisistratean columns. Naturally such a building could not have lasted long, and it was replaced in the Archaic period.

The Sacred House. From the Late Geometric period dates a building, discovered by Kourouniotes outside the Sanctuary of Demeter, immediately to the south of its fourth century peribolos wall (Fig. 4, No. 60). It is almost in front of the south gate of the Sanctuary (Fig. 4, No. 33) but is not aligned with it.[8] It stands on a terrace oriented from north to south, and is composed of a series of three contiguous rooms opening to a long corridor that runs through the entire length of the structure and a small triangular area beyond the south room. Beyond the corridor there is a paved court. The north room is the largest (4.80m. x 4m.). A slab, found almost in the center of the room, served apparently as a base for a wooden column. In the northwest corner stands a small bench, and in the opposite corner a small area is set aside by a row of stones forming an arch. The middle room is the smallest, and has a maximum width of 2m. In the southwest corner was built a well-like bothros raised one meter above the floor level. From the base of the bothros a covered drain, to be seen under the floor, passes under the threshold of the room and terminates in the court below. The third room, with a maximum width of 2.75m., is divided in two compartments by a cross-wall. In the two smaller rooms were found piled a number of vases filled with ashes, apparently the remains of sacrifices. The vases can be dated to the beginning of the seventh century, thus indicating that the building was constructed shortly before, i.e., at the end of the Geometric period. There can be little doubt that the structure served some religious purpose. Kourouniotes believed that in it was housed a cult for ancestors, and consequently called it the Sacred House or Ἱερὰ οἰκία.

This interesting building seems to have been destroyed early in the seventh century; but at the beginning of the sixth, in front of the wall of its court, was built a small square chamber containing an altar. In and around the chamber were found masses of black-figure pottery and figurines, proving its use and the continuation

[8] K. Kourouniotes, *Praktika*, 1937, pp. 42ff.

of the religious rites into the Archaic period. Among the small finds are fragments of painted terracotta tiles similar to those of the Telesterion of the Early Archaic period.

In 1952 we uncovered a structure comparable to the Sacred House a little beyond the northeastern corner of the foundations of the Stoa of Philon.[9] It included a bothros and a number of small rooms, the floors of which were covered with ashes, and it was used from Late Mycenaean times to the end of the Geometric period. The structure seems to have been associated with the well, which we have identified as the Kallichoron of the Hymn, and the ashes could be attributed to sacrifices performed in connection with the ceremonies held around the well. Since the erection of the Stoa and the Kimonian retaining walls destroyed a good deal of the structure, we have little information about it.

Kourouniotes, in 1937, discovered under the floor of the temple of Artemis Propylaia, or Artemis of the Portals (Fig. 4, No. 6), the foundations of a large apsidal building which seems to belong to the end of the Geometric period. The structure was not cleared entirely and its excavation is still to be completed, but it proves that apsidal buildings, like the apsidal Telesterion, were being constructed at Eleusis in the eighth century. The clearing of what Travlos called the "Asty Gates" and its territory revealed fragments of walls of houses of the Geometric period. Publication of these will have to await the complete excavation of the territory. As a matter of fact, we have practically no remains of the Geometric city of Eleusis, and its existence in proto-Geometric as well as Geometric times is proved by the graves found.

Cemetery. On the south slope of the hill Skias, in 1845, explored an extensive cemetery previously tested by Philios. He proved then that cremation was concurrently practiced with inhumation in proto-Geometric and Early Geometric times.[10] His conclusions were confirmed by our discoveries in the west cemetery where we obtained additional information regarding the way in which burials by cremation were conducted. Apparently the pyre was prepared over the area to be used as the grave. After cremation, the ashes and the remnants of the bones were collected and placed

[9] G. E. Mylonas, *Praktika*, 1952, pp. 56-57.
[10] A. Skias, *Ephem*, 1898, pp. 29ff and 1912, pp. 1ff.

in a fair-sized amphora or urn.[11] Then an oval trench was dug (ca. 1.50m. x 0.70m.). By means of a thin wall, the length of the trench was divided into two compartments; in the smaller and deeper compartment was placed upright the amphora containing the ashes. Its mouth was covered by a small vase, usually a skyphos. In the other larger, but shallower compartment were placed the gifts, consisting mostly of vases (Fig. 9). Sometimes the cinerary urn was placed in an older grave, a practice followed especially in the inhumation of adults. In our Figure 8 we have a striking example of an inhumation laid in a Mycenaean earth-cut chamber tomb, which was revealed when its roof collapsed.

Late in the Geometric period was revived the old custom of burying children in large pots. It was then that the graves were furnished with a greater number of gifts, sometimes of considerable value. The richest grave found thus far was cleared by Skias in 1895. It is known as the "Grave of Isis" from a small statuette of Egyptian porcelain found in it representing that Goddess.[12] Among its furnishings were three scarabs and beads of Egyptian porcelain.[13] These Egyptian objects raise the question of the identity of the woman buried in the grave. Was she an Egyptian established at Eleusis, or an Eleusinian who had traveled to Egypt and wished her souvenirs to be buried with her? The latter conjecture seems to us the more plausible. The grave and its contents certainly cannot indicate an Egyptian provenience for the Mysteries of Eleusis or even Egyptian influence on the cult, because they are too late in date; they belong to the end of the Geometric period.[14]

Unfortunately, since the erosion of the soil has carried away the upper part of the graves, we cannot know whether a small mound was erected over them nor have we found the markers that must have indicated these graves. But apparently, from what was recorded by Philios and Skias, over each grave a mound of earth and

[11] G. E. Mylonas, *Praktika*, 1955, pp. 74-77, and pls. 23b, 24, 25. A good many examples of urns are exhibited in the vase-room of the Museum of Eleusis (cf. Fig. 86).

[12] A. Skias, *Ephem*, 1898, pp. 31ff.

[13] The finds, now exhibited in the National Museum of Athens, include 68 vases, 7 bronze fibulae, gold earrings embellished with amber, an ivory pin, bronze bracelets, 10 rings of silver, bronze, and iron.

[14] For an excellent discussion of the grave and its contents cf. R. Young, *Late Geometric Graves and a Seventh Century Well in the Agora*, *Hesperia*, Suppl. II, pp. 234-236 with bibliography.

broken small stones was piled.[15] Occasionally a plain slab of stone or a vase was placed as a marker over the grave, but not the typical large Dipylon vases used as markers in Athens towards the end of the Geometric period. And one wonders whether the lack of Dipylon vases indicates that Eleusis was not as yet very closely connected with Athens.

It is interesting to note that the people of the Geometric period treated the remains of older burials with greater respect than the Mycenaeans, who often enough threw the bones of ancestors out of the burial chambers to make room for subsequent interments.[16] Apparently the respect for the bones of ancestors, which underlies the hero worship characteristic of the early centuries of the Historic era of Greece, began during the Geometric period. A striking example of this reverence came to light in 1955 in section Γ of the west cemetery.[17] In clearing a pot-burial we found that, in the course of digging a trench for it, the people who placed it there had inadvertently destroyed the skull of a previous interment. Instead of removing it, as the Mycenaeans would have done, they changed the direction of their trench, so that the skeleton would not be disturbed further, tried to reassemble the broken pieces of the skull and, as an expiatory offer, placed by it a beautifully decorated oenochoe, or wine jug, with a trefoil lip (Fig. 10).

From the Geometric period also dates the custom of attributing accidentally found graves of a bygone and forgotten age to heroes or legendary figures of the locality.[18] It was during this period that a number of graves found at the western end of the west cemetery were surrounded by a wall; their area was excluded from further use and they were identified as the sepulchers of the heroes who, at the instigation of Polyneikes, son of Oidipous, undertook the fateful war against Thebes a generation before the Trojan war. This *heroon* was pointed out to Pausanias when he visited the site, and it was one of the many historic landmarks the visitor could see at Eleusis.[19] These, perhaps, were the graves which Euripides

[15] *Ephem*, 1898, pp. 86-87.

[16] For the Mycenaean burial customs cf. G. E. Mylonas, "Homeric and Mycenaean Burial Customs," *AJA*, 52 (1948), pp. 56-81.

[17] G. E. Mylonas, *Praktika*, 1955, p. 76, and *Alivizatos Festschrift*, pp. 6-9.

[18] G. E. Mylonas, *Studies Presented to David M. Robinson*, I, pp. 104-105.

[19] G. E. Mylonas, *Praktika*, 1953, pp. 81-87. Cf. Pausanias, I, 39, 2 and

had in mind when he was composing his *Suppliants*. To a similar ancestral worship was dedicated the Sacred House cleared by Kourouniotes.

Apparently during the Geometric period the sanctuary area was surrounded by a peribolos wall, a small section of which was found to the east of the northeast corner of the Stoa of Philon (Fig. 6, E6). It consists of a foundation or socle ca. 1.50m. in height, built of small stones laid in clay mortar; the superstructure was of sun-dried brick. It measures ca. one meter in thickness and was uncovered for a length of 12m. A good section of it runs under and across the Peisistratean Inner Gate. The wall follows the level area over which, in later years, retaining walls and periboloi were constructed.

THE ARCHAIC PERIOD TO PEISISTRATEAN
TIMES (Z), CA. 700-550 B.C.

The political history of Eleusis of the seventh century remains unknown. We may assume that in the days that followed the ill-fated attempt of Kylon to become the master of Athens (ca. 632 B.C.) the people of Eleusis regained their independence, taking advantage of the internal strife of the Athenians. We may even find an echo of another war in Solon's statement to Kroisos regarding Tellos who "crowned his life with a most glorious death; for in a battle between the Athenians and their neighbors at Eleusis he attacked and routed the enemy and most nobly died there."[20] It is not clear, of course, whether those "neighbors" were Eleusinians, but we have no record of a war of Athens against any of the other people to the west of the City who could have been considered "neighbors."

In the days of Solon Salamis was taken by the Athenians. Apparently Eleusis also was then brought into the orbit of Athens, for we hear that the Mysteries were among the Athenian sacred rites provided by Solon's special law. Andokides states definitely that according to Solon's law the Athenian Council had to meet in the Eleusinion the day after the Mysteries were held to hear the report of the officials regarding the conduct of the celebration. We also

---

Plutarch, *Theseus*, 29. The area of the graves was generously purchased by the Greek Archaeological Society of Athens to be preserved as a historic monument.

[20] Herodotos, I, 30.

find specifications for the sacrifices to be held in Athens in connection with the celebration of the Mysteries in an inscription that contains the re-edition of the sacred law of Solon.[21] Apparently during the time of Solon the Hymn was composed.

Solonian Terrace. In the course of the Early Archaic period a monumental temple was constructed, perhaps at the instigation of Solon himself, which for convenience we shall call the Solonian Telesterion. Remains, both of this temple and of the terrace on which it stood, have survived and they can be easily identified because in their construction the Lesbian-polygonal style of masonry was used. The blocks employed in this style, as a rule, are of a polygonal shape with sides not straight but curved, and are fitted carefully (Fig. 16).[22] In corners, blocks more or less rectangular in shape are employed (Fig. 12,Z).

In the course of the seventh century B.C., the Geometric terrace was enlarged to the east and south providing a larger area for the Temple of Demeter and its altars and a spacious court to the east and south of it. Remains of the retaining walls of the new terrace were revealed by Philios and therefore have been known for quite a while. On the north side, the Geometric retaining wall (Fig. 14,a) was extended to the east (Fig. 14,b). The extension is now preserved to a length of 3.50m. and at its highest point it rises 2.60m. above the rock. It was broken and a section of it was destroyed when, in the fourth century B.C., the foundations of a stoa, known as the Stoa of Philon, were lowered across it. Beyond those foundations, however, we find its continuation to the eastern end of the terrace (Fig. 6, Z10; and 23, Z10). There it rises almost to the floor level of the court of the temple. Perhaps this retaining wall served also as a peribolos and this function would be ascribed to the polygonal wall Z11 (Figs. 6 and 28) which runs diagonally across the extreme projection of the retaining wall. At the point where the extension was cut by the northeast corner of the Philonian Stoa, the wall is recessed (Figs. 18r and 6W, 23W). This recession was taken by Noack to be a small door opening to a stairway which was presumed to have led, through the fill, to the level of the court; the hypothetical stairway was restored with some twenty-five

---

[21] Andokides, *de Myst.*, 111. J. Oliver, *Hesperia*, 4 (1935), pp. 21ff.

[22] Noack, *Eleusis*, p. 16, based on Aristotle's passage, *Nik. Eth.*, 1137b, 30. R. L. Scranton, *Greek Walls*, p. 27.

steps. The height of the recess, 1.96m., was considered adequate for a small door. The complete clearing of the area in 1952, how-ever, disclosed the real function of the recess and proved that it is not a doorway, but a niche built around the well W identified as the Kallichoron of the Hymn.[23]

Beyond the niche, built around the Kallichoron, is the rounded eastern extremity of the terrace. At this point the retaining wall is fairly well preserved. Re-examining it in 1932 Kourouniotes and Travlos brought to light the fragment of an older polygonal wall that apparently formed the side of a gate (Fig. 23, Z12).[24] It is constructed of Eleusinian stone and in the Lesbian-polygonal style; it rises to a height of ca. one meter and apparently above it stood a superstructure of sun-dried brick. By its base the hard-pressed surface of a road was revealed. There can be little doubt that the fragment belongs to a peribolos wall that enclosed the area of the temple. Unfortunately, neither the extent of that peribolos nor its exact date can be determined, but it certainly belongs to the Early Archaic period. Perhaps toward the end of the seventh century, there was built over the line of the earlier peribolos a strong retain-ing wall that served to support the east end of the new Archaic terrace of the temple. In that retaining wall the fragment of the peribolos was incorporated. The new retaining wall was also built of Eleusinian stone and in the Lesbian-polygonal style. A good portion of the terrace supported by it, most of the addition to the Geometric terrace, was destroyed by later construction, but enough survived to permit us to determine its shape (Fig. 23, Z20).

The south section of the retaining wall of the Archaic terrace has been preserved to a considerable length under the floor of the Periklean Telesterion (Figs. 6, Z6; 12, Z6; and 23, Z6).[25] It is built of Eleusinian stone, averages one meter in thickness, and stands on a foundation of three or four courses of small unworked stones (Fig. 16). Above that foundation its lower courses are con-structed in the Lesbian-polygonal style, while its upper courses are stepped and built of more or less rectangular blocks (Fig. 12, Z6).

[23] Noack, *Eleusis*, pp. 28-29, and pl. 20e. G. E. Mylonas, *Praktika*, 1952, p. 55. Cf. above p. 45.
[24] K. Kourouniotes, *Deltion*, 14 (1931-32), Parartema, pp. 15-18 and fig. 21.
[25] Philios, *Praktika*, 1884, pp. 75-76 and pl. Δ. Noack, *Eleusis*, pl. 14, B-B3; cf. his p. 23. K. Kourouniotes, *Deltion*, 13 (1930-31), Parartema, pp. 26-27.

The recessions of the stepped part range from 0.23m. to 0.35m. Apparently, above the stone socle, which acted as a retaining wall, stood a superstructure of sun-dried brick that could have served as peribolos.

The entire length of the wall to the southwest is not preserved; it exhibits a gap (Figs. 6, Z7; and 23, Z7) which perhaps formed an entrance or an ascent to the terrace, corresponding to the similar entrance of the Geometric times. Beyond the gap, and between the later columns I4 and I5, the wall is well preserved. It proceeds in a south-southwesterly direction under the steps and the south wall of the last Telesterion and is traceable beyond it and in the south court of the Sanctuary where in places it stands only 0.60m. above rock level. In his plans Noack assumed that the wall turned to the west and terminated against the slope of the hill. However, the scanty fragments uncovered prove that it proceeds in a southerly direction until it disappears under the later Peisistratean wall. (Fig. 6, Z8). Now, if we take into consideration the retaining walls of both the Geometric and the Early Archaic periods, marked E and Z respectively, we shall easily perceive that the Geometric terrace, perhaps at the end of the seventh century B.C., was enlarged to the east and to the south, while its north side remained the same and its west side was placed against the slope of the hill (Fig. 23).

Sacrificial pyre. Ascent to the enlarged terrace was apparently obtained from the southwest where we find the gap in the retaining south wall. In the vicinity of this wall not far east of the assumed ascent to the terrace (Fig. 6, Z7 and 23, Z7), sacrifices seem to have been held in a manner similar to that noted for the Geometric period. Remnants of sacrificial pyres containing pottery and figurines were unearthed both by Philios and by Kourouniotes and on the face of the wall are still discernible traces of smoke and fire of sacrifices. The segment excavated in 1931 by Kourouniotes and Threpsiades in front of the eastern extremity of the preserved wall contained in the top layers black-figure ware, from the earliest to the most developed, and terracotta figurines of types found in the pre-Persian fill of the Akropolis of Athens. The majority of these figurines represent a seated or a standing Goddess, perhaps Demeter. The bottom layer yielded Corinthian and even some proto-Corinthian pottery.[26] These objects prove that sacrificial rites began to be held outside the Archaic terrace at a period when the proto-Corinthian vases became rare and Corinthian vases were common, and continued to the last years of the black-figure style; in other words, the area was used for religious rites possibly towards the end of the seventh century B.C. and throughout the sixth century to the beginning of the fifth. The remains of the earliest pyres naturally indicate the date of the construction of the Lesbian-polygonal terrace wall outside and against which they were piled; these place its construction towards the end of the seventh century B.C. We recall that outside the Geometric south retaining wall was an area where sacrifices were held almost to the end of the seventh century B.C. Now it becomes evident that the area for the sacrifices of the Geometric era was abandoned when the early Archaic retaining wall Z6 was constructed and that sacrificial area was abandoned because it had to be filled in to make possible the enlargement to the south of the terrace and court of the temple. The polygonal retaining wall on the south side of the temple seems to have remained uncovered and in use even after the Early Archaic era and after the Telesterion of the Peisistratean times was constructed.

Solonian Telesterion. On the enlarged terrace stood the Telesterion of the Early Archaic period; the building erected to replace the Geometric temple (Fig. 23,Z). We do not know who was responsible for its construction, but it is tempting to attribute it to Solon as suggested above (p. 64).

The southeast corner of this Telesterion was revealed by Philios in his early excavations and was cleared again by Noack in 1906.[27] At least the lower part of the building was constructed of the bluish-gray Eleusinian stone in the Lesbian-polygonal style. Towards the corner, rectangular blocks were employed for greater strength (Fig. 12,Z). The upper part of the building was apparently of sun-dried brick. The wall stands on a foundation composed of a single row of flat, oblong blocks based on a hard earth surface, perhaps on the floor level of the Geometric terrace (Fig. 13,Z). The southeast corner has been preserved to a maximum height

[26] *Ibid.*, p. 27.
[27] Noack describes this temple minutely and excellently, *Eleusis*, pp. 16ff.

of 1.15m. and its wall exhibits a width of about one meter. From that corner what we may call the south wall is preserved to a length of some 10m., but its foundation can be traced to a length of some 13m. Its east wall was noted by Noack as having a length of 18m. No traces of the north wall have been preserved. It was calculated by Noack that the building measured approximately 18.37m. from north to south and 13.53m. to 14m. from east to west. The position of its rear or west wall could be suggested by an outcrop of rock, marked on the plan of Figures 6 and 20 as area Y, and this outcrop is some 14m. from the façade of the building.

To the remains noted by Philios and Noack we must now add Kourouniotes' later finds. In 1933 Kourouniotes disclosed a small section of a wall built in the Lesbian-polygonal style and exactly in line with the east wall of the temple farther north from the end of that wall marked by Noack. This fragment, preserved below the threshold of the easternmost doorway of the last Telesterion,[28] proves that the temple extended farther north than has been assumed. According to Travlos its length from north to south measures some 24m. The building would, therefore, have an estimated length of at least 24m. and a width of approximately 14m. These measurements indicate that the Archaic Telesterion has an oblong plan instead of the accepted square (cf. Fig. 26,A).[29] It exhibits, therefore, a plan nearer to that of the traditional Greek temple and different from that of the hypostyle halls of later years. The position of its entrance door remains uncertain. I believe that it should be placed near the north end of the long east side of the building facing the triangular court which spreads before that side. On that triangular east court stood the altars of the Goddesses, as they did in the later periods. It is interesting to note that the Eleusinion of Athens, now revealed by Homer A. Thompson and his collaborators, seems to have its entrance on the long east side.[30]

No traces of interior supports were found within the building, nor any other indications suggesting its interior arrangements.[31]

[28] *Deltion*, 14 (1931-32), Parartema, p. 7.

[29] J. Travlos, *Ephem*, 1950-51, p. 10, fig. 10,A. Cf. for example Frazer's *Pausanias*, II, p. 504, where the Solonian Telesterion is given a square plan.

[30] For the Eleusinion see *infra*, p. 247 and Travlos, *Athens*, fig. 33,B. In Travlos' plan the entrance of the Solonian structure is restored on the north side; but I believe that it should be placed on the east side.

[31] It is interesting to note that no objects of a religious nature were found

Based upon the evidence of the later Telesteria, Noack restored a series of wooden steps, a flight for each side of the temple, and in the middle of its cella he placed the Anaktoron, small enough to allow room for passage around it.[32] Not the slightest evidence for these arrangements exists and there is no assurance even for the steps. It seems more probable that the steps were another innovation of the Peisistratean builders; certainly we have no steps in the earlier Mycenaean temple. The size of the terrace on top of which the temple stood suggests that now, in the Archaic period, part of the service was held indoors. It is evident, therefore, that within this Archaic temple we must have an Anaktoron where the Hiera were kept hidden from the pilgrims until the very end of the initiation when a radiant Hierophant in the glow of a brilliant light exhibited them. The assumption of Noack, therefore, that an Anaktoron existed in the Archaic temple is valid; the position he suggests, however, seems doubtful. Travlos suggests that the Anaktoron occupied the depth of the temple along its southwest side (Fig. 26,A). This position, as he says, almost coincides with the position of the Anaktoron in the later Telesteria, and occupies part of the area of the inner room of the Megaron (Fig. 27).[33] It is reasonable to assume that through the centuries the architects of the successive temples tried to build the holy of holies over the same area which, according to the prevailing tradition, was sanctified by the sojourn of the Goddess herself. We may now note that, according to Travlos, in the Eleusinion of Athens a small apartment was formed at the end of its cella.[34] There, it seems, the Hiera were kept during the first four days of the celebration of the Mysteries until their return to Eleusis. A number of such *adyta*, as they are called, placed at the end of the cella are known.[35] The

---

within the structure which could prove its sacred character. This fact does not and should not cast any doubt upon its identification as the Temple of Demeter. However, for the Geometric building and for the Mycenaean Megaron B the process of reasoning which is found adequate to prove the sacred character of the Solonian edifice is by some considered inadequate.

[32] Noack, *Eleusis*, p. 21. Around the Anaktoron he leaves a space of 4.50m. for steps and passages.

[33] Our drawings by Travlos (Figs. 26 and 27) indicate his latest conclusions on the matter.

[34] Cf. J. Travlos, *Athens*, pp. 66-67 and fig. 33B. H. A. Thompson, *Hesperia*, 29 (1960), p. 336.

[35] *Ephem*, 1950-51, pp. 14-16.

Anaktoron of the Archaic temple thus conceived is a comparatively small room (3m. x 12m.), but it was adequate for its function.[36]

Noack suggested that the temple had a flat roof.[37] Kourouniotes, however, found a number of its tiles and they indicate that the roof had a double slope ending in triangular pediments on the two narrow façades.[38] We may note that Anti's restoration of the plan and inner arrangements of the temple are entirely fanciful and are contrary to the evidence as known today.[39] We must also note that Noack suggests for this temple and its terrace a peribolos wall enclosing a considerable area. That peribolos wall has been proved to belong not to the Solonian but to the Peisistratean and Kimonian rearrangement of the Sanctuary area. We have no evidence indicating that the Solonian Telesterion had a peribolos wall. We have seen that in the earlier years of the Archaic period a peribolos wall did exist, but in those years the Temple of Demeter apparently stood on the Geometric terrace, and when in later years that terrace was enlarged the peribolos was incorporated into the retaining terrace walls. Perhaps on top of the retaining wall was built a free-standing wall of sun-dried brick or of stone, acting as a peribolos.

Altar and stepped podium. In the Archaic period, beyond the terrace of the Telesterion some construction was carried out. Sometime about the end of the seventh and the beginning of the sixth century, as we have seen, a small structure was built to replace the older building of the Sacred House. To the Archaic period seems to belong an altar to be seen to the south of the easternmost projection of the Archaic terrace (Figs. 6, Z13; and 23, Z13). That altar was so revered that in Peisistratean times when the peribolos wall was being built, it was made to go around it, thus enclosing it in a well-constructed rectangular niche. When that part of the Peisistratean wall was rebuilt after the Persian wars, the rectangular niche was repeated (Fig. 6, Z13). This brings to mind the niche built in Archaic times around the well that we identified as the

---

[36] To avoid repetition we are postponing the fuller discussion of the question of the Anaktoron to a later chapter, cf. *infra*, p. 83.

[37] See Noack's interesting reconstruction, *Eleusis*, pl. 17a, which, however, is wrong in the inclusion of a peribolos wall that does not belong to this period.

[38] *Deltion*, 14 (1931-32), Parartema, p. 4 and J. Travlos, *Ephem*, 1950-51, p. 10. The lantern or opaion, placed over the roof by Noack to correspond to his Anaktoron is also unwarranted.

[39] C. Anti, *Teatri Greci arcaici da Minosse a Pericle*, 1947, p. 45, fig. 11.

Kallichoron. There can be little doubt that some ritual was held around the altar even after the enlargement of the Geometric terrace.

To a religious function should also be attributed a rather interesting stepped podium found in 1931 by Kourouniotes not far from this altar.[40] It lies some 23m. to the east of the easternmost projection of the retaining wall of the Archaic terrace, outside of the Kimonian doorway (Fig. 4, F5) and along the Periklean wall, in the area marked as Z14 in Figure 23. It is made up of three steps and its disclosed length amounts to 8.40m. (Fig. 19). It has not been ascertained whether its south end, destroyed and covered by the Periklean wall, continued beyond the Periklean construction. The height of the structure, measured behind its east side, amounts to 1.05m., but the top step is only 0.55m. above the level on which stands the lowermost step. This difference in height indicates clearly that the podium was built on inclined ground, sloping from west to east. The steps are made of Eleusinian hard stones, ranging in length from 0.45m. to 1.60m. Their width also varies from 0.41m., the two lower steps, to 0.58m., the top. The rise of the steps averages 0.20m. The north face of the podium is built of polygonal masonry and is well preserved. The steps opened onto what seems to be a broad court with a well-packed floor contiguous with the bottom step. But below the floor Kourouniotes revealed an older floor level belonging to a court that existed before the construction of the podium. In the fill between the two floor levels he found the fragment of a Corinthian aryballos, or oil-flask, whose date is a *terminus post quem* for the construction of the podium. The fill immediately below the floor of the older court contained Mycenaean sherds only. Kourouniotes was also able to observe that the Kimonian floor level came to about the upper surface of the top step, while the Peisistratean reached the top of the second step. Thus he was able to prove that the stepped podium must antedate these periods, that it must belong to the Early Archaic period, to the seventh century B.C. In Kimonian times at its north end a statue, perhaps of Hermes Propylaios, was erected. Kourouniotes believed that the stepped structure was contemporary with the peribolos, a fragment of which he found incorporated in the Archaic

[40] K. Kourouniotes, *Deltion*, 15 (1933-35), Parartema, pp. 34-41, figs. 38-41.

retaining wall of area Z12. Thus, the general date of this strange structure can be established with some degree of accuracy. The discoverer, however, was unable to determine or suggest its function.

The study of the general area in which the stepped podium is to be found will indicate the proximity of its destroyed south end to the altar Z13 (ca. 25m. distant) and to the well (ca. 23m. distant) that we have accepted as the Kallichoron of the Hymn (Fig. 23). The middle of the preserved section of the podium is about 20m. from the easternmost projection of the Archaic terrace and of the somewhat earlier Archaic gate. It is possible to assume that the altar, the well, the podium, and the court formed part of a unified arrangement. We can visualize the arrangement as a large court on the southwest corner of which stood the altar, on the northeast corner the well, and along its east side the stepped podium (Fig. 23). That podium could have served only as a stand from which people could have followed a spectacle, or rites held in the court. Its construction was perhaps imposed by the slope and the need to look towards the west, to the well perhaps and the terrace beyond, which afforded no standing room. Since the floor of the court sloped from west to east, it may well have been difficult for people standing on its east side to obtain a good view of the slope except from a position on the stepped podium. That they were viewing a spectacle or rites held around the well is indicated by the subsequent history of the area.

In Peisistratean times the use of the podium was discontinued, as proved by the rise of the fill to the top of the second step. But in the same times a strong peribolos wall was built across the court (Fig. 6, H29, H25, H23) shutting off the section of the well from that of the podium and making the court between the altar Z13, the well, and podium unusable. This combination of facts proves that the spectacle or rites held in that court were discontinued in Peisistratean times; consequently the need the podium was built to serve no longer existed and the structure was abandoned. It also proves that the rites were connected with the well since its separation from the podium brought about the abandonment of the latter.

The sacred dances. Is it possible to reconstruct the spectacle or the rites witnessed from the podium? The traditions of the site and the position of the well help us suggest such a reconstruction.

We recall how the Goddess pointed to the Kallichoron above which her temple was to be constructed. Our well W fits the specifications to be found in the Hymn. Again, Pausanias has preserved the tradition according to which the well was called Kallichoron, the Well of Fair Dances, because in front of it "the Eleusinian women first danced and sang in honor of the Goddess."[41] It seems to us that the explanation of the name given by Pausanias suggests the beginning of a rite that survived to his day, the rite of dancing in honor of the Goddess. A court stretching in front of the early Archaic gate and below the Archaic temple of the Goddess, a court outside the sacred precinct where part of the public section of the ritual could have been held, a court flanked by a stepped podium from which spectators could watch the rites and at the edge of which we find an altar and a well—this certainly is the court indicated for the sacred dances in honor of the Goddess performed by the women and watched by the initiates. The discovery of the floor of an earlier court below the one served by the stepped podium indicates that dances were performed there before Archaic times. That dances in honor of the Goddess and as a part of the Mysteries were held in much later times, even in the fourth century, is indicated by the dancing woman initiate represented on the Niinnion Tablet to be discussed in a later chapter.[42] The remnants of the structure with the bothros we discovered to the northeast of the Well, still in use in Geometric times, served perhaps the earliest ritual of these dances. The building activities of later generations altered the setting and imposed an end to the use of the court, of the Well, and of the podium for the dances held in honor of Demeter. But they could not have brought to an end the rites themselves. These formed part of the tradition of the cult and had to be continued. The only reasonable conclusion to be adduced from the available indications is that the rites were transferred to another area of the site when the Peisistratean peribolos wall was being constructed.

Burials and pot-burials of children. The picture of the Sanctuary of the Early Archaic period to the days of Peisistratos, is reasonably

[41] Pausanias, I, 38, 6.

[42] Cf. *infra*, p. 213 and Fig. 88. Lucian, *On Dancing*, 15, categorically states that no mystery was ever celebrated without dancing. See also Polydeukes, IV, 103; Athenaios, XIV, 629d; Aristophanes, *Frogs*, vv. 382-387.

clear. This is not the case with the city of Eleusis of the Archaic period. Thus far, houses have not been found, not even traces of them, although some graves were discovered in the west cemetery. The most interesting of these are pot-burials of children. In 1954 we found one of the most outstanding examples of a pot-burial belonging to the first half of the seventh century, and consequently to our period.[43] The receptacle, a monumental amphora, was found on its side some 0.25 to 0.30m. below the present surface of the soil and among burials belonging to the Prehistoric era. Apparently it was broken by the ploughs used in the cultivation of the area over the centuries, and some of its broken pieces were dragged away by the plough-share and destroyed. Most of it, however, survived. The bones of a boy ten to twelve years of age were found in it. The amphora, now in the Museum at Eleusis, stands 1.42m. in height and its entire surface, front and rear, is covered with a decoration painted in black with touches of white. On the rear side a bold floral pattern decorates the body of the vase, while a group of vertical connected spirals were painted on its neck. On the front of the neck is represented the blinding of the Cyclops Polyphemos by Odysseus and his companions (Fig. 29). The hero in white color stands next to the seated giant. An ornamental lion attacking a spirited wild boar is painted on the shoulder, while the story of Medousa, the Gorgons, Athena, and Perseus is depicted on the body. Between the human and divine figures are painted filling ornaments in the manner usual to the times. To discuss this unique amphora fully would be beyond the scope of this volume, especially since this has been done elsewhere.[44] But we must note the extraordinary ability of the painter to render the strong, athletic human form, his successful effort to impart the excitement and uneasiness of "wily Odysseus", the agony and pain of Polyphemos, the fantastic rendering of the heads of the Gorgons framed with serpents, and their nimble movement contrasting with the static, xoanon-like appearance of Athena. Our admiration for its artist must increase when we recall that this is perhaps the first time the Gorgons are

[43] G. E. Mylonas, *Praktika*, 1954, pp. 60-62.
[44] G. E. Mylonas, Ὁ πρωτοαττικὸς ἀμφορεὺς τῆς Ἐλευσῖνος, published by the Greek Archaeological Society of Athens, 1957.

depicted in Greek art; the first time to our knowledge that an artist tried to give a concrete form to the vague notions held by the people of Greece from Homeric times regarding these legendary creatures.[45] With an extraordinary amount of imagination he used elements known in his time to represent their mask-like heads, cauldrons from the rims of which grow griffin and lion heads, a favorite votive offering of the times. Facial features were borrowed from those of the awe-inspiring and rapacious griffins. Grinning mouths were painted suggestive of poisonous exhalations, and geometric patterns stand for hair and beard. Unfortunately, the figure of the fleeing Perseus is not completely preserved; that of the decapitated Medousa occupies the extreme left of the composition. Perhaps we may point out that in painting the scene of the blinding of the Cyclops the artist had in mind the story as told in the *Odyssey*,[46] but for the Gorgons he probably had to draw from his imagination, and from the vague notions of the legends, since his creation antedates the known representations of the story in art and the oldest literary description of Perseus' encounter with the Gorgons. This occurs in the poem of the *Shield of Herakles*, which has come down to us under the name of Hesiod but which seems to have been composed about 600 B.C.

The amphora is one of the best examples of the proto-Attik style of vase painting that has come down to us; in fact we believe it to be one of the best vases ever found on Greek soil. It was painted between 675 and 650 B.C. by a most gifted painter, whose name remains unknown. We have called him, for identification purposes, "the Polyphemos painter." His work, rendered with freedom escaping the rigidity of vase painting and approaching monumental art,[47] will give us the measure of artistic excellence reached in the first half of the seventh century by the artists of Athens, for there can be little doubt that the amphora is the work of an Athenian artist employed by a wealthy citizen of Eleusis.

[45] *Iliad*, V, 738-742; VIII, 349; XI, 33-38. *Odyssey*, 11, 634-635. These are only vague references to the dread-inspiring appearance of the head or eyes of the Gorgon; a description neither of the features of the head nor of the entire creature is given.

[46] *Odyssey*, 9, 381-398.

[47] As a matter of fact, the height of the frieze of the Gorgons is 0.52m. and the length 1.75m. These are dimensions appropriate to monumental painting.

We may indicate briefly another, smaller amphora from the cemetery used for the burial of an infant, because it too is one of the best examples of its type (Fig. 30). It stands only 0.53m. high and was made and painted towards the end of the seventh century, perhaps around 610 B.C. at the time the Solonian Telesterion was being built. We are familiar with its painter from other examples of his work, although we do not know his name; he has been called the "Chimaira painter."[48] Again the surface of the vase is completely covered with decoration. On its neck a lion and a panther or two panthers are depicted and on the body on one side a sphinx and on the other a lion.

[48] G. E. Mylonas, "Une amphore du peintre de la Chimère," *Latomus*, 28 (1957), pp. 357-362. Also J. D. Beazley, "Groups of Early Attic Black-figure," *Hesperia*, 13 (1944), p. 40; *Black-figure Vase Painters*, pp. 3-4.

CHAPTER IV

THE PEISISTRATEAN PERIOD (H)
CA. 550-510 B.C.

THE second half of the sixth century and the beginning of the fifth is one of the great periods in the life of the Sanctuary of Demeter at Eleusis. Then its reputation became panhellenic and admission to its Mysteries seems not to have been strictly confined to the Athenians. The words of the Hymn "Happy is he among men upon the earth who has seen these Mysteries" could be considered as an indirect invitation to the entire Greek world, and Herodotos, towards the middle of the fifth century B.C., stated that "this feast is kept by the Athenians every year for the honor of the Mother and the Kore, and whatever Greek will, be he Athenian or other, is then initiated."[1] Tradition indicates that in earlier years those from other states who wanted to be initiated not only had to find an Athenian sponsor, belonging perhaps to the great families of the Eumolpids and the Kerykes, but they had also to be adopted by the Athenian state as its citizens. Thus, Herakles became an adopted citizen through Pylios, while the Dioskouroi were adopted by Aphidnos.[2]

The ever-increasing fame of the Eleusinian cult naturally resulted in an increase in the number of initiates and the need for enlargement of the facilities for initiation. By the middle of the sixth century perhaps, the Solonian Telesterion proved inadequate to meet the demand. Extensive construction became necessary and with this has been associated the name of Peisistratos, the ambitious aristocrat who conceived the plan of developing his beloved Athens into the leading city of the Hellenic world. We have no evidence to prove this association, but it seems reasonable to believe that he initiated the great works carried out during the time when he was active in determining the politics and policies of Athens, that is from 570-565 B.C., when he led the Athenians against Megara and wrested

---

[1] Hymn, v. 480, and the poet continues: "but he who is uninitiated and who has no part in them, never has lot of like good things once he is dead, down in the darkness and the gloom." Herodotos, VIII, 65.

[2] Plutarch, *Theseus*, 33, 2.

Nisaia from his enemies, to 527/6 B.C., when his son Hippias succeeded him in the tyranny of Athens. Peisistratos, following the example of Solon, must have appreciated the political advantages that would accrue to the city in the development of Eleusis into a panhellenic religious center, the shrine to which the Hellenic world looked for spiritual guidance. The man who reconstituted the Panathenaic festival on a magnificent scale, because he realized its political significance, who raised Theseus from the status of a provincial leader to national preeminence comparable to that held by Herakles, who caused the Homeric poems to be recorded for the first time, who gave a monumental appearance to the public buildings of Athens—such a man would scarcely have failed to take advantage of the possibilities offered by the Mysteries. Again, as a military leader, he would have realized the strategic importance of Eleusis to Athens. When we find that the architectural activity of the period at Eleusis was directed towards two objectives, religious and military, we cannot help but conclude that Peisistratos was responsible for that activity.

THE PEISISTRATEAN TELESTERION

First of all, the facilities for initiation had to be enlarged. The comparatively small Solonian Telesterion was therefore pulled down, and in its place was constructed a larger and more monumental building. Extensive remains of that Telesterion, which we shall call Peisistratean, are preserved, making possible the reconstruction of the Temple with great accuracy. The terrace on which the Solonian Telesterion stood, the Early Archaic terrace, was considered adequate for the enlarged temple; but now it was extended westward against the slope of the hill, a small portion of which must have been quarried away. The foundations, both of its outside walls and of its front portico or prostoon were lowered to the rock through the fill and the older remains, and a new plan was invented to serve more adequately the function of the temple as an initiation hall. It may not be amiss to recall that the Temple of Demeter differed in its use from the other Greek temples, and that in function it somewhat parallels the Christian church, the Jewish synagogue, and the Moslem mosque. The Greek temple served as the edifice in which the cult statue was to be sheltered;

it did not have to provide a hall where services could be held. All rites, such as sacrifices, to be attended by many people were held beyond its walls and around the altar usually built in front of the east side of the temple. Within the Telesterion, the Temple of Demeter at Eleusis, the sacra were sheltered; but in addition there was held a service attended by a large crowd of initiates. The architects of the period, realizing the peculiar need not required of the regular Greek temple, devised a different ground plan for the new sacred building.

The new temple, the Peisistratean Telesterion, is square in plan and is roughly oriented from east to west, with doors and a front portico or *prostoon* as it is called in inscriptions, on the east side (Fig. 20, 4). It is built of excellently worked poros blocks, but its foundations were constructed of the harder limestone, reddish in hue and known as Kara stone, which, according to Dörpfeld, is a material characteristic of Peisistratean construction. The position of the outer walls of the temple can be determined with accuracy. The south wall is preserved to its entire length (Figs. 12, H; and 15, H). The east side was fronted, as we have seen, by a portico with well-preserved floor and foundations. The north side is buried under the north side of the Telesterion of the fifth century B.C. Nothing has survived of its west side, but on that side and at right angles to the end of the existing south wall cuttings in the rock made to receive the lowest course of the west wall give us its exact position. Consequently, we can say that we have the exact plan and the dimensions of the building. Within its walls were found the foundations of the columns that supported the roof, remnants of steps along its walls, and fragments of its roof structure. More architectural parts were found built in a late wall on the north side of the Sanctuary area. We have, therefore, enough material to reconstruct its appearance in a general way. This material was studied very ably by Noack who pointed out the excellent technical qualities of the stone work of the building.[3]

The wall foundations, to a little below the floor level, are made up of a number of courses of hard, irregularly hewn and not completely worked limestone, each course averaging 0.47m. to 0.50m. in height (Fig. 13, H). On top of the limestone construction two

[3] Noack, *Eleusis*, pp. 48-70, where a complete description of the building is given.

courses of poros stone were laid; the lower of these is part of the foundations. The upper served as the *euthynteria* on which rested the masonry of the walls made of poros stones laid in ashlar fashion. In the portico, the top poros course served as the bottom step.

The front portico (27.15m x 4.55m.), was accessible on its three sides by three steps, the bottom one of which is the top poros course of the building's foundation (Fig. 20, H1). A great part of the pavement has survived and it is made up of poros blocks of uneven size excellently fitted. On this pavement stood the columns that supported the roof. No remains of these columns have survived. That they were of the Doric order of architecture can be proved by the discovered fragments of metopes and the profile of the sima from its entablature. Again we can be sure that the portico was two columns deep; however the number of the columns in the façade itself is undetermined. Noack suggested three possibilities of eight, nine, and ten columns in front but finally declared himself in favor of nine columns.[4] Kourouniotes and Travlos believe that ten columns stood in the façade.[5] A decastyle arrangement agrees better with the measurements and the architectural members found in the latest excavations.

The entablature is of the Doric order, and from its members survive fragments of triglyphs, of metopes, of the cornice made of poros stone, of the raking cornice, and of the sima made of Parian marble. Ornamental rams' heads were placed at the corners of the simas. The example found by Philios (Fig. 21) proves that they were of solid marble and lacked the usual channel for rain water. The top of the head presents the flat surface necessary for the placing of a finial, but none was ever placed on it since the block bears no marks for attachment. The roof tiles were of Parian marble and only the cover tiles of the façade ended in anthemia gaily colored; the petals were painted red and were separated by blue lines. The sima too, was decorated with painted anthemia alternating with lotos blossoms. The outlines of the ornament were cut with a sharp tool; its details were filled with blue and red color. The apex finial was floral. The decoration is typical of a Late

---

[4] The solution of the nine columns is accepted by W. B. Dinsmoor, *The Architecture of Ancient Greece*, p. 113.

[5] Kourouniotes and Travlos, *Telesterion*, p. 75.

Archaic Doric temple and it as well as the use of Parian marble, which was not used by the Athenian builders in the fifth century, help to indicate the general date of the construction of the temple.[6]

The carved and painted decoration is characterized by the sensitiveness usual in the sixth century. We should note especially the head of the ram (Fig. 21). Ringlets, placed closely together, convey the feeling of softness of the animal fleece and emphasize, in contrast, the bony structure of the nose, muzzle, and horns. Wavy lines and a dented outline give these horns the appearance of brittle hardness and extraordinary plasticity. Here indeed we have a fragment of nature full of vigor and decorative quality, rendered with love and sensitiveness that can hardly be surpassed.[7] The modeling was accentuated by color, traces of which still existed at the time of its discovery. Red was used for the eyes and blue for the soft hair.[8]

Three doors led from the portico to the large naos. They average 1.30m. in width and the axis of the central door corresponds exactly to the middle of the steps (Fig. 26, B). The naos built of well-worked poros blocks, is a large, almost square hall (25.30m. x 27.10m.). Its roof was supported by a number of columns; the foundations of some of these columns survive and are indicated by dotted squares in Figure 20. The columns of the east rows stood upon artificial fill and their foundations, made of four blocks of poros stones laid in two courses, were not lowered to the rock, but stood on the fill itself. The stones of the foundations are in many instances re-used blocks and a number of them bear anathyrosis on their short sides. Their number and their size would indicate that they were taken from a large building, and since such an edifice does not seem to have existed at Eleusis in that or the preceding period, it is probable that the blocks were brought from elsewhere, probably from Athens, along with the Kara stone used for the foundations. In the base of the foundation of column d2 a badly weathered poros block was found bearing an inscription dating from the first half of the sixth century. This gives us another chronological indication, a *terminus post quem*, for the building.

[6] For a full description of the anthemia and of the ram's head cf. A. Orlandos in Noack's *Eleusis*, pp. 63-68.

[7] H. Winnefeld in Noack's *Eleusis*, p. 69.

[8] D. Philios, *Praktika*, 1883, p. 63.

In the foundations of column d4 Kourouniotes and his collaborators found a poros block on which the name NAYSIKA was inscribed in letters of the same period.

Philios was the first to suggest that a total of twenty-five columns, in five rows of five, were used to support the roof of the naos.[9] Actual foundations, or traces of such on the rock, for only seventeen columns can be seen today; the rest had to be restored in the plan. Dörpfeld so pictured the interior of the Peisistratean Telesterion in his drawings, and his and Philios' reasoning was accepted by all scholars. Noack in his plans also places twenty-five columns in the naos. Recently, however, Travlos has demonstrated that only twenty-two columns were used originally.[10] The north wall of the Anaktoron, acting as a support, eliminated the necessity for columns at the south end of rows 1, 2, and 3, as indicated in his restoration of the Sanctuary area (Fig. 26, B).

Although the columns in the naos have not survived, Noack calculated that their lower diameter should be 1.31m., since the platform-foundation on which they stood measured at most 1.365m. in width. Their height depends on the order used. In an inscription that recorded the building material obtained from an older, demolished building, and entrusted to the overseers of the Sanctuary for the year 408/7 B.C., we find recorded fifty-four drums of columns and sixteen bases of the Ionic order (called σπεῖραι in the inscription).[11] Using that information, Noack ingeniously concluded that the columns erected in the interior of our building were of the Ionic order. The possible height for the Ionic order would have obviated the need for a superposed arrangement of columns and would have eliminated the use of thick lower columns and the crowding of the hall. The same inscription tells us that the rafters were of wood, as was the entire roof structure with the exception of the tiles, which were of Parian marble. This Ionic element in a Doric temple agrees well with Peisistratean practices as known from other contemporary buildings in Athens. We may then assume

[9] *Idem, Praktika*, 1884, pp. 73-75, and Noack, *Eleusis*, pp. 54ff.

[10] Travlos, *Anaktoron*, p. 10 and fig. 10B, and our Figs. 20 and 25 where the foundations of the columns that can be seen now, are indicated by dotted squares; the rows are numbered 1 to 5 from west to east and "a" to "e" from south to north.

[11] *IG*, I², 313/4. *Ephem*, 1888, pp. 49ff and 1895, pp. 62ff and *AM*, 19 (1894), pp. 190ff. Noack, *Eleusis*, pp. 59-60.

that twenty-two Ionic columns were used to support the roof of the hall.

The Anaktoron. There is no indication that an *opaion* or lantern was placed on the roof of the Peisistratean Telesterion. As a matter of fact, the position of the central row of columns would exclude such an arrangement.[12] Perhaps the hall was lighted, if that was necessary, by windows placed on the upper section of the external north and south walls. Such a solution is suggested by Dinsmoor. The lack of the lantern would in turn indicate that a central position for the Anaktoron was not envisioned by the architects. Recently Travlos has proved that the Anaktoron occupied the south-western corner of the hall.[13] At the western end of that corner, marked as "Y" in our Figures 6 and 20, the rock projects some 0.32m. above the floor level even of the Periklean Telesterion. As early as 1833 Philios noticed this projecting rock and wondered why they left it "when they leveled the rock for the floor of the Periklean naos." And he asked, "Was an altar built there or a structure useful for the machinery employed by the priests in the telete?"[14] Noack concluded that the rock was covered by the steps placed along the wall of the temple. He failed, however, to explain why the steps were not cut in this rock as they were cut on the north side, and why we do not have traces of a bed on this rock for the setting of the steps? Furthermore, Travlos has proved that the steps of the west wall stopped at the point where the rock projects. The projecting rock can be explained only if we place the Anaktoron at that corner of the naos. It is interesting to note that in the construction of the Megaron-altar of Demeter at Lykosoura, excavated by Kourouniotes, a fragment of projecting rock was left in the nucleus of the structure, forming almost half of its body, while the other half was made up of ashes left from sacrifices.[15] Could we then assume that the projecting rock was left purposely to symbolize some aspect of the Goddess? Rubensohn has recently suggested that this rock may be the omphalos some-times associated with Demeter.[16] On the basis of the dimensions

[12] W. B. Dinsmoor, *op.cit.*, p. 113.
[13] Travlos, *Anaktoron*, pp. 1-16.
[14] D. Philios, *Praktika*, 1883, pp. 54-55.
[15] K. Kourouniotes, *Ephem*, 1912, pp. 146 and 150.
[16] O. Rubensohn, "Das Weihehaus von Eleusis und sein Allerheiligstes," *Jahrbuch*, 70 (1955), pp. 36-37.

of its later walls, Travlos has figured out that the Anaktoron occupied the area of three intercolumniations in length and of one in width; an area 12.50m. in length from east to west and a little over 3m. in width from north to south, inner dimensions. Its position at the end and not in the middle of the south side would indicate that its placement was imposed by the position of the Anaktoron of the preceding building (Figs. 26, B and 27).

The dimensions of this room seem to some scholars incompatible with the name given to it. The word anaktoron, they say, like its equivalent palace, brings to mind a large, impressive building, and our room is neither large nor impressive. Now let us forget, for the time being, the name and consider carefully the function of the holy of holies, as far as we can know it. Its primary function was to serve as the repository of the Hiera of the cult. Its doors were opened at the close of the initiation when the Hierophant stood in front of them to exhibit the Hiera, or some of them, to the attending initiates. It was also opened on the 13th day of Boedromion for a short time to remove the Hiera for the annual visit to Athens, and on the 20th of the same month, to return them. The Hiera do not seem to have required much space. We hear in this connection that they were carried, at least across the Rheitoi bridge, by the priestesses,[17] and consequently they could not have been heavy or bulky. The Hiera were relics of a remote past and were handed down from generation to generation; presumably they went back to the early years of the cult if not to its very beginning. Those early years are now proved to have extended into the Mycenaean age and in that age we do not seem to have monumental religious representations or bulky religious equipment.[18] In all probability therefore, the Hiera were small, requiring little space even though they may have been numerous, and they were kept hidden even from the initiates until the very end of the

[17] Cf. the Rheitoi inscription, *IG*, I^2, 81 (our Fig. 69). Aelian, *Fragm.* 10, p. 192, 4ff.

[18] No life-size cult statue, for example, is known from the Mycenaean age, but only small figurines; cf. M. P. Nilsson, *Minoan-Mycenaean Religion*, 2nd ed., p. 113, fig. 32 (contents of the shrine of Asine), p. 79, fig. 13 (shrine of the Double Axe of Knossos); cf. *BSA*, 8 (1901-2), p. 97, fig. 55; and Sir Arthur Evans, *Palace of Minos at Knossos*, II, p. 338. Contents of Shrine of Gournia, Nilsson, *op.cit.*, p. 81, fig. 14. Idols of Koumasa: S. Xanthoudides, *The Vaulted Tombs of Messara*, pp. 49ff and pl. XXXIII. Idols of Ghazi: Sp. Marinatos, *Ephem*, 1937, pp. 278-291.

ceremony. Further, the Anaktoron was used neither as a gathering place nor as a *sanctum* to be visited by worshipers. No one but the Hierophant entered it on the few occasions noted. Consequently the space required for the Anaktoron was limited and the size of the room postulated by Travlos is adequate. The position of the room apparently was imposed by tradition. It had to occupy approximately the same area as the Anaktoron of the preceding Telesterion, which could be seen and was well remembered. That Anaktoron was over the southwest corner of the Mycenaean Megaron in which, according to tradition, the Goddess herself lived for a time (Fig. 27).

We have already said that some scholars maintain that the name anaktoron would have been applied to a sumptuous and large building and not to a mere segment of the temple. The most important exponent of this view is the late Professor Ludwig Deubner who maintained that the term indicated the entire Telesterion and not a mere chamber within it.[19] Pointing out that the word anaktoron signified the dwelling of the anax, the king, he concluded that in the area where the later Telesteria were constructed there was originally a dwelling of the King of Eleusis, possibly the palace of King Keleos mentioned in the Hymn. In the course of time, Deubner maintained, the place of the palace was taken over by the Telesterion which thus came to be known as the anaktoron. However, the palace of King Keleos or of any other ruler of Eleusis, in accordance with Mycenaean architectural practices, would have been built on top of the hill and not on its slope where the later Telesteria stood. Furthermore, below the Telesteria of the Historic era the latest and final excavations of the area have revealed only Megaron B which by both Deubner's and Mycenaean standards could not have been the palace of the anax. Nor is there a chance of finding such a palace in the future because the slope has been excavated to its natural rock level. Consequently Deubner's view based on his "palace of the ruler" theory does not seem to be substantiated by the facts as revealed by the spade of the excavators. Further, the passages from ancient authors which he cites

[19] L. Deubner, *Attische Feste*, pp. 87ff; *Deut. Akad. der Wissensch. zu Berlin*, (-Abh. Berl.) 1945-46, No. 2. O. Rubensohn, *AA*, 1933, pp. 316ff; *Gnomon*, 9 (1933), p. 417 and *Jahrbuch*, 70 (1955), pp. 1ff.

do not confirm his conclusions, for they support the opposite view equally well. The word anaktoron in these passages, especially when used in plural, κατὰ συνεκδοχήν, could indicate not the holy of holies but the whole Sanctuary including the Telesterion, exactly as the word megaron in the plural indicates in epic poetry not a single unit but the entire palace complex. Finally, there are two ancient testimonies which prove Deubner's position untenable. Aelian states definitely that only the Hierophant had the right to enter the Anaktoron and this in accordance with the law of the telete.[20] Certainly the entire Telesterion could not have been the Anaktoron, since that structure was entered by all the initiates at the very beginning of the telete. Then again Athenaios,[21] drawing on Hegesander, tells us how Demetrios, the grandson of Demetrios of Phaleron, at the time of the celebration of the Mysteries had a throne placed beside the Anaktoron "for his hetaira friend Aristagora," threatening that whosoever tried to prevent it would be sorry. Certainly the position he chose for Aristagora was one of advantage; such was not a place outside the Telesterion during the celebration of the rites, but within it.

The available evidence, both archaeological and literary, indicates that the term Anaktoron was applied to a special section of the naos or hall of the Telesterion. A reconsideration of the early history of the Sanctuary will provide a reasonable and tenable explanation of the name. We can with reason maintain that not only its use, but also its name was derived from the first temple erected by the Eleusinians at the command of the Goddess in Mycenaean times. That first temple, as we have seen, was in the form of a megaron and, like its secular counterpart, served as the dwelling of the Goddess during her sojourn at Eleusis. With reason, therefore, it could have been called the megaron—the dwelling place—of Demeter, by the people of Eleusis and the priesthood, who were naturally anxious to maintain the tradition that the Goddess lived among them in the heroic past. But this dwelling of Demeter, her megaron, became her temple and so naturally the Temple of the Goddess was known as the Megaron. In this connection it is interesting to recall that some of the known

[20] Aelian, *Fragm.* 10, p. 192, 4ff.
[21] Athenaios, IV, 167 F (*FHG*, IV, 415).

temples of the Goddess built in other parts of Greece in a remote past were known as the Megaron of Demeter.[22] Perhaps from Eleusis the name came to be applied to the early temples of the Goddess wherever they were built. It is reasonable to maintain that when more rooms were added to the Mycenaean building, the name Megaron was reserved for the original structure in which, according to tradition Demeter actually lived. Then the single room of that structure, sanctified by the divine presence, was transformed into the holy of holies where the Hiera were kept, which no profane eye could behold and which even the initiates could see only at the end of the celebration. Thus *the room* became known as the Megaron.

We may now note that in the Historic era the holy of holies of the Temple of Eleusis was sometimes called Megaron and more often Anaktoron and this seems to indicate that for some time the small inner room might have been designated by two names, an earlier and a later; Megaron being the earlier name since, as we have seen, it goes back to the Mycenaean age. The later name Anaktoron was perhaps introduced early in the fifth century B.C. and in imitation of the ways of the tragedians who in their dramas stopped using the word megaron and instead used anaktora, domoi, and more commonly *melathra*.[23] We hear that in the same century the Hierophant and other priests of Eleusis adopted more ornate vestments in imitation of the elaborate costumes given to his actors by Aischylos, who was an Eleusinian.[24] In a similar manner they could have used the term Anaktoron, following the innovation of· the dramatists, to indicate the Megaron of the Goddess or the holy of holies, the adyton of the Telesterion where the very Hiera of

[22] Pausanias, I, 40, 6 states that the most ancient temple of Demeter on the akropolis of the town of Megara was known as the Megaron and that it was built by the legendary king Kar. He also calls the shrine of the Goddess at Lykosoura a Megaron (VIII, 37, 8).

[23] Hesychios: Ἀνάκτορον τὸ τῆς Δήμητρος ὃ καὶ μέγαρον καλοῦσιν, ὅπου τὰ ἀνάκτορα (read τὰ ἱερά) τίθεται. Ammonios of Lamptrae: τὸ δὲ μέγαρον ἡ περιῳκοδομημένη ἑστία ἔνθα τὰ μυστικὰ Δήμητρος. The conception of the μέγαρον as an underground room is very late in date. For an excellent discussion of the term Megaron cf. N. Kontoleon, "Μέγαρον" in *Melanges offerts à Octave et Melpo Merlier*, pp. 5 and 17 where bibliography and succinct discussion.

[24] Athenaios I, 21E "Aischylos, too, besides inventing that comeliness and dignity of dress which Hierophants and Dadouchoi emulate, when they put on their vestments. . . ." Cf. G. H. Pringsheim, *Archäologische Beiträge zur Geschichte des Eleusinischen Kults*, pp. 1ff.

the Goddess were kept. Thus, when used in the singular, anaktoron, the term could have indicated a small room serving a most sacred purpose and not a very sumptuous agglomeration of apartments and rooms. When used in the plural, the term could have applied to the Telesterion in general or even to the entire Sanctuary.

Recently Rubensohn advanced the ingenious suggestion that the Anaktoron was so called because it was the home of the *anassa*, an epithet and title given to Demeter in the Hymn. We find, however, that in the Mycenaean age the title was given even to nymphs and, presumably, the queen of a city could have been called *anassa* since her husband was the *anax*.[25] It would therefore be impossible to prove that *anassa* was an exclusive title of Demeter, and this is essential if from that title we attempt to derive the name Anaktoron. Furthermore Rubensohn's ingenious derivation will not explain why the Anaktoron was also called Megaron.

Along the lengths of the south and west walls beyond the holy of holies rose tiers of nine stone steps and a similar number of steps along the entire length of the north wall. On that side they were partially hewn out of the living rock and partially built. It has been assumed that steps were also built along the east wall, between the doorways, but the latest excavations have disproved this. Steps existed only along the three sides of the hall. The built steps were of limestone excellently joined and smoothed. They, as well as those hewn in the rock, ranged from 0.264m.-0.273m. in height and 0.30m.-0.31m. in width; apparently they were too narrow for use as seats. By standing on them, however, the initiates could follow the rites held in the hall. The floor was covered with slabs of poros stone some of which survive in their original position.

Destruction of the Telesterion by the Persians. The Peisistratean Telesterion was apparently so extensively damaged by fire that a new building had to be constructed to take its place. Some of its walls were utilized in the construction of the new building. The destruction by fire of the Peisistratean Telesterion is connected with one of the most dramatic experiences of the people of Greece—the long-rumored invasion of Greece by Xerxes, the Great King of the Persians. The battle of Thermopylai was fought and lost in

[25] O. Rubensohn, *Jahrbuch*, 70 (1955), pp. 48-49. T. B. L. Webster, *From Mycenae to Homer*, pp. 47-48. M. Ventris and J. Chadwick, *Documents in Mycenaean Greek*, p. 120.

spite of the bravery of Leonidas and his warriors. The leaders of
the Greek armies and navies were huddled together in a council
of war trying to decide whether they should fight the Persians in
the Bay of Salamis. Then "there came a man of Athens bringing
news that the barbarian was arrived in Attika, and that he was
wasting it all with fire. For the army which followed Xerxes
through Boeotia had burnt the town of the Thespians (who had
themselves left it and gone to the Peloponnesos) and Plataia likewise, and was arrived at Athens, laying waste all the country
round": for it was predestined "that all the mainland of Attika
was to be made subject to the Persians."[26] One after the other the
strongholds of the Athenians were lost and finally the Akropolis
itself fell to the foreign invader and was ruthlessly sacked. But
the battle of Salamis, so expertly maneuvered by Themistokles
and fought right across from the Eleusinian coast, marked the
beginning of the end of the Persian effort to subjugate Greece.
Xerxes fled in dishonor after his mighty armada was annihilated
in the straits of Salamis. Some time later, his regent, Mardonios,
withdrew from Athens and Attika, "but first he burnt Athens,
and utterly overthrew and demolished whatever wall or house or
temple was left standing." On his way to Boeotia, he heard that a
force of a thousand Lakedaimonians had arrived at Megara and
on hearing this "he turned about and led his army against Megara,
his horse going first and overrunning the lands of that city."
Eleusis is on the way to the lands of Megara and probably its territory and whatever else was left standing was "overrun" by the
soldiers of Mardonios. To these same soldiers a strange and "marvelous thing" happened after their defeat at Plataia. "Though the
battle was hard by the grove of Demeter, there was no sign that
any Persian had been slain in the precinct, or entered into it; most
of them fell near the temple in unconsecrated ground; and I
judge," writes Herodotos, "if it be not a sin to judge of the ways
of heaven, that the Goddess herself denied them entry, because
they had burnt her sanctuary, the Anaktoron at Eleusis."[27]

[26] Herodotos, VIII, 50 and 53.
[27] Herodotos, IX, 13-14 and 65. When the historian states that they burned the
Anaktoron he wants to emphasize the enormity of the crime. The Persians burned
not only the Sanctuary but the very holy of holies of the Goddess. They therefore
deserved an extreme punishment.

We can certainly identify the people who destroyed the Peisistratean sanctuary. They were the soldiers of the armies of Xerxes and Mardonios. We cannot, however, be sure of the exact date of the destruction. It could have happened either in 480 B.C., when Xerxes conquered Attika, wasted the whole of the land, and sacked the Akropolis, or in 479 B.C., when the cavalry of Mardonios turned towards Megara and wasted the lands between it and Athens. The Persian soldiers, who were refused consecrated ground by the Goddess after the battle of Plataia, presumably took part in all the actions of the army, under the leadership of Xerxes first and then of Mardonios. Consequently, the destruction of the Peisistratean Telesterion could be placed sometime between the summer of 480 B.C. and the spring of 479 B.C.

It can be considered as certain that the Hiera of the Goddess were transported from Eleusis to a safer place when the Persian menace was drawing near. The cult statues and ritual objects from the Akropolis were transferred to Salamis, Aigina, and Troizen in a similar manner. When the Persians were thrown out of Greece, when the freedom of the land was won, the Hiera were returned to the Sanctuary of the Goddess to be placed among the ruins of her Anaktoron. Shortly afterwards a new Telesterion was constructed.

An inscription dating from 422/21 B.C. informs us that the building material of the destroyed Peisistratean Telesterion was salvaged and was carefully stored to be used wherever a need for it arose. It tells us how some of its poros wall blocks were to be used in the construction of a bridge across the Rheitoi so that the priestesses carrying the Hiera could safely cross the current.[28] Interestingly enough the inscription calls the Peisistratean Telesterion the ancient temple, thus proving that to the officials of the Sanctuary of Eleusis the Telesterion and the Temple of Demeter were one and the same building. The notion therefore of the existence of two separate sacred edifices for the cult of Demeter at Eleusis is again proved untenable.[29]

Altars of the Goddesses. The Peisistratean Telesterion stood on the Archaic terrace. The north side of that terrace was some five meters from the temple, thus leaving a somewhat wide passage

---

[28] The Rheitoi inscription, *IG*, I², 81.
[29] *Supra*, pp. 39 and 42.

between it and the north wall of the Telesterion (Fig. 6). The
south retaining wall almost touched the extreme southwest corner
of the portico, but as it veered to the west it left a widening court
beyond the south wall of the Telesterion that must have reached
a maximum width of some 14m. at the point where we have postulated the southwest ascent to the Archaic terrace. In front of the
portico, however, the terrace forms a triangularly shaped court,
over 25m. in extreme length, where the altars of the Goddesses
must have stood (Fig. 25). Euripides, with the Periklean Telesterion in mind, speaks of twin altars of the Goddesses, and an
inscription dating from 446-440 B.C. (known as the Koroibos
inscription) mentions two altars for the Goddesses placed so near
each other that officials could take oaths standing between the two
and holding their hands over them.[30] Of course both the inscription
and the statement of Euripides apply to the post-Persian Telesterion, but it is reasonable to assume that in the Peisistratean period
similar conditions existed.

Peisistratean Peribolos and its gates. In Peisistratean times the
Sanctuary of Demeter was enclosed by a strong peribolos wall,
remains of which were uncovered by Philios in the early days of
the excavations.[31] Noack wrongly attributed a good section of it to
the Early Archaic period, and wrongly maintained that it was
contemporary with the Early Archaic retaining terrace walls.[32]
The excavation of Kourouniotes brought to light the entire surviving length of this peribolos wall. As a matter of fact only small
sections of it are missing, and these because later structures were
built over them. A mere glance at our general plan of Figure 4,
where the Peisistratean walls are indicated in solid black, will illustrate the point. Its extensive remains enable us to determine its
course and its structural peculiarities, and these in turn help us to
distinguish it from the walls of other periods.

The peribolos wall of the Peisistratean times consisted of three
parts. A not too high foundation made of large, unworked, and

[30] Euripides, *Suppliants*, v. 33. K. Kourouniotes, *Eleusiniaka*, I, pp. 176 and
179, ll. 16-17. Cf. also *IG*, II², 1672, l. 141 and *IG*, I², 76, ll. 36-37.

[31] Cf. plan attached to *Praktika*, 1887.

[32] Cf. Noack, *Eleusis*, pl. 15, where the Early Archaic walls are indicated in
blue and the Peisistratean in red and compare that plate with our plan Fig. 4
where the Peisistratean walls are indicated in solid black.

flattish blocks of limestone forms the first and lowest part. On this stands a socle averaging 0.85m. in height built of Eleusinian gray stone in the polygonal style. The third part is the superstructure made of sun-dried brick. In the area of tower H25 is preserved the most conspicuous example of this brick superstructure (Figs. 6 and 24b). It is also excellently preserved below the steps of the Periklean Telesterion; there Kourouniotes uncovered it to a height of 1.30m. above its socle and determined the measurements of its bricks averaging 0.45m. x 0.45m. x 0.09m.[33]

Our drawings (Figs. 4 and 25), show that the peribolos wall enclosed not only the Sanctuary but also the city of Eleusis. We can follow it from its southwest end (H40 in the upper left-hand corner of Fig. 4), along the south slope of the hill of Eleusis, below the modern Museum and workroom to the ancient southern ascent of the hill indicated in the plan. A square tower, H39, guarded the gate through which the people entered the area of the citadel. The tower is well preserved and the opening of the gate, some 3.50m. wide, is clear. From that point the wall followed an easterly direction into what in later years became the South Court of the Sanctuary. At point H38 (Fig. 4) we find a stretch of wall starting perpendicularly from the peribolos towards the slope of the hillside. Originally, perhaps, this wall continued until it met with the north and south wall closing the Telesterion area from the higher points of the hill. It is possible to assume that the "north and south" wall was no other than the Mycenaean fortification wall of the citadel, acting as a cross-wall or diateichisma. Such a cross-wall undoubtedly existed.[34]

Some five meters to the east of H38 Kourouniotes uncovered the South Gate of the Sanctuary area, "the gate towards the sea." It is some four meters wide and it was guarded by a large square tower, part of which survives.[35] From the gate the wall proceeds in an easterly direction to the point where it was demolished to accommodate the Stoa of Philon built in the fourth century B.C. In front of that Stoa was revealed the broken end of the wall H29 still to be seen below a protecting roof of zinc. From H29 we can follow its

[33] K. Kourouniotes, *Deltion*, 14 (1931-32), Parartema, pp. 8ff.

[34] This arrangement is clearly indicated in Travlos' drawing (Fig. 25).

[35] Again we should note how wrongly Noack interpreted the segment of the tower and gate that was visible in his time, *Eleusis*, p. 40, fig. 17C5 and pl. 15.

socle proceeding eastward to the terminal square tower H25 (Fig. 6). When we look at that section of the peribolos wall (Fig. 28) we realize that over the socle we have a stone wall built in a very different technique from that followed in the construction of the other parts of the peribolos, evidently a later repair made necessary by the destruction of the brick superstructure. The destruction can undoubtedly be attributed to the soldiers of Xerxes and Mardonios. As we stand on the small platform built by the archaeological service (Fig. 44g) and look down on this repaired wall, we can, perhaps, see the very spot through which the soldiers of the great King of Persia poured into the Sanctuary area in their mission of plunder and destruction.

From the terminal square tower H25, which marks the easternmost projection of the peribolos and which measures some seven meters on each side, the direction of the course of the wall is changed; it proceeds to the North Pylon or Gate, with another square tower almost in the middle of its course (Figs. 4 and 6, H21).

The North Gate, known as the North Pylon, the main gate of the sacred precinct, was very appropriately located below the northeast end of the rocky spur of the hill and at a short distance to the east of a natural cave formed in the pointed end of the spur. The gate was completely covered in the first century before Christ by a later magnificent gateway, known as the Lesser Propylaea (Fig. 4, No. 15) so that today we cannot see its remains. However, its position is well defined by the square tower, H18, which guarded its approach. More than half of that tower can be seen along the east side of the Lesser Propylaea deep below the floor level. Traces of a stairway, which led to the top of the wall and tower, survive along the west face of the peribolos wall (Fig. 4, H19). We cannot be sure of the details of the North Pylon, but its probable form is indicated in the restoration given in Figure 25. The cave was left within the sacred enclosure and apparently during the Peisistratean period a small temple was built within it, which was identified as the temple of Plouton. From it the cave is known as the Ploutonion (Figs. 4, No. 20, and 50). Noack terminated the peribolos against the east side of the Ploutonion. However, in 1931 Kourouniotes discovered a section of the peribolos to the northwest of the gate (Fig. 4, H17) in the small court between the Lesser Propylaea and its more magnificent companion of Roman Imperial times, the Greater Propylaea. A single course of its socle survives, but its nature is unmistakable.

Again the wall disappears below the third column of the inner portico of the Greater Propylaea only to emerge from under the northwestern corner of that building. From there it continues to the northeast and can be seen along the edge of the paved outer court of the Sanctuary. Noack thought that this part of the wall along the outer court belonged to the Early Archaic period, but its masonry definitely proves it to be Peisistratean. Some 33m. from the Propylaea, a postern gate is guarded by a square tower (Fig. 4, H14). From the nature of its superstructure, a mass of concrete-like *opus incertum* seen above the floor level of the court, it was assumed that the tower was of Roman date and that the walls of Eleusis ended somewhere near here. Kourouniotes' work of 1931 disclosed that the Roman concrete superstructure was based on a foundation that belonged to the Peisistratean era (Fig. 22). From the northwest face of the square tower, now proved to be Peisistratean, the wall proceeded in a northwesterly direction. On and on we followed it, wondering where it would lead, until some 40m. beyond tower H14 it led to a wide gate guarded by another square tower (Figs. 4, H10, H12; and 31). That tower marked the northwest corner of the wall of the city of Eleusis, and the gate it guards proved to be one of the main gates of the city.[36] From tower H12, the wall proceeds to the west and south apparently on its way to enclose the hill of Eleusis along its north side as indicated in Figure 32. Both the wall and the gate, when uncovered, exhibited repairs made between the second half of the sixth century B.C. and Roman Imperial times, but the polygonal Peisistratean socle remained their foundation.

The Great Gate, identified by Travlos as the Asty Gates, because it is turned towards the city of Athens, the Asty of Attika, is very interesting (Fig. 31). In spite of the fact that its opening was blocked by a wall in Late Imperial times, it can be measured accurately because both its door jambs are well preserved. The width amounts to almost 4m. Immediately behind the opening we have

[36] K. Kourouniotes, *Eleusiniaka*, I, pp. 203-204.

an enclosed court some 7m. in length and some 5.40m. in width with a door opening on its southeast side that measures about 3m. (Fig. 4, H10). This results in a double gate very strategically arranged. The double-gate-and-court arrangement is not unusual in Greek architecture, but perhaps this is one of its earliest examples dating from the second half of the sixth century B.C. The strategy underlying its construction of course was to serve as a cul-de-sac for an attacking army by limiting the number of soldiers who could maneuver against the inner door of the fortification. The level of the gate and its court was raised from time to time, of course, until in Roman times it stood some 0.75m. above that of the Peisistratean period.

It is interesting to note that built into the wall of a small house of Roman Imperial times Travlos found a fragment of a decree ordering the repair of the wall and gates of the city of Eleusis.[37] It dates perhaps from the second half of the fourth century B.C., but the structures it mentions were built long before. From that inscription we learn the names of the various gates of Eleusis and we can deduce their possible location, especially since the gates are mentioned in a definite order corresponding to the ruins brought to light thus far. The first lines of the inscription are missing but Travlos assumed, with reason, that they dealt with repairs to be done to our gate which he believed was named in the missing lines. Then the gate towards Megara is named, a postern gate near the corner tower towards the sea, the gate by the Stadium, and the South Gate. Near the South Gate the inscription mentions a small gate, a *pylis*, and finally it refers to a colonnaded structure and to a Propylaion. It is evident that the gates of the Sanctuary were not included in the repairs ordered by this decree. If we now turn to Travlos' drawing (Fig. 32), we can find, reading counter-clockwise, all the gates mentioned in the inscription in an exact sequence. It is interesting perhaps to note that the *pylis* by the South Gate must have been one through which people could enter the southwest corner of the Sanctuary. If we compare Figure 32 with our general plan of Figure 4, where the Peisistratean peribolos wall disclosed by Kourouniotes is marked in solid black, we shall be obliged to

---

[37] Published by Kourouniotes in *Eleusiniaka*, I, pp. 189-208.

conclude that it was in Peisistratean days that the city of Eleusis was surrounded by the fortification wall which served her through-out her life.

The inscriptions and the archaeological discoveries especially of the last thirty years prove that the area of Eleusis was clearly distinguished into two parts, the Sanctuary and the city. Where did the one end and the other begin? We have no remains showing how the Sanctuary area immediately to the west and beyond the south court of the Telesterion was separated from the city that extended to the west along the south slope of the hill and from its akropolis. Beyond the west side of the Telesterion there must certainly have existed a cross-wall, a *diateichisma*, which separated the Sanctuary from the akropolis. In describing the southwest sec-tion of the Peisistratean peribolos we noticed a spur wall by the Southwest Gate of the Sanctuary (Fig. 4, H38). Perhaps after leaving a door opening where it is terminated now, that wall pro-ceeded toward the slope of the hill to end against the Mycenaean wall. Thus it served as the cross-wall or *diateichisma*, separating the Sanctuary from the city to the southwest and from the akropolis towering over it. This is clearly shown in Figure 25. Solid walls enclosed the south and east sides of the Sanctuary. But how was the Sanctuary separated from the north section of the town in the area of the Asty Gates?

Noack terminated the Peisistratean peribolos wall at the Plou-tonion and the North Pylon; but we have seen that this has been proved incorrect. Apparently the area to the north and west of the Pylon was attached to the Sanctuary in Peisistratean times to serve as an auxiliary area where perhaps administrative buildings were located and the dwellings of the officials were grouped. Unfortu-nately that area was very much disturbed in later times, especially during the Roman Imperial period, and as a result very little of what survived could, with any degree of confidence, be attributed to the Peisistratean period. It is certain, however, that the long and narrow building marked H50 in Figure 4 belongs to that period (cf. Fig. 25). In spite of wall L16 built across it in very late Roman times, its plan is clear. The building (25.45m. x

8.75m.) was entered on the short east side. The use of this long building could not be determined from what was found in it, but we believe that Travlos is right in suggesting that it served for the storing of the first-fruit offerings, that it was a σιρός to use the name given to such storehouses or silos by the inscriptions of the times. Along its north side a road was revealed (Fig. 4, No. 17), used to the end of the Roman period but apparently first laid in the days of the construction of the storehouse. The road terminated at its east end in a small door opening, a *pylis*, through which perhaps one could enter into the Sanctuary area. At its west end it merged with a street (Fig. 4, No. 19), which ended at the *pylis* of tower H14. At the junction of Streets 17 and No. 19, a single lane continued to the west for some 16m. and then branched in two directions; the main lane continued to the northwest in the direction of the Asty Gates, while a secondary lane turned sharply to the south and, becoming stepped, climbed the slope of the hill to end ultimately on the northeast corner of the akropolis. The course of Street 19 and of the lane from the *pylis* to the akropolis perhaps marked the line where a cross-wall stood separating the auxiliary area of the Sanctuary from the rest of the city. In the wall of a later house, in the area skirted by the lane in its climb to the akropolis (Fig. 4, No. 18), was found, perhaps *in situ*, what we may call a street sign, a rectangular block of marble bearing the inscription ΟΡΟΣ ΙΕ[Ρ]Ο, boundary of the Sanctuary. This boundary stone is late in date, but it indicates that in later times the auxiliary area of the Sanctuary extended to the lane.[38] Perhaps that was the case in the Peisistratean period also. In that period, we may be sure, the custom was begun of attaching to the Sanctuary a semi-sacred, auxiliary area.

The "Kallichoron" well. Returning to the North Pylon, we note the well to be found some 40m. to the northeast of it, at the southwest corner of the outer paved court of the Roman period (Figs. 4, No. 10, and 33). It was discovered and cleared by Philios in 1892 and has been recognized as the Kallichoron mentioned by Pausanias along with the temple of the "Propylaia Artemis" and

---

[38] In our discussion we follow Travlos' suggestions and conclusions, often discussed on the spot. For the boundary stone cf. J. Threpsiades, *Deltion*, 14 (1931-32), Parartema, pp. 31-32; K. Kourouniotes, *Deltion*, 15 (1933), Parartema, p. 17; J. N. Travlos, *Hesperia*, 18 (1949), p. 142.

"Father Poseidon."[39] The sides of the well are lined in the polygonal style with Eleusinian stone and its round opening is surmounted by two concentric circles of well-cut stone with a total height of 0.59m. Eight stones secured by or connected with double-T clamps form the lower ring (ca. 2.85m. in diameter); four blocks, also clamped, form the upper ring (1.46m. in diameter). The opening of the well at the surviving top is 0.88m., while its diameter at the base of the lower ring is 1.08m. Its depth is now 6m. The floor on which it stands is well paved with large slabs and it is some 1.35m. below the floor level of the Roman Court. The area around it was elliptical, circular at one end and squared at the other. It was surrounded, in the fourth century b.c., by a beautiful parapet wall made of poros slabs set vertically, carefully worked and fitted. Two doors, averaging 0.75m. in width, gave access to the area of the well. The one on the north side of the enclosure is under the south edge of the Roman Court. The other, seen in Figure 33, measures 0.60m. in width. The ancient wall built in the fifth century and strengthened in the fourth was made to encircle the well, and the area it enclosed was respected both by the builders of the Greater Propylaea, at the northeast corner of which the well stands, and by the artisans who paved the Roman Court; for the lowest step on the east side of the Greater Propylaea was cut away so as not to infringe on the area of the well, and the side of the court was stopped at its outer parapet wall. The well, therefore, could be seen at all times as an important landmark of Eleusinian topography. At a later period, perhaps in Roman times, the entrance to the area of the well was fitted with a door, about one meter in width, which opened onto the bottom step of the Greater Propylaea, where its traces can easily be detected. Perhaps a wooden stairway led from that door to the court.

The date of the well, the second half of the sixth century b.c., has been deduced from its construction and its clamps; it is generally considered as contemporary with Peisistratean constructions. In 1931 we cleaned the interior of the well and searched its depth in the hope of finding evidence to verify the date derived from its structure. The well, however, was used throughout the centuries even to the end of the Ottoman occupation and its interior had

[39] D. Philios, *Praktika*, 1892, p. 33; 1893, p. 11; Noack, *Eleusis*, pp. 73ff.

been cleared repeatedly in the course of its use. Its exploration gave us valuable experience and a feeling kindred to that which must have filled the heart of Persephone when she was going up and down to the Lower World, but no actual finds to serve our objective. The pottery we found in its depth belonged to late Byzantine and Ottoman times. So its date has to be deduced from its construction and this seems to place the well in the Peisistratean period.

The Temple of Plouton. When the initiates entered the North Pylon, they would find themselves at the north end of the inner Sacred Way that leads to the Telesterion. Immediately to their right they would see the cave with the temple of Plouton above which tower the rocks of the eastern extremity of the Eleusinian hill (Figs. 2, 3, 4, No. 20, and Fig. 50). Apparently the temple of Plouton was in Peisistratean times established there for the first time. Perhaps at this time there was created before the broad opening of the cave the distinctive triangular court, still supported by retaining walls built in the fourth century B.C. The foundations that are visible today belong to the temple of a later period, but below them we have scanty remains of an older temple composed of a few blocks of Eleusinian stone. These older remains belong to Peisistratean times and to a small shrine composed of a chamber or naos (2.90m. x 2.50m.) fronted originally by an open portico in antis.[40]

There can be no doubt that the shrine is the temple of Plouton mentioned in the inscription of 329/8 B.C. In the fill of the cave was found a votive relief, dedicated by Lysimachides to the God and the Goddess. It represents Plouton and Persephone dining, and the crowning of Demeter by Persephone, who holds two torches; apparently the composition represents the reconciliation of Demeter with Plouton.[41] Both the inscription and the relief are later in date, but they indicate that in the fourth century B.C. the cave was sacred to Plouton; it must have been dedicated to that divinity before that century and in Peisistratean times because within it a shrine was built in those times, and because we have no

[40] D. Philios, *Ephem*, 1886, pp. 29-31; Noack, *Eleusis*, p. 79.
[41] *Ephem*, 1883, pp. 113ff; 1886, pp. 19ff; P. Foucart, *BCH*, 7 (1883), pp. 388-390. Cf. *Sylloge*[4], vol. 3, No. 1050.

tradition that speaks of Plouton taking over the shrine and replacing another divinity. It is obvious that the site was well chosen for a temple to Plouton; the deep cavern could give to the spectator the impression of a χάσμα γῆς, a chasm in the earth, and even suggest to him the "gates of Hades."[42]

The inner gate and the hollow road. From the Ploutonion the inner Sacred Way proceeded northward almost in a straight line along the foot of the east side of the rocky spur of Panaghitsa and in an easy ascending grade reached the north side of the terrace on which stood the Telesterion (Figs. 2 and 4, No. 25). A line of polygonal stones to be seen along its right side shortly before it ends (Fig. 4, No. 26) indicates the right edge of the Way.[43] The North Pylon was the starting point of another road which, branching from the Sacred Way, went to the southeast along the peribolos wall to reach the easternmost corner of the terrace. In the area H24, where the road reached the eastern end of the terrace, and a short distance from the Kallichoron of the Hymn (Fig. 6, W), it passed through an inner gate constructed in Peisistratean times (marked H24 in Figs. 4 and 6). The antae of this inner gate are well preserved and are easily identified. The east anta (Fig. 17, e) is at the end of a wall that projects from the body of the peribolos wall some 3.50m. and has a width of 2.38m. The west anta (Fig. 17, a) was attached to the Early Archaic retaining wall, the face of which was lined with a pseudo-isodomic construction of Eleusinian stones, more or less rectangular in shape but of uneven length and height (Fig. 17, b). That lining apparently was finished on top with a well-profiled cornice two blocks of which survive in position (Fig. 17, c). It should be noted that the west anta, preserved to a height of 1.50m., is not a solid stone construction (Fig. 17, a). Its face only is built of rectangular blocks leaving a space in the heart of the anta to be filled with smaller stones, earth and pebbles. In front of the antae and at their south edge are the stone blocks into which the wooden doorposts were inserted. Beyond doorway H24,

---

[42] The Orphic hymn to Plouton refers to the cave of Eleusis as the gates of Hades: Kern, *Orphicorum fragmenta*, 1922, p. 115. Cf. *infra* for additional discussion of the Ploutonion.

[43] This edge would certainly indicate that from the North Pylon, the later Lesser Propylaea, the Sacred Way went in an almost straight line to the terrace of the Telesterion and will cast doubt on the suggested meandering arrangement of Noack's *Eleusis*, pl. 15.

Noack postulated a "defensive court" to the south and west (indicated by the letters DC, Figs. 6 and 24), and another door that shut off the court. Kourouniotes' investigations of the area proved that such a defensive court did not exist but that the road, passing through gate H24 and around the east end of the Early Archaic terrace, proceeded to the west between that terrace and the south section of the peribolos wall until it reached the south court of the Sanctuary and the south gate.[44] Thus this road, a veritable κοίλη ὁδός (hollow road), could be considered as an inner service road connecting the north pylon with the south court and the south pylon, a road of great use, especially to the personnel of the Sanctuary.

The projecting stone foundations H30 (Fig. 6), clearly seen in the photograph of Figure 24, perhaps formed the footing of a small bridge connecting the east court of the Sanctuary and the top of the peribolos wall as indicated in Travlos' drawing of Figure 25. Such a connection could prove valuable in times of stress. In several sections, stairways built along the sides of the ancient walls gave access to the top. We have already noticed the stairway H19 leading to the top of the wall and tower H18 guarding the North Pylon. Across the inner doorway H24 there is another stairway (indicated in Fig. 4) that led to the top of the fortifications.

The Successor to the Sacred House. The excavations give us a clear picture of the Sanctuary and a general idea of the extent of the city of Eleusis, but they have failed to bring to light the remains of the houses of the people of the period. In fact the only structure worth mentioning, found outside the Sanctuary, is a small building that apparently was built to take the place of the "Sacred House" (Fig. 4, No. 60). During the Peisistratean period the area of that house was terraced carefully and a peribolos wall of polygonal masonry was built around its precinct.[45] The terrace now assumed a trapezoidal shape imposed by the desire to include in it as much as possible of the ground originally belonging to the "Sacred House," and by a roadway that meandered along the west side of the precinct. The terrace thus enclosed measures some 15m.

---

[44] Noack, *Eleusis*, pp. 30ff for his ingenious "zwingertoor" proved wrong by K. Kourouniotes, *Deltion*, 14 (1931-32), Parartema, pp. 10ff.

[45] K. Kourouniotes, *Guide*, p. 50 and *Praktika*, 1937, p. 42ff.

from east to west and 17m. from north to south. On the old foundations, following the older lines of the "Sacred House," a new
building was constructed of poros stone, only a few blocks of which
have survived. Unfortunately they are inadequate to determine its
plan. But they as well as the marble tiles of the structure, which
are of the same type as those of the Peisistratean Telesterion though
smaller in size, help to prove that the structure belongs to the
Peisistratean times.

To this building apparently belongs the beautiful statue of a
fleeing maiden illustrated in Figure 34. It is of Pentelic marble
and stands 0.645m. high.[46] There can be little doubt that the statue
belonged to a pedimental group whose theme must have been the
abduction of Persephone by Plouton. Our figure is one of the "deep-
bosomed daughters of Okeanos" with whom Persephone was playing and gathering flowers on the fateful day of the abduction.
Evidently she is running away from the scene of action, the center
of which naturally would have been occupied by Persephone and
Plouton. But as she turns to look at the wondrous deed that is
taking place, she moves hastily away. She is wearing a Doric peplos
and a high crown indicating her royal birth. The charm emanating
from this figure can hardly be described in words. The forward
movement, indicated by the sweeping folds of the drapery below
the knees and by the slanting position of the body, is masterfully
designed, while the suggested desire to look back and see the action,
a natural desire indeed, gives the artist the opportunity to model
in a fresh and crisp way a beautiful maiden form in a restrained
movement. We look in vain for an indication of terror or anxiety
on the features of the face. In spite of her flight the maiden is
restrained and dignified; she exhibits qualities that apparently were
highly valued even in pre-classical times. Her deep concern is adequately conveyed by the movement which adds to the sweetness
of her face. A few details only in the rendering of the eye, the
mouth, and the folds of drapery prove that the artist, in spite of his

[46] K. Kourouniotes, *Praktika*, 1937, p. 4; *Guide*, p. 67; *Art and Archaeol.*, 21,
p. 113; Noack, *Eleusis*, p. 219 and figs. 87-88; E. Buschor, *Antike*, 2 (1926),
pl. 13; Noack maintained that the statue belonged to the pedimental composition
of his Temple F. This statement was proved wrong by the discovery of the statue
in the area of the Sacred House. We shall see that Temple F belongs to the Roman
period and could not have possessed pedimental sculpture of the early fifth century.
The statue is now to be seen in the small north room of the Museum of Eleusis.

skill in modeling, was still under the influence of the archaic tradition. This indicates that the statue was made at the beginning of the fifth century, perhaps in the years between the victory of Marathon and the destruction of the Telesterion by the Persians, in other words 490-480/79 B.C. It was then that the small sacred structure was destroyed and its pedimental sculpture was smashed; from that catastrophe only our maiden survived to bring us the tale.

Orientation of the Sanctuary toward Athens. It may be advisable to summarize our story of Eleusis and its Sanctuary in the Peisistratean period (cf. Figs. 25 and 32). A new monumental Telesterion, larger than any of its predecessors, was constructed on the Early Archaic terrace. The Sanctuary area was surrounded by a peribolos wall and to it was added an auxiliary area to be used for storing tithes and for other administrative purposes. The city of Eleusis as well was surrounded by fortifications and its area, as defined by these walls, seems to have remained the same throughout the centuries which followed. At any rate the fortifications now constructed and later constantly repaired served Eleusis to the end of its life. Peisistratos, realizing the strategic position of the site, apparently transformed it into a fortified outpost of the state of Athens. By increasing the facilities of its Telesterion, he enabled Eleusis to play a greater role in the religious life of the Greeks for the greater glory of Athens. During this period the ties between the two cities were multiplied and made secure and hereafter the people of Eleusis had to turn to Athens for direction and support. Indeed, Eleusis has now become a deme of Athens and its people belong to the Hippothoontis tribe. To strengthen this tie, Peisistratos, I believe, or the people who were responsible for all the architectural and other activity of the times, so designed their works as to make it evident that Eleusis was part of the Athenian state.

We have noticed that in Geometric and Early Archaic times the main ascent to the terrace of the Telesterion was placed on the south side of the Sanctuary, the side away from Athens. We also noticed that what we believe to have been the area of the sacred dances held in honor of the Goddess was in the direction of the sea. Now Peisistratos or his builders turned the main entrance of the Sanctuary towards Athens, although, in an effort to follow tradition they also made a "Gate towards the Sea" on the south side. But do we know that the North Pylon became now the main gate of the temple? The way in which all the landmarks of the Eleusinian tradition are collected in the north side seems to prove this change. By the North Pylon was the Kallichoron well and its sacred dances; not far from it the Ploutonion, where for the first time a small temple or shrine was built; near it is the locality where the Goddess was assumed to have been found by the daughters of King Keleos, the place that was developed into the "Mirthless Stone." The Sacred Way, leading to the Sanctuary from the outside world is now on the north side and in the court at which it ended scanty but revealing remains of a large structure, perhaps an altar, which in Roman times was replaced by the *eschara*. An inscription of the fourth century speaks of the Propylon of Demeter and Kore, which most probably was erected on this side when Kimon built the outer North Pylon. All existing and recognizable indications seem to suggest rather definitely that the North Pylon was now developed into the main gate of the Sanctuary; and that gate is now turned towards Athens.

We have already recognized another important element. We have seen that the south section of the Peisistratean peribolos wall was built right across a court in which, we have every reason to believe, ritualistic dances were held in honor of Demeter from time immemorial. Those ritualistic dances could not be discontinued; and yet the traditional court in which they were held could no longer be used for the purpose, because of the construction of the wall. Another court had to be provided right away even by the builders of the Peisistratean peribolos. Since dances were held near a well, a very important landmark of the Eleusinian tradition, in the new court a well had to be constructed if it did not already exist. At a short distance from the main gate of the Sanctuary, the North Pylon, constructed by those who built the peribolos wall, we find a well which if it was not actually built at this time at least was now restored to a monumental form. In front of that well we have a court in use until the very end of the life of the Sanctuary. We note in our plan of Figure 4, how the well (No. 10) is to be found almost straight across the end of the Sacred Way (No. 1) which connected Eleusis and Athens. Between the two we have a free area, the new court. Certainly in this court were held the dances suggested by Pausanias and illustrated on the Niinnion tablet (Fig. 88). To this court, therefore, the dances were transferred, away from the direction of the sea and in the direction of Athens. It seems to us that a conscious effort was made to construct the walls and gates of Eleusis so as to make it evident that the site and the cult were closely associated with Athens. This conscious effort we can certainly attribute to Peisistratos who is reputed to have introduced many ingenious devices for the aggrandizement of his beloved Athens.

A final indication of a turn towards Athens is the lack of graves of the period in the west cemetery. It is a well-known fact that the ancient Greeks placed their cemeteries along the main roads leading to their cities, that they placed their important cemeteries along the important road. Now we may note that the west cemetery runs along the road from Eleusis to Megara, and that no graves of this period were found in its excavated areas. Does that suggest that the people buried their dead in a different cemetery, one that was placed along another road, perhaps the road to Athens? Unfortunately the road from Eleusis to Athens, which seems to coincide with the Sacred Way, in the neighborhood of Eleusis is covered by buildings and gardens and thus is unavailable for exploration. We cannot therefore prove that the burial ground of the period was also changed to the direction of Athens. But the lack of remains in the west cemetery seems to suggest this strongly.

CHAPTER V

THE KIMONIAN AND PERIKLEAN ERA
(F AND I) CA. 480-404 B.C.

AN ACT of revenge piled high the burned ruins of the temple of Demeter which Peisistratos built. Fate had decreed, however, that the perpetrators of those acts of impiety were to be defeated and their victims were destined to return victorious to their devastated homes. The outcome, considered as a triumph of civilization against barbarism, filled the Greeks in general and the Athenians in particular not only with the exultation of a victory achieved on the battlefield, but also with pride in their culture and with determination to cultivate the arts which made them superior to others. When the Athenians returned to their Akropolis they found their sacred buildings transformed into heaps of smouldering ruins, and we can imagine the consternation of the Eleusinians, when on their return they found the precinct of Demeter, the sacred temenos of the world, devastated by fire. After the battle of Salamis, in the first flush of victory, the Greeks took a solemn oath not to rebuild the sanctuaries destroyed by the Persians but to let the ruins stand as a memorial of their barbaric conduct: "I will not rebuild any one of the sanctuaries which have been burned or destroyed, but I will let them be and leave them as a reminder to coming generations of the impiety of the barbarians."[1] But could Eleusis and Athens leave the Sanctuary of Demeter in ruins? Could they have moved it to another site? The strong belief that the temple had to occupy the area sanctified by the divine presence so long ago would not permit them to change the site,[2] and the Hiera of Demeter could not have stayed homeless for long. The Mysteries had to be celebrated again in the fall. How could they leave homeless a Goddess who had come to their aid when needed most? The tale told by

---

[1] Diodoros, XI, 29. For a complete bibliography see W. B. Dinsmoor, in *Hesperia*, Suppl. V, p. 158 n. 332.

[2] The importance of the cult depended upon the fact that the initiates found themselves in the same spot visited by the Goddess and could see the sacred landmarks sanctified by her sojourn. This of course would have tended to keep fresh and exact the memory of the past.

Herodotos[3] regarding the vision seen by Damaratos the Lakedai-
monian and Dikaios the exile from Athens was public property.
Everyone knew that Demeter gave the victory to the Greeks in
the Battle of Salamis. Besides, did not Herodotos emphasize "this
other coincidence, that there were precincts of the Eleusinian
Demeter on both battlefields; for at Plataia the fight was held
hard by the temple of Demeter, . . . and so it was to be at Mykale
likewise."[4] After this divine intervention, how could the Athenians
leave homeless the Hiera of Demeter?

KIMON'S CONSTRUCTION

We do not have the story of the reconstruction in the writings of
the ancient authors; they had, perhaps, to refrain from mentioning
it. But we hear of the man to whom the beginning of the reconstruction of Athens is generally attributed. Kimon, the son of
Miltiades the hero of Marathon, devoted to public works a great
deal of his and the public wealth, which he augmented by Persian
spoils.[5] Certainly Kimon seems to have been the right instrument
which divine providence would have used for the reconstruction of
the great Sanctuary. Perhaps this took place between the years 479,
after the victory of Plataia, and 461 B.C. when Kimon was ostracized. His work can now, after the clearing of the site, be defined
with precision. Apparently he repaired the fortification wall
breached by the Persians; then he laid out the court of the Telesterion and at the same time began the rebuilding of that edifice.

The Persians apparently had broken through the brick superstructure of the Peisistratean peribolos wall at a point between H29
and the square tower H25 (Figs. 4 and 6). That part of the wall
Kimon rebuilt. The fragments of the brick that survived on top
of the stone socle were removed and the latter was used as the
base on which a pseudo-isodomic wall of limestone was constructed.
The stones were laid in a stretcher and header arrangement that
can easily be seen today, since the entire length of this repair has
been cleared and left to view (Fig. 28). The pseudo-isodomic wall
presents a finished face on the outside, but its inner face is unfinished

[3] Herodotos, VIII, 65.
[4] Herodotos, IX, 101.
[5] Plutarch, *Kimon*, 13, 7-8.

and it is evident that it was not left to view (Figs. 17 and 24, F1).
Apparently it was now used as a retaining wall to support an enlargement of the east court of the Sanctuary, the court that spreads in
front of the Telesterion. The deep area between the Early Archaic
retaining wall and the Peisistratean peribolos wall, which formed
the "hollow road" in the preceding period, was filled in as well as
the area of the inner gate and of the well. It was possible to fill in
the area around the well and the well itself, because its function
and the dances held in its vicinity had been transferred in Peisistratean days, as we have seen, to the well by the North Pylon.
Even the area to the north of the well was included in this enlarged
court, and had to be artificially filled and leveled. For that purpose
a good section of the east Peisistratean peribolos was used as a
retaining wall, from Gate H24 to the square tower H21 (Fig. 4).
To serve this purpose better the thickness of the Peisistratean peribolos was increased from two to four meters by the addition of a
brick wall built in front of it. This addition is well preserved; the
brick courses, as well as the bricks, were clearly distinguishable at
the time of the excavation.[6]

From Tower H21 almost due west in the direction of the Sacred
Way we find a well-built wall in polygonal style, now preserved to
a length of 9.50m. (Fig. 4, F3). That wall must have served as
a terminal retaining wall to the north for the fill of the enlarged
court of the temple. Thus we find that the Early Archaic terrace
on which the destroyed Telesterion stood was extended to the east,
to the south, and the north, to the Peisistratean peribolos, transformed now into a retaining wall.[7]

Gate F5 and the outer North Pylon. Beyond the east Peisistratean
peribolos (H25, H21 and H18) half the length of which was
transformed into a terrace retaining wall, an oval area was now
added to the Sanctuary ca. 110m. in length from north to south

[6] Cf. K. Kourouniotes, *Deltion*, 14 (1931-32), Parartema, p. 19 and fig. 22.
In Fig. 4 the addition is indicated by the white area limited by a single line in
front of the body of the wall, from H24 to H21 and in Fig. 6 by the checkered
area.

[7] The space added to the triangular Archaic terrace transformed it into an almost
square court some 50m. in extreme width. The south side of the court was formed
by the Peisistratean wall H25 to H29; the east side was formed by the Peisistratean
wall H25 to H21 reinforced with brick; the north side is marked by the retaining
wall F3 that reached the Sacred Way at point 27 (Fig. 4).

and ca. 30m. in width from east to west (Fig. 4,A) known as the Kimonian extension. This new area was enclosed by a peribolos wall (Fig. 4, F6) which started from the Peisistratean tower H25, proceeded northeastward for a short distance and then turned north to terminate beyond the well that Pausanias called the Kallichoron (Fig. 4, No. 10) by the Greater Propylaea. At its southern extremity, by the northeast corner of the Peisistratean tower (H25), was constructed a gate (F5 in Fig. 35), which was revealed in 1884 by Philios; it was cleared again in 1906 and studied minutely by Noack, and it was finally re-examined by Kourouniotes.[8] Noack maintained that this was the oldest pylon of the Sanctuary and placed it in the Archaic period. Kourouniotes' work definitely proved that it belongs to the Kimonian era of reconstruction. The north pilaster of the gate stands to almost its original height and it is composed of two rectangular stone shafts (3.60m. high) set about 0.60m. apart and connected above by a single lintel (Fig. 35, p) 0.46m. in height. These shafts stand at the end of the socle of the new east peribolos wall. The empty space between them was filled with sun-dried brick, which bound the pilaster with the brick superstructure of the peribolos (F6 in Figs. 4, 6, 35). The other pilaster, set against the northeast corner of the Peisistratean tower H25, is not so well preserved, but enough of it survives to a height of 1.40m. above its base to define the width of the gate and its details. Before the inner corner of the pilasters, we find the stone footing of the wooden posts of the gate (Figs. 35, d and 36, d); between them, almost in the middle of the gate opening, we have a somewhat flatter stone (0.22m. x 0.41m. x 0.44m.) which acted as the base for the two wings of the wooden door (Figs. 35 and 36). The width of the gate measures three meters. Since the door jambs were placed at the inner end of the pilasters, a small porch, a prothyron, was produced on the outside. In the interior a small propylon was made with two columns standing at a distance of some 2.60m. from the gate opening. The southwest column base with a shaft standing on it, is still in its original position (Fig. 36, f); the other, still to be seen, has been moved from its place. At a later age, Gate F5 was blocked off by a brick wall (remains of which can be seen in

[8] D. Philios, *Praktika*, 1884, pl. Δ; Noack, *Eleusis*, pp. 32ff, pls. 14 and 15. K. Kourouniotes, *Deltion*, 15 (1933-35), Parartema, pp. 33ff.

our Fig. 35, C). At a short distance from the gate was erected a statue, most probably of Hermes Propylaios, the base of which was found at the end of the stepped podium of an earlier era (Fig. 19, b).

Beyond the gate the new peribolos wall extended to the east and north, as we have seen, to terminate a little to the northwest of the Kallichoron well (Fig. 4, No. 10) under the Greater Propylaea. Between its end and the eastern corner of the Peisistratean wall there remains a small space that was most probably closed by a gateway. Before that gate perhaps stood the Propylon of Demeter and Kore mentioned in a fourth century inscription.[9] Gate F5 possessed such a Propylon and it is reasonable to assume that a similar arrangement would be followed in the building of a contemporary and a more important gateway. Additions and repairs around this gate were evidently made late in the fourth century when a square tower (Fig. 4, K20) was added to its north end and when the wall was strengthened on either side of the tower. It was then that the court of the Kallichoron well was paved and its parapet was erected. At an even later date, in the closing years of the life of the Sanctuary, the thickness of the new peribolos wall, amounting to only 1.80m., was almost doubled; and for this Late Roman repair all kinds of materials were employed, giving to the outer face of the wall a rather slovenly appearance. The Roman face of the wall is the one we see today as we go along the east side of the enceinte. Because of it the entire wall was often taken to belong to Roman times, although both Philios and Noack indicate the existence of the older peribolos behind the facing wall. However, Noack attributed that original wall to the Early Archaic period. Kourouniotes definitely proved that it belongs to Kimonian times and was able to remove a short section of the facing Roman construction to reveal the older wall behind it just to the southeast of Tower K20. In the era that followed the Persian destruction we have, therefore, an inner and an outer gate or pylon on the north side of the Sanctuary, in the direction of Athens. The inner pylon was the one originally built by the architects of Peisistratos; repaired, perhaps after the Persian destruction, it continued to serve the Sanctuary to the first century B.C. The outer pylon with its

[9] *Sylloge*[4], vol. 3, No. 956, line 25.

propylon, constructed possibly by Kimon, must have added splendor to a Sanctuary that was already famous.

The Sacred Way within the Sanctuary was naturally extended from the inner to the outer north pylon. Beyond the south side of the outer pylon, however, a road branched off the Sacred Way and proceeded southward along the outer, eastern face of the Peisistratean east peribolos now serving as a retaining wall; it ended at the Gate F5. This road served the Kimonian extension, a new auxiliary area, and the small dwellings built in it for the use apparently of the sacred personnel. Remains of these dwellings were found especially near Gate F5. To facilitate communication between the auxiliary area and the Sanctuary the small gate, Pylis F7, was cut in the Peisistratean wall to the north of Tower H21.

Kimonian Telesterion. The reconstruction of the temple presented a much more pressing need and to that Kimon applied himself with diligence. It seems reasonable to suppose that on their return, after the defeat of the Persians, the officials of the Sanctuary first tried to find a shelter for the Hiera. Perhaps the Anaktoron of the Peisistratean temple was repaired and used temporarily for that purpose. At the same time plans were made for the construction of a Telesterion even more magnificent than that built by Peisistratos and destroyed by the Persians. We know comparatively little about that new building. Our information comes from its surviving remnants and since the building was never completed and the remnants are few, our knowledge of it is necessarily incomplete. Apparently Kimon's architects decided to use as much as possible of the Peisistratean Telesterion, at least to begin with. In their plan, therefore, they used the foundations of the south and north outer walls and those of the prostoon. Thus they kept the width of the old temple, but they extended its length to the west for some 17.50m. This required extensive quarrying of the rocky slope, and it seems that now for the first time the hillside was extensively cut away. The extent of that enlargement to the west was determined by the position of the Anaktoron. A glance at the restored plan of the temple (Fig. 26, C) will indicate that in the new structure the Anaktoron occupied a symmetrical position and encompassed the same area of ground as before; as a matter of fact it seems that the building was designed around the old Anaktoron.

The prostoon was included in the naos or hall of the Telesterion (compare Fig. 26, B and C), which acquired again a long and narrow form measuring almost 50m. in length from east to west and 27m. in width from north to south. It has been suggested that this was only half of the designed building, the other half, exactly symmetrical to it was to be added at a later time along its south side. This may have been the intention of the architects, but we shall never know. The fact remains that from what has survived we can conclude that in the days of Kimon a building of the plan indicated in Figure 26, C was started. Of the few remains of this building the most enlightening are the foundations of the columns which were to support the roof of the edifice.

The interior columns were arranged in three rows of seven. Their architectural order remains hypothetical since no remnants survived, but Dinsmoor believes that the drums and Ionic bases of the inscription of 408/7 B.C., mentioned earlier (p. 82), belong to these columns; consequently he suggests that the columns were Ionic. The arrangement of the columns would not allow a lantern over the middle of the roof of the building, since the fourth column of the second row comes exactly in the middle of the hall. Again the position of that column would indicate that the Anaktoron did not occupy the central area of the Telesterion. The columns were based on the rock, and wherever they were set over a fill their foundations were lowered to the rock below the fill. These foundations are constructed of large slabs of Eleusinian stone, perhaps the stone quarried from the westward extension of the temple, placed horizontally in irregular courses. The sides of the slabs are unworked and irregular, and in many of them are visible traces of the wooden wedges employed in quarrying them.

Along three of the walls of the hall—west, north, and south—as was the case with the Peisistratean building, tiers of seven stone steps were erected. Of course the steps along the south side were interrupted by the Anaktoron, which seems certainly to have occupied that position and to have been identical in size to its predecessor. On the east side of the hall, perhaps, were left two door openings, corresponding to the three doors of the Peisistratean hall. No provision for a prostoon is apparent in the remains; whether or not such a prostoon was to have been provided later remains uncertain. Again we cannot know how far the construction of this Telesterion had gone before it was stopped and the project abandoned. Of one thing, however, we can be certain: the Anaktoron would have been the first part to be completed. We may assume that the project was discontinued when Kimon was ostracized in 461 B.C.

CONSTRUCTION IN PERIKLEAN TIMES

Even more impressive than Kimon's was Perikles' contribution to the greatness of Eleusis. When we think of the magnificent edifices constructed on the Akropolis of Athens during the administration of that remarkable statesman, we may well wonder that he found time to think of Eleusis also. But since the Sanctuary of Demeter too "brought most delightful adornment to Athens, and the greatest amazement to the rest of men," it too "testified for Hellas that her ancient power and splendor, of which so much is told, was no idle fiction."[10] It was natural therefore, for the great statesman, who was responsible for a Parthenon, to wish to erect for Demeter an edifice worthy of her eminence and of her contribution to the greatness of Athens.

The Iktinian Telesterion. The building begun by Kimon, no longer satisfied the ambitions of the ruler and people of Athens.[11] We learn from Vitruvius and Strabo that Iktinos, one of the two architects of the Parthenon, was commissioned to draw the designs of a new building.[12] The remains we have on the site seem to indicate more than one effort to build the Telesterion at this time;[13] and these indications are corroborated by literary evidence. In Plutarch[14] we find that "it was Koroibos who began to build the Telesterion at Eleusis and that he placed the columns on the floor and yoked together their capitals with architraves; on his death

[10] Plutarch, *Perikles*, 12, 1.

[11] It is interesting to note Thoukydides' comment on the rule of Perikles: "Athens in name was a democracy, in reality was ruled by its foremost citizen" (II, 65, 9-10).

[12] Strabo, IX, 1, 12, "Then one comes to the city of Eleusis, in which is the hieron of the Eleusinian Demeter, and the mystic *sekos* (or hall) which Iktinos built, a temple capable of accommodating a crowd of spectators." Vitruvius, *Praef.*, VII, 16: "Eleusine Cereris et Proserpinae cellomi immani magnitudine Ictinus dorico more sine exterioribus columnis ad laxamentum usus sacrificiorum pertexit."

[13] Accurately noted by Philios in the early days of the excavations.

[14] Plutarch, *Perikles*, 13, 5.

Metagenes, of the deme of Xypete, carried the diazoma and the upper tier of columns, while Xenokles, of the deme of Cholargos, set on high the opaion over the Anaktoron." The participation of Koroibos in the construction is indicated by a building inscription dating from the years between 446 and 440 B.C. published by Kourouniotes.[15] In that decree Koroibos is mentioned as the architect of the Sanctuary. Thus our literary and epigraphical evidence seems to indicate that two different buildings were attempted during the Periklean age: one designed and built, as Strabo and Vitruvius say, by Iktinos, and another built by three cooperating architects who directed the course of construction successively. The evidence preserved at the site proves definitely that an unfinished building was replaced by another which was completed. The unfinished building must be the one designed by Iktinos, for the testimony of Plutarch speaks clearly of the various stages of the structure that was completed. On the basis of this evidence scholars have been able to determine quite accurately the design of the two buildings of the Periklean age.

It was indeed natural for Perikles to have entrusted one of the architects of the Parthenon with the design of the Telesterion of Demeter, and it is equally natural to assume that Iktinos exercised all his ingenuity and love of innovation in the designing of this temple. It seems that he kept the depth of the Telesterion begun by Kimon, but he almost doubled its width, extending the building to the south. Thus he reverted to the square plan of the Peisistratean architects. But he seems to have been the first to introduce the opaion or lantern over the middle of the structure. He limited the internal supports required for the roof construction to four rows of five columns in each row, thus allowing only twenty columns in the interior (Fig. 26, D). The foundations of some of these columns survive in the area of the Telesterion which was artificially filled in, and they reveal the extraordinary care taken for their construction. They were built of rectangular poros blocks, well worked and carefully laid in horizontal courses. Even the rock on which the foundations stand was not only smoothed, but it was carefully cut to make even beds for the lowest course. The excellent

---

[15] K. Kourouniotes, *Eleusiniaka*, I, pp. 173ff, to be referred to hereafter as the Koroibos inscription.

work and the use of poros instead of the local limestone differenti-
ate the Iktinian from the Kimonian building.

According to the design, the Telesterion would have been composed of a square hall or naos, measuring 51.50m. in length, from
east to west, and 49.45m. in width from north to south. Its west
side was cut deeply into the rock of the hillside, while its east wall
was placed along the outer line of the Peisistratean prostoon.
Around its four walls were designed tiers of eight steps, wider
than the ones built before, and six doorways, two on each side
except the west. Noack, to whom we owe the complete plan of the
Telesterion, estimates that the diameter of the columns at the
bottom would amount to about 1.90m., but their height cannot
be determined.

Iktinos' design had to be abandoned, perhaps, as some believe,
because of the death of Perikles, but more likely because of the
difficulties presented by its structural details. The spans between
its columns are immense and they would have required a venture-
some spirit as well as special materials for the construction of the
superstructure which they would have been required to support.
Noack has calculated that the spans range from 8.41m. to 10.06m.[16]
When we recall that the span of the ceiling beams above the lateral
aisles of the Propylaia of Athens, which provoked so much admiration, is only 5.49m. we realize the problem presented by Iktinos'
requirements. Again the erection of the lantern over the central
area, must have presented difficulties. At any rate, for whatever the
reason, Iktinos' design was replaced by another, and carried to
completion by Koroibos, Metagenes, and Xenokles.

There is another problem connected with the Iktinian Telesterion. Was that building to have a prostoon, a portico on its east
side? Noack believed that the original plan envisaged not only a
front portico, but a colonnade, or *pteron*, which fronted the east
side and went around and for a considerable distance along the
north and south sides (Fig. 41a).[17] Then the colonnade was to be
continued along the rest of the length of those sides by walls to well

[16] Noack, *Eleusis*, pp. 139ff.

[17] Cf. Noack's restoration in his pl. 9 and his fig. 71. Noack's restoration found
favor with scholars until recently and even Robertson, *Greek and Roman Architecture*, pp. 171-174 and figs. 75-76 makes use of Noack's plans; but see Dinsmoor, *The Architecture of Ancient Greece*, p. 196.

beyond the hall to close the sides of the terrace which was to extend
at a higher level behind the west side (Figs. 4, No. 28 and 2). To
that terrace led stairways cut in the rock and placed at the side
of the hall at its northwest and southwest ends. Noack's reconstruction of the Iktinian plan is very ingenious and interesting (Fig.
41a), but it does not seem to fit the evidence. His impressive
arrangement is based on two general conceptions: 1) on the stairways cut in the rock at the northwest and southwest end of the
Telesterion, and 2) on the foundations of the hall (Figs. 4 and 6,
K16 and K17). Both these assumptions were proved wrong by
Kourouniotes and Travlos. In two masterful studies[18] they showed
that the stairways are much later than the Iktinian Telesterion and
had nothing to do with the buildings of the Periklean age, and
that the foundations projecting like arrow heads from the corners
of the hall were built with blocks taken from the south section of
the Periklean peribolos wall when that was demolished in the first
half of the fourth century; that consequently the foundations were
constructed long after the Periklean Telesterion was built. Thus
both assumptions on which Noack's ingenious design was based
were proved wrong and what remains from his reconstruction is
the general plan of the almost square naos and the position of the
widely spaced columns within it. Even that hall was not completely
finished, as we have seen, and it was replaced by a different structure.

It is perhaps admissible to think that when the new architects,
whose names are preserved by Plutarch, were called upon to make a
new design for the Telesterion, they tried to utilize the work already done simply by doubling the Kimonian plan. They designed
an almost square hall the roof of which was supported by seven rows
of columns with six columns in each row. In trying to establish the
contribution of Koroibos, Dinsmoor suggested that about the middle
of the fifth century it was he who attempted to double the Kimonian
temple and laid out the great square hall which has survived,
augmenting the three rows of seven columns into seven rows of
seven columns, thus producing a large square room the roof of
which was supported by forty-nine columns. This scheme was again
abandoned, according to Dinsmoor, because of the lighting prob-

[18] Kourouniotes-Travlos, *Telesterion*, and *History of the Eleusinian Telesterion*.

lem.[19] In view of Plutarch's definite statement, however, this suggestion seems doubtful.[20] It is possible, indeed, to assume that the modification of the Iktinian design was made by Koroibos, who, as we learn from the building inscription of 446-440 B.C., was the architect of the Eleusinian Sanctuary, and who, according to Plutarch, began the construction; but it seems that the building which was actually completed and not the one postulated by Dinsmoor was his work.

The Telesterion of Koroibos. The Telesterion which Koroibos, Metagenes, and Xenokles constructed is a vast square hall some 51.20m. in length from north to south and 51.55m. in width from east to west, inner dimensions. A good part of its west section was cut out of the living rock and that side is very clearly seen in all the photographs of the Sanctuary (Fig. 44). In Roman times, when the building was restored, its length was increased by some 2.15m. so that the hall as we see it today has a total length from east to west of 53.70m., inner dimensions. The roof of this immense hall was supported by forty-two columns arranged in six rows of seven columns in each row;[21] thus the span was reduced considerably from that envisaged by the Iktinian plan and the number of columns made possible the oblong central lantern which Xenokles placed on the top of the building. The floor columns supported a second tier of lighter columns by means of which the height needed for the roof was attained.

Plutarch has preserved the information that Koroibos began the construction and "placed on the floor the columns and connected them with architraves." Death overtook him at that point and Metagenes built the "diazoma" and the upper row of columns. We can understand the latter part of Metagenes' contribution, the erection of the upper row of columns. This was the usual procedure in the construction of a Greek temple and we can see its application both in the temple of Poseidon at Paestum and in that of Athena

[19] W. B. Dinsmoor, *op.cit.*, pp. 195-196 n. 1, attributes to Koroibos "the abortive cuttings in the rock floor at the back of the left hand half showing that it was once intended that there should be forty-nine columns." However, we do not know when these cuttings were made; they may be due to a later attempt to alter the plan, perhaps during the Roman reconstruction.

[20] Plutarch, *Perikles*, 13, 5, quoted above p. 113.

[21] Usually the rows are numbered with Latin numerals from south to north and with Arabic from west to east (cf. Fig. 27).

Aphaia on Aigina where some of the columns of the upper tier have been preserved in their original position or have been restored with accuracy.[22] But what was the "diazoma" that he constructed? Philios' belief that the "diazoma" was a second story is unsubstantiated. Noack and Kourouniotes suggest that it refers to a balcony built over the steps and around the central part of the naos at the level of the architraves of the floor columns.[23] One may question, however, the use of such a balcony in the Telesterion and wonder what need it might have served. As far as we know, the ritual does not seem to have required a balcony going around the sides and the space offered by the floor level of the naos is adequate for the accommodation of a large crowd gathered in the Telesterion to watch the Mysteries enacted there in the middle of the hall. People on a balcony could have seen the spectacle only if they had stood about its parapet or railing at its outer edge; as a result only a comparatively small number of people would have been in a position to follow the telete from a balcony. Foucart's supposition that the initiates had to wander through staged narrow passages, simulating conditions in Hades,[24] that they had to go up to and descend from a second story, as he believed, or a balcony as might be suggested now, is too fantastic and is based on the statement of a late writer who confused Christian and Orphic beliefs and practices. On the other hand we should remember that when Pausanias described such a balcony in the temple of Zeus at Olympia, he did not call it a "diazoma": "Within the temple also are pillars, and there are galleries up above (στοαί . . . ὑπερῷοι), through which there is an approach to the image." The term diazoma as applied to the broad corridor separating the seats of a Greek theater is foreign to our situation. We have to seek another meaning for the term.

Athenaios, in his inimitable way of seeking the unusual and strange, has preserved the description of a river boat built by King

[22] The restoration of the upper tier of columns in the temple of Athena Aphaia in Aigina is being carried out by the Greek Service for the Preservation and Restoration of Ancient Monuments under the direction of Professor A. K. Orlandos (until recently) and Dr. E. Stikas (at present).

[23] Kourouniotes, *Guide*, p. 40. Noack, *Eleusis*, fig. 112. Philios' belief was vehemently denied by Svoronos, *JIAN*, 8 (1905), pp. 131ff.

[24] Foucart, *Les Mystères*, pp. 414, 417.

Ptolemy Philopator as recorded by Kallixeinos in the first book of his work *On Alexandria*.[25] The larger cabin of that boat had columns with architraves in gold, over which was affixed a "diazosma" "with striking figures in ivory . . . remarkable in their lavish display." There can be little doubt that the word diazosma there meant a frieze. Perhaps the slight variation in the word diazosma for diazoma may have caused Noack not to accept its evidence. However, we find that Theophrastos uses the exact term diazoma to indicate the frieze of a structure.[26] Perhaps we should understand the diazoma built by Metagenes as a frieze placed over the architraves previously built by Koroibos, and this is indicated by the verb ἐπέστησε (stood on top of). It is true that neither the temple of Aigina nor of Paestum has a frieze. In both temples, the upper tier of columns is placed directly on the architraves of the columns below them. However, that does not prove that it could not have been done elsewhere or that architects were forbidden to do so in their arrangements of the interior of their temples. We may suppose that by adding a frieze, made up of triglyphs and metopes brightly painted in contrasting colors, on top of the Doric architrave, Metagenes relieved the austerity of the interior structural assemblage, used columns reduced in bulk both on the floor level and on the second tier and still attained the necessary height. We would like, therefore, to suggest that Metagenes built a frieze over the architrave, and not a balcony around the walls and over the steps.

According to Plutarch, over the Anaktoron, Xenokles built the opaion, or lantern, that important section of the roof structure, through which air and light were introduced to the hall. All scholars agree that the lantern was over the central part of the building. They disagree, however, as to its exact form, and their opinions are based on purely hypothetical grounds since no evidence whatever has survived. According to Noack, the roof was pyramidal with pierced tiles normally covered but opened and

---

[25] Athenaios, V, 205 C.

[26] Theophrastos, Περὶ λίθων, 7. Foucart, *op.cit.*, p. 352, accepts the *diazoma* as a frieze. Also Busolt, *Gr.Gesch.*², III, 473 and Fabricius, in *RE*, IX, 996, 15. Noack enumerates these references but still maintains that the *diazoma* must have been a balcony.

temporarily curtained before the celebration of the Mysteries.[27] For the final act of the celebration the curtains would suddenly be drawn and the strong daylight would pour through. Dinsmoor, with reason rejected this supposition, and suggested that the lantern "probably consisted of a series of piers forming a clerestory above the main roof . . . which formed a ridge with pediment in front and rear, like that of a later date at Delos."[28] Kourouniotes too, seems to be in favor of a clerestory arrangement over the central portion of the roof. We believe that such an arrangement would fit the situation best.

The Telesterion contained the Anaktoron, centered in the naos under the lantern. Noack pictured it in the form of a raised rectangular platform separated from the rest of the hall by curtains hanging from ceiling to floor.[29] When the Hiera were to be shown by the Hierophant, the curtains were drawn and the interior of the Anaktoron, filled with light, was revealed to the initiates. Noack's conception was proved wrong by a fragmentary inscription published by Kourouniotes and containing among others, the statement πρὸς τῷ τοίχῳ τοῦ ἀνακτόρου, by the wall of the Anaktoron.[30] Walls, therefore, and not curtains surrounded the holy of holies. We have to envisage it as a comparatively small room similar to that in the older Telesteria, now placed in the middle of the naos (Fig. 26). Remains of that room perhaps exist in the foundations to be seen between the central columns IV, 3, 4, 5 and V, 3, 4, 5.[31] They form a rectangle 14.20m. by 5.60m. (Fig. 26, E), a small enclosed area indeed, but adequate, as we have seen, for its function.[32] Outside its northeast corner are to be seen foundations on which stood a niche containing the throne of the Hierophant. One of its sides, formed of a single marble slab bearing the inscription "Hierophantes" in large capital letters, has survived and is now to

[27] Cf. Noack's figs. 72 and 112, and his discussion, pp. 156ff.

[28] W. B. Dinsmoor, *op.cit.*, p. 196. G. LeRoux, *Exploration archéologique de Délos*, II, *La Salle hypostyle*, pl. v.

[29] Cf. Noack, *Eleusis*, fig. 111. Incidentally that restoration shows how heavy the appearance of the interior would have been and how it would have been lightened by a *diazoma*-frieze.

[30] K. Kourouniotes, *Deltion*, 10 (1926), p. 146. Rubensohn has suggested that the phiale mentioned in the inscription must have belonged to a seated figure holding a phiale, *Jahrbuch*, 70 (1955), p. 39 and *AA*, 1933, pp. 324ff.

[31] *Ephem*, 1950-51, pp. 6-10. Travlos was able to prove convincingly the existence of these foundations denied or ignored by other scholars.

[32] *Supra*, pp. 83-85.

be seen in the court in front of the Museum at Eleusis.[33] Of course the inscription and the foundations of the niche are Roman in date; but below the Roman relics do exist two poros blocks proved by their clamps to belong to the Periklean Telesterion. These indicate the existence in that position of the Anaktoron, by the side of which stood the throne of the Hierophant; they will also explain why people began to grumble when in that position, which was reserved for the Hierophant, Demetrios seated his hetaira.

Along the walls of all four sides of the naos were arranged tiers of eight steps, now wide enough to be used as seats if that was desired.[34] Wherever possible, they were hewn out of the living rock, and these have survived; the majority, made of poros stone, have disappeared. Since the entire west side of the naos was cut out of the living rock, the steps on that side are well preserved and form a conspicuous element of the Telesterion as we have it today (Figs. 37, 38 and 44). Six doorways, built of Eleusinian stone, two on each side except the west, gave access to the naos (Figs. 45, e and 47, e). They average 2.90m. in width and open to the hall through the wide corridor formed by the interruption of steps along the walls (Fig. 37, e).[35] The sides of the corridors were lined with marble blocks. The same gray-blue stone of Eleusis was employed in the construction of the walls, which average 1.15m. in thickness. The lowest course is formed by orthostates, preserved here and there and ranging in height from 0.88m. to 1.15m., excellently cut, fitted, and smoothed (Figs. 45, b and 48, f). As a matter of fact, the workmanship of the entire building was exceptional. Its exterior aspect, with its solid unbroken walls of gray-blue stone unrelieved by columns, solemn and austere, must have been awe-inspiring, well suited to its mystic function.

Behind the west side of the Telesterion and some 7.35m. above its floor a wide terrace is cut in the rock some 11.45m. in width (Figs. 2 and 4, No. 28; 44, a and 38). The terrace, at least in the

[33] For a restoration of the Anaktoron see Travlos, *Ephem*, 1950-51, fig. 1.
[34] The width of the Periklean steps varies from 0.60m. (topmost eighth step) to 0.72m. (1st, 3rd, and 4th).
[35] The measurements of the openings of the preserved doorways taken for me again by Dr. J. N. Travlos and Sp. Iakovides are: northwest doorway (Fig. 45,e) 2.60m., width of corridor 3.44m.; northeast doorway (Fig. 55,c) 2.60m., corridor 3.44m.; southwest doorway (Fig. 47,e) 2.40m., corridor, 3.35m. I wish to express my indebtedness to my colleagues for the measurements.

form we have it now, must be considered later than the Periklean Telesterion for a most obvious reason. There can be little doubt that beyond the west side of that temple must have existed a cross-wall, a diateichisma, separating the Sanctuary area from the akropolis. The Mycenaean fortification wall, which apparently long served as a cross-wall, had to be removed when Kimon began to cut into the hillside to increase the length of his Telesterion. And the removal of the Mycenaean wall imposed the construction of a new diateichisma. If the terrace was part of the Periklean Telesterion, then that diateichisma should be found beyond the terrace to the west or on its edge; such a Periklean cross-wall does not exist. Instead we have a fourth century wall at the edge of the terrace. We have, therefore, to conclude that the Periklean diateichisma stood where the terrace is now and that it was removed when the fourth century wall was constructed. This naturally proves that the terrace is later than the Periklean Telesterion and it could not have formed part of its design.

The Periklean diateichisma was replaced by a fourth century wall usually called Lykourgian diateichisma. The wall, like the Telesterion itself, remained in use as long as the Sanctuary. We may therefore suppose 1) that either the terrace was cut in the fourth century, when at its west edge the so-called "Lykourgian wall" was built, or 2) that the terrace was cut in Roman times when the length of the Telesterion was increased by projecting the hall to the west by some 2.15m. and was brought to the point where the diateichisma stood. I am inclined to believe that the rocky terrace was cut in Roman times. It is reasonable to assume that the diateichisma would have been constructed at some distance from the rear wall of the Telesterion and its terrace if the terrace was either contemporary with, or preceded the building of the diateichisma. However, if the terrace was made after the construction of the diateichisma, and that terrace had no relation to the Telesterion, it was natural for its builders to have used all the space available and to bring its western edge immediately under that cross-wall. This would have been the case especially if the terrace was cut as part of the design of the Roman temple L10.

The function of the terrace also inclines us to prefer a Roman date. It has been assumed that the terrace was cut to be used by the initiates to get into an upper story of the Telesterion. Before we accept such an assumption, we have first to prove that the Telesterion had a second story. But, as we have seen, the existence of a second story has been rejected by the majority of scholars interested in the site. We have already emphasized the fact that even if we admit a balcony, as Noack and Kourouniotes suggested (see above p. 118), we have to explain why instead of using a simple and comparatively inexpensive wooden stairway in the interior of the naos, the builders undertook the cutting away of the hillside and the creation of a rock-cut terrace requiring immeasurably greater labor and expense. Furthermore, to get to that terrace they had to construct exterior stairways again cut in the rock. Interior wooden stairways were provided for the temple of Zeus at Olympia to enable people to go from the ground floor to the balcony and the same would have been provided at Eleusis, if they had been required. It seems evident to us that the rock-cut terrace had no relation to the Periklean Telesterion. That temple remained in use and served the same unchanged function until its partial destruction by the Kostovoks in the summer of A.D. 170. Neither in the fourth century nor at a later time did its function require the construction of the terrace. The rock-cut terrace must be related to another structure on the hill; namely, the Roman temple (Fig. 4, L10). Thus all possible indications point to a Roman date for the terrace. We may wonder perhaps why the Periklean diateichisma was removed and another built in the fourth century B.C. when the west side of the Telesterion remained unchanged. We must recall that the south section of the Periklean peribolos wall was demolished in the same century and a new wall was built to replace it. The new wall was constructed farther to the south to provide more space around the Telesterion. For a similar reason a new diateichisma was built farther west to provide more room behind the Telesterion.

The Periklean Telesterion had no prostoon before it. That a prostoon across its east side was contemplated in the design that Koroibos began to execute may be indicated by the fact that the foundations of the naos project a little to the east. It is interesting to note that in the *Suppliants* of Euripides Adrastos is pictured as sitting in front of the doors of the Telesterion, not of a prostoon.[36] Such a prostoon was added in the fourth century, as we shall see later. In front of the east façade of the Periklean Telesterion extended the east or main court of the temple and on it were to be found the two altars of the Goddesses near each other as is indicated by the Koroibos inscription.[37]

Fortification walls. The court of the Telesterion in Periklean times was extended both to the east and to the south, and this required the construction of new walls beyond the line of the Peisistratean. The identification of the Periklean fortification-retaining walls is easy because of the individual way in which they are constructed. They have a lower section or base built of rectangular blocks of Eleusinian stone placed in isodomic courses (Fig. 39). The face of the blocks is roughly worked, often bulging with the edges better cut, but they have excellent anathyrosis for the joints with blocks at each side. On this lower section stands a superstructure of poros stone excellently worked and exhibiting a characteristic beveling along the edge (Fig. 39, a). These blocks too are laid in isodomic courses excellently fitted. The whole work gives the impression of consummate workmanship and solidity; a certain amount of the picturesque is also added by the contrast between the rough aspect of the base and the smooth superstructure with the beveled, softer poros stone.

The southeast section of the Periklean wall survives in its entire length between Tower I12, marking its south end and Tower I14, marking its east end (Fig. 4). This wall also acted as a retaining wall for the enlarged east court of the Telesterion, which has now attained a length of almost 40 meters. Because of that additional function, the solid stone wall has a width of some 4m., while the diameter of its terminal towers is between 9 and 10m. From Tower I14 a narrow segment was built to the Peisistratean Tower H21, closing the Sanctuary area to the southeast and leaving beyond it the Kimonian extension. On the south side of the Sanctuary area and from Tower I12 the Periklean wall followed a westerly direction and some 45m. beyond formed Gate I10, some 3m. in width (Fig. 4). That gate, the Periklean South Pylon, was guarded

[36] Euripides, *Suppliants*, v. 104.
[37] K. Kourouniotes, *Eleusiniaka*, I, pp. 176 and 179, ll. 16-17.

by a square tower, I11. The whole southwestern section of the Periklean wall, however, beyond I12 was demolished in the fourth century B.C., but its course can clearly be made out from the bed of its lowest course, which was cut in the rock. Within the gate and to the left of the square tower we have two poros blocks still *in situ*, which indicate that the level of the south court was reached from the opening either by a ramp or by a stairway. An inner propylon with two columns stood immediately behind the gate, following the example set in Kimonian times. The foundations of both columns are preserved to a height of 0.90m. and apparently the Peisistratean wall was partly used as a foundation for the west column.[38] This southwest section of the wall was also used as a retaining wall for the south court, which had to be extended to the south and west because of the construction of the south corner of the Telesterion beyond the terrace supported by the Peisistratean wall (Fig. 4).

Storehouses, or Siroi. On the east side, since the terracing completed by Kimon and his east peribolos wall were considered adequate, very little new work was done. However, some changes were made. First of all the Kimonian Gate F5 was blocked by the east end of the southeast section of the Periklean peribolos. Even the opening of the gate was filled up by a brick wall (Fig. 35, c). The comparatively narrow east wall, built diagonally from the round tower I14 towards the Peisistratean square tower H21, cut off part of the Kimonian extension and the separated triangular space immediately below the east side of the main court of the temple and at a much lower level from it was apparently used for the construction of a building with a very special purpose (Figs. 4, No. S, and 36). Of that building we find a number of square pillars arranged in three rows (Figs. 35, s, and 36). All five pillars of the north row survive to a height of 6.50m. above their stylobate; the pillars of the middle row, four in number, are not preserved but their foundations can still be seen, while the three pillars of the south row survive to a height of three courses.[39] The founda-

[38] The two small squares beyond Gate I10 in the plan of Fig. 4 are the foundations of these columns.

[39] In Fig. 35S, we can see the three pillars of the south row, the foundations of at least three pillars of the middle row (the view of the fourth is blocked by the pilaster of the Gate F5, but one of its corners can be seen by the side of the inner top corner of the pilaster), and four of the five pillars of the north row. All pillars in the figure are marked with the letter *s*.

tions of these pillars are built of rectangular poros blocks. Some 2.80m. above the stylobate the pillars of the north row exhibit three rectangular cuttings apparently for the insertion of wooden beams. Perhaps at a height of 5.55m. from the stylobate another series of wooden beams may have supported the roof, which seems to have been level with the main court of the Telesterion. The maximum length of this triangular area by the Peisistratean wall measures about 33m., while its maximum width at the south end amounts to some 13.50m.

Noack happily recognized the triangular area and its structure as the storehouse, the σιροί of the inscriptions, where the first-fruit offerings were stored.[40] He further suggested that the roof of this structure formed an extension of the court of the temple and that therefore the storehouse could be considered as underground. Entrance to it was obtained, according to Noack, through a trap-door on the roof and a ladder. These conclusions of Noack have been accepted widely. However, one correction has to be made. Travlos was able to prove that an entrance to this underground building existed on the ground level at the west end of the Periklean diagonal wall (Figs. 4 and 36, S1).[41] He not only revealed the opening of this door, but he even found its threshold *in situ*. At this door ended the road from the north pylon made in the days of Kimon to connect that pylon with Gate F5.

The approach to the Sanctuary from the north remained the same through the outer Kimonian and the inner Peisistratean pylon. The Kimonian extension was of course preserved, and, perhaps, to that auxiliary area were now transferred the buildings which had stood in the section taken over by the σιροί. In Periklean times, therefore, the area of the courts to the east and south of the Telesterion was increased, a new storehouse for the tithes was erected, and on the east and south sides of the Sanctuary a new peribolos wall was erected that acted as a retaining wall for the courts of the Telesterion. The construction of a new and very large Temple of Demeter, the great Telesterion, was also completed to

---

[40] Noack, *Eleusis*, pp. 189ff and fig. 76 on which is based our Fig. 36. For the inscription see pp. 193ff. Prott-Ziehen, *Leges sacrae*, II, 1 19. *Sylloge*⁴, vol. I, No. 83. *IG*, I², 76, l. 10.

[41] K. Kourouniotes, *Deltion*, 14 (1931-32), pp. 28-29.

take the place at last of the Peisistratean. Also a diateichisma was built beyond the west side of the Telesterion which, however, does not survive.

Date of Periklean Construction. Exactly when in the Periklean age this building activity took place is debatable. Some scholars believe that work at Eleusis must have begun after the completion of the great building activity on the Akropolis of Athens, that it could not have been carried out concurrently. To strengthen their view they use the inscription of the σιροί, which Körte dated about 418 B.C. This inscription refers to the building of the σιροί; to an activity intimately connected with the Periklean rearrangement and design of the Sanctuary. Of course one could counter that the construction of the σιροί might have been the last in a series of undertakings that lasted for a number of years. Körte's conclusions, however, are not universally accepted and it has been pointed out recently that the inscription could be and has been placed chronologically anywhere between 435 and 421 B.C.[42] It is maintained that Perikles and his Athenians had to wait until the works in the city of Pallas were completed before undertaking construction in the shrine of Demeter. But who can tell what the great statesman of Athens aspired to do? Why could he not undertake the rebuilding of the Sanctuary at Eleusis along with the reconstruction and beautification of the Akropolis? The center of the cult of Demeter had especial attraction for all the Greeks and was the means of proclaiming to the rest of the Hellenic world the excellence of the Athenian State and its citizens who were the first to receive the gifts of the Goddess and who unselfishly passed them on to the rest of mankind. If one of the purposes of Perikles was to glorify Athens, at Eleusis he had a great chance. The cult of Demeter could become the instrument for the unification of the Greeks under the hegemony of Athens, whose prominence in activities of lasting value and of cultural renown would be enhanced by the undertakings at Eleusis. Plutarch pointed out the enthusiasm, the pride, the divine zeal with which the people of Athens carried out the Periklean projects and went beyond the limits possible to the uninspired.[43]

[42] A. Körte in Noack's *Eleusis*, pp. 313ff, and Kourouniotes-Travlos, *op.cit.*, pp. 88-89.
[43] Plutarch, *Perikles*, 13, 1-4.

It is not unreasonable, therefore, to conclude that in those days of inspiration as well as creation the works at Eleusis were carried out, that the third quarter of the fifth century witnessed the beginning, at least, if not the completion, of the Periklean projects in our site.

Burials. The west cemetery of Eleusis was used again for burials during the last three quarters of the fifth century B.C. Of the graves explored, a good number were those of children. For these, in addition to the practice of pot-burial already established during the fifth century, the custom developed of burial in terracotta coffins known as *larnakes* (Fig. 7, b). One of these larnax burials was removed intact and can now be seen in the Museum of Eleusis (Fig. 43).[44] On the cover of the terracotta coffin (0.95m. x 0.35m.) were found a number of knucklebones originally placed in a line along the longitudinal axis of the larnax. More knucklebones and two lekythoi were found in the coffin along with a bronze strigil. The inclusion of the latter proves that the child was a boy.[45] Outside and by the head of the larnax were found a *chous* (a small jug) and a cup, perhaps the parting gifts of a disconsolate mother to her beloved child. With the knucklebones on the cover were found eggshells, often considered as emblematic of regeneration.

The adult burials include both inhumations and cremations. In this period stone sarcophagi were used for the more important burials, but boxes made of cedar wood were equally valued. The bodies of common people were laid in trenches and under tiles so placed as to form a pyramidal cavity over the supine body. After cremation the ashes and the remnants of bones as well as the burned gifts were sometimes left in the area of the pyre and covered with earth. At other times the ashes and charred bones were collected in an urn usually made of clay and beautifully painted; the urn was then placed in a trench and covered with earth. Occasionally

---

[44] The area of the cemetery in which this larnax was found is one of its most interesting and instructive sections. The Archaeological Society of Athens generously purchased the land and is preserving the area and its many graves for the students and the scholars who may wish to study the development of Greek grave architecture from the original monuments.

[45] In the Classical era the strigil became emblematic of athletics and the emblem of the athlete. Since as a rule men only were engaged in athletics it became emblematic of the male sex.

urns were made of bronze and deposited in stone receptacles square on the outside, cylindrical on the inside. We removed to the Museum of Eleusis one of these bronze urns with its contents intact and its stone receptacle perfectly preserved. In another, we found a linen stole (ca. 2.20m. x 0.50m.), the only piece of linen cloth surviving from the Classical era; it also is now exhibited in the Museum of Eleusis.

CHAPTER VI

THE FOURTH CENTURY AND THE
HELLENISTIC ERA (K)

CA. 400-146 B.C.

THE Fourth century witnessed an expansion of the area of the
Sanctuary and considerable building activity, in spite of the fact
that the early years of the era were years of financial straits and
internal upheaval for the State of Athens. This was the period that
followed the Peloponnesian war which, after thirty years, ended
with the defeat and surrender of Athens to Lysander in the spring
of 404 B.C.; the period that followed the bitter civil war in Attika of
404-403, which ended with the recognition of Eleusis as a govern-
ment independent from Athens and under the rule of the Thirty,
who established themselves there. But when democracy was restored
in Athens and the disastrous rule of the Thirty was brought to an
end in the spring of 403, Eleusis resumed its close ties with Athens
and became again a member of the Athenian State. It was during
the civil war that one of her Kerykes made the memorable appeal
for peace preserved by Xenophon.[1] They were the years that followed the death of Sokrates, awesome proof of the depravity to
which public conscience had descended. Yet, in a short period after
the end of the fifth century the spirits of the Athenians revived
and with it their effort to make their places of worship as remarkable and as expressive as possible of their great faith in culture.

The building activity of the fourth century can be surmised from
the existing remains and from inscriptions. Both indicate that the
south court of the Telesterion was extended; that a new peribolos
wall was built around the south side of the Sanctuary, thus elimi-
nating the need for the existence of the Periklean south wall; that
a portico or stoa, known as the Philonian Stoa, was planned and
placed in front of the Periklean Telesterion. Scholars agree in
accepting these developments; they disagree, however, in the
equation of inscriptional evidence with the remains of the stoa.

[1] Xenophon, *Hellenika*, II, 4, 20-22.

We have already noted the foundations projecting like arrow heads beyond the northeast and southwest corners of the naos of the Periklean Telesterion (Fig. 4, K16, K17). These foundations are earlier than those of the Philonian Stoa because blocks of the stoa rest on them. They are, on the other hand, later than the demolition of the Periklean south wall, because in their construction were used blocks taken from the demolished wall. These are the facts established by the surviving remains. If we now turn to the inscriptions from Eleusis, we find at least two which are pertinent to our problem. The first is known as the decree of the Sacred Orgas, from the beginning of the archonship of Aristodemos, 352/1 B.C.[2] We learn from it that the God of Delphi was asked if the Sacred Orgas should be cultivated and the income from it be used for the building of the prostoon and the repair of the Hieron of the Goddess. By prostoon, of course, was meant the portico in front of the Periklean Telesterion. This inscriptional evidence indicates that by 352 B.C. the building of such a portico was contemplated.

The second and earlier building inscription, dating from 356/5 B.C., gives specifications for blocks to be used in the construction of a prostoon and the digging of its foundations.[3] Davis has shown that this inscription refers not to the Philonian Stoa, but to an earlier one of the same size and plan as the Philonian. Scranton on the other hand maintained that it refers to a stoa to which belong the foundations K16 and K17, and he has actually projected such a stoa in front of the Telesterion and along its sides. Kourouniotes and Travlos, in their study of 1936, proved that the building inscription could refer neither to the Philonian Stoa nor to the foundations K16 and K17, since the former calls for a foundation of 2.45m. wide, and the latter are 3.60m. wide, and since the foundation in the inscription was to be built only in front of the Telesterion. They argue further that the foundations K16 and K17 were actually built to support a platform in front of the east side of the Telesterion. The building of that platform had become essential by the extension of the court to the south and the raising of its level which resulted from the demolition of the Periklean south wall and the construction of the fourth century peribolos wall. As a result they postulate, and rightly I believe, a platform instead of a portico in front of the east façade of the Periklean Telesterion which extended around the corners for a short distance on either side (Fig. 41b). Because of this arrangement Vitruvius could describe that Telesterion as one without exterior columns.[4]

Whether we agree that a portico or a platform was placed in front of the Periklean Telesterion, the fact remains that the foundations K16 and K17 constitute the earliest attempt to build such an addition to the edifice of the fifth century. If we accept the view, which I share, that they antedate both the building inscription and the Sacred Orgas decree, then they should be placed before 356/5 B.C. The date of the construction of the platform in front of the Telesterion is very important for the story of the Eleusinian Sanctuary because it helps to establish the chronology of the works of the fourth century B.C. Its construction certainly took place after the demolition of the Periklean south wall. And it is self-evident that the demolition must have occurred after the so-called Lykourgian peribolos wall had been constructed; otherwise the Sanctuary would have remained open on the south side, and this is inconceivable. Thus we reach the conclusion that the so-called Lykourgian wall must be placed before the middle of the fourth century B.C., in fact sometime before 356/5; and that it is not the work of Lykourgos, whose public service reached its zenith in the year 328 B.C.[5] Is it possible to determine its date more definitely?

[4] Vitruvius, VII, praef. 16; Cf. *supra* Ch. v n. 12.

[5] Lykourgos (died 324 B.C.) to whom the wall has been attributed was elected three times administrator of the finances of Athens and Pausanias (I, 29, 16) tells us that "he brought into the public chest 6500 talents more than Perikles the son of Xanthippos had amassed; he made processional vessels for the goddess (Athena) and golden figures of Victory, and ornaments for a hundred maidens, and arms and missiles of war and four hundred ships of battle. Of buildings he completed the theater (of Dionysos) which others had begun, and during his administration he built the ship-sheds in Peiraeus, and the gymnasium near what is called the Lyceum." A decree in honor of Lykourgos proposed by Stratokles in the archonship of Anaxikrates (307/6 B.C.) set forth the many services which Lykourgos had rendered and concluded with a list of the honors to be conferred to his memory. Apparently Pausanias, and pseudo-Plutarch as well (Life of Lykourgos *Vit. X. Orat.*, pp. 844, 852) drew their information from that decree. On his motion bronze statues of Aischylos, Sophokles, and Euripides were set up in the theater of Dionysos. Because of this remarkable record of public works, it was believed that he was responsible for the construction of the fourth century wall of Eleusis.

We have already seen how the first two decades of the fourth century were the years that followed the disastrous end of the Peloponnesian war and of the civil strife brought about by the rule of the Thirty. Naturally in those decades no great project could have been undertaken. It is true that during those turbulent years the Athenians tried to rebuild the Long Walls connecting Athens with Peiraeus; but that was an urgent necessity on which the very life of the commonwealth depended. To demolish an existing wall, strong and adequate for its purpose only in order to replace it with another was certainly a piece of luxury which the Athenians could not afford. The project must be attributed to a period during which Athens had regained some of its ancient prosperity and prestige, when the dreams for greatness of the Athenians were revived. Such a period we find between the years 375 and 360 B.C. During those years able leaders and generals won for Athens victories that reestablished her in the role of one of the leading cities of Hellas. The work at Eleusis was an undertaking of great prestige; to it of course other Hellenic cities and their allies could have contributed, but the main burden had to be borne by a prosperous and once more ambitious Athens. The so-called Lykourgian wall must be placed in the decade of 370 to 360 B.C.[6] Its construction was followed by the demolition of the Periklean south wall and by the building of the platform in front and on the sides of the Telesterion.

The Stoa of Philon. The construction of the platform probably did not for long satisfy the architectural ambitions of the Athenians. They began to think of a portico of a more monumental nature, worthy of the Temple of Demeter and her Mysteries. To that portico the inscriptions refer. The Athenians may have started the construction soon after 360 B.C., but they were not able to carry through their plans until finally, in the days of Demetrios of Phaleron, a portico was built by the architect Philon, which is known after him as the Philonian Stoa. A building inscription that may be dated either 336 or 326 B.C. contains a record of payments for the transportation of column drums from the quarries on

---

[6] Scranton, *op.cit.*, p. 128, shows preference for the previously accepted date of 330 B.C. for this wall. However the facts disclosed by excavation, cited above, prove that his conclusion is untenable.

Mount Pentele.[7] This inscription most probably is connected with a motion by Lykourgos proposing the renewal of an abandoned plan of building a portico rather than the undertaking of a new plan, and the selection of the architect for that work, presumably Philon. The construction of the portico must have started sometime after that motion; but apparently the work was carried out intermittently, if the stoa was completed during the rule of Demetrios of Phaleron (317-307 B.C.) as Vitruvius states: "cum Demetrius Phalereus Athenis rerum potiretur, Philo ante templum in fronte columnis constitutis prostylon fecit."[8]

Of the stoa built by Philon, we have today the foundations, the stereobate or the floor of the portico (Figs. 44, e; 45, d), some drums, and some fragments of the superstructure.[9] The foundations were built of poros stone of different varieties and hardness and everywhere are lowered to bedrock. At places, therefore, they reach to a great depth. Philios counted 18 courses at the southeast corner of the foundations;[10] in front of the east side of the Telesterion they reach a depth of eight to nine meters (Fig. 44, f). On some of the stones of the foundations we can still see the masons' marks deeply cut (Fig. 18, c). The stereobate and the three steps of the portico were made of Eleusinian gray-blue limestone.[11] Above its floor the stoa was built of Pentelic marble. It measures at the stylobate ca. 54.50m. in length and 11.35m. in depth. It was prostyle dodecastyle in form with two intercolumniations at the flanks. The columns were of the Doric order and had a diameter at the bottom of 1.97m. Of the fourteen columns employed in the construction of the Stoa, only fragments of the lowest drums have survived. Around the base-line of these drums are visible elliptical channels or flutings cut for a short distance (Fig. 44, i). These, along with similar channels cut on the top drum were to serve as guides in the fluting of the shafts of the columns and prove that this work was contemplated. However, it was never carried

[7] *IG*, II[2], 1673. For the dating of the inscription cf. Glotz, *REG*, 31 (1918), pp. 207-220. Noack, *Eleusis*, p. 116.

[8] Vitruvius, VII, praef. 17.

[9] For a detailed study cf. Noack, *Eleusis*, pp. 112ff.

[10] Philios, *Praktika*, 1882, pp. 86ff.

[11] The steps have a width ranging from 0.33m. to 0.39m. and a height of 0.40m. for the top two and 0.32m. for the bottom.

out, since the preserved drums above the height of the channels present a round, unfluted face.

The surviving few fragments of the entablature help us to establish its height. One of its metopes was found intact by Philios, who noted that no traces of color or sculptured decoration were evident on its surface at the time of discovery; none seems to have existed. The immense pediment terminating the entablature also seems to have been left without decoration. Noack calculated that the height of the stoa's façade amounted to about 15.50m. The stoa was damaged during the devastation of the Sanctuary by the Kostovoks in the summer of A.D. 170, but it was repaired shortly after the departure of the barbarians. The Stoa of Philon, constructed in the last quarter of the fourth century, remained in use to the end of the life of the Sanctuary.

Peribolos Extended to the South. The construction of the new peribolos along the south side of the Sanctuary formed the other important undertaking of the fourth century (Fig. 40). As we have seen, it was the earliest work attempted in that century and perhaps took place in the decade 370-360 B.C. The wall is excellently preserved and its construction is interesting, although somewhat imitative of the style of the Periklean builders. The wall has a base of gray-blue Eleusinian stone with pointed outer surface, on which were set tooled blocks of yellowish poros stone in a typical isodomic style. The precision of the jointing and the care and accuracy with which the courses were laid are remarkable and make of this wall one of the best preserved samples of ancient fortification work (Fig. 42). The wall averages some 2.55m. in thickness and is furnished with two towers, a round one at its southwest corner (K7), and a square one (K6) guarding the south pylon. The round tower, some 10m. in diameter is remarkable for its workmanship (Fig. 40). Its base of four, slightly receding courses is completely preserved.[12] Above it we still have five courses of poros blocks laid in a header-and-stretcher arrangement in alternate courses. The wall between the towers, some 32m. in length, is preserved at places

[12] The aggregate height of the four courses of the base is 1.35m. The recessions range from 0.05m. to 0.06m. The aggregate height of the preserved poros courses is 2.22m. The length of the stretchers averages 1.32m. while that of the headers 0.65m. In Figure 4 the fourth century wall is indicated by crosshatching.

to a height of 7.50m. The square tower K6 (Figs. 40 and 46) is also well preserved and stands to a height of some 4m. at its southeast and 1.60m. at its southwest corner. It measures 6.48m. by 5.35m. at the top of its base wall. A narrow stairway, averaging 1.30m. in width, starts from the inner passage of the pylon and leads to a small chamber in the upper section of the interior of the tower.

The square tower K6 guarded the South Pylon, or the Gate towards the Sea, a gate that traditionally had to be placed on the south side of the hieron (Fig. 46). The width of the gate between the two ends of the peribolos amounts to almost four meters. In front of the two ends we have the door posts and at their base, the pivot stones; in one of these is still preserved the bronze sheath in which the door posts turned. This gate was used to the end of the life of the Sanctuary, but as is natural it was repaired often and its threshold level was raised. Two thresholds on top of the original one are still in position (Fig. 46).

The northeast end of this peribolos wall of the fourth century was made to terminate against the round Periklean tower I12 (Fig. 4). From there on to the east and north, the Periklean wall limited the Sanctuary. To the northwest the fourth century peribolos was made to abut against the Peisistratean (Fig. 4, K4). Beyond the Peisistratean wall, however, from point K4 to northwest, it was continued at a reduced width, of some 0.85m. only, and served as a cross-wall, separating the Sanctuary area from the city to the west of it. This cross-wall, known as the Lykourgian diateichisma, was continued to the north for some 25m. and then turned to the northeast (Fig. 4, K2) to enclose the west side of the Sanctuary and separate it from the akropolis area (Fig. 4, K1). A few courses of this wall survive above the west edge of the rock-cut terrace (Fig. 48, d). We must remember that it was not constructed by Lykourgos, but is contemporary with the rest of the south wall of the fourth century. It was constructed to replace the wall built in Periklean times and to increase the space behind the Telesterion. That space is now taken by the rock-cut terrace No. 28 of Roman times (Figs. 2 and 4).

The construction in the second quarter of the fourth century of a new south wall and of the west diateichisma made possible the enlargement of the south court of the Sanctuary and added more space behind the Telesterion. In the space thus added to the Sanctuary we find three interesting and very conspicuous and problematical elements often attributed to this period.

Stepped Platform in the South Court. The first, is the broad stepped platform (Fig. 4, No. 29; Figs. 2 and 47), hewn out of the living rock between the south wall of the Telesterion and a stoa that apparently existed along the inner side of the fourth century peribolos. It has a maximum width at its base of 26.50m., reduced at the top to 20.70m. Shallow steps are interrupted at intervals, by broad zones. In the upper half of the structure a cubic projection of rock was left, like a bema or speaker's platform, with a width of 5.20m. at its top (easily seen in the air view of Fig. 2). A single step leads from here to the rock-cut terrace above it. Steps to the south court of the Sanctuary are cut at either end of a long, elevated platform, some 5m. wide, rising vertically some 2.30m. above the rocky floor of the court before it (Fig. 47, d). Some 4.20m. from the south wall of the Telesterion the front of this platform is interrupted by a niche (Fig. 47, c) 2m. wide, with a low rock-cut shelf on its three sides. The floor of the niche is 0.73m. above that of the south court, and in Roman times it was covered with plaster. Its use is undetermined; perhaps a small statue or other sacred object was placed in it at certain times. At some distance from it but in line with it and on the floor of the court are to be seen worked blocks and rock-cuttings indicating perhaps the position of an altar. Skias attributed that altar to "good classical times."[13] Some 2.30m. to the north of the niche, we find a narrow stairway with ten steps averaging 1.90m. in width (Fig. 47, a). The lower end of the stairway could have been blocked by a wooden beam the ends of which could be placed in deep cuttings made on its rocky side walls. A similar, though wider, stairway is to be found at the south end of the platform.

Noack assumed that the broad, stepped platform, or the part of it that could be seen in his time, formed part of the Iktinian design of the Telesterion. Kourouniotes and Travlos, however, proved that this assumption is not substantiated by the facts.[14]

[13] *Praktika*, 1895, p. 164. There is no way of determining its exact date now.
[14] Noack, *Eleusis*, pl. 9 and pp. 152ff. Kourouniotes-Travlos, *Deltion*, 15 (1933-35), pp. 91ff. *Supra*, p. 116.

The platform was conceived and constructed as a unit at a time much later than the Iktinian Telesterion. It is evident that it is related to the south court of the Sanctuary; it presupposes the fourth century peribolos wall and certainly is later than that wall. As a matter of fact the stairway agrees with the later Roman re-arrangement of the area adjoining the fourth century peribolos wall. The workmanship of the rock-cuttings and of the steps can only be attributed to Roman rather than to earlier Greek times. Consequently it does not belong to our fourth century rearrangement of the south area of the Sanctuary.

Another indication of its later date is provided by a few blocks of the south wall of the Periklean Telesterion standing in their original position. On the outer face of some of the blocks turned to the stepped platform the bosses or knobs useful in handling the stones remain. As a rule these knobs were cut off and the face smoothed after the completion of a building. They would certainly have been removed from the blocks of a building of such importance and structural excellence as the Periklean Telesterion. The fact that they were left indicates that the wall could not be seen because it was laid against the slope of the hill, not as yet cut away to form the stepped platform. The knobs indicate that the platform was not cut in the fourth century, because it is inconceivable that the crafts-men who built the round tower K7 and its wall with such consum-mate skill and pride would have allowed the knobs to remain if they had cut away the hillside to form the platform. The sensitivity towards perfection characterizing the work of the masons of the fourth century had declined, if it had not disappeared altogether, in Roman times and to such a decline we can attribute the survival of the knobs left in spite of the fact that they had become visible. All indications therefore point to a Roman date for the stepped platform.

It has been assumed that the platform was to be used as an ascent to the rock-cut terrace and through it to an assumed second story in the Telesterion. But of the entire broad structure only a small part could have served such a purpose; the stairs at the northeastern end of the platform, stairs only 1.90m. wide. This narrow stairway would scarcely have been adequate for the crowd of the initiates presumed to be desirous of reaching the hypothetical and non-existent second story of the Telesterion (*supra*, p. 118). The narrowness of the stairway proves that it was never intended for such a purpose. Those of us who have time and again seen large crowds of students or tourists struggling to come up to the Museum through that stairway have realized how impossible this narrow stairway is for the purpose. The people who undertook the construction of such a monumental project were certainly capable of making broad steps for a crowd; nor would such an enterprise be prohibitive in cost. Besides, what would have been the purpose of the rest of the broad platform if the narrow stairway was considered adequate for the ascent? What purpose would have been served by the bema? Certainly this broad platform's primary function was not that of serving as a means of reaching to a presumed upper story or balcony in the Telesterion. What then was its purpose?

In our effort to determine the function of this structure we must first note two facts: 1) the long elevated platform rises vertically some 2.30m. from the court level. 2) The stairway commands a complete view of the large south court. The steps, the broad zones, and the bema in its upper section, all seem to point out that the platform served as a θέατρον, in its original meaning of the word; as a place from which a large crowd could follow a performance or a spectacle in the court that spreads before it. The narrow stairway at its east corner would have been adequate as access to such a θέατρον, the way the narrow stairways of theaters were adequate. The broader stairway at the southeast end could serve as auxiliary. What then could have been that performance? Did it have any relation to the dromena, that part of the celebration in which the abduction of Persephone and the wanderings of Demeter were enacted? We doubt that any relation existed between the dromena and the spectacle of the south court. If the dromena were partially held outside the Telesterion, as we maintain, the part presented in the open air would have certainly been enacted in the north section of the Sanctuary where all the sacred landmarks pertinent to the story were to be seen. At a short distance beyond the North Pylon is the Kallichoron, and inside the Sanctuary is the "Mirthless Stone" not far from the well, and the Cave of Plouton, the very "Gates of Hades." There was no need whatever to bring the pageant across the Telesterion to the south court. We may assume therefore that some other performance was held in front of our stepped platform.

We hear of a strange festival held at Eleusis known as the βαλλητύς, "pelting with stones." Athenaios again makes Ulpian, one of his characters, state: "I know, indeed, of a festival held in my own Eleusis which is called βαλλητύς (Pelting). But I will not say a word about it unless I get a reward from every one of you."[15] That this "pelting" meant pelting with stones is evident from what led up to the statement. In spite of the fact that Ulpian was given all the information he had asked about the story of Hegemon's inviting the spectators to pelt him with stones in the theater, he does not in the end explain the Eleusinian festival. Why? Is it because it could not have been divulged as part of the acts held within the Sanctuary of Eleusis? It seems unlikely that we shall ever know.

Hesychios explains the term βαλλητύς as: "a festival in Athens, held in honor of Demophon the son of Keleos."[16] The name of Demophon connects the festival with Eleusis, and perhaps to a festival of this kind refer the rather enigmatical words of Demeter: "On Demophon unfailing honor shall always rest, because he lay upon my knees and slept in my arms"; but then the Goddess added, "as the years move round and when he is in his prime, the sons of the Eleusinians shall ever wage war and dread strife with one another continually."[17]

It seems to be a well-attested practice among primitive agricultural communities to throw stones or even to kill by stoning in order to moisten the earth with blood and induce a more plentiful harvest.[18] This could have been the case at Eleusis, and this the

[15] Athenaios, IX, 406d.
[16] Hesychios, s.v. βαλλητύς. His "in Athens" would certainly mean in the territory of the Athenians.
[17] Hymn, vv. 263-267.
[18] L. R. Farnell, *The Cults of the Greek States*, III, pp. 93-94 where bibliography. Cf. the festival of "throwing of stones" held at Troizen in honor of Damia and Auxesia, divinities akin to Demeter, mentioned by Pausanias II, 32, 2. Cf. Herodotos, V, 82ff. According to J. G. Frazer, III, p. 267, on Pausanias II, 30, 4, stone throwing is a special feature of spring and midsummer customs of European peasants (see his bibliography). Hesychios, s.v. Μόροττον: ἐκ φλοιοῦ πλέγμα τι, ᾧ ἔτυπτον ἀλλήλους τοῖς Δημητρίοις, has preserved the tradition of people beating each other in connection with agricultural festivals.

meaning of the *Balletis*. In this connection we may recall that a priest of Eleusis was called Λιθοφόρος, the stone-bearer. We may picture a crowd of people standing on the stepped platform to witness the casting of stones. Perhaps because of the danger involved the platform was left as a way of protecting the front rows of spectators from an accidental stone pelting. For the same reason, in the Roman amphitheaters, the front row of the seats was raised considerably above the floor level of the arena. This detail may again suggest a Roman date for the construction of the platform. Perhaps the need for a more substantial structure from which people could follow this Balletis arose in Roman times when spectacles of a violent nature became very popular.

Was this ceremony held at the same time as the Mysteries? We do not know. I am inclined to believe that it was held whenever needed. But could the Sanctuary area be entered by a crowd at a time other than that of the Mysteries? In Euripides' *Suppliants* Theseus' mother sacrifices to the Goddesses not in the course of the celebration of the Mysteries, but at another time.[19] We may with reason assume that the people who participated in the casting of stones as well as the spectators, had been initiated into the Mysteries before the occasion and had the right to go into the Sanctuary area. Further, they would use the south gate and would not go beyond the south court where no sacred landmarks related to the Mysteries were to be seen. The staging of the event within the precinct could be justified by the belief that Demeter, the Goddess of the precinct, was the giver of plentiful harvests. Whether or not the *Balletis* was held in front of our stepped platform, the fact, I think, remains that some kind of a spectacle was held there witnessed by the crowd of Eleusinians and Athenians standing on the broad steps above the level of the court. The high bema could have been reserved for the officials of the Sanctuary.

Stairway to Terrace. The second element of interest is the broad, rock-cut terrace behind the Telesterion (Fig. 4, No. 28), which, however, seems to belong to Roman times, as we have seen (p. 122). The third element is the narrow stairway (Fig. 4, No. 26), cut in the hillside along the northwest corner of the Teles-

---

[19] We may note in this connection the presence in the Sanctuary of the Argive women and even Adrastos before the gates of the Telesterion itself: *Suppliants*, vv. 92-94; 33ff; 104.

terion[20] (Figs. 2 and 48). Its 30 steps of uneven depth cut in the rock vary in width, from 2.90m. to 3.30m. At its summit, it circumvents the grand stairway of the Roman temple L10 (Figs. 4 and 48, c) in a narrow and difficult side-passage, some 1.30m. in width, that led between the rear wall of the Telesterion and the Roman temple to the rock-cut terrace. Through the middle of the top steps passed an open drain serving the rocky terrace. The bottom of the stairway could be blocked by a wooden beam placed across it at a height of 1.45m. above the level of the court, in a manner similar to that used for the narrow stairway of the stepped platform No. 29. At that height and on the rocky right-hand side of the wall we can find a square cutting in which the end of such a beam would rest (Fig. 48, h). The dimensions of the steps are not uniform. After the 24th step there is a broad platform 2.20m. wide at its right or north end and 1.70m. wide at its left or south end. Furthermore, the steps are not cut sharply and vertically from the living rock, but left slanting at the corners. In these and in other details of workmanship they contrast sharply with the rock-cut steps of the Telesterion. Their surface does not present appreciable wear indicating their use by a big crowd over a long period of time. These considerations seem to suggest a Roman date for the stairway.

Now let us observe once more the termination of stairway No. 26 at the top and its connection with the rock-cut terrace No. 28 (Fig. 2). If we assume that people used the stairway to reach the rock-cut terrace as access to a second story or a balcony in the Telesterion, we shall have to explain why it terminated in a narrow passage, reduced further by an open drain, that must have proved very uncomfortable for its users, who would have been numerous; it certainly proves difficult and uncomfortable today. It could of course be suggested that the original arrangement was blocked and its course changed when the Roman temple L10 was constructed; but this suggestion is untenable. A passage of such importance would not be blocked or infringed upon by a later building, especially in a period when the number of pilgrims had increased considerably. All indications point to the conclusion that the rock-cut stairway No. 26 was not related to the Telesterion; that it did not serve great crowds; that it was cut to connect the Roman

[20] This is fully described in *Deltion*, 15 (1933-35), pp. 97-98.

temple L10 and its terrace with the Sacred Way; that it was to serve the few who went to that temple, the few who actually used it; that its summit was determined by the grand stairway of L10; that therefore it was cut in Roman times and most probably in the second half of the second century of our era.

Rock-cut Platform by the Sacred Way. To the fourth century seems to belong another stepped platform or exedra cut in the hillside. It is to be seen in the north section of the enceinte, by the side of the Sacred Way and immediately to the south of the Cave of Plouton (Figs. 2, 49, and 4, No. 21). From the latter it is separated by a ledge of the rock of the hillside left as a natural boundary (Fig. 2). The stepped platform is roughly rectangular in shape and measures approximately 10.50m. in maximum length from north to south and 6.25m. in depth from east to west. Two of its sides, the west and south, are stepped. Two steps cut along the front of its east side separate it from the Sacred Way (Fig. 49, SW) and lead to a broad landing 1.45m. wide at the south end and only 0.65m. at the north end. Over the landing rise eight steps on the west side and six on the south. These steps, with the exception of the second, range from 0.30 to 0.40m. in width and have an average rise of 0.32m.; the second step is 0.98m. in width. All the steps of the west side are cut in the rock and they lead to a terrace averaging 3.15m. in width and about 9.50m. in length (Fig. 49, b). Behind the terrace the hillside was cut in a stepped pattern (Fig. 49, c); the projecting cubes of rock could serve either as bases for statues or as beds to support a wall; no traces of such walls, however, remain. They could be used as stands from the top of which people could watch any procession or spectacle held on the Sacred Way. The floor of the terrace towards its south end is cut to form a circular shallow pit 0.92m. in diameter and about 0.35m. in depth. To it leads a channel, 0.35m. in length and only 0.07m. wide, from an irregularly oval depression 0.30m. in greatest diameter. At the time of its excavation a large cottage stood on the terrace; because of this Philios suggested that the circular pit was not an ancient bothros but a mediaeval or modern wine press. Svoronos explained the pit and other cuttings on the terrace as an altar, but his identification as the altar of the Goddesses was proved wrong by later finds. No one today follows Svoronos' interpretation and I agree with Philios that the pit is of modern date.

The south side of the platform is reached by six steps partially hewn out of the living rock and partially built of poros stone. At the end towards the Sacred Way, the steps are faced by poros blocks well-cut and fitted, and that facing forms a vertical wall rising above the level of the Sacred Way (Fig. 49, e). The steps of the south side lead, through an opening measuring 1.40m. in width, to a terrace or court, rising some 2m. above the level of the Sacred Way, the west side of which is cut in the rock. On this terrace we find the scanty foundations of a small rectangular building constructed of poros stone (Fig. 4, No. 22). It measures 2.90m. in width, and we may assume, since its walls are not preserved to their entire length, that its length amounted to some 6m. It may have had a portico in front of its small chamber. It has been suggested that this is one of the two treasuries of the Goddesses known to have existed within the Sanctuary.[21] Its entrance remains uncertain, although one could assume that its access was obtained by means of the rock-cut platform. Beyond its northwest corner still stands a large boulder on the upper side of which we find an artificially produced circular cavity some 0.53m. in diameter (Fig. 49, t and 45, t). Perhaps, as was suggested by Tsountas, this is a *Thesauros*, a donation box for small money gifts to be left by the pilgrims. Its opening was closed by a large stone that left a fissure at the side big enough for the coins to find their way into the cavity, but too small for pilfering fingers.

The date of the stepped platform No. 21 cannot be determined with absolute certainty. Noack suggested that it does not belong to the Greek period.[22] The workmanship of the rock-cut steps, however, is much superior to that of the stairways attributable to Roman times and approaches that of the steps of the Periklean Telesterion. Furthermore, the poros stone construction of the south steps and their facing find a parallel in the retaining wall of the Ploutonion with which they seem to be contemporary. The stepped platform apparently is related to the small treasury No. 22 built of poros stone. That treasury in turn compares with the later temple in the

[21] *IG*, II², No. 1672, ll. 300 and 302.
[22] Noack, *Eleusis*, p. 85.

Ploutonion built of the same material. The treasury and the stepped platform apparently belong to the same project which resulted in giving the Ploutonion the aspect of a triangular inner sanctum. To that project belongs the retaining wall of poros that supports the court of the Ploutonion and separates it from the Sacred Way. These structures of the Ploutonion are generally placed in the fourth century B.C. Their contemporary structures, i.e. the small treasury No. 22 and the stepped platform No. 21, therefore must be placed in the same century. That they cannot be placed in Roman times is proved by the fact that no lime or "Roman concrete" was used in the construction of the east end of the south steps nor in its facing, as was employed in other Roman buildings in the Sanctuary, for example, in the steps of temple L10, of the temple of Artemis and Poseidon, of the Greater and of the Lesser Propylaea.

The purpose served by the platform also would indicate a fourth century date. What was that purpose? Noack suggested that it formed the last station of the pompe, the procession of the pilgrims from Athens to the Sanctuary of Eleusis. Here the train of initiates was stopped for the last time before they entered the sacred area of the inner court of the Sanctuary. However, when the initiates reached the stepped platform they already were on sacred ground; they had already seen some of its sacred landmarks—the Ploutonion, the "Mirthless Stone." The last station of the pompe must have been in front of the Kallichoron well in the outer court of the Sanctuary, before the outer north pylon and not within the sacred enceinte. Some years ago I suggested that "the stepped cuttings served the same purpose as the similar stepped cuttings in the Telesterion, i.e. as a stand from which people could follow some action performed in the area which they overlooked";[23] and this action I assumed to be part of the sacred pageant enacted in the course of the celebration of the Mysteries. I further assumed that the initiates standing on the steps would be able to see the Goddess of the pageant arriving at Eleusis and seating herself on the "Mirthless Stone," where she was to be found by the daughters of Keleos. Certainly that part of the drama was important and formed the initial stage of the proceedings. Perhaps the sacred pageant began in front of the stepped platform, and perhaps on

[23] Mylonas, *Hymn*, p. 89.

the worked piece of rock projecting above the pavement of the Roman Sacred Way (Fig. 4, No. 25) may have been the "Mirthless Stone," where the Goddess waited to be found and welcomed. We recall that Kallimachos places the "Mirthless Stone" by the Kallichoron. Pausanias does not mention the stone although he discusses the well. Since he avoided the mention of any structure within the enceinte, although he named the temple of Artemis and Poseidon of the outer court, it is reasonable to conclude that he did not mention the stone because it was within the enceinte. But it had to be near the entrance to the enceinte, near the inner north pylon, so as to be near the Kallichoron as stated by Kallimachos. The position we suggested fills the requirement. If we recall that Kallimachos' *floruit* was in the reign of Ptolemy Philadelphos (285-247 B.C.), his statement would indicate that at least by the beginning of the third century B.C. the position of the "Mirthless Stone" was definitely established in the north section of the enceinte. And, since it is mentioned in a fourth century inscription, we could maintain that even before that beginning, in the fourth century, its position was set and around it the first part of the drama was enacted.[24] The construction of the stepped platform in that century would have filled a real need; it would have provided the stand from which at least a good many of the initiates could have followed the development of the traditional pageant.

The Ploutonion. Adjoining the stepped platform and between it and the Lesser Propylaea, of a later date, is to be seen the cave in which stood the temple of Plouton, the Ploutonion (Figs. 2, 3, and 4, No. 20). As a matter of fact the Ploutonion was the first sacred area or landmark the initiates would see to their right as they entered the enceinte by the inner north pylon. We have already seen how in Peisistratean times a temple was erected in that cave. In the fourth century B.C. the Ploutonion was rearranged and its area apparently was defined. A well-built retaining wall of poros blocks was constructed in front of the opening of the cave to support a court that now assumed a triangular shape (Figs. 3 and 4, No. 20). A narrow side entrance by the southeastern end of the terrace, projecting into the Sacred Way, gave access to the court surrounded by a peribolos standing on the top of the retaining wall.

[24] *IG*, II², No. 1672, l. 103.

From an inscription we learn that in later times even a railing was placed on the peribolos. Within the triangular area and in the cave was constructed a small temple dedicated to Plouton, to replace the smaller Peisistratean edifice which may have been destroyed by the Persians. The surviving foundations indicate that it was built of poros stone (cf. Fig. 3, No. 20). The shrine evidently was a *templum in antis*, with a front portico and a naos measuring 2.98 by 3.77m. inner dimensions. The total length of the temple amounts to 6.64m.

Some three meters diagonally across from the east end of the north wall of the temple Philios found in the rocky floor of the court a shallow round pit, one meter in diameter. This he attributed to an abandoned effort to dig a well (Fig. 3, No. 20). Svoronos believed it to be a bothros. Of course neither the date nor the purpose of this pit can be determined now. That the temple in the cave was constructed in the fourth century is proved by an inscription dating from the archonship of Kephisophon, 329/8 B.C. It refers to the purchase of boards of elm wood for the construction of the doors of the shrine, the cost of polishing the antae and of painting their capitals, etc. Foucart has ably associated the temple with the inscription and concluded that the temple had just been built and was receiving its final touches in 329/8 B.C.[25] Two votive reliefs bearing scenes related to Plouton and Persephone and found in its enclosure prove that the cave and its temple was the Ploutonion.[26]

We must now examine the cave more carefully. Plouton's temple built on the floor of the cave stands some 2m. above the level of the Sacred Way. People standing on the Way and kept at some distance from the temple by its peribolos would have been able to see only the upper part of the interior of the dark cavern and the entablature of the temple, but would have had a complete view of the entire width of its interior. The cave has in its depth two deep cavities or chambers. In front of the larger chamber, the more southerly, stood the temple of Plouton. The other cavity is shallower and extends to the west of the temple. The two chambers are separated by a rocky ledge (Fig. 50). On the north wall of the

[25] *BCH*, 7 (1883), pp. 387ff. *Sylloge*[4], vol. 3, No. 1050.
[26] The Lysimachides and Lakratides relief: *supra*, p. 99 and *infra*, p. 197.

smaller chamber we find a roughly elliptical opening, measuring approximately 1.30m. by 0.54m., visible from the level of the Sacred Way (Fig. 51). To that opening the rocky floor of the cave ascends and immediately in front of it the rock has been cut so as to accommodate an elementary stairway. If we pass through the elliptical opening, not too difficult a feat for a person of normal measurements, we find ourselves outside the cave and at the top of a stairway of six steps cut in the rock[27] (Fig. 52). The stairway leads to a small triangular area completely separated from the court of the Ploutonion by its retaining wall (Fig. 4, a). In that triangular area there is now a well-like pit, 0.78m. in diameter, almost round in shape. It seems apparent that no water was ever found in that pit. We cannot now determine the date of the pit or of the stairway, but it is reasonable to maintain that, if they were not already in existence, they were cut at the time the temple of Plouton was rebuilt and its court was defined by the poros retaining walls. We cannot know definitely whether or not the elliptical hole was a natural or an artificial opening; perhaps a smaller natural hole was widened artificially to make a passage. There can be little doubt that a specific use was made of the opening, of the stairway, and perhaps even of the pit; possibly all these elements together served a single purpose. The obvious explanation is that they served for the portrayal of the fortunes of Persephone in the sacred pageant which, we have every reason to believe, formed a part of the telete. Perhaps they were used in the staging of the passage from the lower world, in providing for Persephone's ascent to Eleusis. Certainly the setting is both impressive and suggestive and a priestess impersonating Persephone could ascend the stairway and emerge through the elliptical opening into the view of spectators on the Sacred Way, thus heightening the sense of reality and the dramatic appeal of the action.

It must be remembered, however, that this passage cannot be considered as the original gap through which Plouton carried Persephone to the lower world in spite of the Orphic pronouncement "the cave at the deme of Eleusis where are the gates of Hades."[28] The Hymn specifically places the abduction in the plain

[27] The steps average 0.27m. in width and 0.60m. to 0.70m. in length. Their rise ranges from 0.20m. to 0.24m.
[28] *Orphic Hymn*, XIX, 12ff.

of Nysa and the best the Eleusinians could do was to create the tradition that Plouton carrying Persephone descended to the lower world at Erineos, on the bank of the Eleusinian Kephisos.[29] However, Persephone was believed to return annually and to partake of the celebration of the Mysteries, and it is natural to suppose that her return formed part of the sacred drama enacted in the Sanctuary. The cave with its temple of Plouton, its elevated position above the Sacred Way, and its opening offered a magnificent setting within the precinct for the staging of the annual return of Kore; we believe that this was the purpose served by the simple but telling arrangement of steps and opening. Perhaps the composer of the Orphic verse had in mind this act of the sacred drama, when he placed the gates of Hades by the cave of Eleusis.

In the fourth century the area of the Peisistratean Kallichoron well was rearranged. That area was surrounded by a parapet made of slabs of poros set upright and its floor was paved.[30] The Kimonian peribolos wall behind its court was strengthened and tower K20 was built (Fig. 4). It is interesting to note how some of the sacred landmarks of the Eleusinian tradition in the north section of the Sanctuary received special attention in this period. The Kallichoron well, the Ploutonion, perhaps the "Mirthless Stone," were rearranged and beautified. Around these landmarks revolved a considerable part of the sacred pageant. This consideration would strengthen the attribution of the stepped platform to the fourth century; it forms part of the general pattern of the Eleusinian activity in that century.

Construction in Auxiliary Area B. Beyond the Ploutonion to the northwest in the auxiliary area B (Fig. 4), some construction work took place but only scanty remains survive. By now the storage

---

[29] Pausanias, I, 38, 5. Cf. R. Foerster, *Der Raub und die Ruckkehr der Persephone*, p. 46. Suidas, *s.v.* Σαλαμίνος, states that Theseus sat on the "Mirthless Stone" before his descent to Hades. This will also indicate the proximity of the "Mirthless Stone" to the cave that could be considered the Eleusinian passage to the lower world. Pausanias (II, 35, 4-11) mentions the temple of Demeter Chthonia at Hermione where it was believed that a chasm existed which formed a "short cut" to the lower world. So short, indeed, and private it was that the people of Hermione would not provide their dead with the customary fare for Charon (Strabo, VIII, 6, 12, or p. 373). Again Pausanias (II, 36, 7) saw at Lerna near Argos "an enclosure of stones": "they say that when Plouto, as the story goes, abducted Demeter's daughter, he descended here to his subterranean realm." Of course there are many other traditions claiming a different locality for the event.

[30] *Supra*, p. 98.

building of Peisistratean times was in ruins and its north wall was used to retain a terrace on which a building was constructed. In Roman times over that building was erected a large structure that destroyed its predecessor almost completely. In the course of the fourth century the north retaining wall was added to and extended so as to enclose the southwest half of the auxiliary area B (Fig. 4, No. 18). Again scanty remains of the structure built in that area have survived because they were destroyed in later times when other buildings were constructed. Of the fourth century remains most important is a rock-cut cistern of a type appearing now for the first time.

Structures in the South Court. We must now go back to the south section of the Sanctuary to study two structures built in our period. Along the inner face of the east section of the fourth century peribolos, from the Periklean round tower I12 to the fourth century tower K7, a long structure (40m. x 8.25m.) was revealed by Skias (Fig. 4, No. 30),[31] divided by cross-walls into six compartments. Its floor was at a much lower level than that of the court of the temple. The use of the structure is problematical. It may have been used as a dwelling by the most important members of the personnel of the Sanctuary or for the storing of the tithes. The Periklean storeroom on the east side of the Sanctuary was filled in when the Philonian Stoa was constructed and this created a pressing need for storage space. We may assume that the long building along the peribolos wall was then built to provide for that need.

Skias pointed out that along the south section of the peribolos wall a long stoa was built in the fourth century. The bases of two columns and fragments of a wall were revealed by his excavations. Unfortunately these scanty remains are not sufficient to make possible the reconstruction even of the plan of the stoa.

Cisterns. Before we close our discussion of the building activity in the fourth century we must examine briefly the water supply, a problem as acute in antiquity as in modern times. Pindar's ἄριστον μὲν ὕδωρ, water is most excellent, voices the general esteem in which water was held. At Eleusis from Prehistoric times to the fourth century B.C. water was obtained from wells. Most famous of these are the Parthenion and the Kallichoron of the Hymn. In

---

[31] A. Skias, *Praktika*, 1895, pp. 159-193, pl. 1, walls in yellow color.

addition to wells in the fourth century a number of cisterns of a particular type were built, one of which was revealed in the auxiliary area of the Sanctuary, as we have mentioned above. Another of the better known is located on the south slope of the hill of Eleusis, some 75m. to the southwest of the entrance of the Museum (Figs. 4 and 5, No. 71). It was generally accepted as a Mycenaean beehive tomb,[32] until further study and the discovery of other similar examples on the spur to the west of the akropolis enabled Kourouniotes to prove that the so-called beehive tomb of Eleusis is a cistern and belongs to the fourth century.[33]

The round chamber of the cistern, with a diameter at the base of 3.10m. and a height of 4m., opens from its south side into a passage (1.70m. in width and 3.15m. in height) roofed over by a corbel vault. The round chamber is partially hewn in the living rock to about three quarters of its height; it is completed by large stones placed in such a way that each course projects a little beyond the one below it, thus forming an elementary vault or tholos. On the top of the vault, but to the side of its apex, we find an opening 0.38m. in length and 0.28m. in width, through which the water of the cistern was drawn. The walls of the room and of the corridor are covered with watertight plaster. A rock-hewn cistern of a similar form, but with two round chambers connected by a passage, was found and cleared by Kourouniotes on the spur to the west of the akropolis of Eleusis. The diameter of the round chambers at the base amounts to 4.05m. and their height to 4.17m. In section they are conical in form and the circular opening on top measures one meter in diameter. The passage connecting the two rooms (11.50m. x 1.60m.) was entirely hewn from the living rock. There can be no doubt about the use of this double cistern. On the floor of the chambers were found fragments of broken pottery, proving its construction in the fourth century and its continued use to Roman and even Christian times. Similar cisterns with one round chamber and passage are known from Athens.[34]

[32] *Idem, Ephem*, 1912, p. 18 and pl. 3 where plan and section. Noack, *Eleusis*, p. 15. Fimmen, *Die Kretisch-mykenische Kultur*, p. 61. Against this identification, Ch. Tsountas, Μυκῆναι καὶ μυκηναῖος πολιτισμός, p. 123. P. Kavvadias, Προϊστορικὴ ἀρχαιολογία, p. 309.

[33] K. Kourouniotes, *Eleusiniaka*, I, pp. 237ff.

[34] *Ibid.*, figs. 23-26.

THE HELLENISTIC PERIOD

The death of Alexander the Great and the struggle for supremacy of his generals, the Diadochoi, mark the closing quarter of the fourth century and the beginning of what is known as the Hellenistic period. That quarter century as well as the third century were periods of debasement for the Athenian State. The gallant efforts of Demosthenes against the dictatorship of Philip had come to an end and his place was taken by politicians ready to flatter and to grovel to maintain a pitiful existence. Macedonian garrisons had to be accepted for Eleusis, Mounychia, and even Athens;[35] Demetrios Poliorketes was lodged in the Parthenon itself; the rules of the Mysteries were suspended to make possible his initiation to all the degrees the same day and without the traditional preparation. That unglorious period of the Athenian State was not conducive to great public works and little was achieved worthy of note. Early in the third century the top of the akropolis of Eleusis was surrounded by a fortification wall, a good section of which was found high along the north edge of the hill (Fig. 4, K30) starting from the northwest corner of the Roman temple L10 and proceeding westward some 48m. The socle only of that wall survives. It averages some two meters in width and it is built of Eleusinian rectangular and rather flat blocks laid in horizontal courses.

The Small Fort on the Hill by the Sanctuary. To the same years apparently belonged the fort placed on top of the west hill which dominated the sea and the western approach to the city. There until recently stood the foundations of a wall enclosing its triangular top with rectangular towers at each of the corners of the triangle. Over the foundations of this Hellenistic fort a tower was constructed in mediaeval times during the Frankish occupation of Attika. That tower until recently was a conspicuous landmark of the site of Eleusis (Fig. 53). Unfortunately this landmark as well as the small fort was removed by the quarrying activities of the

[35] In September of 322 B.C. Antipater placed a Macedonian garrison in Mounychia for the first time. Demetrios occupied Eleusis and his lieutenants held that city until 285/4 B.C. when it was retaken by the Athenians. For Demetrios' initiation cf. Plutarch, *Demetrios*, 26.

cement factory which was permitted to operate in the neighborhood of the Sanctuary. Whether or not the small fort was connected with the walls of the city of Eleusis is not known; but I believe that in some way its communication with the city was insured.

Of that city very little has been explored. Remains of houses, of a road, and of an artificially retained terrace were revealed on the plateau to the west of the akropolis (Fig. 53), but these remains are too scanty to provide a definite picture of the town of Eleusis or even of one of its Hellenistic houses.

Hellenistic Bouleuterion. The most important building within the Sanctuary area of the third century is the one discovered by Skias in 1895-1898 along the southeastern section of the fourth century peribolos wall; he identified it as the Bouleuterion of the inscriptions.[36] It occupies the area along the inner face of the fortification wall from its terminal round tower K7 to the South Pylon (Fig. 4, No. 31). It is a large rectangular structure (34m. x 14m.) divided by cross-walls into three compartments or rooms. The central room, which is the widest, was apparently the important part of the building since it has a semicircular wall at its back (southwest side), the ends of which are connected by a cross-wall. The side rooms are rectangular and, according to Skias, had no doors to the court but were accessible only through the central room. In front of the central room, some 3.50m. north of its front wall, a parallel wall was found; the space between the two walls was filled in and paved with rectangular stone slabs. Thus a broad platform was formed in front of the central room of the building. Skias suggested that the room was open and that it fronted on a colonnade of six small columns between antae. He also maintained that columns stood on the interior cross-wall which connected the ends of the semicircular wall in the depth of the room. Perhaps we should note that the northwest corner of the west room was cut off by a wall to surround the passage leading from the corridor of the South Pylon to the room in the square tower K6.

The function of the building is indicated by its form; it is a Bouleuterion. That a Council House already existed within the

[36] A. Skias, *Praktika*, 1895, pp. 174ff. W. McDonald, *The Political Meeting Places of the Greeks*, pp. 187-189, pl. VIII. Cf. Fig. 2.

Sanctuary in the fourth century we learn from at least one inscription,[37] but it is doubtful that it might have existed earlier. It has been suggested that the Sacred Gerousia held its sittings here. This, however, has been proved unfounded by O. Rubensohn and especially by James Oliver, who have shown that it was used by the City Council only.[38] Occasionally perhaps it was used by the Council of 500, as is indicated by an honorary degree of ca. A.D. 40-42 in which we find the formula " Ἄρειος πάγος ἐν Ἐλευσῖνι."[39]

In front of the Bouleuterion were erected stelai honoring individuals for special services. A rather late Attik decree, dating from about A.D. 220 and concerned with the restoration of the Mysteries to their former magnificence, specifies that the decision should be inscribed on three stelai, one of which was to be set up "in the hieron in front of the Bouleuterion."[40] In Late Roman times this structure was replaced by another.

To the north of the South Pylon Skias brought to light the remains of a wall (Fig. 4, No. 32) built in the polygonal style similar to that used in the construction of the east wall of the Bouleuterion. The surviving small section cannot prove that the wall belongs actually to a building. Skias suggested that it was part of a retaining wall for a terrace at the north end of which a ramp perhaps led to the akropolis of Eleusis.

[37] *CIA*, III, 5. Philios in *AM*, 19 (1894), pp. 179ff. in l. 2. Cf. *BCH*, 4 (1880), pp. 225ff.

[38] Rubensohn, *op.cit.*, pp. 81ff. J. Oliver, *The Sacred Gerousia, Hesperia*, Supplement VI, pp. 6-7, 30, 43.

[39] *IG*, IV², 83, l. 8.

[40] *IG*, II², 1078, ll. 40-43. *Sylloge*⁴, vol. 2, No. 885.

CHAPTER VII

ELEUSIS IN ROMAN TIMES (L)

THE ROMAN PERIOD was an era of further expansion of the cult and the extension of its benefits to the citizens of the Roman Republic first and the Empire later. This extension of the privilege of initiation was reflected in the construction of auxiliary buildings and in the multiplication of dedicatory offerings. The Sanctuary area was preserved and the Telesterion restored in the form established in the fifth and fourth centuries. A number of structures were added in Roman times, but these were mostly to replace others of lesser importance and monumentality, and to express more fully the enhanced prestige enjoyed by the cult, especially in Roman Imperial times. The increased importance of the cult is indicated by the increased sanctity of the Hierophant,[1] especially by the fact that the Emperor Nero avoided a visit to Eleusis and a demand for initiation which might have been denied to him.[2] At the same time the mighty rulers of Rome were flattered with titles and dedications; Sabina first and then Faustina were named Demeter the Nea, and an ephebic festival, known as the Antinoeia, was regularly held in honor of Hadrian's favorite Antinoos, whose statue was erected perhaps in the outer court of the Sanctuary (Fig. 79).[3]

[1] This is proved by the strict enforcement of "hieronymy," the rule forbidding under severe penalty the calling or mentioning the Hierophant by his personal name. This was not prevalent in earlier times. In Isaios, VII, 9, we find the Hierophant Lakratides mentioned; a fourth century B.C. inscription honoring the Hierophant Hierokleides mentions him by name (*Ephem*, 1897, p. 33); an inscription dating from ca. 275 B.C. gives us the name of the Hierophant Chaeritios (*Ephem*, 1883, p. 81. *Sylloge*[4], vol. 3, No. 1019). But in Roman times the Hierophant became such an exalted personality that to call him or to mention him by name became a punishable sin (cf. Lucian, *Lexiphanes*, 10). And so the Hierophant Apollonios, in an epigram carved on the pedestal of his statue, asks the initiates and the people not to inquire about his personal name for, as he says, he lost it on entering the sacred office—"the mystic law wafted it away into the sea"; however, after his death, his children would disclose the name. And so they did (*Ephem*, 1883, p. 79). As late as A.D. 396, Eunapios believed that he could not disclose the name of the Hierophant who initiated him (*in Maximo*, p. 52). Cf. Foucart, *Les mystères*, pp. 173-175. The same rule applied to the priestesses known as *Hierophantides*.

[2] Suetonius, *Nero*, c. 34, 4.

[3] P. Graindor, *Athènes sous Hadrien*, pp. 100, 101, 171, 266 where bibliography. Cf. *infra*, p. 202 and Fig. 77.

The most important event in the life of the cult was the partial destruction of the Sanctuary by the barbaric hordes of the Kostovoks in the summer of 170 B.C.[4] The effect of that destruction on the minds of the pagan world is reflected in the speech of Aristides, written in a single hour under the impact of the news, and delivered before the assembly of the people of Smyrna.[5] As soon, however, as the barbarians were gone, the Sanctuary was rebuilt and the celebrations continued without interruption. The heroes of the hour were the Emperor who undertook the reconstruction and the Hierophant who, as we learn from an inscription, "saved the rites for his people."[6]

The Lesser Propylaea. A number of buildings were constructed in the course of the Roman period, the oldest of which is the monumental North Gate to the Sanctuary, known as the Lesser Propylaea. It was constructed over the Peisistratean inner North Pylon, to the east of the Ploutonion (Figs. 3 and 4, No. 15; 54).[7] From the Latin inscription cut on its architrave we learn that this monumental gateway had been vowed to Demeter by Appius Claudius Pulcher in his consulship of 54 B.C., but that it was erected or completed after his death by his two nephews.[8] This intention of Appius to build a Propylaeum is referred to by Cicero in two of his letters addressed to Atticus in 50 B.C., and his references seem to suggest that at the time of the writing of the letters the gateway was either not begun or at least not finished.[9] It is worth noting that Appius' undertaking stirred Cicero to conceive the idea of commemorating himself by building a Propylaeum to the Akademy, a design that he never carried out. The remnants of Appius' gateway were cleared first by the Society of the Dilettanti, in whose publication we find the earliest complete description of the building, and then by Lenormant and Philios. Its site was evident even before

---

[4] A. von Premerstein, *Klio*, 12 (1912), pp. 145-164. J. Oliver, *The Sacred Gerousia, Hesperia*, Supplement VI, p. 28.

[5] Aristides, Λόγος 'Ελευσίνιος.

[6] *IG*, II², 3639. He is the same official who later initiated Marcus Aurelius: cf. D. Philios, *BCH*, 19 (1895), pp. 119ff.

[7] Society of Dilettanti, *The Unedited Antiquities of Attica*, London 1917. G. Libertini, "I Propilei di A. Claudio Pulcro ad Eleusi," *Ann.Scu.Ital.*, 2 (1916). H. Hörmann, *Die inneren Propyläen von Eleusis*, Berlin 1932.

[8] For the inscription cf. F. Lenormant, *Recherches à Eleusis*, pp. 291ff, No. 137.

[9] Cicero, *Epist. ad Atticum*, VI, 1, 26; VI, 6, 2.

the excavations and, as we have seen in our Introduction, its remains were taken to be those of the Temple of Demeter by Wheler, Chandler, and other early travelers.

It was constructed of Pentelic marble on a krepis or foundation of regular "Roman concrete" faced by blocks of conglomerate and in the upper parts by blocks of poros stone. A forecourt (ca. 9.80m. x 10.35m.) paved with large slabs, most of which have survived, was flanked on the west, east, and south sides by walls and approached on the north by two steps (Fig. 54, a). Hörmann, to whom we owe a minute description of the building, restored rather thick walls with an entablature molding. In this he followed the ideas of Libertini. However, a number of fragments of Ionic columns and capitals were found at the site by the Dilettanti expedition, and Bedford, in 1812, recorded these carefully and noted that the backs of the capitals were uncarved, a characteristic detail also of the blocks of the architraves belonging to the lateral walls. As Dinsmoor has observed,[10] there is no other building at Eleusis to which these Ionic fragments could be attributed; they cannot be assigned to the Greater Propylaea and, in view of the careful measurements of Bedford, they cannot be assumed as confused records of the Ionic columns of that building. There can be no doubt that their dimensions and properties will only admit their association with the architraves of the lateral walls. Consequently, we have to admit that the narrow wall now running along the length of the lateral walls was a podium on which stood Ionic attached columns, perhaps four in number, as indicated in Dinsmoor's plan, which reached the ornamental architrave of the walls.

A broad doorway, some 2.95m. in clear width, was symmetrically placed at the depth of the forecourt, and this doorway was sheltered by a roofed narrow structure equipped with two columns and two antae on the outside and two Caryatids on the inside. Thus a vestibule was formed on the inside and a prothyron on the outside before the door opening. The prothyron is some 4.40m. in depth and had two Corinthian columns, of which only the bases and capitals survive. The bases are *in situ* (Fig. 54, c) and have a diameter of 1.03m. indicating that the columns they supported were

[10] W. Dinsmoor, *The Architecture of Ancient Greece*, p. 286. Cf. *supra*, p. 10 for account of Ionic fragments in writings of early visitors.

of average height. Their capitals, as well as those of the antae, exhibit an unusual and elaborate decoration carried out with freshness and vigor; among the corner tendrils they exhibit winged animals, lions and bulls perhaps (Fig. 55) and are crowned with unique abaci, hexagonal in plan. The entablature supported by the Corinthian columns also exhibits peculiar features, Ionic and Doric details mixed. The architrave and the frieze are made of the same block of pentelic marble, and on the usual Ionic-Corinthian architrave with its three fasciae we find the Latin dedicatory inscription (Fig. 57). The frieze is composed of triglyphs and metopes, characteristic of the Doric order, and on these we find carved in low relief some of the emblems of the cult of Demeter: cists and sheaves of wheat on the triglyphs, bukrania and stylized poppy flowers on the metopes. The imposition of a carved ornament on the triglyph, of course, is foreign to the Doric order and reflects the Ionic norm. Since the ends of the block are broken, we cannot know whether there were included in the ornamentation the crossed torches and pomegranates symbolic of the cult. We find these two elements in the ornamental frieze from Eleusis illustrated in the publication of the Dilettanti and discussed by Lenormant, and we recall that Chandler noted crossed torches on what he stated to be a pedestal, but which may well have been part of the inscribed architrave and frieze of the prothyron. Above the frieze we have the regular Ionic-Corinthian dentils. The pediment seems to have been undecorated, but the ceiling was coffered.

The central doorway was closed by a massive two-valved door with pivot holes, rectangular in shape, visible at the inner corners of the opening. To facilitate manoeuvering the massive door, rollers were provided which moved in well-cut quadrands (Fig. 54). Running through the door opening we find two other grooves parallel to each other and some 1.40m. apart. They are preserved to a length of 2.90m. These have been widely accepted as ruts made by chariots and as proofs that chariots could enter the precinct. However, we note that no traces of ruts are to be seen on the pavement of the forecourt beyond the point where the grooves stop; that the grooves are cut only where the pavement bulges slightly upwards, and that beyond the point where the grooves end, the floor of the forecourt slopes slightly to its outer edge. Furthermore, the two steps across the front of the forecourt would have been difficult if not impossible for wheeled traffic and they show no signs of wear and tear caused by chariots. With all these facts in mind, we can only conclude that the grooves are not ruts made by chariots, but were intentionally cut on the floor to act as drains to facilitate the passage of the rain water which, coming down the slope of the Sacred Way, would naturally accumulate behind a closed door.

On either side of the prothyron were created two blind niches which were perhaps used for statues. Similarly, two corresponding niches were made in the vestibule in the inner section of the Propylaea. The niches of the vestibule seem to have served at the beginning as fountains, and we can imagine them equipped with two spouts in the form of lion heads from which the water poured into shallow basins or troughs, two in front of each of the still extant niches (Fig. 54, t).[11] At a later time, through the niches were cut lateral doorways, thus giving the Propylaea three door openings.

The inner side of the doorway facing the Sanctuary area also had a distyle porch corresponding to the outer *prothyron*. In this porch, however, instead of columns were flanking parastades at the end of which were two colossal Caryatids. The podia for these are still to be seen *in situ* (Fig. 54, m). The upper part of the statues have been preserved. One of these, the less well preserved, was carried to England by Clark[12] while the other is exhibited in the Museum of Eleusis (Fig. 56). The Caryatids of pentelic marble represent maidens carrying on their heads the mystic Kiste. The Kiste is cylindrical in form and bears on it in highly decorative relief the emblems of Demeter's cult: head of wheat, the poppy, the lidded Kernos, peculiar to the cult, flanked by small flower rosettes reminiscent of the pomegranate flower, a molding representing perhaps the Bacchos, symbol of the Mysteries, made up of myrtle leaves bound together by strands of wool (the rectangles spaced among the leaves being the stylized representation of the strands), a molding of beads and reel, and around the base of the cist a molding of wavy ribbon and dot interrupted at the sides by an acanthus leaf. The destroyed part of the Kiste was

[11] The troughs range from 0.64m. to 1.145m. in length, 0.33 to 0.35m. in width and 0.115 to 0.13m. in depth. Between each pair there is a drain 0.085m. wide in the southwest side and 0.095m. in the southeast.

[12] *Supra*, p. 11.

perhaps covered by tendrils and acanthus leaves. The maidens wear the sleeveless chiton decorated with a Gorgoneion in front. The modeling is crisp and direct and imparts to the forms a beauty unusual for the period.

Hörmann assumed that the Caryatids of the inner façade occupied two successive positions; that first they were placed farther apart and directly against the wall; later they were moved out from the wall and placed slightly closer together. In the former position the inner parastades are assumed not to have been built and a horizontal entablature was carried from Caryatid to Caryatid. In the second stage the parastades were built and a horizontal entablature and ceiling were carried clear across, the Caryatids being *in antis*. Zschietzschmann demonstrated that even in the first stage the flank parastades of the inner vestibule must have existed, like those of the outer vestibule, but assumed that Hörmann's first position of the Caryatids was correct.[13] Dinsmoor refuses to accept a first stage even for the Caryatids. He writes: "Not only would they have made a ridiculous appearance under the horizontal entablature, but their eventual (and probably original) positions show such careful planning with relation to the outer Corinthian columns, as to suggest that they likewise supported a similar entablature and pediment in the form of a distyle porch."[14]

This monumental gateway in Pentelic marble with an outer forecourt and prothyron and an inner vestibule with a distyle porch, built for Appius Claudius Pulcher by his descendants, was a distinct ornament to the Sanctuary of Demeter, adding considerably to its monumental appearance. It is the only structure built in Roman Republican times.

Reconstruction of the Telesterion. In the Imperial era other buildings were constructed and the Telesterion, damaged considerably if not destroyed by the barbarian Kostovoks was restored to its ancient glory. We can detect the restoration from the foundations of a number of columns built of all kinds of stones in a very slovenly manner. The top course of the foundations of the column in the northeast corner of the naos is composed in part of two re-used blocks of marble one of which bears an inscription from the

---

[13] *AA*, 48 (1933), p. 336, "Die inneren Propyläen von Eleusis."
[14] W. B. Dinsmoor, *op.cit.*, p. 286 n. 4.

end of the first century A.D., thus providing an approximate chronological limit after which the destruction occurred and the restoration was undertaken.[15] Perhaps the important change made by the restorers was the extension of the Telesterion to the west by some 2.15m. That extension required further quarrying of the rock of the hillside. I believe that at this time the rock-cut terrace above the west side of the Telesterion was also hewn, Temple L10 was built, and the stairway and the platform on either side of the west side of the Telesterion were made. Again it is possible to assume that it was during this reconstruction that the seats of the Telesterion were covered with marble, traces of which can be detected especially on the stairs of the west side. Repairs can also be detected on the surviving fragments of the entablature of the Stoa of Philon. These and the fact that the columns of the naos had to be built again on foundations constructed now for that purpose seem to indicate that the destruction of the Telesterion was very extensive if not complete. The fires started by the invaders, fed by the massive timbers used in the construction of the architraves, diazoma, and the roof, must have resulted in a tremendous conflagration that apparently destroyed completely the interior of the naos.

Who was responsible for the reconstruction of the Telesterion cannot be definitely proved. The Emperors Antoninus Pius and Marcus Aurelius are usually credited with the restoration of the Temple. If, however, we place the Kostovok incursion in the summer of 170, then we shall have to accept Marcus Aurelius as the restorer, since that year falls within his reign. Again, the scholiast of the rhetor Aristides tells us that Marcus Aurelius, who studied philosophy in Athens, honored that city as a pupil honors his teacher and that among his benefactions to the city is included the repair and rich decoration of the temple at Eleusis.[16] Marcus Aurelius was initiated in A.D. 176 and received unprecedented honors. He was made a "Stone bearer" (Λιθοφόρος) by the Sacred Gerousia and a presiding officer of that body and of the family of the Kerykes; he was not a Hierophant or even a member of the

---

[15] Column VII-6. D. Philios, *Praktika*, 1884, p. 80. *BCH*, 19 (1895), pp. 113-119. The builders of the foundation placed the blocks with the letters under. Philios turned the stones so that the letters came on the upper surface and can be seen now. The inscribed block belonged to a pedestal.

[16] Cf. Scholiast of Aristides on the *Panathenaikos*, 183, 2 (III, p. 308, Dindorf).

Eumolpid family and yet he was allowed to enter the Anaktoron, the only lay person ever admitted in that sanctum in the long history of Eleusis.[17] These honors would have been conferred only on a leader who had contributed considerably to the Sanctuary of Demeter. Apparently he did just that. Besides the Telesterion he erected the outer monumental North Pylon, the Greater Propylaea (Figs. 3 and 4, No. 11).

The Greater Propylaea. This entranceway was built over the pylon which was constructed perhaps by Kimon in the second quarter of the fifth century B.C. Part of the dedicatory inscription has survived and even the bust of the Emperor who was responsible for the reconstruction (Fig. 58); but both are so badly preserved that the evidence they suggest cannot be relied upon completely. Hadrian, Antoninus Pius, and Marcus Aurelius, whose name appears on the dedicatory inscription, have been suggested successively as builders of the Greater Propylaea. Kourouniotes seems to favor the belief that construction of the building was begun under Antoninus Pius and completed under Marcus Aurelius. Noack favors Antoninus Pius.[18] I believe that Deubner has convincibly demonstrated that the Emperor in the shield of the pediment (Fig. 58) is Marcus Aurelius; consequently at least the completion of the building should be attributed to him.[19]

The structure is a faithful copy of the central important part of the Propylaia built by Mnesikles on the Akropolis of Athens in Periklean days. It presents but few differences in plan: it lacks the wings of the building on the Akropolis of Athens; it is raised on a podium to bring its outer and inner porticoes to the same floor level, and its flight of six steps on the front façade, extend around its corners. Five of these steps are now preserved. The central ramp of the Propylaia of Athens was omitted from the Eleusinian copy.

The imposing marble building stands on a stepped podium, which rises some 1.70m. above the floor of the outer court of the

---

[17] *CIA*, III, 702. Capitol, *Sept.Sev.*, 3: "Sacrarium solus ingressus est."

[18] Attributed to Hadrian by: J. G. Frazer, *Pausanias*, II, pp. 505ff. A. Hekler, *JOAI*, 19-20 (1919), p. 232. To Antoninus Pius, by D. Philios, *Eleusis*, p. 59. W. B. Dinsmoor, *AJA*, 14 (1910), p. 155 n. 1. A. Orlandos, *Eleusiniaka*, I, p. 223. Noack, *Eleusis*, p. 222. Kourouniotes, *Guide*, pp. 24 and 31. H. Hörmann, *op.cit.*, pp. 114ff, 118.

[19] O. Deubner, "Zu den grossen Propyläen von Eleusis," *AM*, 62 (1937), pp. 73-81, pls. 39-42.

Sanctuary. It faces towards the northeast, the direction of Athens, and it is not placed on the central axis of the court. Its podium was built in typical Roman style with a core in "Roman concrete" faced with ashlar masonry. The visible part of the building was built of Pentelic marble, like its prototype. It is composed of the blocking or curtain wall pierced by five doorways and of two porticoes, an inner and an outer, on either side of that wall of doorways. The outer portico, facing the court, had a front colonnade of six Doric columns which supported an entablature of plain architraves, a frieze composed of alternating triglyphs and metopes, and a tri-angular pediment enframed in its regular Doric cornice. (For a restoration of the northwest corner of the portico, see Fig. 61.) In the midst of the triangular pediment was sculptured in a shield a bust of the Emperor (Fig. 58). Although the features of the Emperor have been destroyed beyond recognition, Deubner has pointed out that on the shoulder strap of the bust was carved a "giant," identical to the one in the same position on a bust of Marcus Aurelius now in the Louvre. The giant symbolized the enemies of the Empire, the barbarian Marcomani, whom Marcus Aurelius defeated in A.D. 172/3. The carving of the bust, therefore, and consequently the completion if not the initial construction of the Greater Propylaea must be placed after that date. The head of the Gorgon on his chest (defaced by a large cross cut over it in a later period) likens the Emperor to Zeus who destroyed the giants. The bust in a shield placed over the center of the gateway instead of the apotropaic head of Medousa, follows the custom established in later Imperial times of the use of portraits of important person-alities and even of Gods in this fashion (*imago clipeata*). The reassembled pediment with its medallion is now displayed in the great court at a small distance from the front steps of the Greater Propylaea (Fig. 58). Two of the reassembled columns of the façade are on either side of the pediment (Figs. 58, c and 59, c) while a great part of the entablature is reassembled in the area to the right of the visitor ascending the steps of the façade. The frag-ments of the dedicatory inscription are now displayed on the sixth century wall of the Peisistratean storage house to the right of the path to the Lesser Propylaea.

The dimensions of this façade are identical to those of the

Periklean Propylaia of Athens. Thus the diameter of the Doric external columns amounts to 1.558m., while their height is 8.8075m. We do not know whether the columns of the inner portico varied somewhat in height, as in the case in their prototype where the height amounts to 8.528m. The height of the entablature would amount to 2.725m. on the front and 2.710m. on the sides. Thus the height of the façade from the floor to the finial over the center would amount to ca. 16m.

The deep outer portico, 15.24m. in depth, has two rows of three Ionic columns supporting the roof structure (Figs. 3, 4, and 54). The six bases of the Ionic columns are still *in situ* and a few battered lower drums stand on those bases. Broken capitals and fragments of the coffered ceiling are displayed in the portico. Pausanias' remarks regarding the ceiling of Propylaia on the Akropolis of Athens would naturally apply to its copy at Eleusis. "The Propylaea has a ceiling of white marble," states the Periegetes in awe, "and the beauty and size of the blocks up to my time has not been matched."[20] One of the tremendous blocks of marble fallen from the ceiling over the lateral aisles measures 5.80m. in length, 0.40m. in height and ca. 0.75m. in thickness. The lateral walls of the outer portico have not been preserved. The curtain wall, or the cross-wall pierced by the doors, is preserved only in its lowest course (Fig. 54, r). In that course, however, we can make out the five door openings and their thresholds clearly from the wear on the thresholds and from attachments for the door posts. The doors were diminished progressively in size, from either side of the large central door (4.19m. x 7.37m.). The threshold of the last small doorway to the left shows the greatest wear; perhaps this was the only one in daily use.

Beyond the curtain wall or cross-wall the inner portico faces the interior of the Sanctuary (Fig. 54, s). This is a comparatively shallow stoa, 7.36m. in depth, fronted by six Doric columns; the lowest drum of the corner column to the west is *in situ*. Whether the height of the east and west façades differed, as was the case in the prototype, we have no means of ascertaining. In Athens the difference was imposed by the sloping ground over which the building

[20] Pausanias, I, 22, 4.

had to be constructed. At Eleusis the podium on which the Propylaea stood compensated for any difference in level.

Of the steps of the front façade, the lowest on the east side was interrupted when it came to the area of the Kallichoron, so as not to infringe upon its sacred ground. At this point a doorway was built to provide access, by means of a wooden stairway, to the well. Sometime in the course of the use of the Propylaea, the Doric colonnade of the front elevation was closed by a thick wall on which was centered a single door. We can still see clearly on the marble pavement the grooves of its rollers. Perhaps this wall, further blocking the entrance to the Sanctuary, was added during the period when the fortifications of Eleusis were strengthened in anticipation of the invasion of barbarians, perhaps of the Goths and the Herules, and could be attributed to the Emperor Valerian (A.D. 252-262) who embarked on the task of fortifying a number of cities, including Athens.[21] On the marble pavement of the Greater Propylaea and on its steps many crosses were engraved in Early Christian times and after the destruction of the Sanctuary, perhaps after A.D. 500. The crosses, presumably, were to be instrumental in driving away the evil pagan spirits which might have haunted the place.

It is possible to assume that during the construction of the Greater Propylaea the outer court of the Sanctuary was paved with rectangular marble slabs. That court has an irregular oblong shape with its greater length from southeast to northwest, amounting to 65m. (Figs. 3, 4, and 59). The width, along an axis perpendicularly drawn to the middle of the central intercolumniation of the outer stoa of the Greater Propylaea, amounts to some 40m. The Sacred Way from Athens entered its northeast corner, and in that section, to be seen behind the small house of the guards, the Way is paved in the same manner as the court (Figs. 3, and 4, No. 1). As we proceed from the Sacred Way into the outer court, we find to our left two structures of interest.

The Fountain House. The first is a small fountain house (Figs. 3, 4, No. 3). Of this interesting structure only the lowest part survives. It consists of the bottom of the water tank lined with burnt brick, in the form of an elongated Greek Pi, with its opening

---

[21] K. Kourouniotes, *Deltion*, 16 (1934-35), Parartema, p. 2. J. N. Travlos, *Praktika*, 1954, p. 70. Cf. Zosimos, I, 29, and Zonaras, XII, 23.

some 11.30m. in length, towards the court. In front of the tank is a marble flooring in which eight small circular troughs indicate the existence, originally, of eight spouts for water. Below a drain cut into a step carried the water under the foundation of the southeast triumphal arch to a main drain below the road along the east side of the east peribolos wall. Apparently the fountain was faced with marble and had the form of an open portico or stoa fronted by six columns, perhaps of wood. Many marble fragments of the facing are to be seen in front and on top of the fountain. Professor Orlandos, some years ago, pointed out that this simple type of fountain was usually built in sanctuaries and in connection with shrines.[22] The exact date of the fountain remains uncertain, and there can be no doubt that it belongs to the Roman period and that it was built either before, or at the same time as the triumphal arch.

Triumphal Arches. Attached to the west side of the fountain a triumphal arch occupied the space of the southeast corner of the outer court, between it and the square tower K20 (Figs. 3, 4, No. 4). Professor Orlandos' most recent study of the monument proves that "with very few unimportant variations" this arch as well as its counterpart on the southwest corner of the court are faithful copies of the triumphal arch of Hadrian in Athens and that they are later than A.D. 129.[23] Kourouniotes, noting that around the arch were found many pedestals of statues dedicated to members of the family of the Antonines, suggested that perhaps the arch was constructed in the years of the reign of Antoninus Pius.[24] Perhaps we can place it a little later and suggest that the Emperor of its inscription is Marcus Aurelius who proved so great a benefactor to Eleusis.

This triumphal arch at the southeast corner of the court is better preserved than its counterpart in the west corner (Fig. 4, No. 5). It is built of pentelic marble and had a single arch, like its prototype in Athens, spanning an opening that measures at the threshold some 4.85m. The lowest part of this entrance is well preserved. The arch sprang from Corinthian pilasters and its façade, to the

---

[22] A. K. Orlandos, "Παραστάσεις κρηνῶν ἐπὶ ἀγγείων," *Ephem*, 1916, p. 101.
[23] A. K. Orlandos, *Eleusiniaka*, I, p. 222 n. 3. These arches as well as the fountain will be fully published shortly.
[24] Kourouniotes, *Guide*, p. 27.

right and left of the pilasters, was adorned by Corinthian columns, one on each side. These stood upon quadrangular bases adorned by sculptured crossed torches, the emblems of the Goddesses (cf. Fig. 59). Pilasters with a Corinthian capital stood at the corners. On the top of the arch and on its curved blocks we have the inscription ΤΟΙΝ ΘΕΟΙΝ ΚΑΙ ΤΩ ΑΥΤΟΚΡΑΤΟΡΙ ΟΙ ΠΑΝΕΛΛΗΝΕΣ: "All the Greeks to the Goddesses and the Emperor."[25] Over the main part of the structure an attic displayed three openings framed by Corinthian pilasters and columns. The pediment of the central one gave it the aspect of a small shrine or aedicula. The fragments of that pediment, reassembled by Kourouniotes near the arch, are illustrated in Figure 60. The entire structure was light and ornate as we can deduce from its many surviving fragments.

The southeast arch separated the outer court of the Sanctuary from an open section of the city where the initiates could find temporary accommodations during the initiation period. The road to the east of the southeast arch was flanked on one side by the peribolos wall; on the other the excavations of 1930 revealed remains of public buildings among which we find thermae (just behind the fountain, Figs. 3 and 4, No. 40), small hostels (Fig. 4, No. 41), and other bathing establishments (Fig. 4, No. 42) with a communal bathing room indicated by basins set in a circle. Under the road was found a well-constructed main drain or sewer with a brick vault and manholes set at fixed intervals. Water was obtained from wells, a number of which were found in this section of the city, and was also piped to the hostels and bathing establishments from an outside source. Some of the pipes were of lead, others of terracotta. All these structures date from the Roman period, the period of expansion when facilities beyond the fortified city had to be provided for the overflowing crowd of pilgrims.

The southwest triumphal arch is not well preserved and its location can be made out only with some difficulty (Fig. 4, No. 5). Through it people could go from the outer court to the Asty Gates (Fig. 4, H10).

The Temple of Artemis and Poseidon. In the paved outer court, almost in front of the Greater Propylaea, stood the temple of Artemis of the Portals, and of Father Poseidon (Figs. 3, 4, No. 6

---

[25] The inscription is to be seen today in the area of the arch.

and 61). The temple was built of marble over a high podium, rising almost one meter above the floor of the court. When the expedition of the Dilettanti visited the site, the temple had already been destroyed and over its podium were built two modest cottages still inhabited. These cottages made impossible the accurate study of the remains and consequently all the early descriptions of the temple are incorrect. We owe its careful study and exact publication to Professor A. K. Orlandos.[26] The core of the podium, the only part still standing in the court, is built of small stones set in pozzolana and lime ("Roman concrete") faced with poros blocks for the part that was not visible. Four steps of marble were placed around the podium leading to the stylobate, which could be considered as a fifth step. The temple itself was built of pentelic marble and had a front and rear portico fronted by four Doric columns. The side walls projected a little beyond the cross-wall forming a somewhat closed prodomos before its rectangular cella (cf. the ground plan on the upper right hand corner of Fig. 61). The length of the temple at the base of its podium is 16.03m. and its width 10.10m. Its columns were monolithic, since their dimensions were rather small (height 4.53m.). The details seem to indicate that the temple was built before the reign of Marcus Aurelius. As a matter of fact the temple was seen and mentioned by Pausanias who visited the site about the middle of the second century of our era.[27] It was built, therefore, before that date. It is noticeable that it is not exactly aligned with the Greater Propylaea. This may indicate an earlier date, but the orientation may have been calculated to permit both sides of the temple to be seen by people entering the court from the Sacred Way. The roof of the structure was of wood and its tiles of terracotta.

The Altars in the Outer Court. Some 3.85m. in front of the temple are the remains of an altar (Figs. 3, 4, No. 7; 58g, 61). Only its marble frame survives, enclosing the foundation of an altar made of small stones set in lime. The dimensions of the frame are 3.10 by 2.48m. inner dimensions, the frame itself being 0.60m.

[26] A. K. Orlandos, " Ὁ ἐν Ἐλευσῖνι ναὸς τῆς Προπυλαίας Ἀρτέμιδος," *Eleusiniaka*, I, pp. 209-223. To Professor Orlandos I am grateful for his excellent drawing of the restored temple, which he has kindly allowed me to reproduce in Fig. 61.

[27] Pausanias, I, 38, 6. It appears that the temple is earlier in date than the triumphal arches and the fountain house.

wide. The position of the altar, in front of the main façade of the temple, and its construction, proving its Roman date, suggest that it belongs to that temple and possibly was dedicated to Artemis of the Portals. Some 1.50m. from the northeast, beside the temple was a second altar (4m. x 3.35m.) of which only a fragment survives. It is reasonable to assume that this altar belonged to Father Poseidon to whom, as well as to Artemis, the temple was dedicated.

In the outer court there seem to have been other altars also, few traces of which survive today. These could have been used by the initiates on their arrival at Eleusis and around them libations may have been poured and rites performed preliminary to the last act of the processional celebrations. That last act, as we shall see later, perhaps comprised singing, dancing, and the bearing of the kernos in honor of the Goddesses.

The most interesting altar in the court is what Kourouniotes has called the *eschara*, or ground-altar, borrowing the term from the wording of inscriptions referring to sacrifices held in honor of the Goddesses.[28] This structure is located near the northeast corner of the temple of Artemis and Poseidon and is separated from the rest of the court by a single row of stones forming a rectangle 7.15m. on the east side and 6m. on the west; 8.50m. on the north and 8.28m. on the south side (Figs. 3, 4, No. 8). The area within was not paved and in its center we find a rectangular ground-altar built of burnt brick set in lime mortar (Fig. 62). It is in the form of a rectangular well (1.43m. x 1.06m. and 1.75m. deep). Half way down a small shelf some 0.15m. wide projects from all four sides. On this apparently was placed the *eschara* or iron grill on which the fire was built and in which the sacrificial animals were placed. In the inner face of the four sides are six vertical channels or flues, 0.21m. to 0.23m. in width, two each, symmetrically disposed on the north and south sides, and one each on the short east and west sides.

There can be little doubt that the *eschara* is of Roman date, and perhaps it is contemporary with the paving of the court. However, it was built over an area where older and perhaps sacred structures stood, possibly altars of an earlier era. Part of a polygonal wall of

[28] Kourouniotes, *Guide*, p. 29.

a building of the sixth century B.C. can still be seen on the northeast corner of the enclosure. It is reasonable to assume that in this
area an altar was built in the sixth century to take the place of
altar Z13 (Figs. 6 and 23), infringed upon by the Peisistratean
peribolos wall, and that the Roman *eschara* is the last of a series
of altars built in the outer court to serve the cult of the Goddesses.
Perhaps on this *eschara* were sacrificed the small pigs whose flesh
had to be consumed entirely by fire.

Other Structures in the Outer Court. The pavement of the outer
court at its northeastern side is interrupted by a projecting rectangular area (Fig. 4, No. 9). Travlos has identified that area as
the shrine of the hero Dolichos, known from inscriptions.[29] That
shrine was composed of a number of adjoining rooms, each fronted
by an open colonnade. At its eastern end the colonnade turned at
right angles and continued along the north side of the court until
it reached the Sacred Way which at that point had a width of 20m.
Near the end of the colonnade on the Sacred Way is a semicircular
exedra (5 x 3m.) where the dignitaries in charge of the celebration may have taken their position during the arrival of the pompe
at Eleusis (Fig. 4, No. 2). It may, however, have served as a
podium for statues. Travlos in his report for 1953 has suggested
that open porticoes or colonnades closed the court along its north,
west, and east sides. A few years ago, and again in 1957, the
foundations of a large structure were revealed in the streets beyond
the outer court by laborers laying water pipes to the village. These
remains, according to Kourouniotes and Travlos, belong to a large
rectangular building which they identify as a Pompeion, a building where the processions from Eleusis to Athens were organized
annually. Unfortunately, it is impossible to clear the structure
because of modern houses built over it.

Auxiliary Areas. We have seen how in the days of Peisistratos
and of Kimon two large areas were attached to the Sanctuary to
serve as auxiliary areas. The Kimonian area, indicated by the letter
A in plan of Fig. 4, was now filled with a number of buildings,
the ruins of which form a regular maze to be seen to the left of a

---

[29] J. N. Travlos, *Hesperia*, 18 (1949), p. 143, figs. 1-2; *Praktika*, 1953,
p. 76. Cf. the inscription of the overseers 329/8, *IG*, II² 1672, 23-25, where the
Dolichos and the House of the Kerykes are mentioned. In the same inscription
are mentioned other buildings useful for the administration of the sanctuary.

visitor entering the Greater Propylaea. Perhaps we may note the long and narrow structure that was built along the east Peisistratean wall (No. 12 in Fig. 4). It is some 66m. in length and 6m. in width and apparently was used for the storage of the first fruits. We have seen how the filling in of the Periklean storehouse necessitated the construction of other buildings for storage.[30] In Roman times, when the prosperity of the Sanctuary increased, more storage room became necessary and the long and narrow building was perhaps constructed to take care of that additional need. The foundations to the east of the long storage building apparently belong to houses used by the officials of the Sanctuary. From the inscription of the overseers for 329/8 B.C., we learn that a variety of structures used for administrative purposes did exist within the general area of the Sanctuary. The bakery and cistern are mentioned and the dwellings of the priestess, of the dadouchos, the vestiary and the house of the priests responsible for the upkeep of the Sanctuary. The foundations in this area, which may belong to the one or the other of these buildings seem to date from Roman Imperial times. The underground Roman cistern to the left of the Greater Propylaea (Fig. 4, No. 13) is of considerable size and its vaulted rooms and stairways are very impressive. Comparatively simple are the two cisterns built to the right of the Lesser Propylaea over the old Peisistratean storage house.

The auxiliary area extending to the northwest of the Lesser Propylaea (B and No. 18 in Fig. 4) was partially excavated by Philios in the early days of the exploration of Eleusis and was more fully investigated and studied recently by Kourouniotes and Travlos. As we have seen, this area, set aside in Peisistratean days, was divided into two unequal sections by a road leading from the north pylon to the city area beyond (Road No. 17 in Fig. 4). The road has a width ranging from 2.50m. to 3m. and in the course of its long use its level was continually being raised. Actually a difference of one meter exists between the Roman and the Peisistratean levels.

Area B underwent many changes from the days of its first use for auxiliary purposes. The northeast wall of the Peisistratean silo,

[30] *Supra*, p. 150. Cf. D. Philios, *Praktika*, 1882, p. 92. *IG*, II-III[2], 1672, dated 329/8 B.C.

Fig. 4, H50, was extended westward in the fourth century B.C. so as to enclose a comparatively large and apsidal area (No. 18 in Fig. 4). Along the west side of the enclosed area a stairway cut in the rock forms part of a lane that terminated at the akropolis of Eleusis. The southern corner of this area is taken up by a rock-cut terrace (originally 12.50m. x ca. 7m.) which perhaps in Late Roman times was divided by walls into many apartments. Above these apartments another rock-cut terrace was used for a number of rooms, in one of which was a rock-cut cistern. The houses, repaired, altered, and rebuilt in the course of long use, cannot be accurately dated, but it is certain that what we may call the peribolos wall surrounding them on the north, east, and west sides was built in the fourth century. In the wall of one of these structures was found a boundary stone indicating that the limits of the Sanctuary extended to this point.[31]

Like area No. 18, that of the Peisistratean storage building H50 underwent many changes. Over it in Roman times was built a large house for the terrace of which the north wall of the storage building was used as a retaining wall. The house was originally cleared by Philios, but it was re-examined by Kourouniotes in 1934.[32] It is divided into two sections, of which the southern section is about a meter higher than the northern. The east side of the house was destroyed by the construction of the late Roman wall No. 16 (Fig. 4). The southern section, with its floor built against the slope of the hill, is divided into three rooms (Fig. 4, L1), of which the middle is the largest and most important (6.20m. x 4.20m.). Its walls were covered with murals, fragments of which survived on its south wall. One of them, revealed by Philios, represented a seated Zeus holding a victory in his extended right hand.[33] On the floor of this room Kourouniotes found a libation trough made of marble slabs and a small square altar made of clay and plastered repeatedly. The plaster was apparently decorated in color and of its decoration we can make out small parts of anthemia

[31] *Supra*, p. 97. Cf. J. Threpsiades, *Deltion*, 14 (1931-32), Parartema, p. 31, fig. 3. K. Kourouniotes, *Deltion*, 15 (1933-1935), Parartema, p. 17. J. N. Travlos, *Hesperia*, 18 (1949), p. 142.

[32] *Praktika*, 1888, p. 25. *Ephem*, 1888, pp. 77ff and pls. 4-5. *Deltion*, 15 (1933-35), Parartema, pp. 2ff.

[33] It was copied by Gillieron père and published in color by Philios in the *Ephem*, 1888, pls. 4-5.

rendered in blue. Apparently there were wall paintings and a libation trough in the adjacent room which, however, is almost completely ruined. The north section of the house is made up of one large apartment.

Philios, in 1888, said that the building could have been a dwelling and his view has been verified by Kourouniotes' discoveries. The trough and altar would indicate the religious nature of the dwelling. Its proximity to the Sanctuary and its position in the auxiliary area are additional indications of its sacred character; it seems to have been a house serving the religious ministrants of the hieron. With reason its excavators identified it with the οἶκος κηρύκων, the House of the Kerykes, mentioned in the inscription of 329/8 B.C.[34] In the large north apartment of the house, the genos Kerykon, the gens, could gather for meetings, while in the south section (Fig. 4, L1), composed of many rooms, its members could hold their religious rites. The dwelling apparently belonged to the Roman period and was erected to replace an older house. It is possible to assume that the surviving structure was built when the Greater Propylaea were erected, at a time when major rearrangements were made in the Sanctuary area. It is also possible to assume that at that time area 18 was added to the house to be used by the members of the sacred gens.

Area B, below the House of the Kerykes and between it and the north peribolos wall (Fig. 4), is filled with foundations belonging to smaller houses of Roman Imperial times. Here and there fragments of earlier walls indicate that the area was covered with structures from the fourth century B.C. at least to the end of the life of the Sanctuary. It seems safe to assume that these structures served the personnel of the sanctuary, and some may have been the buildings mentioned in the inscription we have already noted. The line M, N, O (Fig. 4) indicates the limit of the auxiliary area, and perhaps there existed a cross-wall separating it from the city.[35]

At the time when the east peribolos wall of the Sanctuary was reinforced and a wall was built across the outer colonnade of the Greater Propylaea, a wall (Fig. 4, No. 16) was constructed that starts from the southwest corner of the inner portico of the Greater

[34] *IG*, II-III², 1672.
[35] Travlos' restoration appears in the plan he published in the *Praktika*.

Propylaea and proceeds to the southwest until it abuts against the rock of the hillside behind the Ploutonion. It thus separates completely the auxiliary area B from the Sanctuary. It cuts across the east section of the "House of the Kerykes" and even over the cisterns. It is made up of all kinds of re-used material, large poros and marble blocks taken from other buildings, and was apparently built in a great haste and without regard for skillful workmanship. It may have been built in the days of the Emperor Valerian, who, as we have seen, may have been responsible for the strengthening of the east peribolos wall.

The Sacred Way within the Sanctuary. Within the Sanctuary proper there was considerable building activity during Roman times. In addition to the restoration of the Telesterion, the inner section of the Sacred Way, from the Lesser Propylaea to the Telesterion (Fig. 4, No. 25) was paved with small marble slabs, a good many of which are preserved, especially in the southwestern section of the road (Fig. 45,a). Today this section of the Sacred Way is retained by a modern wall, which apparently follows the line of the ancient original wall. Noack maintained that the line of the Sacred Way beyond the Lesser Propylaea was rearranged and straightened out in Roman times; that the older Sacred Way from Peisistratean times to Roman proceeded southward, not in a straight line, but in wide curves; that beyond the Lesser Propylaea, it veered away from the rock and followed a straight line to its southern terminal.[36] No evidence justifies this assumption. The only surviving remains of the older road were found by Noack some 27m. to the south of the Lesser Propylaea and 0.50m. below the Roman pavement. At the right edge of the Roman Road in the area marked No. 26 in our plan, an edge of stones does exist, belonging to the Peisistratean period.[37] These scanty remains indicate definitely that the road in Peisistratean times followed an almost straight course from the Lesser Propylaea or the North Pylon to the Telesterion and along

[36] Cf. Noack, *Eleusis*, pls. 8, 14-17. Cf. pl. 32d for the photograph of the blocks belonging to the Greek Sacred Way. Before we could accept his walls u-v as forming part of the Greek Sacred Way we have first to prove definitely their date and position. A number of fragmentary walls, of which the function and date remain uncertain, do exist in that area. The difficulty of the problem of the chronology of walls at Eleusis is illustrated by the fact that Noack accepted Peisistratean walls as Early Archaic and Kimonian walls as pre-Peisistratean.

[37] Stones marked x, x, x, by Noack in his pl. 8.

the slope of the hill as in Roman times. The blocks found by Noack below the Roman level, the marginal stones of Peisistratean date, the general nature of the rocky slope as pictured by Noack in his plate No. 13—all this evidence is in favor of a direction for the older road similar to that followed by the Roman paved road, a direction going around the contour of the rocky hillside. The slope was not so sharp as to require a meandering approach but presents an easy, almost gentle grade, especially in the area immediately south of the Propylaea where Noack assumes a wide bend.

Temple F. To the right of the southernmost section of the Sacred Way are to be seen the scanty remains of a building called by Noack Temple F (Fig. 4, No. 24). Between the south wall of that temple and the Telesterion is the narrow stairway No. 26 (Figs. 4 and 48). The building was excavated by Philios in 1882, cleared by Noack, and investigated again by Kourouniotes in our day.[38] For a good many years Temple F was one of the mysterious and controversial buildings of the Sanctuary.

It is built on an artificially constructed terrace, (14.10m. x 11.20m.) half of which was cut into the hillside. Its east section, approximately half of the length, was artificially filled in and leveled, but its fill was unfortunately removed in the early days of the exploration of the Sanctuary when the rock was disclosed everywhere. Scanty remnants of the walls of this temple and rock cuttings used for the setting of its foundation blocks make possible the definition of its general plan. Noack has correctly concluded that it was a *templum in antis,* having a wide stairway in its front elevation, a shallow porch with two columns standing between antae, and an almost square cella behind it. Part of the stairway, which originally was made up of perhaps ten steps, survives and it proves that it acted also as a retaining wall for the artificial terrace of the eastern half of the structure. Of the rest of the building only fragmentary foundations survive. These prove that the temple was constructed in Roman times. Among the remains of walls, however, are a few blocks of poros stone which belong certainly to a very old building. Based on these blocks, Noack maintained that the Roman temple succeeded an earlier building,

---

[38] D. Philios, *Praktika,* 1882, p. 100. Noack, *Eleusis,* pp. 85ff. K. Kourouniotes and J. Travlos, *Deltion,* 15 (1933-35), pp. 72ff.

the construction of which went back to a very remote age. Again, based on these blocks and on the narrow stairway to the south of the building, a stairway reduced in width according to Noack because of the pre-existence of an older building, he maintained that the more ancient building and the rock-cut terrace on which it stands date from pre-Persian days; that in Peisistratean times there existed within the Sanctuary area both the Telesterion and Temple F which he identified as the Temple of Demeter. Thus he revived the conception of the existence of a temple to Demeter separate from the Telesterion. This theory was advanced, as we have seen, before his time by Blavette, Svoronos, and Rubensohn.[39] These conclusions of Noack were widely accepted by scholars; the pre-Persian date of Temple F was almost universally adopted.

Now, however, we have the latest results of Kourouniotes' investigations, proving definitely that Noack's conclusions are not substantiated by fact. The venerable Greek scholar, who devoted his entire life to the exploration and study of Eleusis, examined this temple minutely, cleared small sections here and there within its terrace which had been left unexcavated, removed a "marker" left by Philios some two meters in height, and reexamined the architectural fragments now to be seen. The evidence he thus collected proves that the poros blocks upon which Noack bases his pre-Persian date of Temple F actually belonged to the Peisistratean Telesterion; that they are part of the building material stored after the destruction of that Telesterion by the Persians, to be used for later construction. These blocks, therefore, do not prove that Temple F, in which they were found, was built in pre-Persian days. The available evidence proves definitely that the Temple F must belong to Roman times. In this connection we may point out that neither Philios nor Kourouniotes found among the debris of this temple any object not belonging to the Roman period. Exactly when, in the Roman era, the temple was built it is not now possible to determine; nor is it possible to know to what deity the temple was dedicated. Of course the assumption would be that it was dedicated to the Goddesses of Eleusis, but this again cannot be proved. Rubensohn's contention and Noack's supposition that

---

[39] A long bibliography has piled up for this problem of whether a temple of Demeter existed separate from the Telesterion. Cf. Mylonas, *Hymn*, pp. 28ff.

this was a temple of Demeter, built to take the place of an older temple that stood on top of the projecting spur of the hill—the first Temple of Demeter different from the Telesterion—is now untenable, since it has been proved that Temple F belongs to the Roman period and that no room is to be found for an older temple on the spur in Mycenaean times or even later.

No evidence has survived to prove that buildings, small or large, were constructed along the east or left hand side of the Sacred Way. Of course, the Sacred Way was flanked on both sides with memorials, altars, and statues standing on high, inscribed pedestals, some of which can still be seen along its course; but buildings, treasuries of the type common in Delphi, for instance, do not seem to have been built. Some 30m. from the Lesser Propylaea, the left edge of the Sacred Way of Roman times seems to have been drawn a little more to the west, thus reducing its width. At the point of the reduction stands a large boulder at the side of which a number of steps cut in the rock lead from the Sacred Way to a lower level. Perhaps these rock-cut steps served to bring the visitor or members of the personnel of the Sanctuary to the north end of the high east main court and through it to the east façade of the Telesterion where the altars were located. They may belong to the period of the rearrangement of the court and its enlargement to the east and north, to the Kimonian period. The Sacred Way finally terminated at the north side of the Telesterion, before its northeastern door.

Temple L10. On top of the northeast extremity of the hill, almost above Temple F, another temple (L10) was built in Roman times.[40] For its construction a large section of the rocky spur was hewn and leveled. Access to that level space was obtained by means of a monumental, broad stairway that closed the rock-cut terrace above the Telesterion at its northeastern end (Figs. 2 and 4, No. 28). Most of the steps of that stairway are embedded in and supported by a construction made of a strong mixture of lime, gross sand, and fragments of tiles and stone, typical of Roman Imperial times. The lower six steps have a length of 10m. and almost reach the northwest corner of the Telesterion leaving between them and that corner a narrow passage that led, as we have

[40] For a complete description, cf. *Deltion*, 15 (1933-35), pp. 66-71.

seen, to the top of the narrow rock-cut stairway No. 26. Above the sixth step is a broad landing over which seven steps were made, with the top one extending the whole length of the façade of the building.

The west section of Temple L10 is cut out of the living rock and its west wall is partially formed of hewn rock to a height of 0.80m. and the fourth century B.C. diateichisma. For the rest we have the foundations or the beds cut in the rock for the courses of the wall. Part of its pavement has survived as well as the threshold to its main room with the emplacements for the door posts.

The remains of the temple indicate a front portico and a simple cella roofed by a vault, the weight of which required thick walls, found on the west, east, and north sides averaging 2.50m. in width. The front portico had a separate roof lower than the main roof and apparently not vaulted, since the walls of the portico would not have been thick enough to support a vault. The portico seems to have been tetrastyle in antis, with perhaps four Ionic columns between the projecting ends of the side walls. In depth it is 4.55m. and the dimensions of the cella amount to 18m. x 12m. inner dimensions. Its interior walls were covered with marble revetment. The floor of the cella was paved with large rectangular slabs, some of which survive in their original position at the south-west corner. No evidence of a foundation for the support of a cult statue was found in the cella. The temple, standing on a platform some 4.10m. above the rock-cut terrace behind the Telesterion and approached from it by a monumental stairway, must have been an imposing building, strikingly Italiote in aspect.

Neither the date nor the divinity to which the temple was dedicated are certain. In general the temple can be placed in the Roman Imperial period, and it can be assumed that it was dedicated to the Goddesses of Eleusis. But we have neither inscriptions nor other evidence of a late date pointing to the existence of such temples within the Sanctuary. Rubensohn, years ago, made the happy suggestion that the temple was perhaps dedicated to Sabina, the wife of Hadrian, on whom the degenerating Greeks of the period had conferred the title of "New Demeter." The same title was conferred on Faustina, the elder, the wife of Antoninus.[41] Since we have two Roman temples almost next to each other, Temple F and Temple L10, one may well wonder whether a temple was erected to each of these empresses.

It is perhaps interesting to note that Temple L10 is not exactly aligned with the rock-cut terrace, and yet the rock was cut away expressly for the building of this temple. Why then was the temple not better aligned with the terrace? The answer seems to be that its west side had to be placed on or to the east of the diateichisma to allow the temple to be within the Sanctuary area. Apparently the diateichisma was used for its west wall not only for reasons of economy, but also because conditions described below prohibited building of the east wall beyond the point where it was built. The position of the east wall also was dictated by the terrain available. It is noticeable that in spite of its Italiote aspect, the front portico of Temple L10 lacks the depth usual to Roman temples. The ratio of the depth of the pronaos to that of the cella is 1:4, while, for example, that of the temple of Artemis Propylaia and Father Poseidon is almost 1:2. Room was available to the northeast for a longer temple that would have allowed a deeper portico. But if the length had been increased, then the width also would have had to be increased to avoid a long and narrow building. If the width had been increased, then the east wall of the temple would have had to be placed further east. The fact that the width was not increased would indicate that conditions prohibited a further expansion of the temple to the east, and the only condition that would impose that restriction is the pre-existence of Temple F below the spur over which Temple L10 was being constructed. Further, we may note that Temple L10 was oriented almost from south to north; its orientation does not conform to the general practice followed in the building of temples. Of course, in Roman times and in Roman cities orientation was not as strictly enforced as it was in Greece. But in this instance the temple was built on a Greek site where both the temple of Artemis and Temple F were oriented

---

[41] Rubensohn, *op.cit.*, p. 104. For Sabina, cf. P. Graindor, *op.cit.*, pp. 129-131. For Faustina, cf. Kaibel, *Epigr. Graeca*, No. 1046, pp. 464-467, inscription of Herodes Atticus in honor of his wife Regilla who died in A.D. 161.

from east to west. It seems to us that the pre-existence of Temple F imposed the position, the measurements, and the orientation of Temple L10, and thus prove it to be the later of the two Roman temples.

The chronological sequence of the temples makes possible their attribution. If Rubensohn's and my suggestion is permissible, that they were built in honor of the "New Demeters" Sabina and Faustina, then we may attribute Temple F to Sabina and Temple L10 to Faustina. In spite of its cramped appearance, the location of Temple F by the Sacred Way, almost in front of the northwest doorway of the Telesterion, was more desirable and would have been used first. Sabina was the elder of the two women; her temple was built first and naturally in the preferable spot. Temple L10, furthermore, seems to us to form part of the general plan that governs the rock-cut terrace and the stepped approach to it, a plan that was conceived and carried out at a time when changes were made in the Telesterion itself. We have seen that after the Kostovok destruction the hall of the Telesterion was lengthened, and the rock of the hillside was cut back some 2.15m. We may suppose that at the same time the rock-cut terrace was made and the stepped stairway and platform on either side of the west section of the Telesterion. It was then also that Temple L10 was constructed at the northeast end of the rock-cut terrace.

We may now recall that after the death of Antoninus on March 7, 161, the Senate unanimously agreed to consecrate his memory. On the base or podium supporting his column his apotheosis along with that of Faustina his wife was represented; on that monument, erected by Marcus Aurelius and Lucius Verus, his adopted sons, the deified couple are referred to as *divus* and *diva*. Again we may recall that from his deathbed Antoninus named Marcus Aurelius as his successor and ordered that the golden statue of Fortune, which stood in the Imperial bedchamber, be removed to the room of Marcus as a token of the transference of his power to his successor. Marcus, who indeed had reason to be grateful to Antoninus, in executing important works at Eleusis, restoring its Telesterion and building its Greater Propylaea, may well have conceived a plan of honoring his benefactor by erecting at Eleusis a temple to Faustina the elder, the deified wife, on whom was conferred the title of Nea

Demeter. In so doing, he followed the example set by Antoninus himself, who in A.D. 140, during his Principate, had erected a temple to the divine Faustina at the side of another Sacred Way, that in the Forum of Rome.

The Area of the South Gate. The area around the South Gate received a good deal of attention in Roman times. First of all, the threshold of the gate was raised above that of the fourth century B.C. A course of Eleusinian stones was placed on top of the old threshold and over it the new threshold was laid. On either side of the opening new parastades were built of poros stone, both of which survive (Fig. 46). Thus the opening of the gate was reduced from 3.90m. to 2.80m. Even this level was changed again within the Roman period, for a third marble threshold was placed over the second and new parastades of poros stone were added, of which the one on the right of a person entering the court still survives. With the addition of the new parastades the door opening was further reduced to about 2m. in width.

To the first Roman construction period, to which the second intermediary threshold belongs, we must assign the two lateral walls erected immediately in front of its inner face. These walls formed a corridor (11.50m. x ca. 4m.) with one set of pilasters constructed at its beginning and another midway (Fig. 4, No. 33), dividing the corridor into two sections, apparently not separated by doors. At the south end of the corridor about 1.10m. from the gate a passage through the east wall led to the room in the square tower K6. The floor level of the corridor, of course, was raised from time to time.[42]

The Bouleuterion. On either side of the corridor important buildings were constructed at this time. To the east one and perhaps two buildings were erected over the foundations of the fourth century Council House.[43] The interior row of columns of a large stoa is clearly marked by the foundations. This stoa seems to have had a length equal to that of the early Council House (34m. inner dimensions) but a depth of only some 9m., with the inner colonnade 6m. from its rear wall. To the second structure belong the founda-

[42] A. Skias, *Praktika*, 1895, pp. 178-180. The fourth century level was found 0.90m. below that of the latest Roman period.
[43] *Ibid.*, pp. 182-191. Our Figure 4, No. 31.

tions of two concentric semicircular walls which take up the area of the central and the west room of the Council House. Only scanty remains of the foundations of the outer semicircle have survived; the inner is stepped and its steps, preserved to a height of 0.36m. above the floor of the structure, are made of grayish marble. The opening of the outer semicircle had a façade with two antae at the ends and five columns between. The relation of the stoa to the semicircular foundations is not certain. It is generally believed that the stoa was built first; that later it was destroyed and was replaced by a structure like an odeion with seats arranged on a semicircular plan and reaching from the front to the rear of the building.[44] Skias maintained that stoa and semicircular walls go together and belong to one building, which had just two rows of seats in front of the inner colonnade. Perhaps the idea of the odeion-shaped structure used as a City Council is preferable. Fragments of unfluted, monolithic columns of white marble with Ionic capitals found in the area probably belong to this building, of which the architrave bore an inscription of Late Roman times. At the two ends of the opening of the inner semicircle are two pedestals (Fig. 4, No. 34), evidently later additions to the façade of the building. The statues which supposedly stood on them have not survived. By the eastern pedestal was erected a small water basin.

To the west of the corridor in Late Roman times a short, broad stoa was constructed. Its plan is clear, although in mediaeval times a building (19m. x 12m.) was constructed over it destroying its superstructure. Its well-preserved front supported five columns between antae, of which the base of the column farthest west and the west anta are *in situ*. Its unfluted columns were of grayish marble; their bases seem to have been made of white marble. Of the inner colonnade only the stylobate remains. The inscriptions cut on the drums of the columns place the stoa in the Roman period—the period, according to Skias, of the construction of the Lesser Propylaea. Beyond this portico to the west another stoa seems to have existed, but its remains are too scanty to permit the restoration of its plan.

Dwellings. The Roman period was one of prosperity and apparently of increased population. Buildings were constructed beyond

[44] W. McDonald, *The Political Places of the Greeks*, pp. 188-189.

the fortified area; some were to serve the pilgrims as hostels over the comparatively short period of the celebration of the Mysteries, others to be used as residences of wealthy citizens. Thus villas were built in the neighborhood of the Sanctuary, surrounded with gardens, and provided with floors paved with mosaics and walls covered with murals. An occasional lucky find has indicated the position of some of these but, unfortunately, it has not become possible as yet to excavate a single villa. A very sumptuous home of Roman date (26.50m. x 13.50m.) was cleared by Kourouniotes in the south slope of the hill immediately below the Peisistratean city wall (Fig. 4, L30, see left margin of plan).[45] The rock cut vertically and the Peisistratean peribolos above it form the north wall of the house; the south wall, built over the slope was strengthened by buttresses. On that side and in front of the house proper a terrace may have served as a small garden. Almost in the middle of the house was the atrium with an impluvium in its center made of marble. On the east side of the atrium a long and narrow corridor indicates the area of the stairway that led to the second story. On the other sides are located a number of small rectangular rooms. With the exception of the room faced with marble slabs in the northeast corner, the walls of the rooms were covered with painted plaster. The floors of the rooms, as well as the atrium, were covered with mosaics of Geometric patterns.

Mithraion. Eleusis apparently felt the impact of foreign cults, especially that of Mithras, towards the very end of its life. We have already seen how the last Hierophant from Thisbe was also a priest of Mithras. Perhaps to him we may attribute the Mithraion which Kourouniotes uncovered to the south of the "Sacred House" (Fig. 4, No. L31). The Mithraion adjoins a large square structure of Late Roman times (Fig. 4, No. L32) with a central court surrounded by rooms on four sides and a small propylon in front. Its purpose is not known, but it may have been a gymnasium.

Water Supply and Bridge over the Kephisos. To Roman Imperial times, most probably to the days of Hadrian, belong the large brick cisterns built against the east side of the Periklean and fourth century peribolos walls of the Sanctuary (Fig. 4, No. 43).

---

[45] K. Kourouniotes, *Praktika*, 1936, pp. 34-40. The mosaics of the rooms are now covered with sand for protection.

Only the rectangular chambers of the tanks survive, but originally the façades, with their marble revetments and ornamental spouts, must have been imposing. Hadrian is reputed to have constructed the aqueduct which brought water to the city from the neighboring hills. Of that aqueduct nothing survives today.

Hadrian obtained the gratitude of the Eleusinians by attending to another of their great needs that had to do with Kephisos, the river flowing a short distance to the east of their city. Today we can hardly detect this river, but in antiquity apparently it was a turbulent torrent. Demosthenes speaks of the havoc wrought by its floods to the fields of Eleusis.[46] Apparently after one of these destructive floods Hadrian, who was wintering in Athens and had recently been initiated into the Mysteries, caused embankments to be raised along the course of the river for the protection of the fields against its sudden inundations. Remains of one of the embankments were seen by the Dilettanti, Leake, and other early travelers, and could still be seen until recently.[47] They have disappeared since the area was transformed into an airfield.

Hadrian, however, seems not to have been satisfied with this great contribution to the well-being of the Eleusinians. The hazard to the pilgrims of the sudden inundations of the torrent necessitated the construction of a bridge over its course. From an inscription we learn that in the last quarter of the fourth century B.C. a certain Xenokles constructed at his own expense a stone bridge for the safety of the crowd of initiates coming to the Sanctuary at Eleusis, and also for the safety of the Eleusinians themselves.[48] Remains of an old stone bridge near Eleusis and over the old bed of Kephisos were noted by Philios in 1892.[49] They were to be seen besides the well, known to the modern Eleusinians as the Fair Well or Kalo Peghadi. Philios believed that the bridge belonged to Hellenistic times, that it was perhaps the one built by Xenokles. The same opinion was held by Kourouniotes, who cleared a good deal of it and found out that it was made up of a number of arches

[46] LV, 28, p. 1279.

[47] Frazer, *Pausanias*, II, p. 501. *Unedited Antiquities*, p. 5. Leake, *Athens*, II, pp. 139, 154ff.

[48] *Ephem*, 1892, pp. 101ff.

[49] D. Philios, *Ephem*, 1892, p. 106, and *Eleusis*, p. 106.

and was built of poros stone, carefully fitted.[50] The final clearing of the bridge was effected by Travlos[51] who determined that its length is 50m. and its width 5.30m., that it is made up of four arches, that the span of the central one is the largest, amounting to 6.90m., while the side arches have a span of 4.30m. The bed of the river under the bridge was paved with large rectangular blocks and this pavement acted as a footing for the arches. The pavement and the footing were constructed of hard Peiraeus poros stone. The workmanship is excellent, and this led both Philios and Kourouniotes to attribute the bridge to Hellenistic times. However, the use of lime in its construction, the form of the clamps employed, and the many Roman numerals cut on its blocks prove that it was built in Roman times. Since the numerals are identical with those found on the blocks of Hadrian's Library in Athens, it is apparent that the bridge over the Kephisos of Eleusis was constructed by that Emperor. This agrees with the ancient testimony that Hadrian after his initiation built a bridge over the Kephisos of Eleusis.[52] It was probably built A.D. 124 or 125.

Other public buildings in Eleusis are known to us only from inscriptions or literary references. Pausanias mentions the temple of Triptolemos, his threshing floor, and his altar,[53] and we hear of a theater and a stadium where athletic events were held at fixed intervals and in which the victors were given barley as a prize. The shrines mentioned by Pausanias have not been found, and the location of the theater and the stadium indicated in our Figure 32 is only conjectural.

Burials. The west cemetery of Eleusis was in use during Hellenistic and Roman times, but it seems to have served the poorer citizens. The graves we found contained but few vases, and in Roman times mostly small glass bottles of the type known as tear pots; in these the tears of the mourners presumably were stored and placed in the graves. The types of the graves also were limited to tile graves or mere rectangular trenches. The wealthy perhaps were buried in the cemetery toward Athens and for them more

[50] K. Kourouniotes, *Eleusiniaka*, I, p. 237 n. 1, where the master expressed his intention of turning over the designing of the bridge to a trained architect. His intentions were fulfilled by Dr. Travlos.

[51] *Praktika*, 1950, pp. 122-127.

[52] P. Graindor, *op.cit.*, p. 35, where bibliography.

[53] Pausanias, I, 38, 6.

sumptuous graves were constructed. Such a built grave we cleared in the gardens of the late Korizes,[54] and from even a more sumptuous grave comes the sarcophagus exhibited in the yard of the Museum (Fig. 82). That it is not a unique example of a sarcophagus burial is proved by the lid, which does not belong to it but to another sarcophagus destroyed perhaps in the course of the centuries. Burials in sarcophagi were not unknown in the Classical era. We have found a number of sarcophagi from that era in the west cemetery, but they are undecorated and are made of poros stone. In Roman times as a rule marble was employed and the sarcophagi were covered with reliefs. The example in the court of the Museum, from around A.D. 190, is a good sample of the type employed in Roman Imperial times. It is interesting to note that no Christian burials were found in the west cemetery. Evidently it was abandoned when Christianity prevailed in the district; by that time the area of the Sanctuary was used for burials. A number of Christian graves were found along the side of the cisterns constructed against the fourth century wall from tower K7 to I12. Interestingly enough, in some of these Early Christian graves, built of brick, we found a number of clay vases indicating the continuation of the habit of supplying the dead with funeral gifts.

Those Christian graves symbolize the end of the life of the Sanctuary of Demeter. When the walls of the Sanctuary were ruined by the hordes of Alaric in A.D. 395, they were apparently left in their ruinous state. No Emperor was there with the desire to rebuild them; no statesman had the ambition to restore "the temenos of the world"; there was no priesthood powerful enough and respected enough to impose its will and its desire, no multitude of grateful initiates to contribute to the rebirth of the shrine. The Emperor was now a Christian who had proclaimed dire measures against the mystic cults; the leaders of Athens and its people were no longer worshipers of the Olympian Gods; the cities of Greece had stopped sending their tithes to Eleusis and the source of inspiration provided by the cult had dried up. A new religion controlled the minds and actions of men. The old pagan rites must go and their shrines must be buried in their own debris. It was so decreed; it so happened.

[54] G. E. Mylonas, *Deltion*, 14 (1931-32), Parartema, pp. 41ff.

CHAPTER VIII

ART AND ELEUSIS

THE STORY OF Demeter and Persephone is rich in elements appealing to the sculptor and the painter. Since the famous Sanctuary was crowded with dedications, most of them executed by artists, we would naturally assume the existence of a multitude of works of art inspired by the Eleusinian myth and forming part of the Eleusinian offerings. Unfortunately the Sanctuary was emptied of its treasures before it was completely destroyed and abandoned, and amid its ruins the excavators found comparatively few works of art. Most of these are now in the small Museum of Eleusis. However, works of art were made for other shrines of the Goddesses all over the Hellenic world and artists continued to depict various aspects of the myth throughout the ages. It is not our purpose, in the present general account of Eleusis, to give either a full description or a complete catalogue of the works of art dealing with our site and its Goddesses to be seen in museums the world over.[1] We plan only to discuss briefly a selection of such works as have been found at Eleusis and are now exhibited in its Museum, and a few others not at that site but important for the cult of Demeter. We purposely avoided the discussion of the majority of these art objects in the course of our description of the architectural remains so as not to interrupt the continuous flow of the description. We discuss them here before our account of what we can know of the Mysteries because we do not want that story interrupted or burdened with the current conflicting interpretations of some of these works of art. Of the objects found at the site we shall mention only the most important and our discussions will not be exhaustive but will aim at giving some basic information perhaps useful to the visitor of the site and to the general student. Fuller accounts

[1] Dr. Betty Grossman, of the City Art Museum of St. Louis, has completed a doctoral thesis on the Gods and Heroes of Eleusis in Greek Art, which gives a full account of the works of art inspired by or made for Eleusis and its Sanctuary.

The present arrangement of objects at the Museum of Eleusis was made after the second world war by the then Ephor of the district and now General Director of Antiquities, Dr. John Papademetriou, to whom are due many thanks.

of course will be found in the studies mentioned in the footnotes and in the bibliography.

THE SCULPTURES IN THE MUSEUM

It is remarkable indeed that we have no definite conception of the cult statues of Eleusis. What were they like? That they were different from the articles contained in the Hiera kept in the Anaktoron is indicated by the fact that the latter were carried by the priestesses at least across the bridge of the Rheitoi, and by the fact that the objects forming the Hiera could not be seen by the uninitiated. On both accounts statuary is excluded since statues are too heavy to be carried by priestesses and have to be made in a studio where they can be seen.[2] Yet cult statues must have existed at Eleusis, for a temple without its cult statues would have been inconceivable. We hear that in some places the cult statues of the Goddesses not only could not be named, but they could not be viewed by the worshipers.[3] The Attik workshops of the second half of the fifth and of the fourth centuries seem to have specialized in the making of cult statues; but among those produced by such creators of Gods as Pheidias and Praxiteles, we shall search in vain for the Goddesses of Eleusis. A good many of the Gods are represented on the sculptures of the Parthenon; from these our Goddesses seem to be missing although often enough certain figures are identified on insufficient evidence as Demeter and Persephone.[4]

Ancient sources mention the appearance in temples in other parts of the Greek world of what could be considered cult statues of Demeter and Persephone; and we also have references simply to sculptured representations of the Goddesses.[5] To the first category belongs the magnificent statue of Demeter from Knidos in the

[2] L. R. Farnell, *The Cults of the Greek States*, III, p. 266, pointed out that sculptors would not dare represent the "chief idols" of the Mysteries, and that consequently all efforts to identify them are useless.

[3] At Hermione no one but the priestesses was allowed to see the statue of Demeter according to Pausanias, II, 35, 8. Also the temple of Demeter and Kore on the Akrocorinth did not have "the statues exposed to view," Pausanias, II, 4, 7.

[4] The two seated female statues from the East Pediment of the Parthenon are so labeled in the British Museum; more probably, however, they are representations of the *Horai* or Seasons, the guardians of the Gates of Olympos. On similar identifications, cf. Farnell, *op.cit.*, pp. 261ff.

[5] Pausanias, I, 2, 4; II, 13, 5; II, 34, 8. Pliny, *Nat.Hist.*, 36, 5, 23, mentions a group of Flora (Kore?), Triptolemos, and Demeter in the gardens of Servilius.

British Museum,[6] the most moving example of the *Mater Dolorosa* of antiquity. In the latter category we should perhaps include the statues of Demeter and Persephone in the Museum of Eleusis and other similar examples. It is undoubtedly true that statues of the Goddesses existed at Eleusis and some may have been set in the Telesterion, as the bases noted by Travlos indicate. A special priest, known as the *Phaethyntes*, looked after them.[7] Rubensohn has very ingeniously suggested that the phiale mentioned in the inscription published by Kourouniotes belonged to a statue of the Goddess in the Telesterion.[8] A statue of a seated Demeter holding a winnowing fan on her lap and a phiale in her left hand has been found in the Agora of Athens and the seated Demeter of the Niinnion plate is holding a phiale in her right hand.[9] The statues, however, could have been votive offerings. Pedestals found all over the Sanctuary prove that offerings of works of art were placed in its courts and some must have been placed in the Telesterion itself. The walls of that temple, or even the exterior of the Anaktoron were perhaps adorned with votive reliefs and paintings. We read, for example, in an inscription of the first half of the second century B.C. set up in honor of Satyra, a priestess of the Thesmophoroi . . . that in recognition of services rendered the people decreed to "bestow upon her the crown of myrtle . . . and to grant her the right to set up a painted portrait (of herself) in the temple of Demeter and Kore in accordance with the privilege bestowed upon other priestesses."[10] Art objects such as the Grand Relief of Eleusis (Fig. 68) and the Niinnion tablet (Fig. 88) could very well have been placed on the walls of the Telesterion or on the exterior of the Anaktoron. But the statues and other works of art from the Sanctuary that we may know represent the Goddesses without their

[6] A. H. Smith, *Catalogue of Greek Sculpture in the British Museum*, II, No. 1300. G. M. A. Richter, *The Sculpture and Sculptors of the Greeks*, pp. 46, 104, 147 and fig. 315. B. Ashmole, "Demeter of Cnidus," *JHS*, 71 (1951), pp. 13ff, and pls. I-VII, where bibliography.

[7] The *Phaethyntes* was not entrusted with the care of the *Hiera* because he could not enter the Anaktoron where they were kept.

[8] K. Kourouniotes, *Deltion*, 10 (1926), p. 145; O. Rubensohn, *Jahrbuch*, 70 (1955), p. 39, and *AA*, 48 (1933), pp. 324ff.

[9] T. L. Shear, *Hesperia*, 7 (1938), pp. 352-353. Demeter holds a phiale on a relief from the Agora, H. A. Thompson, *Hesperia*, 17 (1948), pp. 177-178, pls. 54, 2. Also on the Niinnion tablet (Fig. 88).

[10] O. Broneer, *Hesperia*, 11 (1942), pp. 265-267.

mystic emblems and apparently as regular Olympian divinities. Could any of them have been cult statues? We cannot answer this question conclusively; it is safer to maintain that we do not know definitely the appearance of the cult statues in the Telesterion of Eleusis.

Years ago Otto Kern very ingeniously figured out that the cult statues of Eleusis represented a Demeter seated on her cylindrical kiste with Persephone standing by her side.[11] He based his conclusion on reliefs from Eleusis on which the Goddesses are so represented, suggesting that they reflected the monumental cult group. Very important among the examples cited by him is the fragment illustrated in Figure 63. It is exhibited now against the east wall of the hall of the Museum of Eleusis. Demeter is seated on her kiste, dressed in chiton and peplos, with Persephone similarly clothed standing beside her. Unfortunately the hands of Persephone are missing, but perhaps she was holding her characteristic torches as we see her in other representations. The fragment stands 0.47m. high and was carved in the fourth century B.C. Of course it lacks the impressiveness and beauty of monumental sculpture but it is interesting as illustrating a type. This arrangement of the two Goddesses is to be found on other objects of art such as the relief placed over one of the building inscriptions found in the Sanctuary and now exhibited in the third South Room of the Museum (Fig. 64). In this example Demeter, seated on her kiste, gives instructions to a standing man, perhaps the personification of the people of Eleusis, of the demos, regarding building activities. This reflects the tradition contained in the Homeric Hymn of her command to the Eleusinians to build her a temple. Behind her stands Persephone holding aloft two burning torches. Perhaps Kern is right that the cult statues of Eleusis were composed of a seated Demeter and a

---

[11] O. Kern, "Das Kustbild der Göttinnen von Eleusis," *AM*, 17 (1892), pp. 125-142, where all examples found at Eleusis especially are discussed. For other examples cf. W. Froehner, *Notice de la sculpture antique du Musée de Louvre*, p. 24, No. 5. T. A. Overbeck, *Griechische Kunstmythologie*, II, p. 509, No. 6; *Atlas*, XIV, 6, and XIV, 25. On the basis of Kern's work R. von Schneider and especially Max Ruhland (*Die Eleusinischen Göttinnen*) tried to identify the statues of Demeter in various museums. But the characteristics they find are common to all statues of the fifth century and consequently cannot be conceived as peculiar to the representation of the divinities of Eleusis.

Persephone standing by her mother with torches; but certainty on this matter is impossible.

The oldest extant representation of Demeter in sculpture, at least from Eleusis, is on a marble stele (0.78m. x 0.56m. x 0.09-0.12m.) exhibited now in the north room of the Museum of Eleusis against its east wall (Fig. 67).[12] Demeter, wearing a high polos, a sleeveless chiton and a thicker peplos or overgarment, is seated on a throne with her feet on a stool. She holds a scepter in the left hand and stalks of wheat in the right. Her loose hair falls over her shoulders as a symbol of her grief, as described in the Hymn.[13] A maiden approaches her, dressed in a sleeveless Ionic chiton and stole with her hair carefully pressed in a coif, and holding lighted torches.[14] One of these is in an almost horizontal position while the other is held aloft. The maiden is barefoot like Demeter. In spite of the archaic shortcomings, the work is crisp and sensitive and already conveys an air of Attik charm. The solemnity of the occasion is reflected in the attitude of both figures but the benevolence of the mother Goddess is evident.

The standing figure has been generally accepted as the Kore-Persephone, although Ruhland long ago suggested that perhaps it represented a priestess.[15] If the standing figure is Persephone, our relief would represent the reunion of mother and daughter. The throne on which Demeter is seated, instead of on the usual kiste or on the "Mirthless Stone," indicates that she is seated in the interior of her temple. We fail, however, to find the joyful air such a reunion would produce. The seated mother seems aloof and still under the spell of her grief; besides the size of the maiden would cast doubt on the identification. She is approaching barefooted; that was perhaps a requirement of the mystai. We know that in the celebration of the Mysteries in Andania the participants had to attend barefooted,[16] and we shall find them barefoot in the

[12] It was found by Philios in 1894 in the auxiliary area B, cf. *AM*, 20 (1895), pp. 245-255 and pl. 5.

[13] Vv. 279, 302.

[14] The women of red figure representations painted by Hieron and Brygos wear garments similarly arranged.

[15] M. Ruhland, *op.cit.*, p. 60.

[16] *Sylloge*⁴, vol. 2, No. 736, l. 16: οἱ τελούμενοι τά μυστήρια ἀνυπόδετοι ἔστωσαν; cf. the sacred law of Lykosoura, *Ephem*, 1898, p. 249, and L. Deubner, *Attische Feste*, p. 78.

stamnos of Eleusis to be studied shortly. We would expect Persephone to wear sandals since she had come a long distance. Demeter
is represented barefoot because she is in her temple.[17] I believe
that another divinity active in the myth will fit the representation
better. Besides Demeter and Persephone, Hekate figures in the
drama. She, with torches in her hands, was the first to approach the
sorrowing mother with soothing words; she was the first to join
in the rejoicing of the reunion of mother and daughter; the first
to embrace Persephone returned from the lower world—to "embrace the daughter of holy Demeter": and from that time "the
lady Hekate became the minister and companion of Persephone."
Hekate, who is often represented holding lighted torches, is
approaching the Mother in a worshipful attitude and, in a respectful gesture of greeting to a superior Goddess, she has lowered one
of her torches. The stele must be placed in post-Persian times,
perhaps about 480/475 B.C.

To the same general era, although a little earlier, can be attributed the fleeing maiden from the pedimental decoration of the
Peisistratean structure in the temenos of the "Hiera Oikia" (Fig.
34). We have already mentioned this beautiful statue[18] now exhibited in the north room of the Museum of Eleusis. As we have
seen, it dates from the years immediately before the destruction of
the Sanctuary by the Persians, a little before 480 B.C.

To the Periklean age and the period of the activity of Pheidias
belongs the "Grand Relief of Eleusis" (Fig. 68). It was found by
Philios in the pavement of the Chapel of St. Zacharias some 100
yards to the east of the outer court of the Sanctuary area.[19] Fortunately the modeling was placed face down and so it is well preserved. The original is in the National Museum at Athens; a
plaster cast is exhibited in the Museum of Eleusis against the north
wall of the hall. It is generally agreed that the famous mission of

[17] The contrast in the quality of the garments has been noted before. In sculptured works from the middle of the fifth century B.C. onward the elegant clothes
are worn by the Kore. Here we have the opposite. If we interpret the figure correctly as Hekate, there is no reversal or strangeness in her less elegant garment,
since she is a minor divinity.

[18] *Supra*, p. 102.

[19] G. M. A. Richter, *op.cit.*, pp. 169, 180, 231. Lately, R. R. Holloway, *AJA*,
62 (1958), pp. 404-408, who dates it 440/430 B.C. It is a large stele of pentelic
marble measuring 2.20m. x 1.55m., perhaps the largest relief known from Classical
Greece. The work is in low relief.

Triptolemos is depicted on the relief.[20] The hero stands between the Goddesses in the form of a young boy; and he is so represented either because all mortals in the sight of the Gods are but children, or because he had to be young to be able to accomplish his long mission, or because of the general tendency of classical art to reduce to youthful figures the heroes of the past. He wears sandals, indicative of his journey, and holds his mantle over his right shoulder. Demeter, with hair loose and flowing, holds a scepter and hands him the miraculous seeds destined to bring to mankind plentiful harvests and a civilized life. Behind him stands Persephone holding her torch and placing a wreath on his head; the wreath was originally represented in color now completely gone.

The dignity of the composition can hardly be surpassed. We seem to find ourselves before a sacramental rite performed with solemnity and religious grandeur. The artist has differentiated the Goddesses superbly: their clothes, their stance, their coiffure are characteristic of each. It is no wonder the relief has often been attributed to Pheidias, the great master of the Classical period. It has been variously dated from 450 B.C. to 430 B.C., but I am inclined to place it around 445 B.C.

The relief on the upper part of the famous inscription of the Rheitoi (Fig. 69),[21] in the north room of the Museum of Eleusis, is interesting both as a piece of sculpture and as an example of the inscribed decrees dealing with building activities in the Sanctuary. The lower part of the inscription is missing. On its upper register we find at one end Demeter pulling her peplos over her left shoulder, followed by Persephone holding her lighted torches, one of which she has turned towards the earth. The personification of the people of Eleusis, of Demos, is greeted by the helmeted Athena. Perhaps this is a symbolic representation of the eternal friendship that binds together Athens and Eleusis. Persephone is identified by her torches and Athena by her helmet. The relief was

[20] For the story cf. *supra*, p. 20. The relief was interpreted differently by Svoronos (Τὸ ἐθνικὸν μουσεῖον, p. 106), but his views were not accepted.

[21] D. Philios, *AM*, 19 (1894), pp. 163-193. The turning of the torch towards the earth may here indicate the purification and fertilization of the earth by fire. It is interesting to compare the figure of Demeter of this relief with the statue of Demeter attributed to Agorakritos and exhibited in the hall of the Museum; they apparently belong to the same type. Dimensions: height 0.90m., width 0.57m.

carved around 421 B.C., which is the date of the inscription, sixteen lines of which are preserved on the lower section of the broken stele.

In the same north room is exhibited a stele of Pentelic marble (0.57m. x 0.31m.) showing Persephone perhaps acting as a *Hydranos*, an official whose office was to purify the initiates by sprinkling water over their heads (Fig. 70).[22] The Goddess, wearing a chiton and a peplos in her characteristic manner, stands majestically holding a phiale in her right hand from which she pours water over a youthful nude figure. The phiale, or shallow bowl used especially in libations, was made of a different piece of marble or of other material and has been lost. The initiate by her side is rendered in small scale as befits a mortal. The charm of the composition is ruined by the difference in the scale employed in the rendering of the figures. Its interest lies in the information it conveys regarding the rite of purification by water rather than in its artistic merit. The relief was perhaps carved in the first half of the fourth century B.C.[23]

Demeter is represented in a monumental statue now standing almost in the middle of the hall of the Museum of Eleusis.[24] Unfortunately the head and hands are missing, but the rest of the statue is well preserved (Fig. 75). It is of Pentelic marble and somewhat over life size. The Goddess, wearing a sleeveless Ionic chiton and a Doric peplos, was apparently represented with her left hand lifting the edge of her peplos over her left shoulder in the characteristic manner illustrated in Figure 69; the right arm seems to have been extended along the side of the body and perhaps in that hand the Goddess held the edge of her peplos the other end of which can be seen by her right foot. The work is typical of the second half of the fifth century B.C.; the way the chiton falls below the waist in deep parallel grooves, contrasting

---

[22] K. Kourouniotes, *Guide*, p. 19, fig. 7. L. Deubner, *op.cit.*, pl. 6, No. 3. Note the arrangement of the peplos of Persephone.

[23] In the same north room are also exhibited the ram's head from the Peisistratean Telesterion (*supra*, p. 80), set over the restored corner of that temple by Dr. J. Papademetriou; the torsos of two archaic Kouroi; a relief in which we have an interesting representation of a battle between cavalry and infantry in two registers; a huge cinerary amphora of the Geometric period with an interesting aquatic bird painted on its neck.

[24] G. M. A. Richter, *op.cit.*, p. 106, fig. 325; S. Reinach, *Repertoir*, II, p. 242, No. 4. Height of the statue as exhibited is 1.80m.

with the delicate modeling of the V-shaped folds over the chest, the easy stance and the breath of life which seems to animate the marble, the quality of the chiton, not completely diaphanous, which nevertheless allows the plasticity of the body underneath to be felt and seen are characteristic of that period. The statue must have been the work of a good sculptor of the Athenian school, and it or its original has been attributed to Agorakritos, the pupil of Pheidias. If it is a copy, then it must be a very early one almost contemporary with the original; we are inclined to consider it an original.

In the hall of the Museum against its south wall stands a statue of Persephone, also headless (Fig. 76). It is of Roman date, perhaps a copy of a Greek original, made of pentelic marble and preserved to a height of 1.50m. Comparison with the statue of Demeter just discussed will illustrate remarkably well the difference we often find between an original and a copy. Persephone is clothed in a chiton and a peplos arranged in a manner typical of the representations of the Goddess. Perhaps in her right hand she held a torch. She stands in a rather lifeless manner and without the charm that usually characterizes the Kore of the Greek sculptors and painters. That it reproduces an original well-known to the ancients is indicated by its similarity to the representation of Persephone on the relief illustrated in Figure 74, to that on the relief with a sacrifice in the Louvre, and to the statue of Kore in the Galleria degli Uffizi.[25]

The two Goddesses are represented on a number of reliefs of the fourth and later centuries B.C. exhibited in the Museum of Eleusis. Common, but of interest, are the reliefs representing the *apostole* or the mission of Triptolemos. One of the best preserved examples of this type we illustrate in Figure 74. The stele is broken in two main parts and its pieces were found by Philios in 1885 in two different areas; the smaller fragment was found in the Ploutonion, the larger in area B.[26] In the "Grand Relief of Eleusis" (Fig. 68) we have the entrusting of the seeds to a boyish Triptolemos; in the present relief his mission is represented. In the former

[25] Compare our figs. 69 and 70. Overbeck, *op.cit.*, II, 509, No. 4; *Atlas*, XIV, 2T. G. E. Rizzo, *Passitele*, pls. CLI and CLIV, a.

[26] D. Philios, *AM*, 20 (1895), pp. 255-266, pl. VI. The relief measures 1.23m. x 0.75m. Other examples of the mission are exhibited on the north and east walls of the hall.

the figures were placed on the slab without marginal embellishment; here the slab of Pentelic marble is given the form of a *naiskos* or shrine with a roof structure supported by antae at the two ends. Within this frame is the figure composition. A youthful Triptolemos, apparently holding a scepter in his raised left hand, is seated on a winged chariot in the form of a throne, pulled by dragons. The wheel of the chariot, perhaps made of bronze, was secured in the deep cavity around which the dragon is coiled. Demeter stands in front of the hero and Persephone behind him. The Kore is holding aloft burning torches. It is impossible to define the objects, if any, held by her mother, but perhaps she held a phiale and an oenochoe in a manner similar to that found on contemporary vase paintings. The divinities are being approached by worshipers, apparently the members of the family that dedicated the relief. It is interesting to note again the contrast in appearance of the two Goddesses—the mature Demeter and the more elegant young Persephone; the garments with their individual and characteristic arrangement and apparent difference in quality. Triptolemos also presents an interesting contrast to the bearded representations on vases that appear for the first time in the second half of the sixth century. Now he is youthful and of a type envisaged by the artist of the "Grand Relief." There is a difference of opinion among scholars as to whether the departure or the return of Triptolemos is represented on the relief. The youthful appearance of our hero would argue for a departure in spite of his throne-like seat that could be taken to indicate the final rest from his labors. The addition of the missing wheel would reduce considerably the suggestion of the throne and affirm its similarity to the chariot represented on a hydria from Rhodes now in the Archaeological Museum of Istanbul.[27] In our relief we find another important suggestion; it seems to indicate that already at the beginning of the fourth century the hero was included in the circle of divinities to be worshiped. The quality of the modeling, the graceful poses of the figures, the delightful contrasts, the harmonious grouping of

[27] Cf. Farnell, *op.cit.*, pl. xxi. J. E. Harrison, *Prolegomena to the Study of the Greek Religion*, fig. 151. M. P. Nilsson, *ArchRW*, 32 (1935), pp. 95-96, and *Geschichte der gr. Religion*, I, pl. 44, No. 1.

the divinities place this relief in the opening years of the fourth century B.C.[28]

The story of Triptolemos in his chariot, which seems to appear first in sculpture in the fourth century, was very popular with the vase painters long before that date. In the Archaic period (ca. 700-510 B.C.) we find him, as noted above, represented on vases of the black-figure style as a bearded man, heavily dressed, seated on a simplified chariot usually without wings or dragons, holding a scepter and stalks of wheat.[29] In the Transitional period (ca. 510-450 B.C.) the story became popular with the vase painter, perhaps because of its use by Sophokles in a tragedy known as *Triptolemos.* From that period we have at least forty-nine vases on which the hero is depicted.[30] Triptolemos' story continued to be popular with the vase painters of the Classical period (450-400 B.C.) from which we have at least thirty-two examples.[31] We have fewer examples from the fourth century and more elaborate rendering, but at this point the story was taken up by sculptors. There are fewer representations of the story in the Hellenistic and later periods, but the subject was not altogether abandoned as we can judge from the large but fragmentary relief mounted against the west wall of the hall of the Museum of Eleusis (Fig. 71).

It is known as the relief of Lakratides, because it was dedicated by a priest of that name on behalf of himself and the members of his family who are represented as votaries. Fortunately the fragments that survive are sufficient to give us a general idea of its subject.[32] At the left corner we find the seated Demeter (Fig. 71, 2), wearing her peplos over her head and presumably handing

[28] It should be noted that the right shoulder of the male votaries is nude. Perhaps this was a required arrangement for the himation of worshipers.

[29] A good illustration of the bearded Triptolemos is to be seen on the black-figure amphora, formerly in the Lenormant collection, illustrated by E. Gerhard, *Auserlesene Vasenbilder,* I, pl. 49 and M. P. Nilsson, *Greek Popular Religion,* fig. 19.

[30] This number is taken from Dr. Grossman's lists. On the other hand Sophokles' *Triptolemos* may reflect the popularity of the story in his period.

[31] According to Dr. Grossman's lists.

[32] The fragments were found by Philios in the Ploutonion and were described by him in *Ephem,* 1886, pp. 19-31, pl. 3. Cf. R. Heberdy, "Das Weiherelief des Lakrateides aus Eleusis," *Festschrift Benndorf,* pp. 111-116 and pl. 4. J. Svoronos, *JIAN,* 4 (1901), pp. 487ff, where a restored drawing of relief. K. Kourouniotes, *Guide,* fig. 30. A. W. Lawrence, *Later Greek Sculpture,* pl. 79.

stalks of wheat to a youthful Triptolemos seated in his winged chariot (Fig. 71, 5). Between them stands Persephone-Kore holding lighted torches and facing the Mother (Fig. 71, 3). A bearded Plouton, holding a scepter, stands behind Kore (Fig. 71, 4) and then two divinities, one standing the other seated, identified by the inscription as Goddess, Thea, and God, Theos (Fig. 71, 6 and 7); apparently Persephone and Plouton again as the Gods of the lower world.[33] On either side of the Gods we have Lakratides (Fig. 71, 8) and the members of his family. His young sons, Sostratos and Dionysios (Fig. 71, 1 and 9), are represented in the guise of Iacchos and hold in their hands stalks of wheat, apparently the dragmata, the handful of civilized nourishment, that each initiate had to bring to the Sanctuary at the time of his initiation. The relief dates from ca. 100-90 B.C. to judge from its inscriptions.

The divine figures on this great relief are identified by their names carved against the background. That the words Theos, God, and Thea, Goddess, indicated Plouton and Persephone in their aspect as the rulers of the lower world is proved by another relief from the fourth century known as the Lysimachides relief, found also by Philios in the Ploutonion and now in the National Museum of Athens.[34] In that relief two different scenes are represented, each occupying half of the length of the slab. On the right half we find the god and goddess of the lower world seated at a banquet. Inscribed over their heads are simply Theos and Thea. Like many other people, the Greeks in the early years of their cultural activity avoided naming the dreaded Gods of the lower world. This early custom emerged sometimes in later years. The left half of the relief depicts another banquet scene with Demeter and Persephone as protagonists. The whole subject is meant to stand for the reconciliation of the divinities involved in the myth.

On his relief Lakratides states that he is the priest of Theos and Thea, of Eubouleus and Demeter and of the other Gods who share the same altar. We have seen that Theos and Thea were

[33] Svoronos, *loc.cit.*, identified the God and the Goddess as Asklepios and Hygeia (Health) but others see in them the original divinities of Eleusis who were displaced by Demeter. Cf. P. Foucart, "Recherches sur l'origine et la nature des Mystères d'Éleusis," *Memoirs de l'Academie*, 35 (1895). However, no tradition exists of such a displacement. H. Von Prott, *AM*, 24 (1899), pp. 262-263.

[34] D. Philios, *Ephem*, 1886, pl. 3. L. R. Farnell, *op.cit.*, pl. 1.

Plouton and Persephone, but who was Eubouleus? His identity is still a matter of controversy, but I prefer to see in him the Chthonian (or underworld) Zeus, an aspect of the Father of Gods and Men that is somewhat rare. What is of interest to us at present is that in the Ploutonion Philios found a somewhat battered head that has been identified as Eubouleus (Fig. 65).[35] It is of Pentelic marble and has been attributed to Leochares, to Euphranor, and even to Praxiteles, the great master of the fourth century B.C. Most probably it is a later copy of a fourth century original. That it was known and admired in antiquity is indicated by the fact that at least ten copies of the original have survived. One of these, an unfinished head, was discovered in 1959 by Dorothy Burr Thompson in the Agora of Athens. Evelyn B. Harrison, who published the Agora example, argues convincingly that it represents Alexander the Great as a youth. However, the place of discovery of the example from Eleusis, viz. the Ploutonion, the acanthus leaves carved on the base of the Agora example, the maturity of the broad and at the same time long face, the weak chin, and the heavy locks over the forehead, lead us to adhere, at least for the time being, to the old conception that it represents a benevolent divinity of the lower world. There is no evidence whatever indicating that Alexander the Great was initiated into the Mysteries, that he was ever especially honored at Eleusis, as was the case with Antinoos in whose honor the Antinoeia were established. Nor is there any evidence suggesting that the Greeks of the ancient world ever conceived of Alexander as a "doomed young hero" whose early death had to be remembered with sadness, but always as the conqueror of the great Persian Empire, whose achievement flattered the national pride.

The dedication of reliefs in which votaries are represented, such as the Lakratides relief and that of the mission of Triptolemos, was apparently a usual procedure beginning with the fourth century and from that century we have a number of works of art on which

[35] For a discussion of Eubouleus, cf. also infra, p. 309. For the marble head, now in the National Museum of Athens, No. 181, cf. D. Philios, *Ephem*, 1886, pp. 257-266 and pl. 10; A. Furtwängler, *Masterpieces of Greek Sculpture*, p. 330. J. N. Svoronos, *Ephem*, 1911, pp. 39ff; G. M. A. Richter, *op.cit.*, p. 264, fig. 512; Rizzo, *op.cit.*, pp. 103-108. For the Agora example cf. Evelyn B. Harrison, *Hesperia*, 29 (1960), pp. 382-389.

groups of mortals, the dedicator and his family, are represented approaching the Goddesses. One of the most interesting examples is the fragment, some 0.46m. wide, attached to the northwest corner of the hall of the Museum of Eleusis (Fig. 72). Demeter, in the guise of an old woman, is seated on a rocky ground and is being approached by a group of three men, a woman, and a girl bearing on her head a basket. There can be little doubt that here we have "Demeter on the Mirthless Stone."[36] In the Hymn the seated Goddess was found by a group of maidens; consequently, this relief does not represent the scene of the myth. The presence of men would also exclude the possibility of its dealing with the Thesmophoria where women sat on the ground in remembrance of the experience of the Goddess. Can we see in this representation a scene from the sacred pageant where the initiates are approaching the seated Goddess in their role as participants in the Story? In that case the girl would be an ἀφ' ἑστίας initiate. This interpretation is ruled out because no part of the secret celebration of the Mysteries could be divulged either in literature or in art. It seems probable that our relief represents a devotional act of worship, as did the relief of the mission of Triptolemos. Instead of depicting the Goddess as the giver of agricultural wealth, the sculptor of our relief depicts the bereaved and sorrowing mother. The relief is of special interest since it reflects in a way the general character of the Mirthless Stone, which could not have been a large boulder at the side of the road but a small outcrop of rock such as we have postulated in our discussion of the stepped platform and the Ploutonion (*supra*, pp. 145 ff).

Our interpretation is strengthened by the representation on a relief now in the Museum of Naples where Demeter, seated on her Mirthless Stone, is approached by members of a family; a man, a woman, another man, a youth, and two children. The youth is leading a sheep, and the man holds a dove.[37] These are offerings suited to the regular worship of the Goddess and had no place in the sacred pageant of the Mysteries.

[36] O. Rubensohn, *AM*, 24 (1899), p. 46, pl. 8, 1. Mylonas, *Hymn*, pp. 82 ff.

[37] J. E. Harrison, *op.cit.*, fig. 85. The seated Goddess is approached by a group of votaries on a relief found in the Agora of Athens. Cf. H. A. Thompson, *Hesperia*, 17 (1948), pl. 542; there we have a devotional act different from the one represented in either of the reliefs we have discussed.

In our relief of the Demeter on the Mirthless Stone the men have the right shoulder bared and are barefoot. The woman is covered with her peplos. In the large basket carried by the girl were perhaps the offerings to the Goddess or the fruits, etc., needed for the sacrifice. In some cases the votaries bring with them a sacrificial pig. A procession of worshipers bringing their pigs is represented on a fragmentary votive relief found at Eleusis, published by Kourouniotes in 1925.[38] And on a fourth century votive relief in the Louvre, reputed to have been found at Eleusis and for a long time in the Pourtales collection, are represented Demeter and Persephone standing at the side of an altar in front of which we find a pig tended by a boy, followed by his father and mother.[39] Again it is interesting to note how the woman is covered with her peplos while the right shoulder of the man is left bare. The same is true for the men of the procession published by Kourouniotes.

Each initiate, as we shall find later, was obliged to sacrifice a small pig at the very beginning of the celebration, so it is natural to find initiates represented with that animal on reliefs to be dedicated at Eleusis. Sometimes even statuettes of pigs were taken to the Sanctuary as votive offerings. In the doorway between the hall and the North Room of the Museum of Eleusis is exhibited such a statuette (Fig. 66). It is made of pentelic marble and measures 0.40m. in extreme length.[40]

Before we complete the discussion of the representations of the Eleusinian Goddesses exhibited in the Museum, we must note a fragment of a statuette of marble in the third South Room. It may perhaps represent Persephone seated in Demeter's lap (Fig. 73).[41] It is only 0.26m. high and not of high quality, but interesting for its unusual subject.[42]

[38] *Deltion*, 8 (1923), pp. 167-168, fig. 11.
[39] J. Overbeck, *op.cit.*, II, p. 509, No. 4, *Atlas*, XIV, 2. L. R. Froehner, *op.cit.*, p. 265, pl. XXVI.
[40] Kourouniotes, *Guide*, fig. 8.
[41] *Ibid.*, fig. 43. A. Furtwängler, *AM*, 20 (1895), p. 359. Farnell, *op.cit.*, III, p. 231. Some miniature copies of the figures in the West pediment of the Parthenon are kept in the storeroom. They are to be published fully by Travlos and Miss E. Harrison.
[42] In the same room are exhibited a statuette of Poseidon, a headless life size statue of Asklepios that was found in a field a kilometer from our site, a statuette of Dionysos holding a kantharos, and an Archaistic statue of Dionysos perhaps, almost life size, that are worth noting.

The statue of Antinoos, in the second South Room is perhaps the best work of the Roman period exhibited in the Museum (Fig. 79). The deified youth from Bithynia, favorite of Hadrian, is represented as a youthful Dionysos standing by the Delphic omphalos. It is life size, and breathes a melancholy and sad air well suited to the event commemorated by his statue.[43] The idealism of the work is typical of the Hadrianic era and contrasts sharply with the stark realism that characterize Imperial Roman portraits, as illustrated in the statue of Tiberius, as "pontifex maximus," exhibited in the same room against its south wall.

A number of statues belonging to the Archaistic period and style were found in the exploration of the Sanctuary and are exhibited in the first South Room. The term archaistic is usually applied to the style patterned after the work of the sixth century B.C. by sculptors working in the second and later centuries. The most interesting of the archaistic sculptures found at Eleusis are statues of maidens, one of which is illustrated in Figure 77. It is evident that the sculptor took as his prototype the maidens of the Akropolis of Athens dating from the pre-Persian years of Athenian artistic activity. The maiden of Eleusis, measuring 0.75m. in height, is holding before her the water basin to be used by worshipers for purification before they entered the temple. Of greater individuality and less exuberantly rendered is another maiden exhibited in the same room, a votive offering to the Goddesses by the Demos, or people of Athens, as we learn from the inscription on its pedestal. The maiden perhaps was holding before her a basin made of another piece of marble that was secured in the rectangular cutting so conspicuous in the statue. Kourouniotes believed that on either side of the entrances to the Telesterion were placed statues holding real basins of water to be used by the initiates before entering and that belief seems to be correct.[44]

The many pedestals found in the Sanctuary area and the inscriptional evidence indicate that a great number of statues were dedicated to the Goddesses both by the members of the sacerdotal

[43] P. Graindor, *Athènes sous Hadrien*, pp. 266-267, pl. X. The statue was found by Lenormant in his excavations of 1860, apparently in the outer court of the Sanctuary. Antinoos' short life is placed between A.D. 117 and 138.
[44] He was fond of explaining this idea to his collaborators whenever a chance presented itself.

families and by the initiates. Unfortunately almost all of these statues were destroyed. One of the most interesting of the few survivals is a statuette of marble representing a παῖς ἀφ' ἑστίας, a boy initiate (Fig. 80). It is now kept in the small glass cabinet at the south end of the west wall of the Vase Room of the Museum of Eleusis.[45] It stands only 0.25m. in height and its right hand and its feet are missing. It must be the product of the fourth century B.C. The boy, holding a bacchos, wears only an himation that leaves bare his right shoulder. His right arm, now missing, was extended along his body and with his right hand the boy held a small pig also missing, but which can be deduced from the traces of the break. The boy is typically Greek—chubby, round faced, and with abundant hair. The pig, as we have seen, was the sacrificial animal of Demeter necessary for purification. This little statuette is interesting but not unique. At Eleusis we have two other fragmentary statuettes of boy initiates. One holds the pig across his chest; the other holds the pig along the side of the body in a manner similar to that noted for our Figure 80. In addition, the marble heads of two statues of boys decorated with a rope-like wreath were found at Eleusis.[46] A wreath of myrtle is worn by the boy initiate of the statuette in Rome published by Katharine Esdaile.[47] There too, the boy holds a bacchos and a pig but interestingly enough one of his feet is bare while the other is shod in a sandal. Representations of boys who were initiated in the Mysteries apparently were not uncommon in the fourth century B.C. and in Roman times.

The statue of Tiberius, mentioned above, can serve as an example of a dedication made by a man of consequence. But the average initiate could also make a similar dedication, as indicated by the two headless statues standing against the south parapet wall of the court of the Museum. Dating from Roman Imperial times and of minor artistic merit, they exhibit one feature that is of interest. The heads of these statues were meant to be made of a different piece of marble and were to be inserted in the neck specially worked for

[45] Fully discussed by Kourouniotes in *Deltion*, 8 (1923), pp. 165ff, fig. 8; cf. *AM*, 20 (1895), pp. 357-358.

[46] K. Kourouniotes, *Deltion*, 8 (1923), pp. 155-162, figs. 1-5.

[47] *JHS*, 29 (1909), pl. Ia. A fragment of a statue representing a boy wearing one sandal only was found in the Agora (Inv. No. 316); reported briefly by Evelyn B. Harrison, *Hesperia*, 29 (1960), p. 388.

the purpose. The statues belong to the group of ready-made articles to be used by the initiates, and in some way correspond to the ready-made clothing of our times. The making of a statue requires considerable time, but the initiate coming from abroad, especially from the Roman world, perhaps did not have the time to wait for a whole statue to be made; yet he perhaps wanted to dedicate his statue in the Sanctuary. To expedite matters the artists produced a great number of headless statues. When a customer presented himself, the sculptor had only to model a head that could be inserted on the body chosen by the purchaser. The type of garments given to these statues seems to indicate that the prospective customers for whom they were made were Romans.

The third South Room of the Museum is dominated by the Caryatid, dating from the second half of the first century A.D., which was one of a pair that stood in the inner vestibule of the Lesser Propylaea (Fig. 56). The other Caryatid was carried away and is now in the Fitzwilliam Museum in Cambridge, England. We have already studied this impressive work.[48] In the same room we find exhibited a number of monuments we have noted already. In its southwest corner, for example, we have the larnax burial of a child, illustrated in Figure 43, covered by the lid as reassembled. Huge Geometric amphorae, found in the cemetery of the south slope of the hill of Eleusis by Skias, are also to be seen in this room.

In the court of the Museum which commands a magnificent view of the bay of Eleusis and the famous straits of Salamis, a good many sculptured pieces are exhibited. One of the capitals of the Lesser Propylaea is here (Fig. 55) and two immense torches of marble, apparently the dedication of a grateful initiate. The crosses carved on them indicate later use by Christians. The most conspicuous monument in the court is the marble sarcophagus illustrated in Figure 82. It dates from the end of the second century of our era and bears in rather high relief and on its long side the story of the Kalydonian boar hunt.[49] The composition is interesting, although it lacks the spirit usual in heroic battles, and it illustrates the idealistic trends revived in sculpture in the Hadrianic era. Sphinxes are

---

[48] *Supra*, p. 159.

[49] It measures 2.40m. in length and 1.10m. in height. Cf. lately B. G. Kallipolites, Χρονολογικὴ κατάταξις τῶν μετὰ μυθολογικῶν παραστάσεων ἀττικῶν σαρκοφάγων, Library of the Archaeological Society of Athens, 1959, pp. 20 and 56.

represented on the short sides of the sarcophagus. As we have stated before the lid does not belong to this sarcophagus, but was found near it.

A large slab with "Hierophantes" carved on it stands to the right of the door of the Museum. It belonged to the niche of Roman date within which was the throne of the high priest of Eleusis at the side of the Anaktoron and within the Telesterion. Also the head of a horse, of late Hellenistic date, is of considerable interest. By its side originally stood the statue of one of the Dioskouroi, unfortunately not preserved.[50]

SCULPTURES NOT IN THE MUSEUM

Before we bring to an end our discussion of the sculptured remains in the Museum of Eleusis we have briefly to consider two sculptured monuments to be found elsewhere. The first of these is the well-known sculptured marble urn known as the Lovatelli urn after the name of its first publisher.[51] It was found in a columbarium on the Esquiline, near the Porta Maggiore of Rome. It stands 0.294m. in height and its greatest diameter is 0.32m. Its sculptured decoration, entirely filling its surface, divides naturally into three scenes (Fig. 83). At the right hand, is a scene of a sacrifice. Herakles, identified by his lion skin, is holding a sacrificial pig over the altar which is being purified by water poured from a jug by a bearded priest. The heavily clothed priest holds in his left hand a phiale with three poppy heads. There can be little doubt that here we have the beginning of the rites held for the purification of Herakles. It is immaterial whether in the bearded figure we see the Hierophant or Eumolpos, as the legend holds. The second scene deals again with the purification of Herakles: The hero is now seated on a stool covered by his lion skin, with his bare feet resting on a ram's pelt, on the "Fleece of Zeus" as it was called. His head is covered with a heavy cloak. The significance of this is debated, but perhaps Roussel is near the mark when he

---

[50] Ch. Picard, *BCH*, 82 (1958), pp. 435-465.

[51] Published for the first time by Countess E. C. Lovatelli, "Di un vaso cinerario con reppresentanze relative ai Misteri de Eleusi," *Bullet. della Commissione archeol. communale di Roma*, VII, p. 18, pls. I-V. J. N. Svoronos, *JIAN*, 4 (1901), pp. 475-486, where bibliography up to 1900. Lately, P. Roussel, "L'initiation préalable et les symboles Éleusinien," *BCH*, 54 (1930), pp. 58-65.

maintains that it served to exclude the surrounding world and its distractions from the eyes of the person being purified, who thus unmolested could concentrate his attention on penitent and purifying thoughts. Such penitence and humble respect is indicated by the bare feet of Herakles.

Behind the seated hero we find a priestess holding over his head a *liknon* or winnowing-fan. This agricultural tool was used in connection with a number of ritualistic acts of purification. Its purpose was to separate the evil and leave the good in the penitent.[52] The *liknon* was especially used in the Dionysiac rites, but it could have belonged to the worship of Demeter as well. Farnell suggested that the Hiera were placed in the *liknon* and held over the head of the candidate "in order to bring him into rapport with certain mystic 'sacra' of the Goddess."[53] In a similar manner in the Greek Orthodox Church, the faithful walk under the *Epitaphion*, the simulacrum of the Grave of Christ, or bow their head below the chalice in which are the elements of the Eucharist in the belief that they are thus purified and come into a closer communion with the divine. The *liknon* could have contained simply barley which would, in the course of the rite, be sprinkled over the candidate and later offered in the sacrifice. Whatever the implications, the fact remains that our second scene represents a rite of purification; the ram's skin, "the Fleece of Zeus," further proves that the person purified is purified from the taint of blood; the lion skin at the stool indicates that the candidate is Herakles who is being purified.

In the third scene we find Demeter seated on an altar-like seat, covered with a pelt. She is crowned with heads of wheat, in a unique and very Egyptian fashion, and turns her head to Persephone who is approaching her mother with torch over her shoulder. In front of the Goddess we have a youthful figure extending his hand to a serpent, which raises its head to the hand of the youth. The interpretation of this last scene is difficult. Some scholars have recognized Herakles in the youth, and see in the scene the climax of the initiation, happy converse and association of our hero with the Goddess; the implication being that such will be the prize

[52] L. R. Farnell, *op.cit.*, III, p. 238. J. E. Harrison, *Prolegomena*, p. 549. It is interesting to note a similar use of the liknon-fan in Matthew 3:11.
[53] L. R. Farnell, *op.cit.*, III, p. 239.

of every initiate.[54] One cannot be sure, however, that the youth represented in the third scene is Herakles, nor that it forms a sequel to the rites illustrated in the other two scenes. As a matter of fact scholars have variously identified the youth as Iacchos, Triptolemos, or Eubouleus.[55] Furthermore the way in which the wheat is placed on the head of Demeter, among other things, seems to indicate that the composition reflects the Alexandrian rather than the Eleusinian Goddess.

The Lovatelli urn is compared with reason to the representation on the long side of the sarcophagus of Torre-Nova (Fig. 84). In that monument also we have three scenes, in two of which Herakles is one of the main figures.[56] At the right Herakles approaches an altar over which a priest, holding in the right hand a phiale filled with fruit, pours from a jug the purifying liquid. In the central scene, Herakles is seated on a stool spread with his lion pelt, his head covered by a heavy cloth and his bare feet resting on the "Fleece of Zeus." Behind him Persephone, perhaps, performs the rites of purification, not with a *liknon* but with burning torches. In the third scene we have Demeter seated on a sacred kiste looking towards a youthful Iacchos standing before an altar laden with fruit. The figure of Iacchos corresponds to the youth of the third scene of the Lovatelli urn who thus should also be identified as Iacchos. Again the second scene is one of purification this time by fire, fire considered as one of the purest elements with power to destroy all taint. The person purified is Herakles, who had already sacrificed in the presence of the bearded priest.

The Lovatelli urn has been taken to illustrate the three stages of initiation in the Eleusinian Mysteries.[57] Certainly this is not correct. The scene to the extreme left cannot be the Epopteia; the youthful figure is not Herakles, but probably Iacchos who had no relation to the other two scenes where Herakles is the protagonist. This is definitely established by the Torre-Nova sarcophagus. But

[54] J. E. Harrison, *Prolegomena*, p. 546, identifies the scene as the *Epopteia*, the highest degree of initiation.

[55] P. Roussel, *op.cit.*, p. 62.

[56] G. E. Rizzo, "Il sarcofago di Torre Nova," *RM*, 25 (1910), pp. 89-167, especially figs. 5 and 6. L. Curtius, *AM*, 48 (1923), pp. 31-51, where later bibliography. For the purification by fire see in comparison, Matthew 3:11 and Luke 3:16.

[57] J. E. Harrison, *Prolegomena*, p. 546.

it cannot be really proved that even the scenes where we have Herakles belong to the cycle of the Eleusinian Mysteries. The "Fleece of Zeus" was used in the purification of homicides, and perhaps in the second scene in both monuments we have simply the purification of Herakles from the blood taint of the centaur Pholos.[58] That purification had to precede rites dealing with the celebration of the Mysteries. The scene of the sacrifice of a pig could reflect again a preliminary rite held in Athens before the initiates started for Eleusis, or even a preliminary stage to the more important purification by means of the "Fleece of Zeus." Thus we can conclude that neither of the two monuments can be conceived of as illustrating the secret rites of the Lesser or the Greater Mysteries. At best they could be taken as illustrations of the preliminary stages in the initiation to the Lesser Mysteries, indicated by the presence of Persephone, as performed for Herakles, whose blood taint made his initiation a special case. The two monuments in Italy are indeed of great interest, but they do not offer any information regarding the secret rites of the Greater or even the Lesser Mysteries.

VASES IN THE MUSEUM

The vases found at Eleusis are easily accessible in the Vase Room, the southernmost room of the Museum, where they are arranged chronologically beginning with the Middle Helladic period (ca. 1900 B.C.) and ending with Roman Imperial and Early Christian times (ca. A.D. 450). All the known styles of the potters' industrial art are represented in the collection, and some are outstanding examples of their types. We may mention the proto-Attik amphora by the "Polyphemos Painter," illustrated in Figure 29 and the orientalizing amphora by the "Chimaira Painter" of Figure 30. Very few of the vases found, however, can be directly connected with the Eleusinian rites or illustrate those rites. On a fragment from the neck of a black-figure loutrophoros we have two processions which, according to Kourouniotes who published it, may

[58] Diodoros, IV, 25, 4. Plutarch, *Theseus*, 30, 5. Appollodoros, II, 5, 12, 3, tells us how Herakles came to Eumolpos to be initiated: "but not being able to see the Mysteries because he had not been cleansed of the slaughter of the centaurs, he was cleansed by Eumolpos and then initiated." In our scene we seem to have the "cleansing": the initiation will follow.

represent some sacred rite performed under the direction of the Dadouchos in the preliminary stages of the Lesser Mysteries.[59] It is certain that we do not find in this and other processional scenes part of the initiation proper because the sacred law of Eleusis forbade, under penalty of a fine, the initiation in groups.[60] But apparently other sacred rites were held in honor of Demeter by the initiates at Eleusis and in Athens, and one of these may be represented on the vase. It is interesting to note that the Dadouchos holds one of the torches aloft and the other in a horizontal position and that all the figures are barefoot. One wonders whether the group is approaching the statue of the Goddess to which the worshipers are to be presented by the Dadouchos.

A group of worshipers led in the performance of some preliminary sacred rite is depicted on a stamnos of the red-figure style published by Kourouniotes (Fig. 78). It can be placed not later than the second third of the fifth century, and it comes from a grave where it was placed with other vases as furnishings of the dead.[61]

The main panel is decorated by two male and one female figure. The first figure to the right certainly is a Dadouchos, wearing elaborate vestments. A wreath of myrtle can be seen under the ribbons of the *stemmata* on his long hair. He is an impressive figure and contrasts rather strongly with the simply dressed Dadouchos of the black figure loutrophoros just noted. This difference seems to indicate the truth of the statement that officials of Eleusis adopted rich and elaborate vestments following Aischylos' innovations in the theater.[62]

Behind the Dadouchos we find a youthful male figure holding a bacchos, crowned with a wreath of myrtle, and wearing a himation, in the apparently characteristic fashion of a worshiper, leaving his right shoulder bare. He follows the Dadouchos with the same measured step and hieratic attitude. He is also barefoot. The female

[59] K. Kourouniotes, "'Ελευσινιακὴ δᾳδουχία," *Ephem*, 1937, pp. 240-247, figs. 12-14 and 16-18; *Deltion*, 8 (1923), pp. 164ff. and fig. 7.

[60] K. Kourouniotes, *Ephem*, 1937, p. 248. For the sacred law of Eleusis, cf. *IG*, I² 6, 109-114; the fine was set at a thousand drachmai; the same sacred law in lines 125-126, indicates that groups were brought together either in the court of the sanctuary or in the Eleusinion, but not for initiation. Cf. B. D. Meritt, *Hesperia*, 14 (1945), p. 76, who rightly emphasizes the restriction against group initiation imposed by the same law.

[61] K. Kourouniotes, *Ephem*, 1937, pp. 223ff and figs. 1-4.

[62] *Athenaios*, I, 21e.

figure following does not take part in the procession and is rightly identified by Kourouniotes as Persephone. On the rear panel a woman holding a torch is followed by a youth holding a knotty staff and by another woman bearing a torch.

That both representations have some connection with Eleusis is apparent from the torches, the bacchoi, and the wreaths of myrtle. The first figure of the main panel is certainly a Dadouchos. The detailed study of the figures and the literature led Kourouniotes to conclude that the stamnos portrays some preliminary sacred acts performed under the direction of the Dadouchos, which, however, formed no part of the celebration of the Greater Mysteries. That perhaps such preliminary rites were held in the course of the celebration of the Lesser Mysteries is indicated by Persephone's presence in the scene; and the tradition that the Lesser Mysteries belonged to the Kore cannot be denied.

The "mission" of Triptolemos is a favorite story with the vase painter, as already noted.[63] Its many representations prove that the "apostole" of the hero could not have formed part of the secret rites of the Mysteries.[64] In this a good many scholars agree. But there are a few representations on vases in which some scholars see an aspect of the Mysteries held at Eleusis.[65]

Perhaps the best-known and most discussed representation is to be found on a pelike discovered in 1859 in a grave at Panticapaion in the Krimaia (modern Kerch) and now in the Hermitage (Fig. 85).[66] Its style is clearly Attik, its date fourth century, and its decoration is in two panels. In the front panel Demeter wearing

---

[63] *Supra*, p. 197. Years ago L. E. Stephani published a long list of vases bearing the story, *Compte rendu de la Commission impèriale archéologique*, 1859. Cf. J. A. Overbeck, *Griechische Kunstmythologie*, II, pp. 409-529. The list has been greatly augmented since his day and in the latest study of the subject by Dr. Betty Grossman some 468 examples are listed.

[64] In this connection we may recall Reinach's statement (*Cultes, mythes et religions*, v, p. 76) quoted by Roussel (*op.cit.*, p. 65), "rien de ce qui était mystérieux ne peut avoir été mis par écrit ni figuré."

[65] H. Metzger in a recent study, "Dionysos Chthonien," *BCH*, 68-69 (1944-1945), pp. 296-339, maintains that some of these representations prove that Dionysos was worshiped alongside Demeter and Persephone in the Eleusinian cult. My detailed study on this generally held notion, entitled "Dionysos at Eleusis," will appear shortly in the *Ephemeris*.

[66] L. E. Stephani, *op.cit.*, pp. 73-119, pl. II. J. A. Overbeck, *op.cit.*, II. Atlas, pl. XVIII, 18, J. N. Svoronos, *JIAN*, 4 (1901), pp. 284ff. K. Schefold, *Untersuch. K. Vasen*, No. 368. Nilsson, *Religion*, pl. 46, 2.

a well-decorated polos and holding a scepter is represented seated in the center of the composition and apparently talking earnestly, as her open left hand indicates. At her knee stands an infant generally taken to be Ploutos, holding a cornucopia. Next to Demeter stands Persephone holding a torch and crowned with a wreath of myrtle. On either side of the Goddesses two female figures are seated. The winged figure of an infant Eros playing at the feet of the figure on the left suggests that she is Aphrodite. The identity of the seated figure to the right cannot be established. Demeter and Aphrodite are being approached by a youthful figure holding lighted torches, wearing a richly embroidered costume, a wreath of myrtle, and high, elaborate boots. There can be little doubt that he is the youthful Iacchos who, acting as mystagogos, is leading to the Goddesses a youthful Herakles holding a bacchos and his club and wearing a wreath of myrtle. Above the Goddesses a childlike Triptolemos is represented as arriving in his winged chariot. On the right corner Dionysos is seated holding his thyrsos and crowned with ivy. The God is a mere spectator, kept outside of the main and central theme; his presence is explained by the tradition that he too was initiated in the Mysteries some time during his turbulent life. Another tradition stating that Triptolemos acted as Hierophant in the initiation of Herakles will account for the presence of the former. There can be little doubt that on the main panel of the pelike is represented the bringing of Herakles for initiation. The representation, however, does not give us any information as to the rites held in the course of that initiation.

The scene represented on the rear panel of the pelike cannot be conceived as representing any aspect, preliminary or otherwise, of the rites of Eleusis in spite of the ingenious explanations of Svoronos.[67] The presence of Athena in the middle of the representation and of Hermes, acting as the recipient of the object yielded to him by the maiden rising from the ground, would definitely prove that the representation has something to do with Athenian legends but not with the Mysteries. The seated maiden

[67] J. N. Svoronos, *ibid.*, pp. 322ff, holds that we have the representation of the taking out of the *Hiera* from an underground depository in the Ploutonion to make them ready for the trip to Athens. All scholars now believe that this very imaginative theory is untenable. For illustration cf. Nilsson, *Religion*, pl. 46, 1.

with the torches could be identified as Hekate, whose participation in divine events is not limited only to Eleusis.

On a red-figure krater now in the British Museum, known as the Pourtales vase,[68] appears another composition that caused a good deal of argument (Fig. 81). The figures of the composition are disposed on two levels. In the front and lower level Demeter is seated apparently on the ground and next to her is a throne or seat which remains unoccupied. She turns her head to Triptolemos, seated on his winged chariot drawn by dragons, who talks with animation. Between the two we have the standing figure of Persephone holding a lighted torch. Her raised left foot indicates that the Goddess is just arriving to join her mother and apparently the empty seat is for her. To the seated Goddess are brought by two mystagogoi, actually Iacchos painted twice, Herakles, identified by his club, standing near Demeter, and the Dioskouroi identified by the star in the upper right corner. All three youths hold bacchoi and are crowned with myrtle. There can be little doubt that here the legendary heroes are presented for initiation. The participation of Iacchos and the Doric columns in the background, standing perhaps for the façade of the Telesterion, indicate that the scene takes place at Eleusis.[69] Nothing in the composition reveals ritualistic acts held in the course of the celebration of the Mysteries.

Preparatory acts of the Lesser Mysteries seem to be represented on two red-figured hydriai, one found in Capua and the other in Krete. Both date from the fourth century and on both we have a central composition of three divine figures flanked by others whose identity cannot be established. Demeter seated on an altar-like seat and holding her characteristic scepter turns to look at a seated Dionysos towards whom Persephone is moving with lighted torches.

[68] J. A. Overbeck, *op.cit.*, II, p. 669, No. 3A, Atlas, XVIII, 19. J. N. Svoronos, *JIAN*, 4 (1901), pp. 273ff. L. R. Farnell, *op.cit.*, pp. 246-249, pl. XIX. K. Schefold, *op.cit.*, No. 94.

[69] According to the scholiast of Aristophanes' *Ploutos*, 1013, the Lesser Mysteries were instigated to initiate Herakles. From this, and Diodoros, IV, 25, 4, it is usually inferred that Herakles was initiated only in those Mysteries; consequently it is assumed that the representation must be reflecting the rites of the Lesser Mysteries. However, references of an earlier date seem to imply that he was initiated in the Greater Mysteries; cf. Xenophon's *Hellenika*, VI, 3, 6, Plutarch's *Theseus*, 30, 5. At any rate the presence of Iacchos would definitely indicate the Greater Mysteries.

Metzger maintains that the group represents the three divinities pre-eminent in the Mysteries; a holy trinity: the Mother Demeter, Dionysos as her *paredros*, and Persephone. The movement of Persephone with lighted torches indicates, however, that the preliminary purifications for Dionysos' initiation in the Lesser Mysteries are represented on the two hydriai.[70]

The legendary initiates, Dionysos and Herakles, are represented on a hydria from Cumae while on a red-figure cover in Tübingen are added the Dioskouroi mounted on horses.[71] On both monuments Gods and heroes are conversing peacefully and there is no indication of religious rites either mystic or traditional. The birth of Ploutos seems to be represented on a hydria from Rhodes now in the Museum of Istanbul. In the chapter on the Mysteries we shall discuss fully the problem connected with the birth of Ploutos and its relation to the acts performed at Eleusis. Here we may state briefly our conclusion: the birth of Ploutos had no place in the Mysteries and consequently its representation yields no information regarding the sacred rites.

THE NIINNION TABLET

The only document that can be definitely associated with the Eleusinian cult is the so-called Niinnion tablet, painted in the red-figure technique and dated in the first half of the fourth century B.C. (Fig. 88). It is in the form of a *naiskos* or temple with pediment and a palmette or central finial. The composition is framed by antae, made in the form of bacchoi. The tablet, found in nine fragments and pieced together, measures 0.44m. in height to the top of the palmette, and 0.32m. in width. Holes for attachment are to be seen in its four corners. From the inscription scratched on its base we learn that the tablet was dedicated to the Goddesses by Niinnion. At the back of the tablet a number of letters were inscribed when the clay was fresh and before it was fired. Svoronos

[70] Representations on the vases cited are easily accessible and grouped together in L. R. Farnell, *op.cit.*, pp. 245-256, pls. XVII, XX, XXIa, XXIb. Metzger, *op.cit.*, pp. 326ff. In my forthcoming study in the *Ephemeris* I explain fully the reasons that prove his thesis untenable. One may compare this purification scene with that on the sarcophagus Torre-Nova (Fig. 84).

[71] For illustrations see Nilsson, *Religion*, pl. 47 for the Cumae hydria; pl. 45, 1 for the lid in Tübingen; and pl. 44, 1 for the hydria from Rhodes.

sees in them *ephesia grammata*, apotropaic letters, scratched to avert the evil of curses.[72]

The tablet bears figured compositions both on its broad face and on its pediment. Skias, who was the first to publish it, maintained that its broad face presents a unified and single composition dealing with the *prosodos*, or the ceremonial advent, of mystai to the seated Goddesses of Eleusis, a detail of a rite of the Mysteries. Svoronos maintained that the tablet presents two scenes[73] separated from each other by the delicate white line that threads its way obliquely through the different figures, to be seen under the feet of figures 5, 6, 7 and 8. (Fig. 88); the lower scene, represents rites performed in the Lesser Mysteries—the presentation of Niinnion by a Dadouchos to the seated Persephone; the upper scene, rites held in the Greater Mysteries—the presentation of Niinnion by a torch-bearing Persephone to the seated Demeter. Rubensohn[74] very ingeniously recognized in the scenes the rite of the Κερνοφορία, kernophoria, the bearing of the sacred kernos, a conclusion reached independently by Kourouniotes. But Rubensohn maintained that on the tablet was depicted the same pompe, advancing to the temenos of Eleusis. Scholars accepted the one or the other of the main views expressed by Skias and Svoronos. Thus Philios is in favor of the unified and single scene; Pringsheim, and after him Kern,[75] believe that in the main field we have represented a single act, the reception of the mystai in the court of the Sanctuary of Eleusis at the end of the great pompe by the two Goddesses, and that on the pediment we have the dance of the *pannychis*, the night-long merrymaking, which followed the pompe. On the other hand Jane Harrison[76] follows Svoronos in recognizing two scenes, one below from the

---

[72] First published by A. Skias, in *Ephem*, 1901, pp. 1-39 where a color reproduction made by Gillieron père was given. The original is exhibited in the National Museum and a copy by Gillieron in the Museum of Eleusis in the doorway to the North Room. Usually the copy is used for illustrations. We are publishing here a picture of the original as it is today. Fragments of another red-figure tablet with Demeter and Persephone, now in the Museum of Eleusis, was also published by Skias in the same article of the *Ephemeris*.

[73] J. N. Svoronos, *JIAN*, 4 (1901), pp. 268-269. The white line separating the scenes can be seen with difficulty on the tablet today.

[74] O. Rubensohn, *AM*, 23 (1898), pp. 271ff. K. Kourouniotes, *Ephem*, 1898, pp. 22-28. Leonard in *RE*, XI, pp. 271-306.

[75] O. Pringsheim, *Archäologische Beiträge zur Geschichte des Eleusinisches Kults*, pp. 65ff. O. Kern, *RE*, *s.v.* "Mysterien," p. 1229.

[76] J. E. Harrison, *Prolegomena*, pp. 558-560.

Lesser Mysteries and the other, above, from the Greater Mysteries with a revel represented on the pediment. Farnell too follows Svoronos and concludes: "We may accept Svoronos' exposition in the main: Niinnion, who dedicates the picture, has commemorated in it her own initiation, first into the Lesser Mysteries at Agrai, and then her later initiation into the Greater Eleusinia; and in the gable-field she is depicted reveling with her companions, among whom is the faithful elderly man who accompanies her along the sacred way, carrying the travelling bag, and who never leaves her."[77]

It will be too long to mention the opinions of other scholars who in the main follow the one or the other view. But we should mention the interpretation suggested by Nilsson, our main authority on the religious rites of the Greeks. In his latest study, modifying somewhat his earlier suggestions,[78] he concludes that on the tablet we do not have "a direct representation of a scene in the Mysteries, which it was forbidden to divulge not only in words but also in pictures,"[79] and that on the lower zone "Demeter is approached by Iacchos and two mystai, while in the upper Persephone is brought back to her mother."[80] We doubt the correctness of this interpretation. The usual excitement and joy of a meeting and especially of a reunion such as it is pictured in the abduction myth, is absent from this representation. The painter would have certainly attempted by means of gestures at least, to express the joy which filled Mother and Daughter at their reunion pictured so strikingly in the Hymn (vv. 385-390). Further, in the bringing back of the daughter Hermes played an important role and he is absent in this picture. Even in the annual reunions, we would expect the great joy of the occasion to be indicated. The representation cannot be conceived as a "mythical scene," as Nilsson maintains, because we have mortals intermixed with the Goddesses and Iacchos.

The tablet must be reinterpreted and we must, I think, go back to the explanations of Kourouniotes and Svoronos and maintain

[77] L. R. Farnell, *op.cit.*, pp. 241-244.
[78] M. P. Nilsson, "Die eleusin. Gottheiten," *ArchRW*, 32 (1935), pp. 39ff. K. Kourouniotes, *Ephem*, 1937, p. 224.
[79] I agree fully with this part of the conclusion which was pointed out very successfully by Kourouniotes in *Ephem*, 1937, p. 224, in his rebuttal of Nilsson's earlier views.
[80] M. P. Nilsson, *Greek Popular Religion*, p. 55.

that we have in the main broad field and on the pediment three different scenes that have to do with Eleusinian rites. The torches, the bacchoi, the wreaths of myrtle, the kernos, even the poppies strewn in the field indicate that the scenes are connected with Eleusis and its cult. Svoronos' division of the representation into three scenes is correct, I believe. In all three scenes we have the same mortal woman bearing the kernos and the same bearded man accompanying her (Fig. 88). The woman could very well be Niinnion, the dedicator of the tablet. Their size indicates that they are mortals. The other figures, with the exception of a young boy, represent divinities.[81]

Lower Scene in main panel. From left to right we have a bearded man (Fig. 88, No. 10) walking stately and bearing on his shoulders a walking staff from which a bag is suspended. He is wearing a wreath of myrtle and his single garment, a himation, leaves bare his right shoulder. Then comes a woman (Fig. 88, No. 11) also holding over her left shoulder a heavy staff from which a bag is hanging. She extends her right hand holding a spray of myrtle in a gesture of greeting and respect, and advances in a light step and on her toes, in a stance that indicates dancing. She is wearing a chiton and a Doric peplos richly embroidered, a wreath of myrtle on her head on which she balances a kernos decorated with three sprays. She could be the dedicator Niinnion. In front of her we have a youthful figure, richly dressed, wearing high boots, and holding two lighted torches one of which he has turned towards the earth. A wreath of myrtle crowns his head and his long hair falls over his shoulders in curly locks. Svoronos saw in this figure a Dadouchos and a number of scholars accepted his view. However, we now have good illustrations of the Dadouchos, on the black-figure loutrophoros and the red-figure stamnos of Eleusis (Fig. 78) dating from two periods important for the appearance of that official; these are quite different from our youth, who must represent somebody else. We must note further that the youth is represented in the scale used for the divinities; this, his youthful appearance, the peculiar boots he is wearing in contrast to the barefoot male figures pictured in the Eleusinian processions, his costume so similar to the one worn by the torchbearer on the Panticapaion pelike and

---

[81] The broad panel measures 0.27m. in height and 0.32m. in width.

the Pourtales amphora, prove definitely that the divine figure leading the initiate is no other than the reputed leader of the pompe, the youthful Iacchos.

The figure was originally identified as Iacchos by Skias, but Svoronos' interpretation found greater favor among scholars. Others preferred to leave the issue clouded in vagueness and agreed with Farnell that "we had better leave this dadouchos of divine appearance unnamed."[82] I believe that our discussion leaves no doubt that the youthful male figure with the torches is Iacchos.

Between him and the seated Goddess to the right some painted objects are related to the Eleusinian cult. The two crossed elements between the feet of the Goddess and Iacchos, are certainly bacchoi. By the bacchoi we have a flower and some dotted rosettes. Svoronos took these as well as the other rosettes and flowers in the lower scene as indicative of spring when the flowers grow; that consequently on the tablet we have a scene from the Lesser Mysteries celebrated in the spring—in the month of flowers, in Anthesterion. However, the flower is a poppy, and poppies are the symbol of Demeter and could have been used to indicate that rites connected with the Eleusinian cult were represented. We have similar poppies carved on the architrave of the Lesser Propylaea where the emblems of the cult of Demeter were depicted. Consequently they had no connection with spring or any other season. The semi-oval object painted in white above the bacchoi is more difficult to explain. It has been taken to represent an omphalos and some pointed to it as illustrating Dionysiac influence at Eleusis. Svoronos maintained that it represents an altar decked and made ready for the sacrifice. An omphalos at Eleusis he pointed out was not known from Greek literature, nor was Eleusis ever conceived as the center of the earth, as was Delphi the sacred precinct of Apollo and Dionysos. Lately Rubensohn suggested that perhaps it represented the rock left projecting within the Anaktoron of the Goddess, a feature duplicated at Lykosoura;[83] that could have been considered as an omphalos of an earth Goddess. This concept reflects Farnell's thought "that Athens or Eleusis possessed one or more unrecorded local omphaloi, perhaps in the metroon at Agrai or in the city's

[82] L. R. Farnell, op.cit., p. 244.
[83] O. Rubensohn, Jahrbuch, 70 (1955), p. 36. L. R. Farnell, op.cit., p. 244.

Eleusinion or in the sacred enclosure at Eleusis."[84] One wonders, however, whether such a feature included in the holy of holies would have been generally known to the public, and if it were whether it would have been permissible to include it in a picture, especially since Pausanias did not dare even mention the buildings within the sacred enclosure. We cannot of course exclude the possibility of its representing an omphalos believed to be at Eleusis and formed by the projecting rock of the Anaktoron. We rather prefer an explanation we advanced in public lectures some years ago and which was independently reached by Goudis,[85] that perhaps in the white semicircular object of the tablet we have the *pelanos*, the sacred cake of wheat and barley, ready to be offered to the Goddesses as a preliminary sacrifice in the Greater Mysteries. Its decoration finds a parallel in the elaborate and symbolic patterns stamped on the round loaves of bread offered by the faithful and used in the celebration of the mass in the Greek Orthodox Church.

Iacchos is presenting the mystai to a seated Goddess. Could the lowering of the one torch be a gesture of respectful greeting? We have seen it on the relief of Figure 67, and we find it in a number of other representations. The seated Goddess, holding a phiale in her right hand and a scepter ending in a fleur-de-lis in the other, is ready to receive the initiates. She was identified by Svoronos as Persephone but she was correctly called Demeter by other scholars. The scepter she is holding identifies her as the Mother. She is apparently seated on the ground, a feature peculiar to Demeter alone. Near the Goddess a seat has been made ready, but it remains unoccupied. We have seen the same detail on the Pourtales amphora, and there as is the case here, the seat was made ready, we believe, for Persephone who is not present at this reception, but whose coming is anticipated. The absence of Persephone indicates that the scene belongs to the celebration of the Great Mysteries; the Lesser Mysteries belonged, as we shall see, to Persephone and certainly she could not be absent from her own Mysteries. The presence of Iacchos will indicate also the Greater Mysteries, for he was the leader, active in the preliminaries of the Greater Mysteries, and he personified the cries and the enthusiasm of those

[84] L. R. Farnell, *op.cit.*, p. 244.
[85] D. N. Goudis, Tὰ μυστήρια τῆς 'Ελευσῖνος, pp. 56 and 61.

taking part in the pompe, the special feature of those Mysteries. As far as we can make out from the available evidence, he had no place in the Lesser Mysteries. Furthermore, both the bearded man and the woman bearing the kernos hold walking staffs and have bags on their backs; those objects again were part of the equipment of the initiates taking part in the Greater Mysteries. And if we take the white semicircular object to be an omphalos representing the projecting rock of the Anaktoron, again we shall have to place the scene in the Greater Mysteries. The evident conclusion is that the lower scene deals with a rite celebrated in the course of the Greater Mysteries, and I agree with Rubensohn and Kern that it represents the kernophoria, celebrated in the outer court of the Sanctuary of Eleusis at the end of the pompe. Iacchos has brought the procession safely to Eleusis; he is now presenting its qualified participants to the Goddess of Eleusis, to Demeter; after that he will pass out of the picture of the festivities.

The upper scene is taken from rites in the Lesser Mysteries. Again the bearded man, accompanied this time by a youth, and the woman bearing the kernos are led by a female torch bearer, who from her size must be a divinity and hence Persephone, to a seated Goddess, who must be Demeter since she is holding a scepter.[86] It is interesting to note that in contrast to the gesture of Iacchos, Persephone holds both her torches upwards. This is a natural consequence of the relation of the two Goddesses. We do not expect the Kore to approach her mother with the gesture of respect required of mortals and lesser divinities—a respect which, as we have tried to suggest, is indicated by the lowering of one of the torches. In this scene there is no Iacchos, no walking staff, no bags held by the initiates; they were not needed because the event represented is part of the Lesser Mysteries held at Agrai, in Athens itself. It is interesting to note the column painted in the upper left hand corner of the scene. It certainly stands for a temple, and the decoration carried out in dots in the background would indicate the interior of a court surrounded with walls decorated in a festive manner appropriate to the occasion. The temple, connected with the rite represented, is of the Ionic order. In the Sanctuary of Eleusis and

[86] I cannot find a satisfactory explanation for the difference in color in the representation of the face of Demeter. It should perhaps be attributed to artistic license.

at the time of the painting of the tablet, a sacred building of the Ionic order did not exist, nor one in which that order was employed in a subsidiary role. We cannot be sure that a temple did exist in the precinct of the Goddesses at Agrai; but above the rocky bank of the Ilissos, until the days of the visit of Stuart and Revett, stood an Ionic temple which has since disappeared.[87] That temple was located in the general area in which the temenos of the Goddesses at Agrai was established, the temenos in which the Lesser Mysteries were celebrated; and we can accept the suggestion of Svoronos and others that perhaps the Ionic temple of the Ilissos formed part of that temenos. In that case, the column in the left corner would prove once more that the rites represented take place at Agrai and form part of the Lesser Mysteries.

We believe that Svoronos and his followers are correct in interpreting the scene in the pedimental triangle as representing the *pannychis*, or the night-long revel that followed the arrival of the mystai at Eleusis.

Let us summarize our conclusions on the interpretation of the scenes on the tablet. On its main field are painted two scenes: The upper represents a preliminary rite celebrated in the course of the Lesser Mysteries; the lower a similar rite held in the course of the celebration of the Greater Mysteries. In both we have the presentation of the mystai to the Goddess of the cult, to Demeter, and both illustrate the *kernophoria*, or the bearing of the *kernos*, which seems to have formed part of the preliminary exercises in the Lesser as well as in the Greater Mysteries. The presence of Iacchos in the lower scene seems to indicate that the rite in the Greater Mysteries was held at the end of the pompe and marked the termination of that march from Athens to Eleusis, so famous in antiquity; that therefore the rite took place before the actual telete, the actual initiation in the Telesterion. It formed part of the open rites held in public and therefore it could be represented on a work of art exposed to view to many, as it disclosed no secrets. Similarly the rite of the upper scene was not a secret one and therefore it could be represented in art.

One may wonder now whether we can find anything regarding

[87] For the Ilissos temple J. Stuart, and N. Revett, *The Antiquities of Athens*, I, pp. 7-11, pls. I-VIII. Travlos, *Athens*, fig. 32.

the woman Niinnion who dedicated the tablet. Svoronos, in a penetrating study of the problem was able to suggest that the Niinnion of the tablet is the same as the Nannion whose name and activities are preserved in the 13th book of Athenaios. It seems that she reached the height of her popularity in the first half of the fourth century B.C. when she became one of the famous hetairai of her times.[88] Svoronos suggested that in the bearded man we have her lover and keeper Thallos, or Greensprout, who had come to Athens to buy dried russet-figs and take away a cargo of Hymettos honey, "but met Nannion, forgot his plans and attached himself to the hetaira until all his fortune was spent. Hence Nannion became known as the 'she-goat' because she had devoured that tall lover, Greensprout Thallos."

We have treated the Niinnion tablet in greater detail because it is the only work of art which can definitely be linked with the Mysteries and which can give us some information regarding the preliminary rites of the cult of the Eleusinian Demeter. No information can be gleaned from the other works of art which we have briefly discussed or enumerated. Indeed, art provides even less information than literature regarding the famous Mysteries.

KERNOI

We cannot close this chapter without briefly discussing the sacred vessel of the cult, the *kernos*. It was described by Athenaios as "an earthenware vessel, holding within it a large number of small cups stuck together. 'In these,' Polemon says, 'are white poppy-heads, grains of wheat and barley, peas, vetches, okra-seeds, and lentils.' "[89] Shortly afterwards Athenaios repeats that Polemon in his treatise *On the Fleece of Zeus* says: ". . . kernos . . . is an earthenware vessel holding within it a large number of small cups stuck together; and in them are sage, white poppy-seeds, grains of wheat and barley, peas, vetches, okra-seeds, lentils, beans, rice-wheat, oats, compressed fruit, honey, oil, wine, milk, and sheep's

[88] J. N. Svoronos, *JIAN*, 4 (1901), pp. 263-270. Athenaios, XIII, 582e-f, 587a. I am indebted to Professor T. Webster for drawing my attention to his article in the *CJ*, N.S. 2 (1952), p. 21, and to that of Schiassi, *RivFC*, 29 (1951), p. 231. According to the latter Nannion was born about 375 B.C. and was commemorated in plays from 350 B.C. onwards. The dates indicated by Webster and Schiassi are to be preferred and fit with the dating of the tablet around 350 B.C.

[89] Athenaios, XI, 476f.

wool unwashed. The man who carries it, resembling the bearer of the sacred winnowing-fan, tastes these articles."[90] Whether or not the contents of these small cups were as stated in the first or the second passage, the fact remains that this peculiar vessel held within it a number of small cups stuck together, and that the name of that vessel was kernos. In the excavations of Eleusis were found a number of vessels corresponding to the description of Athenaios-Polemon. Some of these were surrounded by a good number of small cups stuck together (Fig. 87). Others have but symbolic tiny cups, and from others the cups are missing; but the similar nature of all these vessels is unmistakable. Their similarity also to the vessel borne by the woman on the Niinnion tablet is evident. Some scholars believe that these vessels were used as incense burners.[91] The lack of traces of fire in their interior definitely excludes this attribution as Kourouniotes and Rubensohn have proved. Apparently the vessels were used to hold a variety of cereals, representing a *panspermia*, that were being offered to the Goddess by the initiates in a service known as *kernophoria*; the worshipers could later partake of these cereals in remembrance of her benevolence to humanity and with the belief that they shared with the Goddess her bounty. In later years kernoi of a votive character were apparently made to be dedicated to the Goddesses and often these were made of marble or with symbolic little cups attached to the body of the vessel.

COINS OF ELEUSIS

A few words about the coins issued by the Eleusinians may be relevant in this general survey of the art of Eleusis. These are made of bronze and have been found in small numbers in the Sanctuary as well as in the city area. Like everything else pertaining to the site of the Mysteries, the coins also present apparently insoluble problems. On the obverse of these coins sometimes Triptolemos

[90] Athenaios, XI, 478d. One wonders which of the lists given by Athenaios and taken from Polemon is the correct one. In the second we have more elements but among these are included beans and wine. The former were forbidden to the initiates and the Goddess abstained from the latter remarking that it was not lawful for her to drink wine. Could then wine and beans have been included in an offering to Demeter? I am afraid that the longer list contained elements added by scribes to an original and shorter list.

[91] H. Von Fritze, *Ephem*, 1897, pp. 163-174. Pringsheim, *op.cit.*, pp. 69ff. Philios, *Ephem*, 1906, pp. 206-207.

appears on his chariot pulled by dragons, sometimes Demeter on a
chariot, or the head of Demeter; and on the reverse a pig facing
right stands on a bacchos. Above the pig is written ΕΛΕΤΣ and less
often ΑΘΕΝ. Head places all these coins in the years between 339
and 322 B.C.;[92] but Cavaignac distinguished them in five series and
maintained that each of these series was struck at Eleusis when that
city was independent of Athens.[93] The first series he attributes to the
occupation of Eleusis by the Thirty in 403 B.C.; the second, to 318
B.C., to the times of the war of Polysperchon against Kassander
and of Kassander against Demetrios Poliorketes. Perhaps during
that war Eleusis became independent of Athens and issued its own
coins. The third series could belong to the year 295 B.C. when
Demetrios occupied Eleusis; his lieutenants held the city until
285/4 when it was retaken by the Athenians. Coins of the fourth
series belong to the second century B.C. and those of the fifth to still
later times. Babelon[94] believes that the coins, of bronze and of
comparatively small value, were issued during the celebration of
the Mysteries to be thrown by the initiates to the crowd lining the
bridge of Kephisos. I am inclined to believe that the right of issuing
coins was conferred upon the people of Eleusis by the Athenian
state as a token of special favor to the city of Demeter, that they
were issued whether or not Eleusis was independent of Athens.

[92] *Historia Numorum*², p. 391.
[93] *Le trèsor d'Éleusis*, pp. 16, 79-80.
[94] *Traitè des monnaies Grècques et Romaines*, III, pp. 127-141.

CHAPTER IX

THE ELEUSINIAN MYSTERIES

"Then Demeter went, and to the kings who deal justice . . . she showed the conduct of her rites and taught them all her mysteries . . . awful mysteries which no one may in any way transgress or pry into or utter, for deep awe of the Gods checks the voice."—*Homeric Hymn* vv. 473-479

SECRECY

IN A FEW VERSES the Hymn indicates the introduction of the cult of Demeter to Eleusis and its secret character. One of the requirements of the cult, apparently very strictly enforced, was the secrecy imposed upon its initiates. They had to keep silent forever about the things they witnessed and heard during the celebration.[1] That obligation was jealously enforced by the Athenian State and the transgressor was severely punished. "You know," states Isokrates, "how the City becomes most angry in matters related to the Gods, if one would appear to be at fault regarding the Mysteries, and of the other matters, if one dared destroy the democracy."[2] Divulging the secrets of the cult was considered comparable to the destruction of democracy. When Alkibiades, in a drunken state, dared to imitate acts of the celebration, he was condemned *in absentia*, his property was confiscated, all the priests and priestesses of the state were called upon to pronounce curses upon him;[3] and this in spite

[1] Sophokles, *Oid. Kol.*, 1050ff. Aischylos, *Fragm.* CCCII, 218, Aristophanes, *Knights*, 282.

[2] Isokrates, *De bigis*, 6.

[3] Plutarch, *Alkibiades*, 19-22. Thoukydides, VI, 27-28, and 60. Xenophon, *Hellenika*, I, 4, 14. It will perhaps be interesting to read again the accusation against Alkibiades as given by Plutarch: "Thessalos son of Kimon of the deme of Lakiadai, impeaches Alkibiades, son of Kleinias, of the deme of Skambonidai, for committing crime against the Goddesses of Eleusis, Demeter and Kore, by imitating the mysteries and showing them forth to his own companions in his own house, wearing a robe such as the Hierophant wears when he shows forth the sacred secrets to the initiates, and calling himself Hierophant, Polytion Dadouchos, and Theodoros of the deme Phegaia, Keryx, and hailing the rest of his companions as Mystai and Epoptai, contrary to the laws and institutions of the Eumolpids, Kerykes, and priests of Eleusis." Plutarch adds that Alkibiades' property was confiscated. It is

of his popularity and the fact that shortly before his conviction he had been entrusted with one of the most important military missions ever undertaken by Athens, the Sicilian expedition. Similarly, Diagoras the Melian was condemned; according to the scholiast of Aristophanes' *Birds*, he had divulged the secrets of the Mysteries, explaining them to all, and even celebrating the Lesser Mysteries. The Athenians issued a decree against him, promising a talent as reward to the person who would kill him and two talents to him who would capture him alive.[4] Andokides, accused of revealing the Mysteries, just escaped being condemned to death.[5] Even in the second century of our era the prohibition was so strong that Pausanias, the traveler, not only avoided explanations regarding certain customs related to the Mysteries, but even refrained from mentioning the buildings to be seen in the sacred precincts of Demeter both at Eleusis and Athens. "My dream," he wrote, "forbade me to describe what is within the wall of the sanctuary; and surely it is clear that the uninitiated may not lawfully hear of that from the sight of which they are debarred." For the precinct in Athens he said: "I purposed to pursue the subject, and describe all the objects that admit of description in the sanctuary at Athens called the Eleusinion, but I was prevented from so doing by a vision in a dream. I will, therefore, turn to what may be lawfully told to everybody."[6]

Even the accidental transgression of the rule was severely punished. Livy has preserved the story of two Akarnanian youths who accidentally wandered into the Sanctuary. They were apprehended and condemned to death in accordance with the *patria*, the ancestral laws.[7] We hear of another man, Theodoros, who tried to make fun of a Hierophant by asking him: "Explain to me, Eurykleides, who are those who are impious in the eyes of the gods?" Eurykleides replied, "Those who expose the secrets to the uninitiated." Theodoros countered, "You are an impious man, you also, since you

---

interesting to note that a number of fragments of an inscription recording the confiscated property of Alkibiades were found by the American excavators of the Agora of Athens, cf. note 114 *infra*.

[4] Aristophanes, *Birds*, 1073-1074; *Frogs*, v. 320 and scholia on the line. Cf. Melanthios in *FHG*, IV, p. 444.

[5] Andokides I and [Lysias] VI.

[6] Pausanias, I, 38, 7 and I, 14, 3.

[7] T. Livius, XXXI, 14.

give explanations to a person who is not initiated." For this sacrilege Theodoros was saved from being brought before the Areopagos
only through the intervention of Demetrios of Phaleron.[8]

According to the prevailing belief, the Goddess herself meted
out punishment to those who did not keep her rule of secrecy. An
Epikourean who had entered the sacred area into which only the
Hierophant could enter, died from an unknown sickness shortly
afterwards.[9] Another, who had climbed on a rock to see the celebration, fell off and was killed.[10] Even those who lived far away
from Greece, and consequently were beyond the jurisdiction of
Athens, kept the secret for fear of the Goddesses. Horace makes
it plain that he would not be in the same ship with a person who
had divulged the secret of the Mysteries, because of the sure destruction to be inflicted on him and incidentally on those who
traveled with him.[11]

It is amazing indeed that the basic and important substance of
the secret rites was never disclosed, when these Mysteries were
held at Eleusis annually for some two thousand years, when a
multitude of people from all over the civilized world was initiated,
and when their content was transmitted orally from Hierophant
to Hierophant over so many generations. Indeed, some information
regarding this celebration has reached us and on this we may base
our knowledge, our assumptions, and our flights of imagination.
This information comes from both literary and artistic sources. In
considering it we shall have to bear in mind two very important
facts. First: the myth of Demeter and Persephone was part of Greek
mythology; it was the precious heritage of all the Greeks. Second:
there were two parts to the Mysteries of Eleusis. The first part was
held in public; it occurred in the open air and initiated and uninitiated alike could witness it; they could see and hear what was said
and what was done. This was especially true for instance of some parts
of the celebration held in Athens: the taking of the Hiera from
Eleusis to Athens, the proclamation, the descent to the sea, the
sacrifice of the piacular pigs, the pompe or Iacchos, the appearance

---

[8] According to the story preserved by Amphikrates in his book on *Famous Men*,
he was condemned to drink the hemlock (Diogenes Laertius, II, 8, 101).

[9] Aelian, *Fragm.* 12 and Suidas, *s.v.*, Hierophantes.

[10] Aelian, *Fragm.* 58, 8.

[11] Q. Horatius Flaccus, *Odes*, III, 2, vv. 25-29.

in their vestments of the Hierophant, the Dadouchos, and the other priestly figures of Eleusis. Our literary references deal almost in their entirety with the public aspect of the celebration. Our inscriptions refer to the duties of the officials known to all. Consequently acts dealing with this public aspect of the Eleusinian cult could be mentioned and could be repeated by writers and recorded on public monuments. That is why when Aristophanes in his *Frogs* sketched details of the pompe or procession and in a marvelous way painted the festive and almost divine character of Iacchos,[12] none of his contemporaries thought of accusing him, because Aristophanes was not disclosing secrets not to be mentioned, or an essential and meaningful part of the secret telete, but was simply describing in a poetic and inspired manner things known to all. In contrast, Aischylos almost lost his life because the people of Athens thought that in his tragedies he was divulging some of the secrets of the Mysteries, that he was revealing details of the second secret part of the celebration.[13] We hear that he was attacked in the theater itself and escaped only because he managed to take refuge at the altar of Dionysos and because members of the Areopagos of Athens intervened for him and begged the crowd to spare him, promising that he would be brought before a regular court for judgment.

We must insist on this distinction and explanation regarding our literary evidence, because recently some scholars have tried to find in the statements of the ancient philosophers details that might expose the real meaning and substance of the Eleusinian Mysteries, and have in fact based on these excerpts elaborate systems of initiation and doctrine which do not correspond to the reality.[14] The references bearing directly on the Mysteries to be found in our ancient authors apply to the part of the celebration held in public and visible to all. We find very few references, and these descriptive rather of ritual than of substance, to the second and

---

[12] Aristophanes, *Frogs*, vv. 324ff. Cf. G. W. Elderkin, *Mystic Allusions in the Frogs of Aristophanes*, 1955. All the allusions deal with the open part of the Mysteries.

[13] Aristotle, *Nik. Ethics*, III, 1, 17. The dramas mentioned are *Archers*, *Priestesses*, *Iphigeneia*, and *Sisyphos* (Scholium of Eustratios, p. 40). The secrecy imposed on the initiates increased with the passing of years as is proved by the "hieronymy" applied to the Hierophant.

[14] Foremost among modern scholars: V. Magnien, *Les mystères d'Éleusis*, 3rd ed., Paris, 1950.

secret part of the celebration, of what happened in the Telesterion during the nights of the secret rites. For example, Plutarch's reference to the brilliant light in the midst of which the Hierophant appeared when the Anaktoron was opened; or the allusion to the alternation of feelings and moods experienced by the initiates; or the statement attributed to Aristotle that they suffered rather than learned;[15] all these are interesting details, but they fail to disclose the substance of the telete.

We must also remember that not all ancient passages on the telete necessarily refer to the Eleusinian celebration. Other secret rites were celebrated in Greece in the Historic era and among them most popular and most energetically pursued were the Orphic mysteries, so much so that their reputed founder, Orpheus, was known as the instigator of all the teletai.[16] His mysteries were better known in later times, because the Orphics had a written literature which was available through the Early Christian era. Again the Orphics were not averse to adding to their own myths and practices others belonging to popular cults, in the hope of attracting more people to their sect. Thus they incorporated in their traditions the myth of the abduction of Persephone by Plouton, although it was incompatible with their basic doctrine of Zagreus, the son of Zeus and Persephone. Before we can attribute to the Eleusinian cult practices suggested by statements in ancient authors, we have first to be sure that they do not refer to the Orphic mysteries. Ever since the beginning of the study of the Eleusinian cult, attention has been drawn to testimonies that seem to give us a glimpse into the substance of that cult. All these testimonies, however, are derived from the writings of the Early Christian Fathers. As we proceed we shall find that their testimony cannot be trusted, that their statements do not correspond to the facts.

The same limitations apply to representations in the various artistic media, as we have seen in the previous chapter. Not every representation of Demeter and Persephone in vase painting or

---

[15] Plutarch, *de profect. virt.*, 81E, Themistios-Plutarch *apud* Stobaios, *Florilegium*, 120, 28 (Meineke, IV, p. 107). Aristotle *apud* Synesius, Dion., p. 48A.

[16] Pausanias, IX, 30, 4 where Orpheus is "believed to have discovered the mystic rites," and had his statue with *Telete* standing by his side. Plato, *Protagoras*, 316D. Euripides, *Rhesos*, v. 943. Scholium on Euripides *Alkestis* 968, etc.

sculpture illustrates an aspect of the Mysteries. The artists, like the writers, found themselves bound by restrictions, and the artist who dared divulge secrets, like Aischylos, would have run the danger of prosecution. We have a number of representations in which myths concerning the two Goddesses are depicted. Indeed, the myth of the mission of Triptolemos proved a most favorite story with the Athenian vase painter. The very fact that these myths are so represented proves that they formed no part of the Mysteries. After all, the myths of Demeter and Persephone would be represented in art as any of the myths belonging to the Olympian Gods, and statues of the Goddesses were created for their temples as it was customary to do for the other Gods. But these representations did not belong to the secret cycle of the Eleusinian cult and cannot be conceived as revealing the Mysteries. At most, they may depict some of the public part of the worship. We must bear in mind these facts when we try to see what actually took place during the celebration. Before we do so, let us consider briefly the priesthood of Eleusis and the people officially connected with the events.

FUNCTIONARIES OF THE CULT OF DEMETER

The management of the order of the celebration, not its religious content, was in the hands of one of the chief magistrates of the city of Athens, of the Archon Basileus or king-archon. He was helped in his office of general supervisor by a *paredros*, or assistant next in command, and four officials, known as the *epimeletai* or superintendents, who were elected for this post by the assembly; one of them from the family of the Eumolpids, another from that of the Kerykes, and two from the citizens at large.[17] They were responsible for seeing that everything went smoothly and they reported to the people of Athens the day after the end of the celebration any infringements of the laws governing the celebration. The officials in control of the religious content of the celebration were the priesthood of Eleusis and this included the following:[18]

The *Hierophant* was the High Priest of the Cult of Demeter

[17] This arrangement was certainly in force in the fifth century B.C. Aristotle, *Const. of Ath.*, 57. For *paredros*, cf. *CIA*, II, 597.

[18] The arrangement echoes the terms of the peace concluded in Mycenaean times between Athens and Eleusis, *supra*, p. 25.

at Eleusis. He was from the family of the Eumolpids and held office for life. He alone, at the most solemn moment of the celebration, could show to the worshipers the Hiera, the revelation that completed the initiation.[19] Hence, he can be considered as possessing the right to final and complete initiation. He alone could enter the Anaktoron.[20] In Roman times especially his personal name could not be spoken; he was a hieronymos, and his sanctity was paramount.[21] His name headed the list of the ἀείσιτοι, of those maintained at public expense in the Prytaneion of Athens. It was he who proclaimed the holy truce and sent messengers, known as *spondophoroi*, to the Hellenic world inviting all Greeks to participate in the celebration and to send the tithes due to the Goddess.[22] The Hierophant, with the other members of his gens, was the interpreter of the unwritten, ancestral laws that governed the celebration and he presided, perhaps, over cases where infringements of these laws were to be determined.[23] In general he had charge of the Sanctuary and was responsible for the celebration. He had the right to erect his statue in the Sanctuary area, and he alone could refuse initiation to those whom he considered unworthy.[24] He could be married,[25] but he kept chastity during the celebration.[26] He enjoyed a *proedria*, a special place of honor, in the theater, and his throne was placed near that of the priest of Dionysos. He was an impressive figure, wearing elaborate vestments,[27] and his sudden appearance, bathed in brilliant light, in front of the opened doors of the Anaktoron, filled the initiates with wonder and awe.

The *Hierophantides* were the Hierophant's chief assistants and

[19] Hesychios, *s.v* ἱεροφάντης.

[20] Aelian, *Fragm.* 10.

[21] For this taboo on the personal name of the Hierophant, the *hieronymy*, cf. *supra*, p. 155 n.1.

[22] *Sylloge*⁴, vol. 3, No. 1019 and vol. 1, No. 83.

[23] [Lysias] VI, 9-10.

[24] We have the instance of Apollonios of Tyana as an example: Philostratos, *Vita Apoll.*, 4, 18.

[25] We hear of sons and daughters of Hierophants: Harpokration, *s.v.* ἱεροφάντης; [Lysias] VI, 54. Isaios (Lakratides), VII, 9. Pausanias, II, 14, 1, has wrongly been taken to indicate that the Hierophant of Eleusis might never marry.

[26] Stobaios, IV, p. 73 (*Meineke*) quoting from Iuncus. Hippolytus, *Philosophoumena*, V, 8, states that the Hierophant was drugged to make sure of his chastity in the course of the celebration.

[27] Athenaios, I, 12, p. 21e: "Aischylos, too, besides inventing that comeliness and dignity of dress which Hierophants and Dadouchoi emulate, when they put on their vestments. . . ."

were two priestesses devoted to the service of the elder and younger Goddess.[28] They took an important part in the initiation. In an epigram a Hierophantid, possibly, by the name of Kallisto speaks of herself as "one who stood near the doors of Demeter and Kore the torchbearer," as one who cherished the recollection of "those nights lit by a fairer light than the day."[29] Another glories in the fact that she had set the crown on the heads of Marcus Aurelius and of Commodus.[30] These priestesses were chosen from the family of the Eumolpids,[31] held office for life, and in Roman times, at least, enjoyed the privilege of hieronymy. They could be married, since we find children and descendants mentioned in inscriptions, and had the right to erect their statues in the Sanctuary area.

The *priestess of Demeter*, who in Roman times was also called the "priestess of Demeter and Kore," belonged either to the family of the Eumolpids or to that of the Philleidae, lived at Eleusis in a dwelling, οἰκία τῆς ἱερείας (the house of the priestess), known as the ἱερὰ οἰκία, "the Sacred House," held office for life and was eponymos at Eleusis for the year, i.e., events and inscriptions were dated by her name. She was paid an obol by every initiate both in the Lesser and the Greater Mysteries.[32] In the sacred pageant she acted the role of Demeter and Kore and her office was so exalted that occasionally she disputed with the Hierophant the privilege and right of celebrating certain sacrifices.[33]

Priestesses Panageis (παναγεῖς) were the all-holy ones. They seem to have been women ministrants of the cult, whose role remains uncertain. Hesychios calls them simply priestesses of the Athenians. They seem to have had the right of "touching the Hiera," and they lived together in special dwellings, situated per-

---

[28] *Ephem*, 1885, pp. 148ff; 1894, p. 175; 1900, pp. 74ff. *BCH*, 19 (1895), p. 113.

[29] *Ephem*, 1883, p. 146.

[30] *Ephem*, 1885, p. 150. Perhaps the Antiope of Athenaios (XIII, 71) who "expounded to the initiates the loud, sacred voice of mystic oracles, as she duly escorted the priest through the Rharian Plain to honor Demeter," was such a Hierophantid.

[31] *Ephem*, 1883, p. 142, *CIA*, III, 900.

[32] *Ephem*, 1883, p. 110, l. 17; 1887, p. 111; 1900, p. 79. *Sylloge*², vol. 2, No. 587, l. 127; and *IG*, II², No. 1672, l. 18. Inscription from second century B.C.: *CIA*, IV, p. 198, No. 834b, ll. 49-50. *BCH*, 19 (1895), p. 113. Photios, *s.v.* Φιλλεῖδαι.

[33] Demosthenes, *Neaira*, 116.

haps in the auxiliary area of the Sanctuary; apparently they were called μέλισσαι or bees, and, like modern nuns, had no communion with men.[34] The title παναγεῖς, all-holy, however, as an adjective was often given to the priestesses and priests of the Sanctuary. Perhaps the "panageis priestesses" were responsible for the carrying of the Hiera to Athens and for their return to Eleusis. We do not know whether they were drawn exclusively from the family of the Eumolpids.

The *Dadouchos*, or torchbearer, was, among the male celebrants, second in importance to the Hierophant. He was chosen from the family of the Kerykes,[35] held office for life, and usually was called either Kallias or Hipponikos, these two names alternating in order. He participated in the celebration of the Mysteries and in the initiation of the worshipers, took part in the purificatory sacrifices, and as a special privilege, he alone could use the "Fleece of Zeus" for the purification of those tainted with blood.[36] He was associated with the Hierophant in the *prorrhesis*, or proclamation, in the offering of prayers for the welfare of the State,[37] and perhaps he was responsible for the lighting effects necessary to the Mysteries. After the beginning of the fifth century, he wore elaborate vestments like the Hierophant, a knot of hair (*krobylos*) on the nape of his neck, and a *strophion*, a head band.[38] He was ἀείσιτος, he was maintained at public expense in the Prytaneion of Athens, had the right to erect his statue in the Sanctuary area, and in Roman times enjoyed the privilege of hieronymy. A house of Dadouchos is mentioned in one of the lists of the expenditures of the Sanctuary. However, he could not enter the Anaktoron, nor could he have a part in the showing of the sacred objects to the initiates. Assisting the Dadouchos was a priestess known as the δᾳδουχοῦσα.[39]

[34] Hesychios, s.v. παναγεῖς. Julian, *Rhet.*, v. 173, *CIA*, IV, p. 203, l. 81.

[35] Andokides, I, 127. Scholium on Aeschines, III, 18 δᾳδοῦχοι δὲ ἀπὸ Κηρύκων. Aristides, *Eleusinios*, p. 417 (Dindorf, I): κήρυκες δὲ δᾳδούχους παρείχοντο.

[36] Hesychios, s.v. Διὸς κῴδιον and also Suidas.

[37] Scholium on Aristophanes' *Frogs*, 369 (Loeb-Dindorf, 372). Isokrates, *Paneg.*, 157.

[38] Aelian, *Fragm.*, 10. Athenaios, I, 21e. Cf. Plutarch, *Aristides*, 5, where we find also the incident of the Persian soldier who, in the battle of Marathon, mistook the Dadouchos Kallias for a king because of his long hair and strophion. For the house of the Dadouchos cf. *Sylloge*[2], vol. 2, No. 587, l. 305.

[39] *CIG*, No. 1535.

The *Hierokeryx*, or, as Xenophon calls him, the Keryx,[40] the Herald, of the initiates was drawn from the family of the Kerykes and his chief qualification perhaps was a clear strong voice. For it was he who actually read the proclamation and ordered that silence which had to be followed by the initiates throughout. He acted as a *mystagogos*, for which service he was paid by each initiate half an obol per day.[41] In Roman times he was eligible to high political office. Apparently he was appointed for life, was ἀείσιτος, and had the right to erect his statue in the Sanctuary area.

The Priest at the altar, ὁ ἐπὶ βωμῷ ἱερεύς, held office for life, belonged to the family of the Kerykes, and although he is rarely mentioned in inscriptions, he nevertheless is among the priests of Eleusis listed in an inscription of late Roman Imperial times.[42] Only in one decree of the Classical period is he mentioned.[43] His duties are not clear, but judging from his title, we may assume that he was responsible for the sacrificing of the animals. In Roman times his office seems to have been an important one, since it attracted persons of high rank. A certain Leukios Memmius glories in the fact that he initiated—meaning, apparently, that he prepared for final initiation—the Emperors L. Verus and Marcus Aurelius and Commodus.[44] As a mystagogos he received half an obol from each of the initiates, he was ἀείσιτος, and he had the right to erect his statue in the Sanctuary area.

These were the most important ministrants of the cult. They belonged to the two great families of the Eumolpids and the Kerykes, who held the right of apostolic succession. How this succession was determined and how heredity was counted we do not know, but apparently these things were decided by the members of the family and by vote. The families formed hieratic castes claiming the instigators of the cult or divinities for their ancestors, and drawing from these claims their privileges and the right of

[40] Xenophon, *Hellenika*, II, 4, 20. Demosthenes, LIX, 78. His throne in the theater of Dionysos bears the inscription "Hierokerykos."

[41] Sopatros, *Rhet. Gr.*, VIII, p. 118, 24 (Walz). J. Prott, and L. Ziehen, *Leges Graecorum Sacrae*, No. 3, col. C., p. 12. *Sylloge⁴*, vol. 1, No. 42, c.

[42] *Ephem*, 1894, p. 176.

[43] Prott-Ziehen, *op.cit.*, No. 3, col. C, p. 12. *Sylloge⁴*, vol. 1, No. 42, l. 130.

[44] *Ephem*, 1883, p. 78. *Sylloge⁴*, vol. 2, No. 872. For the meaning of μυεῖν = initiate, and the problem connected with those who had the right to initiate cf. P. Roussel, *BCH*, 54 (1930), p. 57. Apparently the members of the Eumolpids and the Kerykes had that right.

apostolic succession. The claims of the Eumolpids are clear. They were recognized by the local tradition, as represented by the Hymn, as an important family to whose ancestor Eumolpos the Goddess herself revealed her Mysteries.[45] From Eumolpos his descendants derived the right to perform the Mysteries and to reveal the Hiera to the initiates, a right which, as we have seen in Chapter II, was guaranteed to them by Athens at the close of the wars against Eleusis. The basis for the claims of the Kerykes is not clear. The family enjoyed similar privileges, but was definitely second in order.[46] According to the Eleusinian tradition recorded by Pausanias, their progenitor was Keryx, the younger son of Eumolpos. But the family itself maintained that their ancestor was Keryx the son of Hermes and Aglauros, or Herse, or Pandrosos, daughters of the legendary king of Athens, Kekrops.[47] Because of this confusion in traditions and claims and because of the fact that no Kerykes were residents of Eleusis at least in the time of the reforms of Kleisthenes,[48] scholars tend to believe that the family of the Kerykes was an Athenian family that became connected with the administration of the cult only after Eleusis came under the domination of Athens. The Kerykes presumably recognized Hermes as their ancestral God, and they officiated in the service of Apollo Pythios and Delios, in a cult foreign to Eleusis but peculiar to the Ionians.[49] They had an official house at Eleusis, known as the οἶκος κηρύκων, where they held special rites and council meetings.[50] Down to the fourth century, they are coupled with the Eumolpids, and at least in one inscription they are mentioned as the "genos of the Kerykes and Eumolpids."[51] After that century they are no longer mentioned, and it seems that at least the office of the Dadouchos passed to the family of the Lykomidai, the priestly family of Phlye at

[45] Hymn, vv. 474-476.

[46] Isokrates, *Paneg.*, 157. Aristotle, *Const. of Ath.*, XXXIX, 2 *CIA*, IV, p. 4. Aischines, III, 18.

[47] Pausanias, I, 38, 3. Polydeukes, VIII, 103.

[48] W. S. Ferguson in *Hesperia*, 7 (1938), p. 42, states "the Kerykes were an association, from which residents of the Thriasian plain" i.e. of Eleusis and its territory, "were excluded, organized or reorganized after the conquest of Eleusis to give other Athenians a worthy share in the celebration of the Eleusinian Mysteries."

[49] Foucart, *Les mystères*, p. 14.

[50] Andokides, I, 127. *IG*, II², 1672, l. 25. *Supra*, p. 173 for the ruins perhaps of that official house of the Kerykes.

[51] *Ephem*, 1883, p. 83.

Athens. This may indicate, as some believe, that the family of the Kerykes died out; but statements of Pausanias and Aristides imply their existence in the second half of the second century of our era.[52] Could one suppose that the Kerykes were merged with the Lyko-midai in the fourth century for reasons unknown?

In spite of these uncertainties it cannot be denied that these two families for centuries provided the high officials of the cult and that the Eumolpids kept their privileges and succession intact to the end of the life of the Sanctuary. Plutarch was justified in saying that not only in the past but even in his day it was Eumolpos who initiated the Hellenes.[53] Both the Eumolpids and the Kerykes per-formed functions other than those required by the celebration of the Mysteries. We find them in a commission entrusted with the question of boundaries of the sacred land of the Goddess,[54] taking part in legal actions brought against individuals for impiety. To a group of three Eumolpids, known as ἐξηγηταί or interpreters, was entrusted the special task of interpreting the ancestral laws. For them a carriage was provided at the expense of the Eleusinian treas-ury, when they accompanied the Hiera from Eleusis to Athens.[55] At least the Eumolpids received a share of the sacrifices held both in the Lesser and in the Greater Mysteries.[56] Both families, how-ever, were responsible for the preservation of the sanctity of the cult and for the exclusion from it of all intrusive foreign elements, and together they issued joint decrees.[57]

Besides the officials drawn from the families of the Eumolpids and the Kerykes, we have others less important, whose family connections seem not to have been of consequence. Of these the following are the most important:

The *Phaethyntes* was a special official whose duty seems to have been the cleaning of the statues of the divinities.[58] He was also

---

[52] Pausanias, I, 38, 3. Aristides *Eleusinios*, p. 417 (Dindorf, I).

[53] Plutarch, *de Exil.*, 17.

[54] *Sylloge*[4], vol. 1, No. 204. BCH, 13 (1889), p. 443.

[55] Demosthenes, XXII, 27 and scholium. [Lysias] VI, 9; Andokides, I, 127. *Ephem*, 1887, p. 111. Suidas, *s.v.* ἐξηγηταί. *Sylloge*[2], vol. 2, No. 587, l. 42 and *IG*, II², 1672, l. 41.

[56] *Ephem*, 1890, p. 83. *Sylloge*[4], vol. 3, No. 1050.

[57] Aischines, III, 18. Isokrates, *Paneg.*, 157.

[58] *Ephem*, 1894, p. 176. Polydeukes, VII, 69. *Sylloge*[4], vol. 1, No. 42, l. 130. Such an official is known from very few places. Pausanias, V, 14, 5, mentions the descendants of Pheidias who were entrusted with the task of polishing the chrysele-

entrusted with the task of announcing to the priestess of Athena of the Akropolis of Athens the arrival of the Hiera at the Eleusinion in the city.[59] This mission gave rise to the thought that this official had something to do with the Hiera. This is not substantiated by what we know; the Hiera were kept in the Anaktoron, which could be entered only by the Hierophant. How then could the Phaethyntes have anything to do with the sacred objects? He apparently had to clean and take care of the statues standing in the Telesterion.

The *Iacchagogos* was the special priest who accompanied the statue of Iacchos in the procession from Athens to Eleusis.[60] He was an Athenian and had a seat reserved for him in the theater of Dionysos at Athens.

The *Hydranos* was an official charged with the purification of the initiates by sprinkling them with water, or even pouring water over them. Hesychios calls him the purifier of the Mysteries.[61] In the stele, of the Museum of Eleusis, we have Persephone herself acting in the capacity of Hydranos (Fig. 70).

The *Neokoros*, who was responsible for the cleanliness and decoration of the Sanctuary, occupied a special building known as the Neokoreion.

Polydeukes mentions a number of minor priests and priestesses who were responsible for the singing that accompanied the celebration.[62]

Finally there was a functionary of special interest, the παῖς ἀφ' ἑστίας. He seems to have been a young boy (in later years it could also have been a girl),[63] who belonged to one of the aristocratic and important families of Athens and was elected by vote annually to

---

phantine statue of Zeus at Olympia made by their ancestor. In Athens we hear of a *phaethyntes* of the Olympian Zeus; this official had a seat in the theater of Dionysos at Athens.

[59] *Sylloge*[4], vol. II, No. 885, ll. 16-17.

[60] *Ephem*, 1894, p. 176. Polydeukes, I, 32.

[61] He is not mentioned in the list of the personnel of *Ephem*, 1894, p. 176, nor by Polydeukes and for this reason Pringsheim suggested that the title was given to any one who was qualified to prepare the candidates for initiation, especially to any of the members of the Eumolpids and the Kerykes. *Archäologische Beiträge*, p. 22. This purification corresponds somewhat to the Christian baptism.

[62] Polydeukes, I, 35.

[63] *Ephem*, 1894, p. 176; 1885, p. 145.

be initiated at the expense of the State.[64] The boy evidently was assumed to proceed from the hearth of Athens—his title really meaning "the boy who is initiated into the Mysteries from the hearth of Athens"—to represent the hopes of the city. His participation guaranteed the favor of the Goddesses to the city and perhaps their especial favor to the younger generation.[65] He was expected to perform certain duties not specified in our inscriptions, corresponding perhaps to those of an altar-boy in a Christian church. The office conferred high honor upon the boy or girl chosen and the title was highly valued. Small statues of boys and girls who held the office were allowed in the Sanctuary (Fig. 80).

INITIATION AND THE INITIATES

The initiate was referred to as μύστης (mystes), and he was under the direction of a sponsor who could be the μυσταγωγός (mystagogos), the person who introduced the mystes or even performed some of the preliminary rites, if he belonged to the family of Kerykes and Eumolpids. Initiation was individual; group initiation was forbidden by law. The initiate who partook of the highest degree of initiation was called the epoptes. The ceremony of the Mysteries, the ὄργια, *orgia*, was held in the temple known, as we have seen, as the Telesterion.[66] The initiates had to pay a fee to the various functionaries for their services, and apparently the entire expense for initiation amounted to fifteen drachmai.[67] Thus we find that the Hierophant received from each initiate an obol per day (both for the Lesser and Greater Mysteries), the Priestess of Demeter likewise received an obol per day, the Hierokeryx, as well as the Priest at the altar, the priestesses and the Phaethyntes,

[64] Bekker, *Anecdota*, I, 204. Porphyry, *de Abst.*, 4-5. *Ephem*, 1894, p. 176. Harpokration, *s.v.* ἀφ' ἑστίας μυεῖσθαι.

[65] L. R. Farnell, *The Cults of the Greek States*, III, p. 164. Porphyry (*de Abst.* 4, 5) states in explanation: ὅπερ γὰρ ἐν τοῖς μυστηρίοις ὁ ἀφ' ἑστίας λεγόμενος παῖς ὅστις ἀντὶ πάντων τῶν μυουμένων ἀπομειλίσσεται τὸ θεῖον, ἀκριβῶς δρῶν τὰ προστεταγμένα.

[66] From the verb τελέω (to make perfect); hence *telete* meant making perfect particularly by initiation. It should be remembered that the term and the verb were not applied exclusively to the Mysteries of Eleusis. Other secret rites were called *teletai*, especially the Orphic and Dionysiac rites.

[67] *IG*, II², 1672, l. 207. *Sylloge*², vol. 2, No. 587, l. 207: "μύησις δυοῖν τῶν δημοσίων," 30 drachmai.

half an obol per day from each initiate.[68] In the amount is included the price for a pig that served to purify the worshiper.[69]

The chief divinities. The chief divinities of the Mysteries, of course, were Demeter and Kore or Persephone. Plouton, the God of the lower world, was associated with them. Occasionally we find Plouton and Persephone associated as the Gods of the Lower World and referred to simply as Θεός and Θεά.[70] Iacchos is a divine personality associated with, but not forming a part of, the cult. He was the personification of the shouting and enthusiasm which characterized the procession from Athens to Eleusis. In later years he was confused with Dionysos who was never one of the Gods worshiped in the Mysteries.[71] Again we have a mysterious divinity, known as Eubouleus, whose identity is not completely established and whose role was a very minor one; perhaps in him we have the Chthonian Zeus.[72] Triptolemos received a portion of the sacrifices held, but seems to have been extraneous to the actual secret Eleusinian cult.[73]

Degrees of initiation. The Mysteries are proved to have included various stages or degrees of initiation. Theo Smyrnaios, in an effort to equate his conception of the stages of Philosophy to the initiation, lists five such stages or degrees:[74] 1) καθαρμός, or initial purification; 2) τελετῆς παράδοσις, a mystic communion or communication; 3) the epopteia, or revelation and sight of the holy objects; transmission of the telete; 4) the ἀνάδεσις or στεμμάτων ἐπίθεσις, the crowning with garlands which thereafter become the badge of the one who was initiated in the Mysteries, and 5) the happiness resulting from communion with God. The stages enumerated by Theo have induced some scholars to maintain that there existed five degrees of initiation and for these they devised an elaborate ritual and qualifications.[75] We may point out, however, that the fourth

[68] Cf. Prott-Ziehen, No. 3, p. 12, and col. C.

[69] Aristophanes, *Peace*, vv. 374-375, seems to indicate that the pig cost three drachmai and this is confirmed by the decree establishing the order of the festivals of Athens and the sacrifices by the state finally published by J. H. Oliver, *Hesperia*, 4 (1935), p. 21.

[70] L. R. Farnell, *op.cit.*, pp. 136ff, where discussion and bibliography. *Supra*, p. 198.

[71] Herodotos, VIII, 65. Plutarch, *Alkibiades*, 34. For Dionysos, *infra*, p. 276. Confusion seems to have started in the days of Sophokles, cf. *Antigone*, vv. 1115ff.

[72] Cf. G. E. Mylonas, "Early Christian Fathers on the Eleusinian Mysteries," *Athens Yearbook*, 1959, p. 48 (in Greek). Cf. our Fig. 65.

[73] *Sylloge*⁴, vol. 1, No. 83 dated 423/2 B.C., l. 37.

[74] *De utilit. Math.*, p. 15 (Herscher).   [75] Magnien, *op.cit.*, pp. 238ff.

stage of Theo's account belongs to the second and third stages and forms part of their ritual, since we know from inscriptions that the crowning occurred normally at the very beginning of the initiation. We have seen that one of the Hierophantides gloried in the fact that she set the crown on the heads of Marcus Aurelius and Commodus, and that occurred at the beginning of the telete, for in her epigram she states specifically, ἀρχομένη τελετῶν.[76] The happiness and bliss forming Theo's fifth stage, certainly are part and parcel of both the telete and the epopteia, for as Farnell has stated, "the object of the μύησις (of the initiation in general) is to place the mystes in a peculiarly close and privileged relation with the divinity,"[77] and that relation, of course, brings about bliss and happiness. In connection with Theo's statement we shall do well to bear in mind that he was anxious to justify his view of the development of philosophy and was not particularly anxious to be factual about the Mysteries.

On the other hand references to the Mysteries speak of only three stages. Especially important and interesting is Plutarch's story regarding the order of Demetrios Poliorketes to be initiated into the Mysteries, into the whole of the telete, from the Lesser Mysteries to and including the *Epoptika*.[78] There was nothing more than that, otherwise Demetrios would have wanted to be initiated in the assumed other stages.[79] Thus, we may feel certain in concluding that the Mysteries of Demeter at Eleusis contained but three stages or degrees: the preliminary initiation into the Lesser Mysteries, the initiation proper into the Greater Mysteries, known as the *telete*, and the *epopteia*, or highest degree of initiation.

THE LESSER MYSTERIES

The Lesser Mysteries were held as a rule once a year in the early spring in the month of flowers, the Anthesterion.[80] Occasionally when there were large crowds they were held more than once,[81]

---

[76] *Ephem*, 1885, p. 150.

[77] L. R. Farnell, *op.cit.*, p. 130.

[78] Plutarch, *Demetrios*, 26.

[79] The accusation against Alkibiades mentions only mystai and epoptai and no other degrees, *supra*, p. 224 n. 3.

[80] Scholium on Plato, *Gorgias*, 497c; on Aristophanes, *Ploutos*, 845, Plutarch, *Demetrios*, 26.

[81] Especially in the year when the athletic festival of Eleusis was held, *IG*, II², 847 (215/4 B.C.). *Ephem*, 1887, p. 175. *Sylloge⁴*, vol. 2, No. 540, l. 22.

certainly twice the same year. The Lesser Mysteries were held in Athens at the site of Agra or Agrai, on the east bank of the river Ilissos.[82] Since the Hieron of Demeter is mentioned in this connection without further clarification,[83] we do not know whether a temple of the Goddesses stood there. It seems possible that the Ionic temple of Ilissos, published by Stuart and Revett and no longer existing, might have been the temple of Demeter at Agra.[84] According to the Athenian tradition the Lesser Mysteries were instituted for the benefit of Herakles when he wanted to be initiated into the Mysteries, into the whole of the telete, from the Lesser Hades. Not wishing to refuse their benefactor, as the Scholiast of Aristophanes states the case, but at the same time in an effort to adhere to the custom of not initiating foreigners (i.e. non-Athenians) they instituted the Lesser Mysteries.[85] However, they may have been instituted by the Athenians when Eleusis came under their control, so that the celebration might start at the City. Additional information is provided by the Scholiast of Aristophanes: "The Greater Mysteries were Demeter's and the Lesser Persephone's" and by Douris, the Samian historian, who quotes a fragment of an ode according to which the "goddess Demeter is coming to celebrate her daughter's Mysteries."[86] It seems therefore reasonable to conclude that the Lesser Mysteries were held at Agra in honor and under the direction of the Kore, but that Demeter herself attended them as an honored guest.

We do not know exactly what took place in the Lesser Mysteries, but apparently they served to prepare the participants for the main initiation, to purify and create the attitude required for the communications of the Greater Mysteries.[87] The candidates took part

---

[82] Stephanos Byzantios, *s.v.* Ἄγρα χωρίον. Eustathios, Schol. on Iliad II, 361.36. *Ephem,* 1887, p. 175; *Sylloge*², vol. 2, No. 650, l. 23. Polyainos, V, 17.

[83] Hesychios, *s.v.* Ἄγρα and Suidas. Cf. also Bekker, *Anecdota,* I, 327, 3, on Metroon in Agra.

[84] J. Stuart and N. Revett, *The Antiquities of Athens,* I, pp. 7-11, pls. I-VIII. Travlos, *Athens,* fig. 32.

[85] Apollodoros, II, 5, 12, 2. Diodoros, IV, 14. Scholium on Aristophanes' *Ploutos,* 1013. Cf. Plutarch, *Theseus,* 30. Xenophon, however, seems to indicate that Herakles was initiated in the Greater Mysteries: *Hellenika,* VI, 3, 6.

[86] Aristophanes' *Ploutos,* 1013 (schol.). Athenaios, VI, 253D. Hippolytus, *Philosophoumena,* V, 8. Cf. our interpretation of the Niinnion tablet, *supra,* p. 213.

[87] Scholium on Aristophanes' *Ploutos,* 845. Clement, *Stromat.,* IV, 3, 1: καὶ ἔστι τὰ μικρά ὥσπερ προκάθαρσις καὶ προάγνευσις τῶν μεγάλων and V, 2. For an excellent discussion of the preliminaries to full initiation see P. Roussel, "L'initiation préalable et le symbole Éleusinien," *BCH,* 54 (1930), pp. 51-74.

in individual ceremonies of purification and cleansing from defile-ment,[88] under the direction of the mystagogos, of a member of the Eumolpid family or that of the Kerykes, but always under the watchful eye of the Hierophant. Fasting, sacrifices, sprinkling of water or even bathing in the waters of Ilissos,[89] and singing hymns, formed part of the ceremonies. Apparently the bearing of the sacred vessel kernos at least by women initiates, in a ceremony known as Kernophoria, and dancing formed part of the Lesser as well as of the Greater Mysteries, as we have learned from the tablet dedicated to the Goddesses by Niinnion (Fig. 88).[90] Per-haps other details in the myth of the Goddesses were enacted amid singing and praying and these are described by Stephanos as "μίμημα τῶν περὶ τὸν Διόνυσον."[91] Both Deubner and Foucart be-lieve that the statement of Stephanos proves that in the Lesser Mysteries were enacted myths from the life of Dionysos and thus link that God with the Mysteries.[92] Their suggestion has been widely accepted by scholars. However, no sign of Dionysiac influ-ence on the rites of Eleusis is recognizable; and it would be strange to have the enactment of the story of Dionysos in a performance serving as a preparation for the Mysteries of Demeter and Kore, and to exclude the stories regarding these Goddesses and especially stories of Persephone who was the special deity of the ritual. It should also be noted that Dionysos is not represented on the Niinnion tablet where the presentation of the participants in the Lesser Mysteries is depicted. The real meaning of this statement by Stephanos has, we believe, been made clear by Goudis: in the Lesser Mysteries pageants were performed in imitation of the representations held in honor of Dionysos (in his theater).[93] In that acting particular use was made of the myths of Persephone. Finally we may be sure that public sacrifices were held which the epimeletai, who along with the king-archon were in charge of the management of the celebration, offered sacrifices in behalf of the *Boule* and the *Demos* of Athens.[94]

[88] *IG*, 1², 6, ll. 109-114, and Prott-Ziehen, *op.cit.*, No. 3, col. C, l. 22.

[89] From which its banks are called "mystic." Polyainos, *Strat.*, v, 17.

[90] For a full discussion of the tablet *supra*, p. 213.

[91] Stephanos, Byzantios, *s.v.* Ἄγρα.

[92] Foucart, *Les mystères*, p. 292. L. Deubner, *Attische Feste*, p. 70.

[93] D. N. Goudis, Τὰ μυστήρια τῆς Ἐλευσῖνος, p. 29 n. 2.

[94] *Sylloge⁴*, vol. 2, No. 540. It should be noted that a holy truce was proclaimed also for the Lesser Mysteries, so that people could attend.

If from literature and the inscriptions we turn to art, we shall find little to add to the suggestions obtained from the literary sources regarding the ceremonies of the Lesser Mysteries. The stele from Eleusis (Fig. 70) shows the purification by water; the sprinkling or pouring of water over the head of the initiate. Other acts of purification are represented on the Lovatelli urn and on the sarcophagus of Torre Nova (Figs. 83-84). We have seen how these perhaps deal with the special case of Herakles,[95] and except for the sacrifice of the pig, had little to do with the regular ceremonies held in the Lesser Mysteries. It has been suggested that the procedure illustrated on the urn and the sarcophagus was for persons tainted with a blood guilt, but such persons were normally excluded from initiation and we may assume that the occasional exceptional candidates were purified from the taint even before they were admitted to the Lesser Mysteries. It cannot be conclusively proved that such purifications formed part of the celebration. The representations on the Pelike in the Hermitage and on the Pourtales vase in the British Museum only indicate the bringing of Herakles and of the Dioskouroi to be initiated and tell us nothing of the ceremony; they prove, however, that the Goddesses were believed to attend the rites. The stamnos from Eleusis (Fig. 78) tells us a good deal about the appearance of the Dadouchos and indicates that sacred rites were held in which worshipers participated in groups, but gives no definite information regarding the Mysteries. We cannot even be sure whether or not the scene represents acts held in those Mysteries. Athena, and not the Goddesses of Eleusis, presides over the scene on the hydria from Krete, but Athena took no part in the celebration of the Mysteries. The only pertinent document, as we have seen, is the tablet of Niinnion (Fig. 88), and that deals with the preparatory stages of initiation, and indicates the belief that the initiates are presented to the Goddess herself. We learn from that tablet, however, that the *kernophoria*, the bearing of the kernos, perhaps by women only, was part of the celebration of both the Greater and the Lesser Mysteries. The meaning of the *kernophoria* may be the offering of the first fruits, a form of sacrifice of *panspermia*, of the produce of the earth, from which the initiates also could partake at the end.

[95] *Supra*, pp. 206-208.

The many representations of Triptolemos have nothing to do with the rites of the Mysteries and this holds true also for the vase paintings and sculptured representations of the Goddesses. The only possible conclusion seems to be evident: the representations on objects of art shed no light on the secret rites held in the course of the celebration of the Lesser Mysteries.

Possibly the drinking of a special potion, the kykeon, terminated the fast that must necessarily have formed a part of the purification exercises. Whether or not the winnowing fan, the *liknon*, was a ritualistic instrument used at Eleusis cannot definitely be determined. If the representation on the Lovatelli urn has nothing to do with the regular ritual of the Lesser Mysteries and is only a detail of the purification of a special person tainted with blood, then the use of the *liknon* in the Mysteries becomes very doubtful. On the other hand we hear that the Dadouchos had the right of spreading the "Fleece of Zeus" below the feet of the *enageis*, of people tainted with blood, and this may indicate the admission in certain cases of persons so tainted, after a special purification presided over by the Dadouchos. That function of the Eleusinian official, however, does not necessarily mean that the rite was a regular part of the Mysteries; the purification might have taken place at any time before the person could be admitted to the Lesser Mysteries. The officiating of the Dadouchos would be a guarantee of the complete and satisfactory removal of the taint before admission to the Mysteries was granted.

Our knowledge of the rites held in the Lesser Mysteries is very limited indeed, and we can be sure of only one fact; they served as a preliminary exercise aiming at a complete purification of the candidate.

THE GREATER MYSTERIES

The Greater Mysteries were held once a year and every fourth year they were celebrated with special splendor in what was known as the *penteteris*.[96] The month known as Boedromion was the sacred month of the Mysteries, and this corresponded to September and the beginning of October. To the Greater Mysteries initiates would come from all over the Hellenic world and later from

[96] *Ephem*, 1883, p. 123, l. 46; 1887, p. 36, l. 25.

the Roman world as well, initiates including men, women, children, and even slaves. Before the time of the celebration arrived, special messengers, known as the *spondophoroi*, chosen from among the members of the Eumolpids and Kerykes, were sent to Greek city-states, proclaiming a holy truce and asking for tithes of first fruits, and for official delegations (*theories*) to be sent to the Goddess.[97] For the Greater Mysteries the truce lasted fifty-five days, from the fifteenth day of the month of Metageitnion, which preceded the month in which the Mysteries were held, to the tenth day of Pyanepsion, the month following the celebration; and thus the entire month of Boedromion, the month of the Mysteries, was included. The special envoys were sent by the Hierophant, from whom they received special instructions and who later on had the right to honor them for their services.[98] They would leave Eleusis in groups and at various times, those with the longest journeys leaving first. The expense of the *spondophoroi* was paid by the Treasury of the Sanctuary.[99] A fourth century inscription speaks of the special messengers sent to the islands, and from Polybios we hear the story of a convoy sent to Egypt in the days of the Diadochoi. Again we have the record of a mission to Laodikea of Syria and to Antioch.[100] In response the states visited would send special delegations and tithes in grateful recognition of the benefits received from the Goddess; the benefits of "civilized nourishment, of the ἡμέρου τροφῆς, which is the reason why men do not live like wild animals." On very rare occasions cities would refuse to obey the call; this was the case with the Phokeans, who, because of their refusal, made themselves unpopular for all time.[101] Beside the official delegations private citizens who aspired to be initiated into the Mysteries would go to Athens where they would spend a number of days preparing themselves for the great experience under the direction of their *mystagogos*. The official program of exercises began on the 15th day of Boedromion.

[97] Of course the Roman communities were added later after Greece came under the rule of Rome. Aischines, II, 133. *IG*, II², 1236. *Sylloge⁴*, vol. 1, No. 42.

[98] *CIA*, IV, 2, No. 597C, l. 15. *Sylloge⁴*, vol. 3, No. 1019.

[99] *Ephem*, 1883, p. 110, l. 4. *Sylloge²*, vol. 2, No. 587.

[100] Polybios, XXVIII, 6. *IG*, II², No. 1672, l. 4. *Ephem*, 1883, p. 110; 1901, p. 52. Cf. Foucart, *Les mystères*, pp. 268ff.

[101] Aischines, II, 133. Cf. *Hesperia*, 8 (1939), pp. 5-12 for an Athenian decree in protest against the Aitolian League for the arrest of the *spondophoroi* (4th century B.C.).

On the previous day, the 14th of Boedromion, the Hiera of Demeter were removed from their place in the Anaktoron, and were taken in state to Athens. The procession was headed by the priesthood of Eleusis, and the Hiera were carried by the priestesses. The sacred objects were contained in kistai, special sacred cists, that were securely closed by red ribbons.[102] Thus spectators and participants had no chance to see what they contained. The Caryatids of the Lesser Propylaea (Fig. 56) indicate the shape of the holy kistai: they were cylindrical, pyxis-like receptacles with close-fitting covers that sealed the contents firmly. The kistai are often referred to in the singular, while the Hiera are in the plural, and this gives rise to the problem of the number of the sacred kistai. Both Apuleius and Plutarch indicate that there were a number of them,[103] and more than one kiste is mentioned in the famous inscription of Andania where we read that the sacred virgins led the chariots on which there were to be seen the kistai, containing the sacred objects.[104]

The procession started, perhaps from the Pompeion of Eleusis beyond the outer court of the Sanctuary, after the preliminary sacrifices known as the *prothymata*[105] were held. Originally the procession, including the priests and priestesses carrying the kistai, apparently went on foot. In later years the priestesses at least seem to have gone in carriages certainly part of the way. For in an inventory of effects belonging to the two Goddesses of the year 408 B.C. are mentioned parts of a chariot with four wheels deposited in the Eleusinion.[106] An inscription of the third century contains the instructions given to the *epimeletai* of the Mysteries to prepare the chariots for the Hiera, the expense of which was to be defrayed by the State.[107] In later years it seems that in a different carriage drawn by two animals, rode the three *Exegetai*, or interpreters, of the ancestral law, members of the family of Eumolpids; [108] the expense

---

[102] Plutarch, *Phokion*, 28.
[103] Apuleius, *Metamorphoses*, VI, 2. Plutarch, *Phokion*, 28.
[104] *Sylloge*⁴, vol. 2, No. 736, l. 30.
[105] *CIA*, IV, No. 385d, p. 104, l. 16. *Sylloge*⁴, vol. 2, No. 540.
[106] Cavaignac, *Le trésor d'Éleusis*, pls. II and III, col. a. Cf. Pringsheim, *op.cit.*, p. 48. *Ephem*, 1895, pp. 61ff, *AM*, 19 (1894), p. 192, col. A, 1, 20ff; col. b, 1, 26ff.
[107] *CIA*, IV, No. 385d, p. 104, ll. 17-20.
[108] *Sylloge*², vol. 2, No. 587, l. 42.

for this also was to be borne by the treasury of the Eleusinian temple. Even when the Hiera were borne by carriage, the priest-esses had to walk across the bridge of the Rheitoi. That bridge, as we have seen, was located at the southeastern extremity of the Thriasian Plain towards Athens where stood the ancient boundaries between the two states. Until Roman times a contingent of Athe-nian Ephebes would meet the procession near the Rheitoi lakes, at the shrine or statue of Echo, and escort it into Athens. In Roman times, however, the escort of Ephebes would get to Eleusis on the thirteenth day of Boedromion[109] and officially escort the procession from its starting point, the Pompeion of Eleusis. The Ephebes bore spears and round shields and wore black chlamydes until white ones were donated to them by Herodes Atticus and became the traditional garb.[110]

The procession, thus escorted, would stop for a rest close to Athens, at a suburb known as the Sacred Fig Tree.[111] According to legend Demeter stayed at this place and was cared for by the hero Phytalos, to whom, as a reward for his hospitality, she gave the fig tree.[112] The site belonged to the deme of the Lakiadai and seems to have been near the place where the church of St. Savvas now stands by the Botanical Gardens of Athens. The procession was met at that place by the people of Athens headed by their priests and was escorted in state to the special sanctuary of the Goddess in Athens, known as the Eleusinion in the city, located below the northwest corner of the Akropolis. The Hiera were deposited in that Sanctuary and the *Phaethyntes* of Eleusis was dispatched to the Akropolis to announce the arrival of Demeter to the priestess of Athena.[113] Thus ended the preliminary day of the celebration.

The location of the Eleusinion in the city, long a topic of argu-ment among scholars interested in the topography of ancient Athens, has finally been established by the American excavations of the

[109] Prott-Ziehen, *op.cit.*, No. 7, p. 32. *Sylloge*⁴, vol. 2, No. 885.
[110] *IG*, III, 1132. Philostratos, *Vitae Soph.*, II, 1, 5, p. 58. *Sylloge*⁴, vol. 2, No. 870.
[111] Philostratos, *Vitae Soph.*, II, p. 20.
[112] Pausanias, I, 37, 2.
[113] *Sylloge*⁴, vol. 2, No. 885, l. 16.

Agora. It lies above the southern boundary of the Agora and below the Akropolis, exactly where its position was indicated by the literary sources. There was a comparatively large structure revealed, presumably a temple, enclosed in a precinct. No direct evidence was discovered identifying the sanctuary by name, but the objects found in its area leave no doubt as to its identity.[114]

First Day: Boedromion 15 (Aghyrmos). On the first day the Archon Basileus, the magistrate of Athens who had the supreme direction of the celebration, called the people to a festive assembly at the Stoa Poikile, or Painted Stoa, in the famous Agora of Athens. Because of this gathering the day was officially known as the ἀγυρμός.[115] In the stoa, in the presence of the Hierophant and the Dadouchos, the Hierokeryx repeated the πρόρρησις (*prorrhesis*) or proclamation, as composed by the two functionaries. Then it was that the people were officially invited to take part in the celebration of the Mysteries and to be initiated into them. Exactly what was stated in the proclamation we cannot know, but its sense can be pieced together from a variety of sources. "Everyone who has clean hands and intelligible speech," meaning Greek of course, "he who is pure from all pollution and whose soul is conscious of no evil and who has lived well and justly," the proclamation seems to have stated, could proceed with the initiation; the rest should abstain.[116] Anyone burdened with the guilt of homicide was completely excluded from participation as he was normally excluded

---

[114] For the Eleusinion in Athens, cf.: T. L. Shear, *Hesperia*, 8 (1939), pp. 207ff and 9 (1940), p. 268. E. Vanderpool, *Hesperia*, 18 (1949), p. 134. Among the objects found are fragments of inscriptions listing the confiscated property of Alkibiades that were to be set up in the Eleusinion: K. Pritchett, *Hesperia*, 22 (1953), pp. 225-299; 25 (1956), pp. 178-317; other fragments of inscriptions in which mystai are mentioned as well as the *phaethyntes*: L. H. Jeffry: *Hesperia*, 17 (1948), pp. 86-111; three reliefs, two of which represent the mission of Triptolemos and the other Demeter seated and Athena standing; five shallow pits filled with kernoi. Pausanias, I, 14, 1-4, mentions temples of Triptolemos, Demeter, and Kore without specifying whether or not they were in the precinct. Cf. R. E. Wycherley, *Athenian Agora, III, Testimonia*, pp. 74-85, Nos. 191-228 and Homer A. Thompson, "Activities in the Athenian Agora, 1959," *Hesperia*, 29 (1960), pp. 334-338.

[115] Hesychios, *s.v.* ἀγυρμός.

[116] Libanius, *Or. Corinth.*, IV, p. 356 (Reiske). Cf. also p. 368. Celsus, *apud* Orig., III, p. 149. Cf. Suetonius, *Nero*, c. 34 Theo Smyrnaios, p. 22 (Dupuis). Compare with Aristophanes' *Frogs*, vv. 354-355 and then vv. 369ff.

from religious acts by the Archon Basileus. After the Persian wars, all barbarians were also excluded,[117] because of the sacrilegious acts of the soldiers of Xerxes and Mardonios. Those who could not understand Greek were also excluded, of course, because they could not hope to understand and appreciate the ἱεροὺς λόγους, the sacred formulas, pronounced in the course of initiation. We have already seen how originally the Mysteries were restricted to the Eleusinians and Athenians; then they were opened to the Greeks adopted by the Athenian State; in the days of Herodotos at least they were open to all Greeks who wanted to be initiated; and in the days of Roman preeminence and domination, to all Roman citizens.

In the proclamation no statement seems to have been made regarding the required sacrifices and other preparations, but apparently these were explained to the initiates by the *mystagogoi* in the course of their indoctrination. Perhaps during the day a general inspection and checking of the initiates took place to determine whether or not they were properly prepared, through their participation in the Lesser Mysteries, and were ready to embark in the celebration of the Greater Mysteries. Of course a strict examination aiming at the exclusion of undesirables was impossible, especially in the days of the Roman Empire when large crowds attended the celebration, and apparently the fear of divine punishment rather than the efforts of the officials kept away those who were ineligible. Nero is an excellent case in point.[118] Occasionally of course, a person would be refused participation—for example Apollonios of Tyana who was considered a wizard.[119] Those who were admitted had the right perhaps to enter the precinct of the Eleusinion where the Hiera were kept, after washing their hands with lustral water kept in basins by the door.[120] At the Museum of Eleusis is exhibited the statue of a maiden holding a basin (Cf. *supra* p. 202, and Fig. 77) indicating that lustral rites were usual both at Eleusis and at Athens. It is reasonable to assume that other rites were held at the Eleusinion,[121] but these have remained unknown.

[117] Isokrates, IV, 157. Cf. Polydeukes, VIII, 90 Drako's laws ordered: χερνίβων εἴργεσθαι τὸν ἀνδροφόνον, σπονδῶν, κρατήρων, ἱερῶν, ἀγορᾶς.

[118] Suetonius, *Nero*, c. 34.

[119] Philostratos, *Vit. Apoll.*, IV, 18.

[120] [Lysias] VI, 52: εἰσῆλθεν εἰς τὸ Ἐλευσίνιον, ἐχερνίψατο ἐκ τῆς ἱερᾶς χέρνιβος.

[121] Cf. U. von M. Wilamowitz, *Der Glaube der Hellenen*, II, p. 479.

Second Day: Boedromion 16 (Elasis). This is known as the ἄλαδε μύσται ("To the Sea, oh Mystai,") from the shouts accompanying one of the main acts of the day. Early in the morning the heralds would order all participants to cleanse themselves in the sea and the shout "to the sea, oh mystai" would fill the city. The trip known also as ἔλασις (*elasis*) was under the supervision of the *epimeletai.*[122] Each of the initiates carried with him a small pig, which also had to be washed in the sea, and was accompanied by his mystagogos. We believe that they rode to the sea in carriages, and from this was derived the name *elasis*. We may be able, perhaps, to catch the festive spirit of the *elasis*, in the long trains of carriages and carts of modern Athenians in festive mood, driving to the sea from all directions on Sundays and holidays during summer. The small pigs are no longer here, but the mood and the spirit and the traffic jams, which in antiquity required the presence of the *epimeletai* and today the intervention of the police, are still there and are still enjoyable.

The sea was considered immaculate;[123] it cleansed and purified man from all evil.[124] The initiates probably went to the nearest shore, to the Phaleron coast on the east side, or to the peninsula of Peiraeus, the port town of Athens.[125] After cleansing themselves and their pigs in the blue waters of the Saronic Gulf, they would return to Athens. Probably the pigs had to be sacrificed immediately upon return to the city for to have waited another day would have necessitated a second cleansing of the animal. The blood of the pig was considered a very potent agent of purification with the power to absorb the impure spirit inhabiting human beings.[126] Each

[122] Hesychios, *s.v.* ἄλαδε μύσται, Polyaenus, III, 11. Plutarch, *Phokion*, 6. *CIA*, IV, No. 385d, l. 20, p. 103. *Sylloge*⁴, vol. 2, No. 540.

[123] Aischylos, *Persai*, 577. Cf. also the statement of the Hierophant whose "name was wafted by the sea" (*supra*, p. 155 n. 1).

[124] Euripides, *Iphig. Taur.*, 1193: κλύζει πάντα τἀνθρώπων κακά.

[125] Accidents were not unknown. Plutarch, *Phokion*, 28, tells us how a mystes, washing himself and his pig in the "Kantharos haven," was caught by a "sea monster" (a large fish); and the scholiast of Aischines, III, 130, records the carrying away of a mystes by a large fish. It is not certain whether the scholiast refers to the same accident recorded by Plutarch or to a different event.

[126] Perhaps this power is reflected in the miracle of the possessed in the New Testament. A pig was sacrificed and used for the purification of the sacred field, of the Sanctuary itself and of the house of the priestess; cf. *Sylloge*², vol. 2, No. 587, ll. 120, 126-127 and *IG*, II², No. 1672, ll. 120 and 126-127.

Scholium on Aristophanes' *Peace*, 374, and on *Acharneans*, 747: ἕκαστος τῶν

initiate, therefore, had to sacrifice his pig for himself.[127] Since the small animal became as emblematic of the celebration as the torch and the kernos, we find it represented in the arms of mystai in a number of works of art (Figs. 66 and 80). Its sacrifice must, too, have been a characteristic act of the celebration, and so we find in the *Frogs* of Aristophanes (vv. 377ff) the famous reference to its consumption by fire: "Oh Queen, greatly honored daughter of Demeter, how sweet is the smell of pigs' meat wafted to me."

Third Day: Boedromion 17 (Day of Sacrifices). Scholars do not quite agree as to what happened on this day. It seems to me that in the course of the third day there was held the great sacrifice and prayer for the city and for the other cities who sent *theories* or delegations to the celebration of the Mysteries. Some scholars believe that this sacrifice was held in the afternoon of the second day and on the return from the trip to the sea when the pigs also were sacrificed. There is no evidence whatever suggesting this supposition. It seems to me that the return from the sea, a rather disorderly affair, and the killing and sacrifice of so many little pigs, were not conducive to the solemn atmosphere required for the major sacrifices on behalf of the city. Again, it seems that good organization would have required at least one important act a day, especially since one day of final preparation and expectation would have been sufficient. Consequently it seems logical to assume that the third day, or part of it, was spent for the official sacrifice on behalf of the city. The day takes its name again from the order issued by the officials regarding the bringing of the animals to be sacrificed ἱερεῖα δεῦρο ("*hither the victims*").

On this day the Archon-Basileus aided by his *paredros* and the four *epimeletai*, and in the presence of the representatives of the other cities and of the people of Athens, offered the great sacrifice to the Goddesses of Eleusis in the Eleusinion and prayed for the *Boule* and the *Demos* of Athens, for the women and children of the commonwealth in accordance with the ancestral custom, the *patria*. This must have been an occasion of dignity and of reli-

---

μνουμένων ὑπὲρ ἑαυτοῦ ἔθυε. Jane Harrison (*Prolegomena to the Greek Religion*, p. 16) maintained that a pig was sacrificed because "the pig then as now was cheap to rear and a standby to the poor"; but it is nearer to the mark to maintain that it was sacrificed because of its association with dirt with which evil spirits are often equated and because of its fertility in the case of an agricultural cult.

[127] [Lysias] VI, 4. *CIA*, IV, 2, No. 385d. *Sylloge*⁴, vol. II, No. 540.

gious exaltation that could hardly have been attained at the end of the second day, characterized by hilarity and the squeaks of little pigs being killed. After the sacrifice on behalf of Athens, the various representatives took turns in sacrifice and prayer for their cities and people.

Fourth Day: Boedromion 18 (Epidauria). It was called Epidauria or Asklepieia, in honor of Asklepios and in commemoration of his late purification. For according to the local tradition, the God of healing was late in coming from Epidauros; the proclamation, the purification in the sea had already taken place, and the sacrifices were completed. A special repetition of the rites was held so that the God could be properly initiated into the Mysteries of Demeter. "The Athenians professedly assign to Asklepios a share in the Mysteries and give to the day on which they do so the name Epidauria," states Pausanias.[128] After the precedent set by Asklepios, the day was used thereafter for the preparation of those who had arrived late to the celebration. For the initiates who had normally taken part in the activities of the opening days this was a day of rest. They had to remain at home, Aristotle tells us,[129] and perhaps they were further instructed in what was expected of them.

It is interesting to note that the rites held for the late comers were supervised and directed by the Archon-Eponymos and not by the Archon-Basileus. The latter magistrate took care of the *patria,* the religious rites of ancestral origin; the former was in charge of new elements and rites added in the course of time. The Epidauria was a new element introduced after 421 B.C., when the cult of Asklepios was established in Athens. And we hear that the God was sheltered in the Eleusinion until his temple was completed, indicating his association with the Goddesses of Eleusis. Philostratos has preserved the information that the Epidauria, held after the day of the proclamation and the day of the sacrifices, were celebrated with a second sacrifice on behalf of the city.[130]

---

[128] Pausanias, II, 26, 8. It is noteworthy that Pausanias uses the singular for the day, as Epidauria, thus indicating that one day was devoted to it and not two as is sometimes maintained.

[129] Aristotle, *Const. of Athens,* LVI, 4: πομπῶν δ' ἐπιμελεῖται (ὁ ἄρχων) τῆς τε τῷ Ἀσκληπιῷ γιγνομένης, ὅταν οἰκουρῶσι μύσται.

[130] Philostratos, *Vita Apollon.,* IV, 18. Some take this statement to indicate that the pigs were sacrificed during the day of the great sacrifice; what Philostratos had in mind are the sacrifices on behalf of the city.

Fifth Day: Boedromion 19 (Pompe). This day, known as Iacchos or pompe, marked the culmination of the rites and festivities in Athens. In many respects it was one of the most brilliant days of the celebration, the day of the great procession, the day of the return to Eleusis. The Athenians, masters at arranging brilliant festivals as proved by the Panathenaic procession, clothed this pompe with an awe-inspiring impressiveness comparable to that of the solemn processions through the streets of modern Athens on the night of Good Friday. The visit to Athens had come to its close and Demeter was ready to return home. The Ephebes of Athens, again armed as before, were made ready by the *kosmetes*, the magistrate in charge of the young men, early in the morning to accompany the procession.[131] This time they were crowned with myrtle, with the sacred wreath of the Mysteries.

The initiates with their sponsors collected perhaps at the Pompeion of Athens by the Dipylon Gate. They too wore festive clothes, were crowned with myrtle, and in their hands they bore the mystic bacchos, made up of branches of myrtle tied at short distances with strands of wool.[132] Many carried a thick, knotty staff, specially made for the Mysteries, from the end of which they would suspend the *korykos* or *phaskalos*, a sack containing supplies, or bedding, or the new clothes they would wear during their initiation (cf. the Niinnion tablet, Fig. 88). When supplies were heavy, they were conveyed by pack animals; the donkey was especially used for this purpose and to that use Aristophanes refers when he makes Xanthias exclaim: "By Zeus, and I am the donkey leading the mysteries."[133]

The road to Eleusis is rather long, some fourteen miles; and although originally it was covered on foot, apparently as early as the fifth century some people went in carriages. It was then that the width of the bridge over the Rheitoi was reduced to only five feet, so that carriages could not go over it. This restriction is generally taken to have been aimed at carriages used in the procession; but since it could also refer to wheeled vehicles normally covering the road in everyday life the inscription stating it does not definitely

---

[131] *IG*, II², 1078. *Sylloge*⁴, vol. 2, No. 885, l. 10.
[132] Scholium on Aristophanes' *Knights*, 406.
[133] Aristophanes, *Frogs*, 159.

prove the use of carriages in the procession as early as this. Aristophanes in his *Ploutos*[134] tells us of the coquettish old woman who took part in the procession riding on a carriage and who was beaten by her lover because somebody cast eyes on her. In the course of the fourth century B.C. it became customary for the rich to ride in carriages, and Lykourgos had a decree passed forbidding their use in the pompe and establishing the monetary penalty to the transgressors at six thousand drachmai. He seems to have been the first to pay the penalty, since his own wife was the first transgressor.[135] By the end of the fourth century B.C. the priests also went in carriages provided by the state, and in the same century, as we have seen, a carriage was provided for the transportation of the Hiera.[136] The crowd of pedestrians, the many carriages and pack animals, would certainly have created problems of order and the need for supervision.[137] In the celebration of the Mysteries of Andania there were special officials entrusted with the order and empowered to impose punishment on the troublemakers.[138] Whether similar officials existed in Athens we do not know, but perhaps the *epimeletai*, as well as the escort of the Ephebes, looked after the orderly progress of the procession.

Let us now picture this brilliant event. Early in the morning of the fifth day the priests of Eleusis and the priestesses took the Hiera from the Eleusinion, where they had been sheltered since their arrival in Athens, and following the Panathenaic Way which went by that sanctuary, traversed the Agora, and came to the gate of Athens known as the Dipylon and to the Iaccheion, perhaps situated near there.[139] The wooden statue of Iacchos, bearing a torch and crowned with a wreath of myrtle, was then placed in a carriage and, accompanied by its special priest known as the *Iaccha-*

[134] Vv. 1013ff. The first presentation or "didaskalia," as it was called, of *Ploutos* took place in 408 B.C.

[135] Plutarch, *Orat. Lykourg.*, 842A (p. 173, ed. Vernardakis).

[136] *Sylloge*[2], vol. 2, No. 587, 41, and No. 650, l. 18.

[137] In the narrative of Herodotos, VIII, 65, we have a great cloud of dust as if raised by three myriads of people: but there, of course, we deal with a vision. The Periklean and the Roman Telesterion could accommodate around 3,000 worshipers, the latter a few more.

[138] *IG*, v, 1390, l. 40 and l. 145: Offenders were to be whipped and expenses were provided for the "wand-bearers," the ῥαβδοφόροι. *Sylloge*[4], vol. 2, No. 736, line 150.

[139] Plutarch, *Arist.*, 27.

gogos, took its place at the head of the procession.[140] Meanwhile, the crowd of the initiates with their sponsors, and a good many Athenians, who would escort the Hiera for a short distance beyond the gates, were collected and made ready to start at the Pompeion of Athens situated between the Dipylon Gate and Eridanos or the small Sacred Gate.[141] The procession was ready to start possibly after a last inspection. Iacchos and his priest were at the head; then came the priests and the *panageis*, the all holy, priestesses of Demeter bearing the Hiera in the kistai, perhaps in a manner illustrated by the Caryatids of the Lesser Propylaea. Then came the officials of the state, the *theories* of other cities and foreign representatives, then the mystai on foot—men and women and children with their sponsors, then those in carriages, and finally the pack animals forming the end. The crowd taking part must have been considerable.[142] The procession would advance on the road known as "the road to Eleusis" marked by boundary stones.[143] Further on, the road developed into the Sacred Way.

The procession went slowly but with enthusiasm and animation, and the road and the hills surrounding it echoed and reechoed the festive cry of the participants:

> . . . Come, arise, from sleep awaking,
> Come the fiery torches shaking
> Oh Iacchos, Oh Iacchos,
> Morning Star that shinest nightly,
> Lo, the mead is blazing brightly,
> Age forgets its years and sadness,

[140] Pausanias, I, 2, 4. Polydeukes, I, 32. There was a seat in the theater of Dionysos ἱερέως ἰακχαγωγοῦ.

[141] W. Judeich, *Topographie von Athen*, 2nd ed., pp. 360-362, where Bibliography. I. T. Hill, *The Ancient City of Athens*, pp. 34-35. G. Karo, *An Attic Cemetery*, p. 38. Travlos, *Athens*, fig. 36.

[142] Plutarch, *Themistokles*, 15, speaks of a great multitude. For Herodotos' statement, *supra*, n. 137. Foucart, *Les mystères*, pp. 324ff gives a beautiful account of the pompe. Cf. E. Pfuhl, *De Atheniensium pompis sacris*, Berlin, 1900.

[143] Two boundary stones were found in 1871 and 1874. Cf. 'Αθήναιον, III, p. 598. The general appearance of the pompe is reflected on the sculptured base of the votive statue of Nunnius Nigrinus; on that relief men, women, and children, with the bacchoi in hand, march in parallel rows. See L. Deubner, *Attische Feste*, pl. 6, No. 1.

Aged knees curvet for gladness,
Lift thy flashing torches o'er us,
Marshall all the blameless train,
Lead, Oh lead the way before us . . .

(Aristophanes, *Frogs*, vv. 340-350, tr. B. B. Rogers.)

The role of Iacchos became more important after the Persian invasion of Xerxes, since it was believed that the youthful God helped the Greeks against the barbarians in the battle of Salamis.

The pompe wound its way around the foothills of Parnes, between the Aigaleos and Mount Poikilon, passed one after the other the many monuments flanking the Sacred Way,[144] and reached the height of the pass. There stood the Sanctuary of Apollo, God of the laurel, established by Chalkinos and Deion on that spot of Attika "where they saw a galley running on the land,"[145] and inherited by the Holy Virgin now worshiped in her golden monastery of Daphni. From there the Sacred Way descended sharply towards the sea and in its meandering course opened up vistas of crystalline mountains and blue waters. The modern road follows in general the ancient Sacred Way to the shrine of Aphrodite, only a short distance from the sea. Its ruins to the right of the road, and its niches cut in the rock, are conspicuous landmarks even today.[146]

At the shrine of Aphrodite the Sacred Way diverged from the course now followed by the highway; it went over the hill to emerge behind the lakes of the Rheitoi and to reach the sea by the bridge we have already mentioned. From that point the Sacred Way and the modern road once more coalesce for the rest of the course.

As soon as the initiates had crossed the bridge, a special and

[144] Polemon wrote a whole book about these monuments, of which only scanty fragments have survived: *FHG*, III, p. 108. Pausanias, I, 36, 3ff, names some of the monuments.

[145] Pausanias, I, 37, 7. They were ordered by the Delphic oracle to "sacrifice to Apollo at that place in Attika where they should see a galley running on the land. But when they were at about Mount Poikilon, there appeared to them a serpent hastening to his hole; so they sacrificed to Apollo at that place."

[146] The shrine, mentioned by Pausanias, I, 37, 7, was first recognized and explored by Kambouroghlou and finally cleared and studied by Travlos (*Praktika*, 1937, pp. 25-33). The width of the Sacred Way located by Travlos beyond the shrine and over the hills amounts to five meters.

interesting event would occur. It was known as the *krokosis*, from the legendary Krokos, the first dweller of the territory, whose descendants had the privilege of tying a woolen *kroke*, a ribbon of saffron color, around the right hand and the left leg of each of the mystai.[147] What the meaning of this rite was we do not know, but perhaps it protected the initiates against evil spirits. Deubner maintained that this rite, the *krokosis*, was performed in Athens between Boedromion 15 and 19, to avoid delay which would naturally result if held on the road during the pompe.[148] However, the rite would offer to the initiates the chance to rest; it would serve to fill the time until sunset, and then the pompe could continue its way by torch light. It was perhaps during this period of respite by the seaside that Phryne's famous exhibition took place. "At the great assembly of the Eleusinia and at the festival of Poseidon," states Athenaios, "in full sight of the whole Greek world, she removed her cloak and let down her hair before stepping into the water." The sight inspired Apelles to paint his Aphrodite rising out of the sea.[149]

Before reaching its destination the pompe had to cross the Eleusinian Kephisos. On its bridge waited men with heads covered who hurled insults against important citizens participating in the celebration.[150] They in turn went by silently and there seems not to have been any exchange. The purpose of these *gephyrismoi*, as they were called, seems to have been apotropaic; piling insult on exalted persons so that they would be humbled and would not be visited with the jealous reactions of the evil spirits. Certainly the insults and the clever and gross abuse must have caused a good deal of merriment. And in a joyous mood, with torches lit, the pompe would finally reach the end of the Sacred Way and the outer court of the Sanctuary.[151] Iacchos was then received at the

---

[147] Bekker, *Anecdota*, I, p. 373. Pausanias, I, 38, 2. P. Foucart, *op.cit.*, p. 337.

[148] L. Deubner, *op.cit.*, p. 77.

[149] Athenaios, XIII, 590.

[150] Hesychios, *s.v.* γεφυρίς – γεφυρισταί, places the event on the bridge of the Eleusinian Kephisos. Strabo, IX, 400, on the other hand, places it on the Athenian Kephisos. Foucart, *op.cit.*, p. 335, rightly accepts Hesychios' version. Perhaps the two ancient writers refer to two different events. I believe that Strabo's reference applies to the returning initiates while Hesychios' refers to the pompe. Cf. *infra*, p. 280.

[151] That the pompe reached Eleusis late in the evening is indicated by the fact that its day is often called εἰκάς or the twentieth day of Boedromion. Plutarch,

court in a joyful and playful way and his mission and contribution were brought to an end. But if we get any reflection of the events which followed the arrival in the choral song of Aristophanes' *Frogs*, we must conclude that the rest of the night was spent in singing and dancing in honor of the Goddess.[152] In that court, and after the days of Peisistratos, could be seen the Kallichoron well around which such dances were traditionally held, and on the tablet of Niinnion dancing is indicated (Fig. 88). On that tablet the *kernophoria*, the last act of the night is also represented. Perhaps women bearing on their heads the mystic kernos performed a special dance in honor of the Goddess. Kourouniotes suggested that the *kernophoria* was held at another time when the initiates would not be as tired as they naturally were after the long day, after their march and activity. It seems to us, however, that it was the appropriate ending of the pompe, the moment of the arrival at the Sanctuary where the Goddess would receive her worshipers and acknowledge their presentation; the last act in which Iacchos, who is present on the Niinnion tablet, would participate and then disappear from the scene of the celebration. The present-day religious processions and exercises held in the great shrines of Christendom demonstrate that the fervor of the anticipating believer enables him to act even beyond normal human endurance. Yes, the dancing and the *kernophoria* were a fitting end to an exciting day. Finally the crowd would disperse and seek shelter and rest in one or the other of the hostels near the Sanctuary, or find hospitality in the houses and villas of friends. Thus ended one of the most brilliant religious processions and celebrations of the ancient world and one that left the initiates filled with enthusiasm and anticipation.

Perhaps we should note that in the long life of the cult, only once the pompe was suspended, although it had already started; when news of the destruction of Thebes by Alexander the Great reached Athens, the celebration was called off. In the course of the

---

Kamil., 19; *Phokion*, 28. Scholium on Aristophanes' *Frogs*, 326: μία τῶν μυστηρίων ἐστὶν ἡ εἰκάς, ἐν ᾗ τὸν Ἴακχον ἐξάγουσι. But this is because the ancient Greeks counted the day from sunset. Thus the 19th would end at sunset and the next day, the 20th, would begin with the sunset of the 19th. The pompe continued into the night and after the sunset of the 19th, hence the 20th was considered as the day of Iacchos.

[152] That it was a παννυχίς, "lasting all night long," is indicated by Euripides, *Ion*, 1074.

Peloponnesian war, when truce was impossible, the ceremonies on the Sacred Way were considerably reduced, and after the occupation of Dekeleia by the Spartans the pompe was carried by sea to and from Athens. Alkibiades, on his return to Athens, dared resume the overland procession, but he had to use the entire army of the Athenians to guard against sudden incursions.

What happened after the pompe, and the night-long revel that followed? When did the real celebration of the Mysteries, the real telete begin? The abundant information contained in inscriptions, which were the official records of the Sanctuary and of the state, and in the writings of the ancient authors regarding the part of the Mysteries conducted openly and witnessed by all, contrasts very sharply with the paucity of evidence for what occurred within the Sanctuary during the sacred nights of initiation.[153]

Sixth Day: Boedromion 20, Night of 20th to 21st (Telete). Apparently the day of the twentieth was spent in resting, fasting, purification, and sacrificing. Fasting was considered most essential for complete purification and for ridding the body of evil. At Eleusis, in addition, it was observed in commemoration and imitation of Demeter's fasting after the abduction of the Kore. Fasting could have been either partial or total. Porphyrius[154] informs us that the initiates were not allowed to eat certain kinds of fish—red mullet, dog-fish, black-tails—domestic birds and especially the cock, sacred to Persephone, beans, pomegranates, apples, the flesh of animals not properly killed, and eggs. They were not permitted to touch a dead body or a woman who had just given birth to a child. They apparently abstained from wine, following Demeter's example in refusing the wine offered to her by Metaneira. Of course, we cannot be sure that Porphyrius' list of taboos applies exclusively to the Eleusinian cult, but similar restrictions aimed at purification

---

[153] Those nights were known as μυστηριώτιδες usually translated "mystic." Since in our terminology "mystic" connotes something different from "nights of the mysteries" we shall avoid the term "mystic nights." The occasional use of the "mystic nights" should be taken to mean "the nights during which the secret rites of Demeter were held at Eleusis." During the day, it seems that little activity took place and that then the initiates rested.

[154] Porphyrius, *De Abstin.*, IV, 16. Cf. Arbesmann, "Das Fasten bei den Griechen und Romern," *Religionsgesch. vers. und Vorarb*, 21.1 (1929), pp. 19ff and 77ff, where the cathartic and apotropaic qualities of fasting are established. The ancients believed that through fasting a purity of body and soul and a spiritual revigoration were obtained.

seem to have been the common property of the mystery cults of the ancient world.[155] The partial fasting, of course, was kept by all the initiates at the instruction and under the supervision of the mystagogoi, and perhaps before they were actually admitted to initiation they would have to declare that they had not eaten any of the forbidden foods.[156]

The total fasting of course would have been in observation of Demeter's total fasting, and perhaps it was kept by the initiates during the first day of their residence at Eleusis. This total fasting perhaps came to a close by the drinking of the kykeon, the special potion of the Eleusinian Mysteries, again in observation of the similar experience of the Goddess who had refused red wine, and requested meal mixed with water and soft mint for a drink.[157] The mixing of a potion was not uncommon in the early years of Greek tradition, and we find it mentioned both in the *Iliad* and the *Odyssey*.[158] In the religious tradition of the people perhaps it started as a rite established by small agricultural communities to end the fasting that was part of an agricultural festival. Gradually it became symbolic of a telete in honor of the Goddess of agriculture. The Hymn, in describing something that already was current, attributed the beginning of the rite to the Goddess herself and made her prescribe its composition. We can understand that fully, but one wonders whether any mystic significance was attributed to the drinking of the kykeon. And the line following the statement of the compliance of Metaneira to the instructions of the Goddess: "δεξαμένη δ' ὁσίης ἕνεκεν πολυπότνια Δηώ (v. 211)," does not help to clarify the point; as a matter of fact it has caused a good deal of uncertainty. A variety of interpretations have been offered in an effort to establish its meaning.[159] Evelyn-White has translated it: "so the great queen Deo received it to observe the sacrament," and

---

[155] Cf. Diogenes Laertios, VIII, 33.

[156] Cf. Libanius, *Or. Corinth.*, IV, p. 356 (Reiske).

[157] Hymn, vv. 49, 200-201, 208ff.

[158] For an excellent and complete discussion of the kykeon see A. Delatte, *Le Cyceon breuvage rituel des mystères d'Éleusis*, Paris, 1955, where complete bibliography. In *Iliad*, XI, 624-641, Hekamede mixed a potion for the wounded Machaon with Prammian wine and on this "she grated cheese of goat's milk . . . and sprinkled . . . barley meal." A similar potion, but for different results, was mixed by Kirke in *Odyssey*, 10, 234.

[159] For a full discussion see Delatte, *op.cit.*, pp. 40ff.

"to observe the rite" is understood by Allen-Sikes. Similar interpretations were advanced by others and to the drinking of the kykeon a sacramental character has thus been attributed. Perhaps Delatte is right in comparing this verse with a passage in Euripides' *Iphigeneia in Tauris* (1. 1461), where a similar expression certainly signifies "en vue de l'etablissement d'un rite et pour que la deesse obtiente les honneurs." Whatever the meaning of that verse, we believe that the act of the drinking the kykeon was one of religious remembrance, of the observance of an act of the Goddess, and implied no sacramental mystic significance.[160] Perhaps it helped to place the partaking initiate in proper mental accord with the sufferings of the Goddess.

We do not know whether the initiates partook of the kykeon individually, in groups, or in a communal arrangement, but it seems possible that the drinking of the kykeon came at the very beginning of the services of the initiation, perhaps in the course of the first day at Eleusis. The timing of this rite had, I maintain, to be in agreement with the experiences of the Goddess. She drank the kykeon at the very beginning of her stay at Eleusis. The mystai, in a similar fashion, partook of the potion at the very beginning of their final initiation, perhaps after sacrifices were held in the Sanctuary that marked the beginning of the celebration.

The main sacrifice in honor of Demeter, Persephone, and the other Eleusinian Gods was again under the supervision of the Archon-Basileus, his *paredros*, and the *epimeletai*, who offered prayers on behalf of Athens and its people. Even the Ephebes took part in this sacrifice offering an ox and a phiale. It was during this period that perhaps the *pelanos*, a large cake made of barley and wheat harvested from the sacred Rharian plain, was offered to the

---

[160] The conception of the communion with the deity realized by the drinking of the *kykeon* was developed by Loisy, *Les mystères paiens et le mystère Chrétien*, p. 69, and the sacramental quality is upheld by Wehrli, "Die Mysterien von Eleusis," *ArchRW*, 31 (1914), 89-98. Jevon maintained that the "wheat and orge" were originally the totems at Eleusis and the drinking of the kykeon was an effort to assimilate the virtue of the spirit of harvest residing in them; when later the totemic conceptions were eliminated, the harvest spirit became the qualities of the two Goddesses whom the initiates believed they assimilated in drinking the *kykeon*. Thus he attributed a sacramental character to the *kykeon* (*Introduction to the History of Religion*, pp. 365ff). This hypothesis, based on anthropological conceptions and primitive parallels, is contrary to the known facts about the Eleusinian cult. Cf. Farnell, *op.cit.*, III, pp. 194ff.

Gods, the Eumolpids having the right to determine how much of it and to what divinity it would be offered.[161] Thus rested, purified, and conditioned by the sacrifices, the initiates were ready to receive the great revelation. To be acceptable they would wear the new clothes they brought for the occasion.

What did take place within the enclosed Sanctuary where the Mysteries were revealed? Can one follow the anticipating pilgrims in their entry to the sacred enclosure? Perhaps at the very outer gates, the Propylaea, the initiates were checked and screened, and their fitness to witness, as developed by the mystagogoi, was established. Perhaps it was then that they were given instructions how to proceed further: "to those entering the temenos of Eleusis the program was stated, not to advance inside the adyton," writes Proklos.[162] It was perhaps then that their names were recorded on wooden tablets kept by the priests, and their wreaths of myrtle were replaced by wreaths with ribbons, the emblem of their consecration to the divinities.[163]

What next? Then the ceremony really began and the initiates apparently went through certain experiences which left them perhaps filled with awe and even confusion, but also overflowing with bliss and joy. What were those experiences? We may feel certain that the rites included three different elements: the δρώμενα (dromena, that which was enacted), the δεικνύμενα (deiknymena, the sacred objects that were shown) and the λεγόμενα (legomena, the words that were spoken). What were these elements? Is there a way of establishing their nature and the meaning which they contained for the initiates? Let us see what we may through the veil of secrecy that has enshrouded them for so many, many generations.

The dromena: There can be little doubt that part of the dromena at least was a sacred pageant, the presentation of the story of Demeter and Persephone. Such a pageant, accompanied with music, singing, and measured steps, but with very few explanatory words and with no dialogue, could have been very impressive and conducive of those feelings of awe, sorrow, despair, and joy which

---

[161] *IG*, II², 140, l. 19. *Sylloge⁴*, vol. 1, No. 83, l. 36 and No. 200, l. 17.

[162] Proklos, Diadochos in *Alkib.*, I, 5, p. 288.

[163] *CIA*, IV, 1, p. 169, No. 25, 1c. along with l. 172, No. 225e. *Ephem*, 1885, p. 150, No. 26, where the Hierophantid crowns the Emperor at the beginning of the telete.

could, as in the tragedy, bring about a *katharsis*. Unlike the people in the theater, who were mere spectators of the tragedies performed, the initiates probably took a certain part in the dromena and thus could share more fully the experiences of the Goddess, and, perhaps because of that, were able to feel closer to her divine presence. They perhaps attained the feelings possible to Christians of our days who follow and even participate in the dromena of Holy Week. The story of the abduction, of the wanderings of Demeter, of her arrival at the very place in which the initiates found themselves, her stay with Keleos and Metaneira, the sorrow and grief which accompanied her days of seclusion in her temple, the rejoicing experienced in the reunion of mother and daughter, and finally the extension of divine blessings and benefits to the initiates who in a way were taking the place of the Eleusinians of old, enacted in the mystic darkness of night and in the light of torches could have been a memorable experience. The story was old and well-known, but so were the myths used by the writers of the Greek tragedies; it was the way in which the story was treated, the meaning attached to it, and its unfolding in the very place sanctified by the Goddess that counted. After all, Aristotle specifically stated that the initiates were not going to learn anything, but they were to suffer, to feel, to experience certain impressions and psychic moods.[164] Certainly the story could produce such experiences especially if the initiates themselves took a certain part in its reenactment. What could that part be? Perhaps the initiates went around searching for Persephone, sorrowing for her disappearance, hopeful of news of her, gladdened by the promise of her discovery, finally elated by her return and her reunion with her Mother; all these taking place right where originally they were supposed to have occurred, in the mystic torch light!

But where could such a full presentation of the story have been enacted? The majority of scholars believe that the entire pageant was staged in the Telesterion. I believe, with Kern,[165] that the story

---

[164] Aristotle *apud* Synesios, *Orat.*, 48: τοὺς τετελεσμένους οὐ μαθεῖν τι δεῖ, ἀλλὰ παθεῖν καὶ διατεθῆναι, γενομένους δηλονότι ἐπιτηδείους.

[165] O. Kern, *Die griechischen Mysterien der classischen Zeit*, pp. 75-76. However, Kern maintained that whatever was enacted was not an ἀπόρρητον, a secret, since some of it was represented on works of art. This conception cannot be true; we cannot have some details of the telete secret and others not. What was represented in art was not part of the telete.

was developed in and out of the Telesterion, around the very land-marks supposed to have been consecrated by the actual experience and presence of Demeter. The objection that they could not have been held in the open because they would thus be exposed to the view of the uninitiated, is not valid, since the part held outside the Telesterion was still enacted in the Sanctuary area, within an area in other words enclosed by high walls, which no one not con-nected with the celebration could enter. And so the initiates could stand on the steps of the terrace by the Sacred Way (Figs. 49 and 4, No. 21) and witness the arrival of the Goddess to Eleusis; they could share her grief as she sat disconsolate on the "Mirthless Stone,"[166] there to be found by the daughters of Keleos; they could then roam over the Sacred Way within the Sanctuary and the main terrace of the temple in an effort to find the Kore; they could assemble again by the opening of the Ploutonion to see Persephone coming from the lower world; they could accompany the Kore to the Telesterion with rejoicing and waving of their lit torches, and they could picture for themselves the joy of the Goddesses at finding each other in their reunion effected beyond the mortal ken, in the Anaktoron, the holy of holies of the Sanctuary. Indeed, the pageant acted in the midst of the night with alternation of light and darkness, with music, and even sang invocations, could have been made into a memorable experience; the participation of the initiates in its unfolding could have remained unique and a source of happy memories and bright hopes for the rest of their lives. Those of us who have participated in the services of Holy Week always go back to that experience with joy and increased hope.

This effort to picture the sacred pageant is not based on fancy alone. Here and there we get a shred of information that goes into the weaving of the entire pattern. Of course, our sources are late and are not very reliable, but still they can be trusted for statements that were not made under the influence of syncretism and of the Gnostics. Clement of Alexandria explains, "Demeter and Kore

---

[166] Interestingly enough the Hymn states that the Goddess sat not on the well, but near the Parthenion well by the road. So the initiates would not have to go beyond the walled area of the Sanctuary to the well that was later called Kalli-choron to see the Goddess newly arrived to Eleusis. The story of the man who climbed on a rock to see the celebration preserved in Aelian, *Fragm.* 58, 8, cer-tainly indicates that part of the celebration was held outside the Telesterion.

have come to be the subject of a mystic drama, and Eleusis celebrates with torches the abduction of the daughter and the sorrowful
wanderings of the mother."[167] A passage of Tertullian, in which
the benevolent Father misinterprets the act, suggests that the
abduction was part of the drama: "Why is the priestess of Demeter
carried off, unless Demeter herself had suffered the same sort of
thing?"[168] asks the Early Christian apologist. Lactantius tells us
that "in the Mysteries of Demeter all night long with torches
kindled they seek for Persephone and when she is found, the whole
ritual closes with thanksgiving and the tossing of torches."[169] The
Scholiast of Theokritos quotes Apollodoros' statement: "the Hierophant is in the habit of sounding the so-called gong when Kore is
being invoked by name."[170] Whatever could be the meaning of
the last three words, the fact remains that some kind of signal was
given in the course of the dromena.

Were the dromena limited only to the presentation of the myth
of the abduction and the wanderings of Demeter? Did they include
other acts? Foucart, the great student of the Eleusinian Mysteries
to whom we owe so much, maintained that more was enacted and
stressed the information contained in a passage from Themistios'
essay "On the Soul," preserved in Stobaios and drawn from Plutarch. "The soul," reads that famous and much abused passage
"[at the point of death] has the same experience as those who are
being initiated into great mysteries . . . at first one wanders and
wearily hurries to and fro, and journeys with suspicion through the
dark as one uninitiated: then come all the terrors before the final
initiation, shuddering, trembling, sweating, amazement: then one is
struck with a marvelous light, one is received into pure regions and
meadows, with voices and dances and the majesty of holy sounds

---

[167] Clement, *Protreptikos*, II, 12.

[168] Tertullian, *Ad Nat.*, II, p. 30. For its interpretation see Appendix, *infra*,
p. 310.

[169] Lactantius, *Div. Inst., epitom.*, 23. Incidentally in the Easter Service of the
Greek Orthodox Church the worshipers bear lighted candles, which they toss up
and down when the glad tidings of the Resurrection are proclaimed by the officiating priest.

[170] Apollodoros, *Fragm.* 36 (Müller). The meaning of the statement is not
entirely clear. We follow Farnell's interpretation (*op.cit.*, p. 175). Foucart
(*op.cit.*, p. 34) explains "when the kore is calling for aid." It is noticeable that
the gong is mentioned with the words "so-called"; perhaps this would indicate the
unusual nature of this instrument and the unfamiliarity of the public with it.

and shapes: among these he who has fulfilled initiation wanders free, and released and bearing his crown joins in the divine communion, and consorts with pure and holy men, beholding those who live here uninitiated, an uncleansed horde, trodden under foot of him and huddled together in mud and fog, abiding in their miseries through fear of death and mistrust of the blessings there."[171]

Especially on the strength of this passage Foucart maintained that the dromena contained also a simulated trip of the mystai through the regions of the lower world, through tortuous ways where in darkness they would see all kinds of apparitions, of *phasmata*, that would cause shuddering, and sweating, and terror. And then the mystai would pass to the smiling meadows of the Elysian plain, lighted by a marvelous light; among those meadows and in the communion of other holy men, they would see the image of a fortunate stay which the Goddesses promised to the initiates. The visions and wanderings of the lower world, he maintained, were enacted in the Telesterion, while the blissful scene was revealed to the initiates on its second story. In passages of Plato[172] he found arguments strengthening his belief, which however, are not capable of disposing the doubts expressed against Themistios' famous passage. We may admit that the pagan writer of the days of Julian reflected some impressions of the Mysteries of Eleusis, suggested apparently by Plutarch, but we can also maintain that he was confused in his information and ideas. We cannot know, for example, where his description applies to the soul, and where to the Mysteries; where assumption ends and reality begins; we cannot know what part of his statement is based on the Eleusinian rites and what on other rites, on the Orphic mysteries for example. The picture of the saintly men in the Elysian plains is typically Orphic and so are the horrors intimated and the suffering and the mud in which the uninitiated dwell in fear.[173] In his description one feels the impact of the preaching and the rites of the so-called *Orphiotelestai*, the itinerant charlatan-priests of Orphism, who inspired so much fear and even terror in the people of Greece.

---

[171] Stobaios, IV, p. 107 (Meineke).   [172] P. Foucart, *op.cit.*, pp. 392ff.

[173] The horrors of Hades were exploited by the Orphics and the *Orphiotelestai* against whom we find a good many harsh statements in the writings of the ancient authors. Cf. especially W. K. C. Guthrie, *Orpheus and Greek Religion*, pp. 156ff for an excellent comparison of Orphic doctrine in relation to the Eleusinian cult.

And we have to recall that when Themistios speaks of the experiences of those who are being initiated into the great mysteries, he does not specify the rites he has in mind; and certainly the Orphic mysteries were considered to be great mysteries.

From his passage two pictures emerge: that of the initiated who live in "pure regions and meadows" and form a "divine communion" consorting "with pure and holy men," and a second picture of the uninitiated, "an uncleansed horde, trodden under foot . . . and huddled together in mud and fog." It is interesting to compare these two pictures with statements made by Sokrates in Plato's *Phaedo* (69 C) and by Diodoros (I, 96). According to the latter "the punishment in Hades of the unrighteous, the *Meadows* of the righteous, and the fantastic conceptions common among the many . . . were introduced by Orpheus in imitation of the Egyptian funeral customs." Sokrates, on the other hand, declares that "those persons to whom we owe the institution of the mystery-rites are not to be despised, inasmuch as they have in fact long ago hinted at the truth by declaring that all such as arrive in Hades uninitiated into the rites shall lie in mud, while he that comes there purified and initiated shall dwell with Gods. For truly, as their authorities tell us, there are many that carry the wand but few among them that are Bacchoi." Olympiodoros clarifies the issue further by commenting that Sokrates parodies the statements of Orpheus even to the extent of quoting the verse on the wand-bearers. Clearly the two pictures of Themistios, the Meadows in which the initiated live and the mud in which the uninitiated lie are proved to be derived from Orphic doctrines.[174]

Themistios' pictures are reflected in the words of Adeimantos to be found in Plato's *Republic*. "Mousaios and his son," that is, the instigators of the Orphic mysteries, "grant to the ὅσιοι more excellent blessings from the Gods than these. Having brought them, in their writings, to the house of Hades, they arrange a symposium of the ὅσιοι where reclining on couches and crowned with wreaths

[174] Cf. Guthrie's conclusion, *op.cit.*, p. 163, that the torment of being buried in filth is connected with the Orphic ideas of purity. To the doctrines of the Orphics and not to the Eleusinian rites refers the well-known statement of the Diogenes the cynic in reply to the urgings of the Athenians to become initiated: "It would be ludicrous if Agesilaos and Epaminondas are to dwell in the mud, while certain folk of no account will live in the isles of the Blest simply because they have been initiated" (Diogenes Laertios, VI, 2, 39).

they pass the time henceforth drinking. . . . But the ἀνόσιοι and the unjust they plunge into mud in Hades and make them carry water in a sieve. . . . And these are charlatans and soothsayers who frequent the doors of the rich . . . and they produce a mass of books of Mousaios and Orpheus . . . they call them *teletai*, these ceremonies which free us from troubles of the other world and if we do not perform their sacrifices an awful fate awaits us."[175] No less a scholar than Plutarch comments that Plato directs the above "at those περὶ τὸν ʼOρφέα."[176]

In contrast, our only literary source for the Eleusinian cult, the Hymn to Demeter, does not threaten the uninitiated with the prospect of a miserable existence in mud and fog. "Happy," indeed, "is he among men upon earth who has seen these mysteries; but he who is uninitiate . . . never has lot of like good things once he is dead, down in the darkness and gloom,"[177] down in Hades. It is generally accepted by scholars that in his *Frogs*, Aristophanes has the Eleusinian cult in mind, that in a poetic language he gives us some reflections of the open part of the Mysteries of Demeter. He pictures Herakles warning Dionysos and Xanthias, his attendant, that on their way to the lower world they would come upon "weltering seas of mud, and ever-rippling dung: and plunged therein, whoso has wronged the strangers here on earth, or robbed his boylove of the promised pay, or swinged his mother, or profanely smitten his father's cheek, or sworn an oath forsworn, or copied out a speech of Morsimos."[178] Dionysos and Xanthias saw in the sea of mud parricides and perjurers. Among the sinners we do not find those uninitiated into the Eleusinian Mysteries, as would have been the case had this conception of a life in mud been a feature of Eleusis. Indeed, a Hades filled with horror and punishment for the morally unclean equated with the uninitiated is clearly an Orphic conception,[179] and from that conception Themistios drew his pictures.

[175] Plato, *Republic*, 363ff.
[176] Plutarch, *Comp. Kimon. et Lucull.*, I, p. 521. [177] Hymn, vv. 480-482.
[178] Aristophanes, *Frogs*, vv. 145ff, and 272-273 (translation B. B. Rogers).
[179] Cf. Plato's Gorgias 493a where it is stated that it was an "ingenious mythmaker, some Sicilian or Italian perhaps, who taught the equation uninitiated equal to foolish, lustful and intemperate. And the mythmaker seized the statement made by some wise man 'that in this life we are dead and that our body is a tomb.' " Certainly the last statement is a basic theory of the Orphics and is reflected in

When from our literary sources we turn to the actual remains of the Sanctuary of Demeter and its Telesterion and try to stage a trip to the lower world with all its attendant horrors and pitfalls, we shall find ourselves in agreement with Noack, who pointed out that such scenes of action would have been impossible in that building; that no machinery to produce the apparitions, the setting, and the effects postulated by Foucart and his followers ever existed; that no mention of expense involving even the most elementary stage-settings is mentioned in the surviving lists of expense inscribed on stone.[180] Furthermore, no underground rooms and passages exist into which the mystai might have descended to get a glimpse of Hades. The confidence developed in the hearts of the

---

Kratylos 400C where a distinction is drawn between *soma* and *sema* and where the followers of Orpheus are directly credited with "holding that the soul is undergoing punishment . . . and has this husk (body) around it, like a prison, to keep it from running away." It seems that the wanderings of the soul and its uncertainty and the hurrying to and fro over tortuous ways reflect Plato's statements that in turn echo Orphic thought. In *Phaedo*, 108, Sokrates, discussing the journey of the soul to Hades, states that some souls, evidently not well-ordered, who "long for the body hover distracted . . . for a long time in the neighborhood of that body and of the visible region with much struggling and much vexation, until at last they are dragged forcibly away by their appointed spirit." The journey to Hades is not easy because the road to Hades is not a clear path as told by Aischylos in his *Telephos* but has many "branchings and forkings of the way" and the danger for one to go astray is real. Here we get the impression which Themistios is trying to convey. However, before making this statement, Sokrates repeats the doctrine of the reincarnation of the soul and its judgment. "Now this is the story: when a man has breathed his last, the spirit to whom each was allotted in life proceeds to conduct him to a certain place, and all they that are there gathered must abide their judgment, and thereafter journey to Hades in company with that guide. . . . There that befalls which must befall; and having there abided for the due span of time they are brought back hither by another guide; and so they continue for many circuits of time" (*Phaedo*, 107E: translation by R. Hackforth, Cambridge 1955). Certainly the theory of reincarnation is an Orphic doctrine and so it seems that Sokrates under the impression of that doctrine made the remarks regarding the wanderings of the soul which we find reflected in Themistios. Commenting on the passages quoted, Professor Hackforth writes: "the first page of the present myth (107D-108C) is an impressive sketch, to be supplemented later (113Dff), drawn from Orphic or Pythagorean doctrine" and he adds the warning that "the eschatological myths are not to be regarded as sheer transcriptions of some Orphic Book of the Dead." The reference to 113Dff is to the ideas expressed regarding the Earth and Tartaros, the bottomless pit, represented as a chasm; there again even the language is Orphic.

Elsewhere (*Gorgias*, 524A) Plato mentions the bifurcation of the roads, one leading to the Elysion the other to Tartaros. The bifurcation, reflected by the tortuous ways of Foucart, is a typical Pythagorean-Orphic conception on which the former based their mystic significance of the Y.

[180] Noack, *Eleusis*, pp. 236ff.

heroes initiated in the Mysteries was not due to their preview of the horrors of the lower world, but to their belief that initiation provided them with a bond of communion and friendship with the august divinities in control of that world. The effects of fear and trembling could have been produced by simple acts, by the various details of the sacred drama, by the darkening and lightening of the hall in the course of the initiation and by solemn music and invocations. It is clear that Dante's *Inferno* or any other inferno did not belong to Eleusis and its Mysteries. After all, the people of the ancient world, especially in the days of the crystallization of the rites of Eleusis, in the days of the composition of the Hymn, were not tormented or even worried with ideas of the lower world like the Christians of mediaeval times. The Mysteries did not provide them with detailed instructions how to get to and how to act in the lower world like the Book of the Dead, or the plates buried with the followers of Orphism.[181] We can, therefore, conclude that Foucart's suggestions are untenable, and a simulated trip to the lower world did not form part of the dromena.

Clement of Alexandria is responsible for the notion that a *synthema* or pass-word was used by the initiates at Eleusis.[182] On the basis of his statement, modern scholars have developed a good many theories of additional activity in the Telesterion during the nights of the Mysteries. We shall examine these theories in detail in the Appendix, because they require thorough scrutiny and analysis. Here we may state that these theories are not substantiated by the facts as we can determine them now.

Some scholars believe, mistakenly it seems to me, that the mission of Triptolemos formed part of the dromena. The very fact that beginning with the sixth century B.C. the mission is so often represented in art proves that it does not belong to the secret rites which no one could utter. If it was not permitted to disclose any part of the rites by word of mouth, how would it have been allowed to disclose them by means of the permanent forms of art? The fact that the mission was not mentioned in the Hymn is proof that it was not part of the *orgia* instituted by the Goddess herself. In this connection we may recall Isokrates' famous statement that

---

[181] Cf. Olivieri, *Lamellae aureae Orphicae*, 1915.
[182] Clement, *Propreptikos*, II, 18p.

Demeter conferred upon the land of the Athenians a double gift, which is the greatest ever given to mankind: the gift of the telete (of the Mysteries) and the gift of the fruits—of the produce of the earth.[183] Triptolemos and his mission do not belong to the gift of the telete, but to that of the produce of the earth. Pausanias in his description of the trip to Eleusis, mentions what belonged to Triptolemos, because Triptolemos and his shrines do not belong to the telete; but the dream forbade him to describe what was within the walls of the Sanctuary that belonged to the Goddess and her Mysteries.[184]

Another important act attributed to the Mysteries can also be disposed of with certainty, although it is held by the majority, if not by the entire body, of scholars; that is the belief that a Sacred Marriage, an ἱερὸς γάμος, was part of the dromena. Such sacred marriages are not uncommon in mystery cults of the pagan world, but, as we are to see in the Appendix, it had no place in the Eleusinian Mysteries.[185]

In Proklos' *Timaios* 293C, we find a remarkable statement which has been assigned a place in the Mysteries of Eleusis. "In the Eleusinian rites," the statement goes, "they gazed up to the heaven and cried aloud 'rain,' they gazed down upon the earth and cried 'conceive.' "[186] The same formula is stated by Hippolytus to be the great secret of the Mysteries. This statement sounds like part of a primitive agricultural rite,[187] but Foucart maintained that the initiates shouted "rain" and "conceive" when assembled before the underground chamber where the Hierophant and the priestess were assumed to hold their sacred marriage and where "on se preparait la naissance de l'enfant divin."[188] However, it is remarkable that on the edge of a well by the Dipylon gate of Athens was cut an inscription that reads: "O Pan, O Men, be of good cheer, beautiful Nymphs, *rain, conceive,* overflow."[189] If the "rain-conceive" was, as Hippolytus states, the great and unspeakable secret of the Eleusinian Mysteries, would they have dared to inscribe it on a well open to public view? The statement fits simple agricultural rites

---

[183] Isokrates, *Paneg.* 28.
[184] Pausanias, I, 38, 6.   [185] *Infra*, Appendix, pp. 311 ff.
[186] Proklos in *Timaios* 293C. Cf. Aug. Lobeck, *Aglaophamus sive de Theologiae mysticae Graecorum causis*, p. 782. Hippolytus, *Philosophoumena*, V, 7, 34.
[187] Cf. Farnell, *op.cit.*, p. 185.   [188] P. Foucart, *op.cit.*, pp. 495-496.
[189] "O Pan, O Month, be of good cheer . . ." *BCH*, 20 (1896), p. 79.

and, if we do not attribute to it a sacred significance, we could accept that it was used during some of the Eleusinian festivities, of which there were so many; but certainly it formed no part of the dromena or of the Sacred Formulae of the Mysteries. Long ago, Lenormant suggested that it was used at the *Plemochoai,* but again the invocation to "Pan," the "Men," and the "Nymphs" of the well does not permit the connection.[190]

Is there a possibility that in the dromena was included a sacramental meal? This has been assumed by many scholars. That there might have been a communal meal in which the initiates would taste of the cereals, the gift of the Goddess to mankind, there is some possibility. That it was a sacramental meal cannot be definitely established. Years ago, Lobeck emended the *Synthema* of Clement to read from "having done my task" to "having tasted," ἐργασά-μενος to ἐγγευσάμενος and Foucart accepted that view and maintained that the initiates "avaient bu le cyceon et goute aux gateaux de la ciste."[191] This view of the pioneers in the study of the Eleusinian Mysteries has been accepted by many. It is strengthened by the obscure statement of Polemon,[192] preserved by Athenaios, which we have already quoted: "after these (the priest) proceeds to the celebration of the mystic rites; he takes out the objects of the 'thalame' (shrine or chamber) and distributes them to those who have borne the *kernos* aloft. . . . And he who has carried them, that means he who has borne aloft the kernos, tastes these articles." The passage is very obscure, and it is not definite that it applies to the Mysteries of Eleusis. It may be permissible to assume that there was a meal, but like the drinking of the kykeon, it was held at the beginning, at the breaking of the fast before the telete; it had no sacramental meaning, and it could have been taken individually or in small groups in commemoration of the great gifts that the Goddess gave to mankind.[193] That people believe that a

[190] Lenormant in Daremberg-Saglio Dictionary, *s.v.* "Eleusinia," vol. II, p. 573 n. 682.

[191] P. Foucart, *op.cit.,* pp. 381-382.

[192] Athenaios, XI, 56, p. 478. *Supra,* pp. 221-222.

[193] The representation on the vase of Naples which is taken to illustrate the meal and Polemon's statement, if it actually represents that meal proves that it lacked sacramental value since it was depicted on a vase. But it has been suggested that it actually represents an *orphiotelestes* in his ritualistic act (Harrison, *Prolegomena,* p. 157). For an illustration of the scene cf. Farnell, *op.cit.,* pl. xvb opposite p. 240.

bond of alliance and friendship is formed between those who partake of the same nourishment, was true in ancient Greek times as it is today; but to proceed from this and maintain that the initiates who consumed the first-fruits considered themselves the vassals and faithful of the Goddess and in return had a right to count on her help is pure assumption. One thing, however, seems certain; the meal had no sacramental significance since even its composition was stated by Polemon, and it did not form part of the dromena.

The survey of the available evidence leaves us with one definite fact regarding the dromena. They included a sacred pageant which dealt with the story of the abduction of Persephone, the wanderings of Demeter, and the reunion of the two Goddesses at Eleusis. Whether or not it contained anything more, as perhaps it did, we cannot prove nor can we know what else it could have included.

The legomena. When from the dromena we turn to the legomena we find a total absence of evidence or even information, however inferential. Scholars agree that the legomena were not sermons, or long religious discourses, but short liturgical statements and explanations, and perhaps invocations. They were brief comments accompanying the dromena. Yet, they were of the utmost importance. A rhetorical exercise preserved under the name of Sopatros gives us the story of a young man who dreamed that he was initiated in the Mysteries; he saw the dromena, but because he could not hear clearly the words of the Hierophant he could not be considered as initiated.[194] This seems to reflect a general belief that without the legomena the initiation was imperfect because without hearing the initiate could not perhaps understand completely all he saw. When an accusation was brought against Andokides, it was because he showed the Hiera and told the things that cannot be uttered.[195] Foucart believes that the legomena also furnished instruction to be used in the lower world comparable to that contained in the Book of the Dead of the Egyptians.[196] The practical objective of this instruction would have been to give the initiate information which could help him in the lower world after death; this filled him with joy and confidence since he had the

---

[194] Sopatros, *Rhetores Graeci*, VIII, p. 110 (Walz).
[195] Andokides, I and [Lysias] VI, 51.
[196] Foucart, *op.cit.*, p. 423.

words that would insure a pleasant hereafter. However, Foucart's belief is based upon his conception of the derivation of the Eleusinian Mysteries from Egypt; new ideas from that district, he maintained, could easily be attached to the body of mysteries originally borrowed from Egypt. But his Egyptian theory is no longer accepted, nor is his belief that the Book of the Dead could have been the prototype of the spoken word of the Mysteries. The legomena were perhaps nothing more nor less than brief ritualistic and liturgical formulae which supplemented and made clear to the initiate the performance he was witnessing. Because of their importance only people who spoke and understood Greek were invited in the proclamation to join the initiates.

The Deiknymena, the objects which were shown, remain equally unknown. Most important of these were the Hiera. The climax of the celebration was attained when the Hierophant standing in front of the Anaktoron and in the midst of a radiant light exhibited the Hiera to the initiates. From that revelation of the sacred objects, the most important function of his office, the high priest received his name: "he who shows the Hiera."[197] The Hiera were kept in the Anaktoron, the holy of holies in the center of the Telesterion, the year round and could be revealed by no one else. What were these sacred objects, the Hiera, so jealously kept from the eyes of the uninitiated? Unfortunately we cannot know. But it is evident that the nature of the Hiera would be the most important secret, the disclosure of which would have been severely punished. And the secret was faithfully kept. The various suggestions and inferences made by scholars both during the Early Christian period and in modern times, studied in the Appendix, certainly are unsuccessful, imaginative efforts to pierce the veil.[198] In spite of all these efforts we have to confess that we do not know what those sacred objects were. We have suggested in an early part of our study that they may have been small relics from the Mycenaean age handed down from generation to generation; such relics must have seemed strange and consequently awe-inspiring to the Greeks of the Historic era. Their age and the unfamiliarity of their appearance would have lent the impression of objects used by the Goddess

---

[197] Plutarch, *De prof. in virt.*, 81E. *Ephem*, 1883, p. 79. Cf. *supra*, p. 84. ἱεροφάντης, Hierophant.
[198] *Infra*, pp. 303 ff. and 295 ff.

herself during her stay in the temple within which they found themselves. It is interesting to note that the kiste borne by the Caryatid of the Lesser Propylaea is similar in form to the pyxis carried by women votaries in Mycenaean frescoes, by the women of Tiryns for example. Perhaps the relics of Eleusis were originally kept in Mycenaean pyxides. We cannot be sure of the appearance and nature of the Hiera, but we can be certain that their revelation was a most important part of the celebration and formed the climax of the rites.

Epopteia. Some of the sacred objects were revealed only to those who were initiated into the highest degree known as epopteia. To that degree mystai were admitted a year after their initiation in the telete. The epopteia was not considered an essential sequel and an imperative step for the completion of the celebration of the Mysteries but was available for those who aspired to a greater degree of understanding and accomplishment. For the great mass of initiates the celebration ended with their participation in the telete; that was considered adequate for whatever they expected to gain from the initiation. The celebration of the special rites of the epopteia were held at Eleusis during the Greater Mysteries and many scholars believe that they were held on the second night of the stay of the pilgrims at Eleusis. Of course, we cannot know what happened during the epopteia nor whether the rites held were long enough to occupy a whole night. I would like, however, to suggest that both the telete and the epopteia were held in the course of the two nights spent in the Telesterion; that at the close of what was prescribed for the first night and for the celebrants of the telete, they would be ordered to leave the Sanctuary in which only candidates for the epopteia remained. Then some preliminary rites were held and the epoptai were prepared for the final and climaxing rites of the morrow. On the second night at the end of the celebration for the telete, the initiates would leave and the epoptai would remain for the culmination of the service. In a similar manner in the Christian ritual of the early centuries we find the catechumens asked to leave the church where the confessed Christians remained for the celebration of the mass; was this another of the many details of the indebtedness of Christianity to the Mysteries held at Eleusis?

We are absolutely in the dark as to what constituted the rites of the epopteia. The ingenious theory that these rites were mainly in honor of Dionysos cannot be seriously maintained.[199] But apparently the showing of the Hiera again formed a most important part of the celebration since the name implies the revelation, the gazing at, and the silent contemplation of objects shown. Hippolytus, who lived in Rome in the first half of the third century of our era, definitely speaks of "the Athenians initiating people at the Eleusinia and showing to the epoptai that great and marvelous mystery of perfect revelation, in solemn silence, cut wheat."[200] Hippolytus begins his statement by saying that the Phrygians considered the "cut wheat" as a mystery and after the Phrygians, the Athenians, and shortly afterwards he calls Attis "the verdant cut wheat." It would be very strange indeed if the Athenians had adopted for their Eleusinian Mysteries this symbolic representation of the Phrygian Attis, the divinity of the Phrygian mysteries which they despised. Of course, it is possible to assume an accidental coincidence of beliefs of two different cults based on the yearly growth of vegetation. But the evidence seems to indicate that Hippolytus mixed his information regarding the mysteries and attributed to the Eleusinian what actually belonged to the Phrygian Mysteries. If the cut wheat was "the great and marvelous mystery of perfect revelation," how is it that we find it carved on monuments exposed to the view of candidates at the very beginning of the telete? We have seen how ears of wheat are represented on the architrave of the Lesser Propylaea and formed part of the decoration of the kiste supported by the Caryatids of the same building (Figs. 56 and 57). According to Himerios, the sophist who lived in Athens in the days of Julian the apostate (A.D. 361-363) and who consequently knew what was going on at Eleusis, "an old law ordered the initiates to take with them handfuls of agricultural produce which were the badges of a civilized life."[201] Surely among these were included ears of wheat. And indeed on the relief of Lakratides the priest, we find his sons with handfuls of wheat (Fig. 71). How can we maintain that the showing of "cut

[199] P. Foucart, *op.cit.*, pp. 433ff. V. Magnien, *op.cit.*, p. 235.
[200] Hippolytus, *Philosophoumena*, v, 38-41.
[201] Himerios, *Orat.*, Z, 2, p. 512.

wheat" was considered "the great and marvelous mystery of perfect revelation" when we find that even the candidates of the telete had to bring with them cut wheat, and when cut wheat is freely exhibited on buildings and works of art?

We have another indication that casts doubt on Hippolytus' assertion. Tertullian of Carthage, one of the most important apologists of Christianity and somewhat older than Hippolytus (perhaps A.D. 160-220), stated that not the wheat but the phallos was the sacred symbol shown to the epoptai: "Tota in adutis divinitas tot suspiria epoptarum, totum signaculum linguae, simulacrum membri virilis revelatur."[202] Whom shall we believe, Tertullian or Hippolytus? What shall we accept, the wheat or the phallos? Neither the one, nor the other. Foucart, years ago, always following his Egyptian mirage, pointed out that in Egypt Osiris was identified with the wheat and that the second part of the Mysteries of Isis and Osiris was presided over by Osiris. At Eleusis Persephone, the second divinity of the Mysteries, could not be identified with the wheat. Dionysos should be considered as the God of the epopteia, the counterpart of Osiris, as Demeter was the counterpart of Isis and the Goddess of the telete.[203] Magnien, in an effort to harmonize the conflicting statements of the Early Christian Fathers, maintained that first the cut wheat, symbolizing illumination, was shown to the epoptai and then the phallus, symbol of the generating force and of Dionysos.[204] But how could we justify the phallus as a symbol of a celebration in honor of Demeter and Kore? Magnien tried to get around the difficulty by accepting Foucart's Dionysos as the God of the epopteia. But this is contrary to the available evidence. Dionysos is not mentioned in inscriptions dealing with the celebration; he is not included in the lists of the Eleusinian divinities to whom sacrifices were due; he does not appear in the Lakratides relief (Fig. 71) where the Gods and heroes of Eleusis are represented; he has no place in the local traditions as given by the Hymn and no Dionysiac influence has been detected in the Eleusinian ritual. Furthermore, to assume that the Goddesses of Eleusis would be entirely excluded from the final degree of

[202] Tertullianus, *Valent.*, 1.

[203] P. Foucart, *op.cit.*, pp. 433ff. Cf. Diodoros, 1, 96, where Demeter is equated with Isis.

[204] V. Magnien, *op.cit.*, p. 235 (2nd ed.).

initiation to their own mysteries held in their honor and in their Sanctuary is impossible. Of course we have Stephanos' statement that the Lesser Mysteries were "μίμημα περὶ τὸν Διόνυσον" which is recalled by both Magnien and Foucart (cf. *supra* p. 241). However, neither the one nor the other explains why Dionysos is evoked at the very beginning of the preparation of the initiates, then dropped and forgotten in the telete, to appear again in the epopteia. Nor do they explain why Dionysos is not included in the list of the Gods to whom sacrifices are due. Stephanos' statement could be interpreted as Goudis suggested:[205] in the Lesser Mysteries pageants were performed in imitation of and similar to the dramas held in the theater in honor of Dionysos, but with Persephone and Demeter as protagonists instead of Dionysos.

Pindar speaks of Dionysos as the God "of the flowing locks who is enthroned beside Demeter" and this of course was repeated later by Aristides.[206] I believe that Pindar's statement finds its true meaning in the following interpretation. The Athenians believed that Demeter and Dionysos came to their city from other countries, were received as guests, and were given hospitality. Plutarch states clearly that it was proposed by Demetrios to be received every time he came to Athens with the hospitable honors paid to Demeter and Dionysos (τοῖς Δήμητρος καὶ Διονύσου ξενισμοῖς).[207] We hear that when Dionysos arrived from Eleutherai he stayed in a small temple in the Akademy before he was brought into the city by Peisistratos. It was then that he occupied, as his fixed habitation, the small temple near the theater. The event was commemorated in the City Dionysia; annually the statue of the God was taken to the small temple of the Akademy and from there it was brought in procession and with pomp and circumstance within the walls of the city.[208] In a way it was reminiscent of the bringing of Demeter

[205] *Supra*, p. 241, Goudis, *op.cit.*, p. 29 n. 2.

[206] Pindar, *Isthmian*, VII, vv. 3-5. Compare Scholium on this and Plutarch in *Comm. ad Arat.*, 7, 818, where an explanation is attempted not based on the conception that they shared the celebration at Eleusis. Aristides, IV, 10. It is interesting that no other classical writer used the term and Aristides was active around A.D. 170!

[207] Plutarch, *Demetrios*, 12.

[208] P. Foucart, *Les Cultes de Dionysos en Attique*, Ch. IX. IG, II², 1006, 1008 and 1028. Alkiphron, IV, XVIII, 16 (Schepers). Pausanias, I, 2, 5; I, 20, 3; I, 29, 2. Schol. Aristophanes, *Ach.* 243. Sir Arthur Pickard-Cambridge, *The Dramatic Festivals of Athens*, 1953, pp. 54-59.

to Athens in the form of the Eleusinian Hiera. This establishment of Dionysos in Athens, I believe, Pindar wanted to extol. Demeter was established in the Eleusinion in the City below the northwest corner of the Akropolis, Dionysos in the theater below the southeastern corner; thus they became *paredroi*, that is, they were enthroned near each other. This establishment had nothing to do with the Mysteries of Eleusis. In a similar manner Erechtheus was *paredros* of the Gods because his palace was on the Akropolis where the temples of the Gods were standing.[209]

For the celebration of the epopteia priests and priestesses were needed. Who could these have been? The Hierophant, the Dadouchos, and the other priests of Eleusis? But those belonged to the old families of the Eumolpids and the Kerykes, to whom was entrusted the celebration and the faithful adherence to the ancestral laws, to the *patria*; they were the functionaries who transmitted to the initiates all the orgies, entrusted to their forefathers by the Goddess herself. Certainly in those orgies the worship of Dionysos was not included. The very value of the celebration depended upon its conservatism and upon the belief that whatever was done and whatever was imparted was what the Goddess herself had instituted. The more we consider the matter the more we come to realize that the epopteia could not have been other than an exclusive ritual held in honor of Demeter and Persephone and of no other divinity. The statements of Tertullian and Hippolytus do not correspond to the facts. Dionysos had no place in the cult of Eleusis.[210] What the ritual of the epopteia was we cannot know, nor what its substance and meaning. Certain sacred objects were revealed to the epoptai who perhaps were supposed to observe them in silence and meditation, but what these were we cannot know.

Seventh Day: Boedromion 21. Night of the 21st to the 22nd.

The second day at Eleusis was perhaps spent in rest and preparation for the ritual of the final night in the Telesterion. The cele-

---

[209] Liddell & Scott, *s.v.* πάρεδρος.

[210] H. Metzger in *BCH*, 68-69 (1944-1945), pp. 323-339, maintains that Dionysos was an Eleusinian Divinity and he bases his conclusions on the representations of Eleusinian themes especially on vases. However, he does not try to explain why the name of Dionysos is not included in the official lists naming the Eleusinian deities. I have refuted his arguments in my study on "Dionysos at Eleusis" to appear shortly in the *Ephemeris*. For the silence cf. Plutarch, *De Profect. Virt.*, 81, E.

bration of the Mysteries was brought to an end in the course of that night; then ended the dromena, the legomena, and the deiknymena. With the revelation of the Hiera the initiation was completed and the mystai, still under the impact of deep emotional feelings but filled with joy and hope, would leave the Sanctuary of Demeter to the epoptai. They, too, in the course of the second night and in the Telesterion would attain the higher degree of initiation and their final glimpse of the most sacred objects of the cult.

Perhaps we should briefly note a mysterious formula with which it is believed that the rites were concluded. It is preserved by Hesychios and reads: "πάξ, κόγξ, ἐπιφώνημα τοῖς τετελεσμένοις" "(pax, konks, an exclamation of those who have been initiated in the *telete*)."[211] The meaning of the first two words is uncertain. It is suggested that they mean "enough, finished" and that they were used at the very close of the initiation. Hesychios does not specify the telete in which the exclamation was used and consequently we cannot be sure that it applies to the Eleusinian Mysteries.

Eighth Day: Boedromion 22. (Plemochoai).

The last day of the initiates at Eleusis was devoted mainly to libations and rites for the dead. Athenaios tells us how in the course of that day each initiate filled with liquid two special vessels known as *plemochoai* and, placing them with face to the east and west respectively, turned them upside down thus pouring their content in libation to the earth. At the same time he repeated a ritualistic formula.[212] From the vessel and the rite the day was known as the *Plemochoai*. Of course this rite was not long enough to occupy the time of the initiates and perhaps we should conclude that a good deal of the day was spent in festivities, in singing and dancing. Plutarch seems to indicate that the day was spent in festivities.[213] Perhaps in the course of the day the majority of the initiates dedicated to the Goddess the new garments they wore in the celebration. Some took them home and used them as swaddling clothes for babies as yet unborn.[214]

[211] A. Lobeck, *Aglaophamus*, pp. 75ff.

[212] Athenaios, XI, 93C, 496A. Hesychios, *s.v.* πλημοχόη. Polydeukes, X, 74.

[213] Plutarch, *Eth.*, p. 769 (Didot): ἐν Ἐλευσῖνι μετὰ τὰ μυστήρια τῆς ἑορτῆς ἀκμαζούσης.

[214] Scholium in Aristophanes' *Ploutos*, v. 845, quoting Melanthios. In the Sanctuary there was a vestiary where the garments were kept. In contrast the candidates

Ninth Day: Boedromion 23.

The return to Athens seems to have occurred on the ninth day, Boedromion 23. It was not made in an organized pompe and all initiates did not have to return to Athens before starting on their homeward voyage; some would start for home directly from Eleusis; others, and of course the Athenians with them, returned to Athens whenever they pleased and in small groups. It was perhaps on the return trip that the *gephyrismoi* mentioned by Strabo occurred;[215] the abuses hurled at the initiates by people standing on the bridge of the Athenian Kephisos.

On the next day, Boedromion 24, the Council of the Five Hundred convened at the Eleusinion of Athens, according to a law established by Solon,[216] to hear the report of the Archon-Basileus and his assistants regarding the conduct of the celebration and to take action on possible reprehensible incidents. We have no word regarding the return of the statue of Iacchos, the leader of the pompe, and this seems to indicate once more that his role ended with the arrival of the procession at Eleusis. Nor do we hear of the return of the Ephebes, the honorary escort of the Hiera.[217] We may assume that they escorted the statue of Iacchos back to Athens.

It may be well at this point to note that with the end of the celebration at Eleusis the special obligations of the initiates to the Sanctuary and to the Goddess came to an end. They were not obliged to return to the Sanctuary periodically to worship; they were not obligated to follow a certain pattern of life or rules of conduct. They were not formed into "thiasoi" or bands or clubs dedicated to the service of the Goddess and of humanity, nor did they belong to what we may call a "church body." They were free to return to their normal life, enriched by their Eleusinian experiences, which helped them, perhaps, to become "more pious, more just, and better in everything" as Diodoros (v, 48) states.

who had been initiated in the Lesser Mysteries continued to wear the garments of their initiation until they were worn out. *IG*, II², 1672, 229.

[215] Strabo, IX, 400.

[216] Andokides, *De Myster.*, 81-83.

[217] The decree recording the order of the transportation of the Hiera to Athens and of the pompe has no provisions for the return to Athens after the telete, although it indicates in detail the role the Ephebes were to play in the pompe (*Sylloge*⁴, vol. 2, No. 885 inscription dating ca. A.D. 220).

What we can learn about the Eleusinian Mysteries is certainly very limited. We know of certain rites that were not, however, part of the secret celebration; we can figure out certain acts that were part of the Mysteries, such as the enactment of the sacred pageant; we know nothing of the substance of the Mysteries, of the meaning derived even from the sacred drama which was performed. Explanations suggested by scholars thus far, and philosophic conceptions and parallels, are based upon assumptions and the wish to establish the basis on which the Mysteries rested. These accounts do not seem to correspond to the facts. The secret of the Mysteries *was kept a secret* successfully and we shall perhaps never be able to fathom it or unravel it.

For years, since my early youth, I have tried to find out what the facts were. Hope against hope was spent against the lack of monumental evidence; the belief that inscriptions would be found on which the Hierophants had recorded their ritual and its meaning has faded completely; the discovery of a subterranean room filled with the archives of the cult, which dominated my being in my days of youth, is proved an unattainable dream since neither subterranean rooms nor archives for the cult exist at Eleusis; the last Hierophant carried with him to the grave the secrets which had been transmitted orally for untold generations, from the one high priest to the next. A thick, impenetrable veil indeed still covers securely the rites of Demeter and protects them from the curious eyes of modern students. How many nights and days have been spent over books, inscriptions, and works of art by eminent scholars in their effort to lift the veil! How many wild and ingenious theories have been advanced in superhuman effort to explain the Mysteries! How many nights I have spent standing on the steps of the Telesterion, flooded with the magic silver light of a Mediterranean moon, hoping to catch the mood of the initiates, hoping that the human soul might get a glimpse of what the rational mind could not investigate! All in vain—the ancient world has kept its secret well and the Mysteries of Eleusis remain unrevealed.

The few details that we know are inadequate to give us a complete understanding of the substance of the rites. What do we know about those rites? We know that different degrees of initiation existed, the most advanced of which was known as the epopteia.

We know that all people of Hellenic speech and untainted by human blood, with the exception of barbarians, were eligible to be initiated into the Mysteries—men, women, children, and even slaves. We know that the main initiation, the telete, included at least three elements: the dromena, the things which were enacted; the deiknymena, the things which were shown; and the legomena, the words which were spoken. The spoken words and the sacred objects revealed by the Hierophant remain unknown. We may assume that the pageant of the wanderings of Demeter, the story of Persephone, and the reunion of mother and daughter formed part of the dromena; that it was a passion play which aimed not only to unfold the myth of the Goddesses to the initiates but also to make these initiates partake of the experiences of the Goddesses to share with them the distress, the travail, the exultation, and the joy which attended the loss of Persephone and her reunion with the mother. Certainly the story of the *Mater Dolorosa* of antiquity contains elements that appeal to the human heart and imagination. "With burning torches Peresphone is sought, and when she is found the rite is closed with general thanksgiving and a waving of torches." We may assume that the fortunes of Demeter and Persephone symbolized the vegetation cycle—life, death, and life again: "the sprouting of the new crop is a symbol of the eternity of life"; that they gave the initiates confidence to face death and a promise of bliss in the dark domain of Hades whose rulers became his protectors and friends through initiation. But can we go beyond this point and imagine more fully the substance of the Mysteries?

There are a good many scholars who believe that there was no more to the Mysteries than the few facts and surmises we have summarized; there are others who believe that their substance was so simple that it escapes us just because of its simplicity. There are even a few who maintain that the secret was kept because actually there was no secret worth keeping. The testimonies of the ancient world would prove untenable the suggestion of the agnostics. I believe that nearer the mark are the scholars who are trying to suggest a meaning which could have appealed to so many people for so long. Of the variety of suggestions made we shall quote but three because they seem to us that they take us as far towards a solution of the mystery as we can hope to go with the available evidence.

Nilsson suggests that the Mysteries based "on the foundation of the old agrarian cult a hope of immortality and a belief in the eternity of life, not for the individual but for the generations which spring one from another. Thus, also, there was developed on the same foundation a morality of peace and good will, which strove to embrace humanity in a brotherhood without respect to state allegiance and civil standing. The hope and the belief and the morality were those of the end of the archaic age."[218]

Guthrie has suggested that the Eleusinian cult was based upon the Homeric (and I would add also Mycenaean) conception of the hereafter and of an existence after death somewhat altered to benefit the initiates.[219] "In Homer," he states, voicing the generally accepted ideas, "dead exist indeed, but they are strengthless, witless wraiths, uttering thin bodiless shrieks as they flit to and fro in the shadowy house of Hades." And we may recall in this regard Achilles' words, "I should choose, so I might live on earth, to serve as the hireling of another, of some portionless man whose livelihood was but small, rather than to be lord over all the dead that have perished," whom he described as "the unheeding dead, the phantoms of men outworn."[220] But Homer also has an Elysium, a very pleasant place indeed, to which went special people for special reasons; Menelaos was destined to go there because he "had Helen as his wife and in the eyes of the Gods he was the son-in-law of Zeus." Guthrie suggests that perhaps this Elysium was promised to the initiates of the Eleusinian cult, and that promise of course filled them with bliss and joy. The suggestion seems plausible, especially since its inception could go back to the Mycenaean age when the Mysteries were established at Eleusis. It holds no punishment for the uninitiated and only the promise of good things for the mystai; the two correspond to the prospects held out by the Hymn. It is simple, but does not seem to have any relation to the Goddesses of Eleusis, whose role was not that of assigning dead to different categories.

"Are we left quite in the dark as to the secret of salvation that Eleusis cherished and imported," asks Farnell, and we may well

218 M. P. Nilsson, *Greek Popular Religion*, p. 63.
219 W. K. C. Guthrie, *op.cit.*, p. 149.
220 *Odyssey*, 11, vv. 476 and 489-491.

join him in his answer. "When we have weighed all the evidence and remember the extraordinary fascination a spectacle exercised upon the Greek temperament, the solution of the problem is not so remote or so perplexing. The solemn fast and preparation, the mystic food eaten and drunk, the moving passion-play, the extreme sanctity of the ἱερὰ revealed, all these influences could induce in the worshiper, not indeed the sense of absolute union with the divine nature such as the Christian sacrament . . . but at least the feeling of intimacy and friendship with the deities, and a strong current of sympathy was established by the mystic contact." Since those deities ruled over the lower world, people would feel that "those who won their friendship by initiation in this life would by the simple logic of faith regard themselves as certain to win blessings at their hands in the next. And this," suggests Farnell, "as far as we can discern, was the ground on which flourished the Eleusinian hope."[221]

Was this conception sufficient to justify the enthusiasm of the ancient world? What was the role and significance of Demeter who was the major deity of the Mysteries and who was not the mistress of the lower world? Plouton the master of that world had from all appearances a very secondary role and Persephone would emerge as the dominant power if the suggestion is accepted. Both Farnell and Guthrie reason well what can be obtained from the available evidence, and give us perhaps a portion of the significance of the Mysteries. I agree with them since I had reached similar conclusions; but I cannot help feeling that there is much more to the cult of Eleusis that has remained a secret; that there is meaning and significance that escapes us.

Whatever the substance and meaning of the Mysteries was, the fact remains that the cult of Eleusis satisfied the most sincere yearnings and the deepest longings of the human heart. The initiates returned from their pilgrimage to Eleusis full of joy and happiness, with the fear of death diminished and the strengthened hope of a better life in the world of shadows: "Thrice happy are those of mortals, who having seen those rites depart for Hades; for to them alone is it granted to have true life there; to the rest all there is evil," Sophokles cries out exultantly. And to this Pindar

---

[221] L. R. Farnell, *op.cit.*, p. 197.

with equal exultation answers: "Happy is he who, having seen these rites goes below the hollow earth; for he knows the end of life and he knows its god-sent beginning."[222] When we read these and other similar statements written by the great or nearly great of the ancient world, by the dramatists and the thinkers, when we picture the magnificent buildings and monuments constructed at Eleusis by great political figures like Peisistratos, Kimon, Perikles, Hadrian, Marcus Aurelius and others, we cannot help but believe that the Mysteries of Eleusis were not an empty, childish affair devised by shrewd priests to fool the peasant and the ignorant, but a philosophy of life that possessed substance and meaning and imparted a modicum of truth to the yearning human soul. That belief is strengthened when we read in Cicero that Athens has given nothing to the world more excellent or divine than the Eleusinian Mysteries.[223]

Let us recall again that the rites of Eleusis were held for some two thousand years; that for two thousand years civilized humanity was sustained and ennobled by those rites. Then we shall be able to appreciate the meaning and importance of Eleusis and of the cult of Demeter in the pre-Christian era. When Christianity conquered the Mediterranean world, the rites of Demeter, having perhaps fulfilled their mission to humanity, came to an end. The "bubbling spring" of hope and inspiration that once existed by the Kallichoron well became dry and the world turned to other living sources for sustenance. The cult that inspired the world for so long was gradually forgotten, and its secrets were buried with its last Hierophant.

[222] Sophokles, *Fragm.*, 719 (Dindorf). Pindar, *Fragm.*, 102 (Oxford).
[223] Cicero, *De Legibus*, 2, 14, 36.

THEORY AND FACT

The Writings of the Early Christian Fathers
and Modern Interpretations

THE PERIOD of transition from paganism to Christianity is one of the most interesting and important chapters in the life of our Western World. It was a period of increased prestige for the cult of Eleusis that gradually waned until it was wiped out by a triumphant Christianity. Perhaps it was fortunate that Christianity appeared at a time when the power of the Olympian Gods had declined and people were tired of the myths of their achievements. The mystery rites, and especially the Eleusinian, still exercized a profound influence on the minds of man and against those rites the crusaders for the New Religion turned their efforts and fire. In their writings the Early Christian Fathers include statements regarding the Mysteries and these rather brief pronouncements inspired the formulation of a number of theories still current among scholars.

The statements begin to appear towards the end of the second century of our era. By then Christianity was firmly established in the Roman Empire and from a struggling brotherhood had developed into a militant church, intent on proving that paganism was not the true religion, but a childish concoction of corrupt conceptions brought together by immoral men. From the polemics composed by learned writers to prove this point emerges an extraordinary fact. None of the Fathers appears to have been initiated into the Mysteries and none claims that he is repeating what was told by initiates converted to Christianity. It is indeed strange that statements of ex-initiates were not available. Does this indicate that among the thousands and thousands of converts, none had been worshipers of Demeter? If true, this would be an extraordinary tribute to the strength of the cult of Demeter. Or, can we assume that the recruits to the new faith, even after their conversion to Christianity kept her secret because they still held the Goddess in awe?

We must remember that a number of mystery cults besides the Eleusinian were current in the early centuries of Christianity and that there was abundant literature on the telete of the Orphic mysteries and doctrines. Furthermore, we must bear in mind that each of the mystery cults had one special divinity in whose honor and under whose special supervision the rites were performed. Occasionally a closely associated divinity was attached to the principal one; this was the case with Demeter and Persephone in the cult of Eleusis. But Demeter and Persephone and no other divinities were the main Goddesses worshiped at Eleusis, and around their experiences and teachings the rites there were held. Plouton, as we have seen, played but a minor role. Demeter had no part in any other mysteries, Orphic, Dionysiac, or Mithraic. The divinity of the Orphic mysteries was Dionysos Zagreus and no other, and he had no place whatever in the Eleusinian cult. Consequently when statements are made of Demeter and her secret cult, they do refer, or are meant to refer, to the Eleusinian Mysteries. Another point to remember is that syncretism and the conceptions of the Gnostics in the early centuries of the Christian era had reached the peak of their popularity, and equating ideas and practices originally independent of each other and even contrary to each other was then a very common practice. The general tendencies, prevalent in their period, the Early Christian Fathers adapted to their own purposes. This was not an extraordinary procedure, since they were not writing scientific or philosophical essays, but polemics against what they sincerely believed to be the established folly of paganism. And so they seem to attribute to the Eleusinian Mysteries whatever they happened to know or to hear regarding the practices of any of the other cults in their attempt to discredit the cult of Demeter.

CLEMENT OF ALEXANDRIA (A.D. 150 - CA. 211)

This capable defender of Christianity is one of the earliest and most important of the Fathers in whose writings we find statements regarding the Eleusinian Mysteries. He had traveled extensively and studied under many famous teachers, both Christian and pagan, before he was established as a presbyter in Alexandria. He had a profound knowledge of ancient literature and philosophy and was thoroughly familiar with the traditions and religious practices of the pagan world, but he had not been initiated into the Eleusinian Mysteries.

The Mysteries of Deo. The statements regarding the Eleusinian Mysteries are to be found in the second chapter of the *Protreptikos*, or his Exhortation to the Greeks p. 13ff (Loeb edition, translation G. W. Butterworth): "The mysteries of Deo commemorate the aphrodisiac, violent attack by Zeus of his mother Demeter and the wrath of Demeter (I do not know what to call her really, mother or wife) on account of which she is said to have been called *Brimo*; also the supplications of Zeus, the drink of bile, the tearing out of the heart of the victims; and unspeakable obscenities. The same rites are performed in honor of Attis and Kybele and the Korybantes by the Phrygians. They (the Phrygians) have spread the myth how Zeus tore off the testicles of a ram and then brought and flung them into the bosom of Deo, thus paying a sham penalty for his violent attack by pretending that he had mutilated himself. If I go on further to quote the symbols of initiation into the mystery they will, I know, move you to laughter, even though you are in no laughing humor when your rites are being exposed. 'I ate from a drum; I drank from the cymbal; I carried the sacred kernos; I stole into the bridal chamber.'"

Deo was the poetic form of the name of Demeter and in literature we find it already in the Hymn. There can be no doubt that the Deo of the passage is Demeter and this of course is stated by Clement himself. But the Father does not state specifically that the "mysteries of Deo" he describes are the Mysteries of Eleusis. Scholars, however, remembering that Demeter was the principal divinity in those Mysteries only, that the Eleusinian were the only renowned mysteries of the Goddess, have assumed that the reference is to the Eleusinian cult and have attached to Demeter the epithet *Brimo*, given by Clement to the divinity of the "mysteries of Deo." Let us see whether the statements in the passage can apply to Demeter's rites held at Eleusis without discussing the question of whether or not Clement wanted to imply such an equation.

The content of the "mysteries of Deo" was "the aphrodisiac, violent attack by Zeus of his mother Demeter and the wrath" of the latter. Was, however, that violent attack the subject of the Eleusinian cult? Fortunately Clement himself gives us the general subject of that cult in a brief statement and in the *Protreptikos* itself: "Demeter and Kore have come to be the subject of a mystic drama, and Eleusis celebrates with torches the abduction of the daughter and sorrowful wanderings of the mother."[1] This subject matter is entirely different from the content of the "mysteries of Deo" of the other passage. Noticeable also is the absence of Kore from the mysteries of Deo. Furthermore, Clement states that the mysteries of Deo commemorate the attack by Zeus of his *mother Demeter*; we must note these three words "πρὸς μητέρα Δήμητρα." According to the *Theogony* of Hesiod, Rhea and not Demeter was the mother of Zeus and the Hesiodian conception of Theogony was followed at Eleusis. In the Hymn to Demeter, which, as we have seen, could be considered as embodying the local Eleusinian tradition, Demeter is the daughter of Rhea and therefore the sister and not the mother of Zeus.[2] The violent attack and the ensuing wrath do not fit the amorous relations of Zeus and Demeter which resulted in the birth of Persephone,[3] but they admirably describe the situation created between Zeus and Rhea taught by the Orphics. According to their doctrine: "Zeus pursued his mother *Rhea*, incensed by her order forbidding his marriage; and when she changed herself into a she-dragon he also transformed himself into a dragon and tying her up in the so-called Heracles' knot he had intercourse with her—and the symbol of the form of this intercourse is the (entwined) staff of Hermes."[4] This violent attack assuredly brought about the wrath of *Rhea*, "on account of which she is said to have been called *Brimo*," and the effort of Zeus to placate his mother.

It is evident that Clement presents not the Eleusinian but the Orphic tradition which applied not to Demeter but to Rhea the mother of Zeus. That this was the case is indicated by the statement: "the same rites are performed in honor of Attis and Kybele and the Korybantes by the Phrygians." Certainly, we cannot even dream of suggesting that the orgiastic rites held by the Phrygians in honor of Attis and Rhea-Kybele, for which the Athenian intel-

---

[1] *Protreptikos*, II, p. 12.
[2] Hesiod, *Theogony*, vv. 453, 458. Hymn, vv. 60 and 75.
[3] Cf. Hesiod, *Theogony*, vv. 912-914.
[4] O. Kern, *Orphicorum Fragmenta*, No. 58 (41), p. 139.

lectuals expressed such disdain, were the same as those held at Eleusis or contained teachings in any way related to the Eleusinian cult. Furthermore, the "tearing off of testicles" applies only to the mysteries of Attis. Here, indeed, Clement is speaking of the Phrygian rites, which in a typical syncretistic manner he equates with the rites of Deo; he is speaking of rites in which Rhea-Kybele was the honored Goddess to whom the title or epithet *Brimo* was given.

The *symbols* quoted by Clement also point to the Phrygian cult. The drums, the cymbals, the bridal chamber are important instruments of that cult. Besides, further on Clement himself defines somewhat differently the "password" or the *synthema*, of the Eleusinian cult. That the "symbols" do belong to the cult of Rhea is made evident by the statement of Firmicius Maternus: ἐκ τυμπάνου βέβρωκα, ἐκ κυμβάλου πέπωκα γέγονα μύστης Ἄττεως: I have eaten from a drum; I have drunk from the cymbal; *I have become a mystes of Attis.*[5] The last seven words leave no doubt that Clement's "mysteries of Deo," were the mysteries held by the Phrygians in honor of Rhea-Kybele-Attis. In equating Rhea with Demeter, Clement again followed the Orphic teachings according to which "the Goddess who before was Rhea, when she gave birth to Zeus became Demeter." Or as Proklos put it: Orpheus taught that Demeter was Rhea; when she was with Kronos before she was Rhea, but when she gave birth to Zeus she became Demeter.[6]

The Story of Baubo. The second statement which is of importance to us and which makes stronger the insinuation that the "mysteries of Deo" were the Eleusinian is Clement's story of Baubo. "Yet how can we wonder," he states, "if the Tyrrhenians, who are barbarians, are thus connected to base passions, when Athenians and the rest of Greece—I blush even to speak of it—possess that shameful tale about Deo? It tells how Deo, wandering through Eleusis, which is a part of Attika, in search of her daughter the Kore, becomes exhausted and sits down at a well in deep sorrow. This display of grief is forbidden, up to the present day, to those who are initiated, lest the worshipers should seem to imitate the Goddess in her sorrow. At that time Eleusis was inhabited by aborigines,

[5] Firmicius Maternus, *De errore*, 18, p. 102 (Holm).
[6] *Orphic. Fragm.*, 145 (106.128), p. 188 (Kern). Proklos on Kratylos, 403e and 401c.

whose names were Baubo, Dysaules, Triptolemos, and also Eumolpos and Eubouleus. Triptolemos was a herdsman, Eumolpos a
shepherd, and Euboleus a swineherd. These were progenitors of
the Eumolpids and of the Kerykes, who form the priestly class at
Athens. But to continue, for I will not forbear to tell the rest of
the story. Baubo, having received Demeter as a guest, offers her a
draught of wine and meal. She declines to take it, being unwilling
to drink on account of her mourning. Baubo is deeply hurt, think-
ing she has been slighted, and thereupon uncovers her secret parts
and exhibits them to the Goddess. Demeter is pleased at the sight,
and now at last received the draught,—delighted with the spectacle! These are the secret mysteries of the Athenians! These are
also the subjects of Orpheus' poems. I will quote you the very lines
of Orpheus, in order that you may have the originator of the
mysteries as witness of their shamelessness:

> "This said, she drew aside her robes, and showed
> A sight of shame; child Iacchos was there,
> And laughing, plunged his hand below her breasts.
> Then smiled the Goddess, in her heart she smiled,
> And drank the draught from out the glancing cup."[7]

For this extraordinary performance Clement quotes from Orphic
and not Eleusinian tradition and literature. Nowhere indeed is he
so indiscreet as to state definitely that the scene of Baubo formed
part of the Mysteries, but the impression he leaves is unmistakable.
The placing of the story at Eleusis; the stay of Demeter by the well
in deep sorrow; her sojourn with the mortal rulers; her initial
refusal to drink the draught presented to her; her final acceptance;
the priestly classes of the Eumolpids and Kerykes characteristic only
of the Eleusinian cult, all these details reflect the tradition of
Eleusis well-known to all because of the Homeric Hymn.[8] Yet, he

---

[7] *Protreptikos*, II, pp. 16-18. It should be remembered that the Orphics had a
voluminous literature a small part of which dealt with the Orphic mysteries. In
their Theogony they included stories and hymns for practically all the Gods. This,
however, does not indicate that all the Gods had a place of importance in the
Orphic mysteries; nor does it indicate that their stories reflected the secret rites that
were held in honor of other Gods like Demeter.

[8] Compare the Orphic with the passage in the Homeric Hymn, vv. 195-205.
In the latter instead of the depraved Baubo we have the trusted Iambe and instead
of the shameful exhibition we have "many a quip and jest" with which the heart
of Demeter was cheered.

does not use the key epithet Eleusinian but instead he exclaims: "These are the secret mysteries of the Athenians." Of course, Clement had to be careful with his statements whose value would have been nullified if he were caught by the pagans telling untruths. But can there be any doubt that he is referring to the Eleusinian rites? I think not. And this may indicate that the "mysteries of Deo" described in the first passage were to be equated with the Mysteries of Eleusis. For otherwise the same Goddess Deo, would have been presented as a protagonist in different mysteries.

We have to examine in greater detail the story of Baubo because modern scholars have based on it their conception of the existence of a "κτείς" or female pudenda, among the sacred objects of the Hiera of the Eleusinian cult. This in turn led them to the "theory of manipulation" to be discussed shortly. It can be stated categorically that the Eleusinian tradition has no place for Baubo at the site of Demeter. Her place of origin has not been established as yet to the satisfaction of all. Malten maintained that the Orphics, but not the Eleusinians, borrowed Baubo from the island of Paros, where she was worshiped along with Demeter and Kore and Zeus Euboleus, and Kern added that the worship of Baubo is known to us from Paros only.[9] Guthrie, following an old suggestion of Gruppe's, projects an Asia Minor-Phrygian origin for Baubo.[10] Our conception of the origin of Baubo must, I believe, be based on firmer ground. The prevalent view now is that the name "Baubo" meant "that which the woman exhibited to Demeter, that is, the female pudenda."[11] If this view is correct, then it is evident that the name was created after the fact, to personify the myth. I suggest, therefore, that the creation of Baubo took place in a locality where the raising of clothes by women and the exhibition of their secret parts, accompanied by banter, obscene language, and gestures, were related to the worship of some God or Goddess. As far as I know, there is no record indicating that such a custom existed

[9] P. Malten, "Altorpische Demetersage," *ArchFR* (1909), p. 441; O. Kern, *RE*, III, pp. 150ff, *s.v.* Baubo. *IG*, XII, 5, 227.

[10] W. K. C. Guthrie, *Orpheus and Greek Religion*, pp. 135-136. Gruppe, *Gr. Mythologie und Religion*, p. 1437 n. 2, and 1542 n. 1. Guthrie gives a good bibliography and a group of figurines which according to him represent Baubo. It is uncertain whether the figurines actually represent Baubo.

[11] A. Dieterich, *Philologus*, 52 (1893), pp. 1ff, and *Eine Mithrasliturgie*, 1903, pp. 125ff. Cf. Hesychios, *s.v.* Baubo.

either in Greece or in Asia Minor. But Herodotos found a similar custom at Bubastis in the Delta of Egypt, where the cat-headed Pasht, equated with Artemis by the historian, was worshiped.[12]

"When the people are on their way to Bubastis," Herodotos wrote, "they go by river, men and women together, a great number of each in every boat. . . . Whenever they come near any other town they bring their boat near the bank; then some of the women do as I have said [i.e. make noise and sing], while some shout mockery of the women of the town; others dance, and others stand up and raising their garments expose their secret parts." And this was done only by the women pilgrims for the women of the riverside towns.

Diodoros also has preserved the tradition according to which, if after the death of the sacred Apis-bull a new one is discovered, only women may look at the God for forty days, but they do this "while lifting their clothes up and showing their private parts to the God."[13] The actions of the pilgrims to Bubastis and of the women ministrants of Apis, reflect a very old established practice that could have given rise to the birth of Baubo and her story. Her actions therefore, as given by the Orphic Hymn and by Clement, cannot be construed as indicating details of the Eleusinian rites and their Hiera.

The Synthema. After telling the story of Baubo, Clement states what he called the *synthema*, thus it seems to me tying the story to the rites of Eleusis: "And the synthema (pass-word) of the Eleusinian mysteries is as follows: 'I fasted; I drank the kykeon; I took from the kiste; having done my task, I placed in the basket, and from the basket into the kiste.' "[14] On this definite attribution, added to the story of Baubo, scholars built a number of theories purporting to explain the very nature of the Mysteries; for many believed that the *synthema* contains the very substance of the secret cult of Demeter. Before we consider its content, however, even before we try to establish whether or not it actually belongs to Eleusis we have to determine, if possible, when the *synthema* could have been spoken by the initiates.

We must note that Clement used the word "symbols" when he

[12] Herodotos, II, 59 and 60. Translation A. D. Godley, Loeb edition.
[13] Diodoros, I, 85.
[14] *Protreptikos*, II, p. 18.

gave the formula of the Phrygian mysteries, but *synthema* when he talked of the Eleusinian. We believe that by the two words the Father indicated two different relations to the telete of the participant. The "symbols," analogous to the *credo* of the Christians, were a confession of faith, a proof of acts accomplished and of complete initiation. The words with which the formula ends in the writing of Firmicius Maternus: "Now I have become a mystes of Attis" definitely indicates this fact. In contrast the word "synthema" means a password, a statement used for recognition and identification. Since the initiates of the Eleusinian Mysteries after the telete were not banded together in *thiasoi* or *colleges*, they had no need of identifying formulas, of *synthemata*. They would not, therefore, have been taught a password at the end of the telete. But they would have had a need of an identifying formula at the very beginning of the Greater Mysteries, indicating that they were properly prepared and ready to receive the blessed revelation. They had completed the purificatory acts of the Lesser Mysteries, they had taken part in the preparations held in Athens in the four first days of the celebration, they had been present at the preliminaries at Eleusis itself, and now they were ready to embark upon the all-important act of complete initiation. Before they were allowed in the sacred precinct they had to identify themselves and state that they were ready for the great event; and the *synthema* would do just that. As a matter of fact the scholiast of Plato's Gorgias (p. 123) states that the "symbols," which he used perhaps instead of the *synthema*, were stated in the Lesser Mysteries!

The theories based on the *synthema* can be divided into two main groups developed out of Lobeck's emendation of the participle ἐργασάμενος of Clement into ἐγγευσάμενος, from "having done my task" into "having tasted thereof."[15] Lobeck's followers maintain that the "synthema" indicated "the eating by the communicant of some sacred food which was preserved in the mystic cista, pain bénit probably with other cereals and fruits."[16] The scholars who retain Clement's wording maintained that the *synthema* indicates the handling of some object or objects kept in the kiste. But what could that object be?

[15] A. Lobeck, *Aglaophamus*, p. 25.
[16] L. R. Farnell, *The Cults of the Greek States*, III, p. 186.

A. Dieterich was the first to maintain that the object taken from the kiste was a phallus; that the initiate, after taking it, placed the phallus in his breast and then replaced it in the kiste. By that symbolic act, he was united with the Goddess, and became her child.[17] This conception became the center of a great controversy and gave birth to even wilder and more obscene fantasies. Scholars refused to admit the phallus in the cult of Demeter and so Körte maintained that not a phallus but the female pudenda, the *kteis*, suggested by the story of Baubo, was contained in the kiste. According to Körte by sliding the *kteis* over his body, the initiate believed that he was reborn, that he became a child of Demeter.[18] Kern, an admirer of Körte's, going a step farther, maintained that the initiate actually came into a symbolic union with the Goddess by manipulating his own genital organ in the *kteis*.[19] Picard projected a mystic union of the initiate with Demeter and Dionysos effected by the manipulation of a phallus and a *kteis*; the phallus was taken from the kiste and placed in a basket where the *kteis* was and vice versa; each initiate performed the operation and thus achieved union with the divinities.[20] Wilamowitz suggested that by merely seeing or touching the *kteis* the initiate was bound to the Goddess with a bond that blessed and sanctified him.[21]

Against these suggestions a number of scholars protested,[22] pointing out that the *kteis* and the phallus are foreign to the Eleusinian cult; that their manipulation would be symbolic of creation and not of rebirth; that adoption required a special ritual, known from the adoption of Herakles by Hera,[23] not indicated by the

[17] A. Dieterich, *Eine Mithrasliturgie*, p. 123, and again in *Mutter Erde*, pp. 110ff (ed. 1925).

[18] A. Körte, *ArchFR*, 18 (1915), p. 116ff.

[19] O. Kern, *Die Griechischen Mysterien der Classischen Zeit*, p. 10.

[20] Ch. Picard, *RHR*, 95 (1927), pp. 237ff.

[21] Wilamowitz-Moellendorff, *Der Glaube der Hellenen*, II, p. 53.

[22] Loeff, *Mnemosyne*, 45 (1917), p. 364. Maass, *ArchFR*, 21 (1922), p. 260. Ziehen, *Gnomon*, 5 (1929), pp. 152ff, Farnell, *op.cit.*, p. 185 n.b. See for discussion of the various views D. N. Goudi's *Tὰ μυστήρια τῆς 'Ελευσῖνος*, pp. 88-93. P. Roussel, *BCH*, 54 (1930), pp. 67ff. L. Deubner, *Attische Feste*, pp. 79ff.

[23] Diodoros, IV, 39. The passage in the pseudo-Platonic *Axiochos* (of early Hellenistic date), 371 A-C, in which is described the abode of the pious, has been pointed out as proving the "theory of adoption." "The initiated," read the crucial lines of the passage, "have a special place of honor (a proedria) there (in the abode of the pious) and there too the holy ceremonies are performed. You (the initiate) therefore, will surely be the first to share the privilege, being as you are a '*gennetes*' of the Gods." The word "gennetes" has strengthened the speculations

synthema or provided for by the manipulation of the genital organs. Of course Theodoretos attributes the *kteis* to Eleusis, but in the same treatise he also states that the *kteis* belonged to the Thesmophoria.[24] We must also remember that he lived in the fifth century of our era (423-458) when the tradition of the Mysteries had grown vague and overburdened with attributions foreign to its nature. Clement, who was much nearer to the pagan tradition and to a period of prosperity of the pagan cult, does not mention the *kteis* among the objects contained in the kiste; as a matter of fact he attributes the *kteis*, as we shall see later, to Ge-Themis. Before we admit Körte's theory we have to prove the existence of these objects in the kiste.

Noack, following the views expressed, maintained that the *synthema* gives us the content of the telete.[25] Each initiate, he states, with head covered, like Herakles on the Lovatelli urn, approached a table on which the kiste was placed. Helped by the Hierophant he performed the handling of the *kteis*, without actually seeing it or the other sacred objects, and then returned to his place. And it was necessary to have his head covered because seeing the sacred objects formed the climax of the telete and none could be seen before. However, the other initiates in the Telesterion would have seen the action, even though the person handling the *kteis* at the time could not see it. Furthermore, the repetition of this individual handling by the hundreds of the initiates would have resulted in a long and tedious performance that would have robbed the telete of its inspirational quality. And then Noack has to prove that a *kteis* was actually among the objects of the kiste.

Other important considerations make these suggestions untenable. The handling of the phallus and of the *kteis* is an unclean act,

---

of those who believe in the "theory of adoption" because it could be interpreted in a way favorable to their view. They maintain that the word means "adopted child of Demeter," or adopted in the family of the Gods through Demeter, through initiation into the Eleusinian Mysteries. However, the true meaning of the word, pointed out long ago by Foucart (*Les Mystères*, p. 365: "toi qui est un des fidéles des déesses"), is: a worshiper of Demeter, one of the group of men who together worshiped Demeter. See Francis R. Walton, "Kinsman of the Gods," *CP*, 48 (1953), pp. 24-28 for a thorough discussion of the problem. *Axiochos*' passage therefore, does not prove a belief in the divine adoption of the initiate.

[24] Theodoretos, Ἑλληνικῶν θεραπευτικὴ παθημάτων, 7, 11 (p. 104) and 3, 84 (p. 51).

[25] Noack, *Eleusis*, pp. 236ff.

no matter how we may try to explain it. And yet chastity was a prerequisite for initiation. Among the initiates we find not only women—young and old, married and single—but even children— boys and girls; and to expose these children to the act would have been criminal. To overcome this difficulty the proponents of the theory of manipulation maintain that it was not held in the telete, but in the epopteia; however, they bring no evidence to justify their assumption. Since, according to their theory, that manipulation brought about the rebirth of the initiates and their adoption by the Goddess, the act could not have been excluded from the telete. We have seen how the telete was actually the important celebration in which all initiates had to participate; the epopteia was optional and for the few who wanted additional enlightenment. The rebirth and adoption were certainly most important and desirable acts and if they formed part of the epopteia only, all the initiates would have been required to participate in that last degree of initiation. We have already seen that the *synthema*, the password, on which these theories were based, more appropriately belongs to the very beginning of the telete. And the telete was certainly attended by boys and girls, the ’αφ’ ἑστίας initiates. Since abstinence from inter- course and purification after it was required even for the average act of worship,[26] how then can we admit even a symbolic act of the kind in the sacred Temple of Demeter? Such an act would scarcely have escaped the diligent Clement, who after all is quoting the *synthema*. I appreciate the fact that the act could be considered as symbolic and that it could be assumed to have been sanctified by its relation to a divinity; but nevertheless it seems extremely inappropriate in the Temple of Demeter and Kore, who in Andania was known as "the chaste." Fortunately, we are not dependent solely on moral theorizing for our refusal to accept the theories of manipulation.

All the testimony regarding the Hiera refers to their *revelation*, and not their *manipulation*. The high priest of Eleusis is called the Hierophant because *he shows* the Hiera. Hesychios defines the Hierophant as the priest *who shows* the Mysteries. According to Plutarch, Alkibiades' impeachment was "for committing crime

---

[26] Prott-Ziehen, *Leges graecorum sacrae*, Nos. 91, 92, 148, 117. Herodotos, II, 64.

against the Goddess of Eleusis . . . by mimicking the mysteries and *showing* them forth to his companions in his house, wearing a robe such as the Hierophant wears when *he shows* the sacred secrets to the initiates."[27] Glaukos the Hierophant "*showed* to all mortals the orgia of Demeter."[28] Pausanias, in an effort to explain the name of Kyamites, states: "anyone who *has seen* the Mysteries at Eleusis or has read what are called the work of Orpheus, knows what I mean."[29] Andokides, addressing himself to those of his judges who had been initiated into the Mysteries, said:[30] "You have been initiated and *you have seen* the Hiera of the Goddesses so that you must punish the impious but save those who have committed no injustice." And the author of the speech against Andokides writes: "This man wearing the robe (of the Hierophant) and imitating him *showed* the Hiera to the uninitiated and uttered aloud the unspoken words."[31] Herakles, being unable *to see* the mysteries because he had not been cleansed from the death of the Centaur, was purified by Eumolpos and then was initiated;[32] and so he glories in Euripides (τὰ μυστῶν ηὐτύχησ' ἰδών).[33] The Dadouchos Kallias, addressing the Spartans, reminds them that Triptolemos *showed* (δεῖξαι) the Hiera of Demeter and Kore to Herakles and the Dioskouroi, their progenitors.[34] Sophokles exclaims: "Thrice happy are those mortals, who, *having seen* those rites, depart for Hades"; and to this Pindar replies: "Happy is he who, *having seen* those rites goes below the hollow earth."[35] Finally we read in the Hymn itself: "Happy is he among men upon earth who *has seen* these mysteries."[36] I believe that all this testimony, brought together at random, is sufficient to convince the serious student of the Mysteries, that the Hiera were shown to the initiates and not given to them to handle. Consequently, the very base of the theories of manipulation is untenable and the hypotheses built on it improbable and unfounded.

[27] Plutarch, *Alkibiades*, 19-22.
[28] *Ephem*, 1883, p. 81.
[29] Pausanias, I, 37, 4. Note the contrast between the "has seen" and "has read."
[30] *De Myster.*, 31.
[31] [Lysias] VI, 51.
[32] Apollodoros, II, 5, 12.
[33] *Hercules Fur.*, v. 613.
[34] *Hellenika*, VI, 3, 6.
[35] Sophokles, *Fragm.*, 719. Pindar, *Fragm.*, 102.
[36] Hymn, v. 480.

Clement states that the *synthema* belongs to the Eleusinian Mysteries. However, he also insinuated that the scene of Baubo was part of the Mysteries of Eleusis, as we have seen. The latter is proved contrary to the facts; the former too may not apply to our Mysteries. We may wonder whether the "Eleusinian Mysteries" of Clement are the Mysteries held at Eleusis in Attika in spite of his statement. We learn from at least two reliable sources that Mysteries of Demeter and Kore were held in a suburb of Alexandria known as Eleusis. Livy defines the locality: "ad Eleusinem . . . qui locus quattuor milia ab Alexandria abest"; and Tacitus tells us that Ptolemy "questioned Timotheos, an Athenian of the clan of the Eumolpids, whom he had called from Eleusis to preside over the sacred rites. . . ."[37] From a scholium of Aratus we learn that the abduction of the Kore was celebrated by the "Egyptians."[38] The *synthema* given by Clement could have belonged to the rites celebrated at Eleusis of Alexandria, which thus could have been legitimately called "Eleusinian mysteries."

Many years ago Pringsheim pointed out that the *Kalathos* of the *synthema* actually belongs to the mysteries held at Eleusis in Alexandria.[39] Indeed, the only known rite in which the *Kalathos* had a mystic role is mentioned in the hymn to Demeter by Kallimachos and it was held in Alexandria. In that hymn the βέβηλοι, the profane and uninitiated, were ordered to "look down," not to raise their eyes to the *Kalathos* carried through the streets of that city on a chariot pulled by four white horses.[40] As far as I know, the Attik-Eleusinian tradition, the references of ancient authors, and even the few representations in art, represent and speak only of kistai. The Kalathos, as it is used by Clement with a mystic role,

---

[37] Livius, XLV, 12. Tacitus, IV, 83.

[38] Aratos, *Phaenomena*, 150. Polybios, XV, 29, 8, mentions a Thesmophorion in Alexandria.

[39] G. H. Pringsheim, *Archaeologische Beiträge zur Geschichte des eleusinischen Kults*, p. 49 n. 1.

[40] Kallimachos, *Hymn to Demeter*, vv. 1-6 and 120-123. Of course there was a festival held in Athens known as τὰ κανᾶ, in which, according to the scholiast of Aischines (περὶ παραπρεσβείας, p. 90, Dindorf), the virgins of Athens carried κανᾶ or baskets on their heads in which were some sacred objects of Demeter and the virgins were called κανηφόροι. But such festivals with girls carrying baskets were held in Athens in honor of other divinities—of Athena, for example, of Artemis and of Dionysos—which had no mystic connotations. It seems that even for a regular sacrifice a girl carried on her head a basket containing the offerings and the utensils needed (cf. Fig. 72).

is unknown to Eleusis. Even Clement mentions kistai only, when he speaks of the Hiera of Eleusis. Recently our main authority on Greek Religion, Professor Martin P. Nilsson, stated that only the first six words of the *synthema*, "I fasted; I drank the Kykeon," could belong to the Eleusinian Mysteries held in Attika. And the rest: "I took from the kiste; having done my task, I placed in the basket, and from the basket into the kiste," the part of the *synthema* used for the development of the theory of manipulation, possibly belonged to the mysteries held in the neighborhood of Alexandria in honor of Demeter.[41] I agree completely with Professor Nilsson.

That new elements and local variations were added to the Mysteries of Eleusis in a number of places after their introduction is a well-established fact. When Pausanias mentions the celebration of "the mysteries of Demeter at Keleai in imitation of the Mysteries observed at Eleusis," he adds, "they celebrate . . . every third year, not annually. The Hierophant is not appointed for life, but at each celebration a new Hierophant is elected, who may, if he chose, take a wife. In these respects their practice differs from that observed at Eleusis."[42] Even greater variations characterize the mysteries held by the Pheneatians in honor of "Demeter surnamed Eleusinia . . . alleging the rites identical with those performed at Eleusis. . . . Beside the sanctuary of the Eleusinian goddess is what is called the Petroma, two great stones fitted to each other. Every second year, when they are celebrating what they call the Greater Mysteries, they open these stones, and taking out of them certain writings which bear on the mysteries, they read them in the hearing of the initiated, and put them back in their place that same night. . . . There is a round top on it, which contains a mask of Demeter Kidaria: This mask the priest puts on his face at the Greater Mysteries, and smites the Underground Folk with rods. I suppose there is some legend to account for the custom."[43]

In the mysteries celebrated at Andania in Arcadia, Methapos, the "deviser of mysteries and all sorts of orgies," seems to have added a number of Gods by the side of Demeter and Kore.[44]

---

[41] M. P. Nilsson, *Greek Popular Religion*, p. 45.

[42] Pausanias, II, 14, 1.

[43] Pausanias, VIII, 15, 1. It is interesting to note that here a priest impersonated Demeter and not a priestess.

[44] *Sylloge*⁴, vol. 2, No. 736. Pausanias, IV, 1, 5 and 7.

It is interesting to note that Pausanias, who was so reticent on the subject of Eleusis and who avoided the mention of even the monuments in the precinct of Demeter, was so free with information regarding the celebration elsewhere, especially at Pheneai. It seems that additions made to the original rites were not guarded with the same strictness. In a similar manner in Alexandria local traditions or other foreign practices could have been added from time to time to the original rites imported from Eleusis. The fact that Ptolemy especially summoned the "Athenian" Hierophant to preside over the secret rites, not to introduce them, seems to indicate a concern over conditions existing in Alexandria, conditions brought about perhaps by innovations and changes made to the original cult. A Eumolpid's specialty was to know the *patria*, the ancestral laws and customs governing the secret rites of Demeter and his duty to see that the rites were celebrated strictly in accordance with the *patria*. In this connection it will be interesting to note a passage in Epiphanios' *Panarium*.

"In Alexandria," he writes, "there is the so-called Korion, and it is a very large temple, that is the temenos of Kore. [The worshipers] having passed the night in vigilance with songs and flute playing, singing to the idol . . . After the call of the roosters they descend with torches in hand to an underground chamber and from it they bring up on a litter a wooden xoanon, seated, nude, bearing on its forehead some seal of a cross, covered with gold . . . and they carry this xoanon around seven times, making a circle around the most central temple with flutes and drums and hymns, and having sang and danced they take it down again to the underground place . . . and they say that at this hour, today the Kore, that is the Virgin, gave birth to the Aion."[45] Even if we tried intentionally to do so it would have been difficult indeed to produce a more complete concoction of diverse and contrary elements than Persephone with the cross on her forehead, becoming the Virgin and giving birth to the Gnostic Aion. Of course it is impossible to prove that Epiphanios' account reflects his version of the Mysteries of Demeter and Kore, but his statement serves to illustrate the ease

[45] Epiphanios was a bishop of Eleutheroupolis of Palestine and Konstantia of Kypros and lived A.D. 367-403. *Panarium* in *Philologus*, 16, p. 354. Cf. L. R. Farnell, *op.cit.*, III, p. 375.

with which traditions and rites of different cults and even of Christianity were fused together in the fourth century.

Summarizing our discussion, we may suggest that the entire *synthema* or at least the second part of the *synthema* beginning with the words "I took from the kiste," was devised in Alexandria and had nothing to do with the rites of Demeter held at Eleusis; perhaps it was concocted in imitation of the Phrygian *"symbols"* at a time when syncretism was at its height and *"theokrasia"* (the confusing and equating Gods) became a common practice.

If we had to admit a *synthema* to the rites of Eleusis, then we could only follow Nilsson and maintain that the password, stated at the very beginning of the telete, actually when the initiates were entering the sacred precinct of Demeter for the first time, and in response to the question of the officials if they had observed the prescribed final, preparatory rites, was: "I fasted; I drank the kekyon," and perhaps the women-initiates would add "I carried the kernos," as we see them do on the Niinnion tablet. These words indeed described acts of piety and preparation immediately preceding the secret rites held in the Telesterion. The theories of Dieterich, Körte, Kern, Picard, Noack, and their followers, are proved, I believe, inapplicable to the rites of Demeter held at Eleusis in Attika, and formed no part of the dromena either of the telete, or the epopteia.

The Contents of the Sacred Kistai. "Consider," Clement states, "the contents of the mystic kistai; for I must strip bare their holy things, and utter the unspeakable. Are they not sesame cakes, pyramids and spherical cakes, cakes with many navels, also balls of salt and a serpent, the mystic sign of Dionysos Bassareus? Are they not also pomegranates, fig branches, fennel stalks, ivy leaves, round cakes and poppies? These are their holy things. . . ." And, he added "In addition, there are the unutterable symbols of Ge-Themis, marjoram, a lamp, a sword, and a woman's comb (*kteis*), which is a euphemistic expression used in the mysteries for a woman's genital organ. What manifest shamelessness!"[46] What

---

[46] *Protreptikos*, II, p. 19. The inclusion of a serpent in the sacra of the kiste proves that Clement had no knowledge of the Hiera of Eleusis. Perhaps he was influenced in his statement by the "cistophoric coins" of Asia Minor that were so common in the closing centuries of paganism. Cf. Charles Seltman, *Greek Coins*, 1955, pl. LVII, Nos. 7 and 9. At best his statement could be accepted as reflecting Dionysiac practices.

Clement assigns to the Mysteries, modern scholars took to belong
to the Hiera of Eleusis, the only sacra that were jealously kept in
a kiste, and these were cakes of a not too definite nature. On this
account and on a rather indefinite passage of Polemon, preserved
in a second-hand rendition by Athenaios,[47] Lobeck based his emendation of the *synthema*, and maintained that it indicates a sacred meal.
Since no authority can be attributed to Clement's list, the Hiera of
Eleusis remain unknown.[48]

Careful consideration of Clement's references to the Mysteries
of Deo and of Eleusis and to what has been attributed to those
Mysteries by modern scholars proves, I believe, that his statements
apply either to the mysteries of Rhea-Kybele-Attis, or to those
celebrated perhaps in Alexandria; that he draws his information in
the main from Orphic sources or from rumored local traditions;
that neither of these two sources had anything to do with Eleusis;
that he equates the rites of different mystery cults, following in
this respect the practice of the gnostics of his time; that in his
Protreptikos he tried to show that "the mysteries are mere custom
and vain opinion, and it is a deceit of the serpent that men worship
when, with spurious piety they turn towards these sacred initiations
that are really profanities and solemn rites that are without sanctity."

It is important to note that Clement, who had no difficulty in
casting aspersions against the pagan rites, could find no evidence of
and made no direct charges of immoral practices held in the celebration of the Eleusinian Mysteries, although he seems to imply
that they stem out of an immoral act, Demeter's violent attack by

[47] Athenaios, XI, 56, p. 478.

[48] Delatte, *Le Cyceon breuvage rituel des mystères d'Éleusis*, suggests that among
the objects contained in the kiste was a grinding stone, perhaps attributed to the
Goddess, whose primitive looks could have inspired awe to the initiate; that the
initiates might have been allowed actually to grind grain on it, thus repeating a
sacred act; the meal from that grinding to be used for a communal dinner. However, millstones and grinding tools preserved their primitive form for a very long
time. L. A. Moritz in his *Grain-mill and Flour in Classical Antiquity*, 1958, p. 41,
concludes that the ordinary saddle quern of the Early Bronze Age, made rather
handier by the elongation of the upper stone and by the introduction of grooving
on both stones, was widely used in Greece until well into classical times and perhaps until the end of the classical era. At Olynthos and in the houses destroyed by
Philip (348 B.C.) the late Professor David M. Robinson and I found saddle-querns
that are no different than those I found at the Early Helladic settlement of Aghios
Kosmas, dating from ca. 2300-1900 B.C. Consequently Mycenaean millstones
would not have impressed the initiates, because they were almost identical to
those used at the time.

Zeus. His famous appeal to the Hierophant and the Dadouchos, often quoted by modern scholars, is a mere rhetorical exhortation; "Quench the fire, oh Dadouchos. The light convicts your Iacchos. Suffer the night to hide the mysteries. Let the orgies be honored by darkness. The fire is not acting a part; to convict and to punish is its duty."[49] On the other hand, in his apostrophe to the Christian mysteries, he uses the terminology of the Eleusinian Mysteries: "Oh truly sacred mysteries! Oh pure light! In the blaze of torches I have an epoptic vision of heaven and of God. I become holy by initiation. The Lord is the Hierophant who reveals the mysteries; He marks the mystes with His seal, gives light to guide his way, and commends him, when he has believed, to the Father's care, where he is guarded for ages to come."[50] Clement would have never dared to commit the sacrilege of calling Christ an Hierophant, if the high priest of Eleusis was, or was rumored to be the perpetrator of immoral acts, as suggested by Asterios. We may therefore conclude that we can learn very little, actually nothing of importance, as far as substance is concerned, about the Eleusinian Mysteries from Clement's statements; but we get from them the conviction that no acts, which even by Christian standards could be considered immoral, were included in those rites.

HIPPOLYTUS

The Cut-Wheat. Hippolytus, the pupil of Eirenaios and the admirer of Origen, is somewhat later than Clement. He lived in Rome as a presbyter during the first half of the third century of our era. Of importance to our quest is the fifth book of his *Laby-rinth*, or *Refutation of all Heresies*, known as the *Philosophou-mena*.[51] In that book we find the following passage of special interest to us: "The Phrygians, the Naassene says, assert that God is a fresh ear of cut-wheat, and following the Phrygians the Athe-nians, when they initiate in the Eleusinia exhibit in silence to the *epoptai* the mighty and marvellous and most complete epoptic mystery, an ear of cut-wheat." Shortly afterwards, Hippolytus

---

[49] *Protreptikos*, II, p. 19.
[50] *Protreptikos*, XII, p. 92.
[51] This work has come down to us under the name of Origen, but there can be no doubt that it was written by Hippolytus. Our references are taken from Migne's *Patrologia*, vol. 16, p. 3150.

states: "In the course of the night, the hierophant at Eleusis in the midst of a brilliant fire celebrating the Great and Unspoken Mysteries, cries and shouts aloud saying, 'Holy Brimo has borne a sacred child Brimos,' that is, the mighty gave birth to the mighty one."

In Chapter IX (p. 275), we have studied the first of these statements and reached the conclusion that actually the cut-wheat could not be what the Father claims. We may here add that in his *Philosophoumena* Hippolytus tried very hard to show that the doctrines of the heretic sect of the Naassenes were derived from the teachings of the Greek philosophers and from the rites of the Phrygian mysteries and doctrines. In the midst of his enumeration of these doctrines unexpectedly and without apparent connection he thrusts his statements regarding the Eleusinian Mysteries. It would be absurd, I believe, to maintain that the Eleusinians followed the Phrygians in the adoption of the symbol of Attis, the cut-wheat, as their most marvelous mystery.

Brimo and the Birth of Brimos. To the second statement of Hippolytus, to his formula of Brimo, has been attributed greater importance. It has been maintained that this formula was stated aloud at the culmination of the telete. We may well ask how the Father could know what took place in the Telesterion when he had not been initiated into the Mysteries. How could he know what the Hierophant said? His description of the Hierophant officiating in the midst of a brilliant fire, recalls Plutarch's "μέγα φῶς" "great light" emanating from the opened Anaktoron when the Hierophant revealed the Hiera.[52] Hippolytus could have known the work of Plutarch, and from many ancient sources, he knew that the most important function of the Hierophant was the revelation of the Hiera. Hence, following the known tradition, he could picture that high priest standing in the midst of a brilliant light, revealing the Hiera. He of course knew that formulae which could not be spoken in public were used in the Mysteries. Did not the Hymn state "awful mysteries which no one may in any way transgress or pry into or utter"? Did not the accuser of Andokides proclaim that the accused committed the great offense of impersonating the Hierophant, showing the Hiera and uttering the secret words which

[52] Plutarch, *De profect. virt.*, p. 81E. For this and the references to the *legomena*, cf. *supra*, pp. 272-273.

must never be spoken? That the legomena, or the words which were spoken, formed part of the telete was generally known and thus Sopatros, in a rhetorical exercise, states that a certain youth who could not hear what the Hierophant said was not considered as initiated, although he followed the telete. All this Hippolytus could have known, but he did not know what actually was revealed and said by the Hierophant. Into this great gap in his knowledge he introduced Brimo and the child Brimos to complete the picture of the officiating Hierophant, whose appearance in a brilliant light was well established.

Scholars agreed with the statement of Hippolytus because until recently they accepted Clement's equation of Demeter with Brimo. But we have seen that the title Brimo does not belong to Demeter but to Rhea; that Rhea is Brimo. The Goddess therefore who gave birth to the mighty Brimos, if such an event was believed to have taken place, is Rhea and not Demeter; consequently the formula could not belong to Eleusis in spite of Hippolytus' specific indication. Scholars also believed that the formula formed a sequence to the acts perpetrated in an underground chamber mentioned by Asterios. But we shall see shortly that Asterios' statement is not based on fact.

We shall reach the same conclusion by following another approach: by asking the simple question, who was this Brimos? In the English translations the formula, as a rule, is rendered with "the sacred child Brimos or the holy child Brimos" and the immediate inference of the sex is not apparent. The Greek reads Βριμὼ ἔτεκε κοῦρον, the Brimos was a boy. If Brimo is Demeter then we must find in the myths a son of that Goddess. According to the known Eleusinian tradition, however, the only offspring of Demeter was not a Kouros but a Kore, Persephone; in the myth of the Hymn a son is not to be found. In the *Theogony* of Hesiod and in the *Odyssey* we find the traditional story of the love of the divine Demeter and the mortal Iasion which resulted in the legendary birth of Ploutos.[53] Is it possible to equate the Brimos of Hippolytus with the Ploutos of Hesiod? I do not think so. Surely, in Hesiod's and Homer's account we have a poetic and allegorical expression of man's belief in the benefits resulting from

[53] *Odyssey*, 5, vv. 125-127. *Theogony*, vv. 969-972.

the cultivation of the soil—Demeter is the mother of Ploutos of wealth. In a similar allegorical trend, the sculptor Kephisodotos represented Peace nurturing Ploutos. We may recall that in the Hymn, both Goddesses are the givers of wealth and not only Demeter.[54] In addition the birth of Ploutos, like the mission of Triptolemos, is represented on vases of the fourth century, B.C.[55] This would have been impossible if the birth of Ploutos was the culminating act of the Mysteries. Isokrates, as we have seen, states clearly that Demeter conferred on the people of Athens a double gift: the gift of the telete (i.e. of the Mysteries) and the gift of the produce of the earth.[56] The two gifts are separate and distinct. Ploutos, like Triptolemos, was part of the gift of the produce of the earth, the main source of wealth in ancient agricultural communities. Ploutos is not mentioned in the inscriptions that give us the names of the Eleusinian divinities and heroes, nor is he represented in the votive relief of Eleusis. He certainly cannot be Hippolytus' Brimos. Triptolemos could not fill the role, since in the Hymn he is included among "the Kings who deal justice." He was already an adult when Demeter arrived at Eleusis and consequently the Goddess could have nothing to do with his birth.

Some scholars recognized in Brimos the Iacchos of the Mysteries. This is completely untenable. Iacchos is not mentioned in the Hymn and is comparatively a late comer to Eleusis; his popularity increased after the battle of Salamis. He was the personification of the shoutings and the enthusiasm of the initiates and his duties were limited to the bringing of the pompe from Athens to Eleusis. He had no shrine at Eleusis and he was a visitor whose hospitality had to be arranged annually by the officials from Athens.[57] In later years he was confused with Dionysos, and in Athens, in the festival of Lenaia, the Athenians hailed him as the son of Semele and not of Demeter.[58] In art, Iacchos is represented as a youthful divinity

[54] For the Kephisodotos statue cf. G. M. A. Richter, *Sculpture and Sculptors of Greece*, fig. 659. Hymn, v. 488.

[55] Cf. the hydria from Rhodes now in the Museum of Istanbul (M. P. Nilsson, *Greek Popular Religion*, fig. 24. L. R. Farnell, *op.cit.*, III, pl. XXIb) the pelike in the Hermitage (Farnell *op.cit.*, III, pl. XVIII) and the Tübingen vase (Watzinger, *Griechische Vasen in Tübingen*, pl. 40) among others.

[56] Isokrates, *Paneg.*, 28. For Triptolemos cf. Hymn, vv. 473-475.

[57] *Sylloge*⁴, vol. 2, No. 540.

[58] Scholium of Aristophanes' *Frogs*, 479. On Iacchos see *supra*, p. 238.

and not as a baby (cf. Fig. 88). Certainly Iacchos could not have been Brimos.

Dionysos could not be a successful candidate for the equation. According to the *Theogony* of Hesiod, that seems to have been followed by the Eleusinian tradition, he was the son of Semele.[59] According to the Orphic tradition, as Dionysos-Zagreus, he was the son of Persephone and Zeus. Then, as we have seen, Dionysos had no part in the Eleusinian Mysteries and all references to his participation are later in date and are the result of his confused equation with Iacchos.[60] In late Orphic tradition, according to Guthrie, Dionysos seems to be equated with Eubouleus.[61] Guthrie's conclusion is based on evidence belonging most probably to the third century of our era, when traditions were confused and *theokrasia* became a common practice in Orphic literature.

At Eleusis we have a divinity known as Eubouleus, to whom was due a portion of the sacrifice of the "first fruits" of the ἀπαρχαί, and Lakratides on his relief calls himself the priest of the God, the Goddess, Eubouleus, Demeter and the other Gods.[62] But we learn from inscriptions found in Paros, Amorgos, Mykonos, and Delos, and from Diodoros that the divine Eubouleus of Eleusis was most probably the Chthonian Zeus and as such he could have no relation with Brimos. Of course Eubouleus the swineherd is not mentioned in the Hymn and even in the Orphic tradition he was the son of Dysaules and Baubo.[63]

[59] Hesiod, *Theogony*, vv. 940-942.
[60] This fact is especially illustrated by the Delphic hymn. *BCH*, 19 (1895), p. 403, and the inscription in *CIL*, VI, 1780, dating from A.D. 342. Cicero's *De Nat. Deor.*, 2, 62, cannot be attributed to the Eleusinian Mysteries with certainty; it most probably refers to the Orphic-Dionysiac rites. Some authorities maintain that Dionysos was worshiped at Eleusis along with Demeter: cf. H. Metzger, *BCH*, 68-69 (1944-45), pp. 323-339, but see my forthcoming study on the subject in the *Ephemeris*. However, no scholar has ever attempted to connect with Eleusis the birth of Dionysos.
[61] W. K. C. Guthrie, *op.cit.*, pp. 179-180. His suggestion is based especially on the inscription on a gold band from a grave of a follower of Orphism found in Rome and now in the British Museum. It dates from the second or third century of our era.
[62] *Sylloge*[4], vol. 1, No. 83. For the Lakratides relief *supra*, p. 197 and fig. 71.
[63] Cf. the story of Baubo, *supra*, pp. 291 ff. The attributions of Triptolemos and others to the unnatural relations of Demeter and her host, projected by later Christian writers are not worthy of consideration. For the Zeus-Eubouleus see Frazer on Pausanias, I, 14, 3, and VIII, 9, 2. Also *AM*, I (1876), p. 334; 16 (1891), pp. 1-29. Diodoros, V, 72. Cf. *supra*, p. 293.

Our brief survey of the Gods and heroes of Eleusis and of the Eleusinian tradition proves that in the myths of Demeter and Persephone we have neither a deity nor a mortal whom we could equate with Brimos. Persephone is the only known offspring of Demeter. Hippolytus' formula consequently could not belong and does not fit Eleusis. It is more suitable for rites in which the new vegetation was personified by a Kouros. At Eleusis only the Kore could be considered as the personification of the vegetation which springs forth in the appropriate season every year; but in the mysteries of Rhea-Kybele in Asia Minor, Attis, a Kouros, was worshiped as the reborn nature. The title Brimo belongs to Rhea-Kybele; the Kouros, Attis, belongs to her mysteries. The formula of Hippolytus therefore should belong to the mysteries of Rhea, if it belonged to any mysteries at all. In a manner typical of the syncretism of the times Hippolytus attributed to Eleusis what belonged elsewhere.

We have already considered Hippolytus' other formula: "the great and unutterable mystery of the Eleusinians; rain—conceive," and proved that it could not belong to the cult of Demeter.[64]

TERTULLIAN

Let us now consider briefly the question asked by Tertullian in his apologetic treatise composed in the year of our Lord 197: "Why is the priestess of Demeter carried off, unless Demeter herself had suffered the same sort of thing?"[65] The first part of the question can be true, without proving the truth of the asserted second part. We have seen how in the sacred drama of Eleusis the abduction of Persephone was enacted (*supra*, p. 262). A priestess of the highest possible standing impersonated the Kore. As far as we know, there was only one priestess of Demeter whose importance and high state are proved by the fact that she served for life and her name was used to date the years; she was *eponymos* at Eleusis.[66] It was that priestess of Demeter who had to impersonate first the one and then the other of the Goddesses. As the priestess of Demeter she enacted the part of Persephone in the abduction scene as recorded in the Hymn; the *priestess of Demeter* was abducted; *but it was in the*

[64] *Supra*, p. 270.   [65] Tertullianus, *ad nat.*, 2, 7.
[66] *BCH*, 19 (1895), p. 113. *Ephem*, 1894, p. 176. *Supra*, p. 231.

role of Persephone that she was abducted. It was, then, a true statement that the "priestess of Demeter was carried off," but a false
assumption that the abduction indicated that Demeter also was
raped; for the priestess was carried off not as *Demeter* but as
Persephone.

It is true that the scholiast of Plato's *Gorgias* writes: "[These
mysteries] were performed in honor of Demeter and Kore, because
Kore was abducted by Plouton, and Deo was joined with Zeus."[67]
But the scholiast was a Christian who lived at a later period and
used as sources not only the ancient pagan authors but also the
writings of the Early Christian Fathers. He must have known the
statement of Tertullian and the writings of Clement. He had read
in the *Protreptikos* the Orphic story of the violent relation of
Zeus and his mother whom Clement identified as Deo.[68] In the
question asked by Tertullian he found the assertion that the rape
of the priestess proved that of Demeter. Since he knew from the
Hymn that Persephone was abducted by Plouton and that this was
enacted at Eleusis, he concluded that the ravisher of Demeter in
the drama was Zeus; and so he made his statement. But both
Tertullian and Clement were wrong in their assertions and attributions as we have seen; consequently the scholiast's conclusion was
also wrong since it was based on false assumptions.[69]

ASTERIOS

The Katabasion and the Sacred Marriage at Eleusis. Another
statement, made by Asterios the bishop of Amaseia in Asia Minor,
remains to be considered. In his *Engomion to the Saintly Martyrs,*
we find:[70] "The Eleusinian Mysteries, are they not the main part
of your religion and the demos of Athens, yea the whole of Greece
gathers to celebrate that vanity? Is not there [in the sanctuary of
Demeter at Eleusis] the katabasion and the solemn meeting of the
Hierophant and the priestess, each with the other alone; are not

[67] On Plato's *Gorgias*, 497C.   [68] *Protreptikos*, II, p. 13. *Supra*, p. 289.
[69] How scholiasts and later Christian writers used the statements made by the
early Fathers and how they confused them and the ancient sources can be demonstrated by a single passage from Michael Psellos' τίνα περὶ δαιμόνων δοξάζουσιν οἱ
Ἕλληνες, Migne, *Patrologia*, vol. 122, pp. 877-880A. See also scholium on Plato's
Gorgias, 497C where the "synthema" of Clement is repeated; a proof of the
scholiast's knowledge of the writings of that Father.
[70] Migne, *Patrologia*, vol. 40, cols. 321-324.

the torches then extinguished and the vast crowd believes that its salvation depends on what those two act in the darkness?" On this statement and its obscene innuendoes, strengthened by Hippolytus' formula of Brimo, scholars built their theory of the enactment of a "Sacred Marriage," and even the birth of a child in the Eleusinian Mysteries. Foucart maintained that the initiates shouted the other formula of Hippolytus, "rain—conceive," assembled in front of the *Katabasion* within which the Hierophant and the priestess "on se preparait la naissance de l'enfant divin."[71]

Before we can analyze Asterios' statement it is necessary to understand the relative positions of Christianity and paganism in the days of the bishop. Asterios lived around A.D. 400, in a period when Christianity was not only well established, but occupied a favored and privileged position in the Roman Empire, both the eastern and the western. The short-lived reign of Julian the apostate (361-362), in the course of which paganism was favored, had gone and any advantages which accrued to the worshipers of the Olympian gods had vanished certainly during the comparatively long reign of Theodosios (379-395). The Christians, especially in the large cities of Antioch and Alexandria, in the days of Asterios became the persecutors and the pagans the persecuted; temples and idols were destroyed by fire and their devotees mistreated.[72] Theodosios issued consecutive Imperial edicts against sacrifices, the worship of the idols, and especially against the secret teletai. Christian services were becoming more and more ostentatious and magnificent, oecumenical synods were held under the auspices of the Emperor himself,[73] and Theodosios submitted to a humiliating public penance imposed by Bishop Ambrosios. Christianity was dominant and in its security lost some of the militant spirit characteristic of the days of Origen and Clement. The efforts of its princes were mainly devoted to defending its doctrines and to strengthening its followers in the faith.

Even a casual comparison of the sermons of Asterios with the works of Clement will reveal the change in attitude of the leaders of Christianity. Asterios' sermons are apologetic, composed to provide the members of his flock arguments in defense of the faith in

[71] Foucart, *Les mystères*, p. 496.
[72] K. Amantos, *Introduction to Byzantine History* (in Greek), p. 173. Then the Serapeum of Alexandria was burned.
[73] In 381 Theodosios convened in Constantinople the second oecumenical synod.

answer to the criticisms of the pagan and the Jew. We may note further that his sermons, and we have a total of twenty-one, are not characterized by the knowledge of ancient sources and traditions for which Clement's works are remarkable. That the bishop was comparatively ignorant of the great works of the past, let alone the authors of minor significance, is widely accepted, but his advocates argue that Asterios' statements must correspond to reality because otherwise he would have been accused by the pagans of telling untruths and that would have been detrimental to the cause he was trying to defend. This argument is valid for the days of Clement, as we have said above, but not for the days of Asterios. His sermons were addressed to his flock, the people of the district of Amaseia. How many of the pagans of his province of the years around 400 had a sufficiently clear, first-hand knowledge of the Mysteries of Eleusis to be in a position to censure the bishop's assertions? Theodosios' laws with their monetary penalties and other punishments, in practice almost for a generation, certainly discouraged the undertaking of a long pilgrimage to a place no longer officially considered holy. The fame of the Sanctuary by then had almost vanished and even its administration had reached the lowest point of debasement, since its last known Hierophant was no longer a Eumolpid, or even an Athenian, but a man from Thespiai who actually was a priest of Mithras. The period of Asterios was safe; the bishop could include in his sermons whatever his fancy or the rumors available to people in high places dictated without fear of censure or contradiction on the part of the pagans.

The solemn meeting of the Hierophant and the priestess is in complete contrast in its innuendoes with what we know of the sanctity and chastity required of the high priest of Eleusis, which Hippolytus himself states was safeguarded by the use of anti-aphrodisiac drugs. Certainly Clement would not have dared give the title "Hierophant" to Christ, if that high functionary of the Eleusinian cult was even suspected of such an act. We cannot assume that Asterios had more information about the Mysteries made available in the closing years of the life of the Sanctuary. His writings do not indicate such knowledge. He certainly had fewer opportunities to come into contact with initiates than did his predecessors. Nor does he claim that his information came from such a source. When Clement insinuated profane practices, he quoted the Orphic hymn which his hearers and readers could consult for themselves. What is the source from which Asterios draws? Was it Epiphanios and his *korion* statement? Was it from rumors regarding the mysteries of Rhea-Kybele-Attis popular in his homeland Asia Minor? Or was it his imagination? We may note his word σωτηρία—the "salvation" of the crowd, which it was believed depended on the act performed by the priest and the priestess, and remark that the idea of salvation was not a pagan but a Christian conception.

In addition, the bishop of Amaseia maintains with certainty the existence of a *Katabasion* in the Sanctuary of Demeter where the Hierophant and priestess met in darkness. In spite of all the explanations advanced by the advocates of Asterios, the word *Katabasion* to the early Christians meant: an underground chamber or crypt to which one descended; "a place for relics under the altar." (Liddell and Scott). If Asterios' statement is true, then such a chamber must exist in the Sanctuary of Eleusis below the floor of the Telesterion, where the initiates collected for the final and most important ceremonies of the Mysteries. The final excavation of the area by Kourouniotes and his collaborators failed to reveal such a chamber.[74] Nor is there a chance for a *Katabasion* to be found in the future; the territory of the Telesterion has been completely cleared and everywhere the rock was reached. We can therefore assert with absolute certainty that at Eleusis there is no *Katabasion*, as Asterios maintains. That underground chamber, the center of his accusation, was the product of his imagination; and so were the acts insinuated as perpetrated in the nonexistent *Katabasion*. Thus his statement is proved not to correspond to the realities as known from literature, history, and especially from the inexorably factual work of modern archaeologists.

On Asterios' statement was based the conception of the existence of a Sacred Marriage at Eleusis. Now that the statement is disproved, the notion of the Sacred Marriage becomes doubtful. The statements of the other Fathers which were taken to contribute to and strengthen the notion are also proved of doubtful value and possibly wrong. Hippolytus' formula of Brimo and Brimos, pre-

---

[74] It has been suggested that the Ploutonion might have been the katabasion. The floor of that cave, however, is some two meters above the level of the Sacred Way, from which pilgrims entered it. When they did so they actually *went up* to it and not *down* as required by the term. The cave could not have been the katabasion.

sumed to follow naturally Asterios' act, cannot be proved to have belonged to the Mysteries of Eleusis; it seems more probable to maintain that it belonged to the Phrygian mysteries. The title Brimo, which seemed to tie up Hippolytus' formula with Asterios' story, is proved from Clement's statement and sources not to belong to Demeter but to Rhea. Tertullian's rhetorical question can be answered by the fact that the abducted priestess of Demeter was impersonating Persephone in the act of Plouton's rape of the Kore. Hippolytus' "rain—conceive" cannot be a secret formula connected with an important act of the Greater Mysteries, because we find it inscribed on a well in Athens exposed to public view. Actually there is no evidence to prove, or even to suggest the existence of a Sacred Marriage in the celebration of the Mysteries of Demeter at Eleusis.

In closing perhaps we should comment briefly on the use by scholars of Lucian's *Alexander the False Prophet*, as evidence for the enactment of a Sacred Marriage at Eleusis. It would be too long to go through that work and to point out its true nature, although reading Lucian's text is a most delightful experience. I have dealt with this assumption at some length in my study on the writings of the Early Christian Fathers, and the reader who is interested in the matter will find there a full analysis of the work.[75] If we read the entire essay and follow carefully the sequence of the events, we find that the mysteries established by Alexander were but a dramatization of his own adventures and teratological claims. His aim was to establish himself as a hero and to emphasize his important contribution to the welfare of mankind by bringing among its members Glykon, τρίτον αἷμα Διός, φάος ἀνθρώπων (Glykon, the grandson of Zeus, bright light to mortals). In those so-called mysteries we have not one but three marriages: that of Apollo and Koronis, of Podaleirios and the mother of Alexander, of the false prophet and Selene, the moon. His purpose was to show his divine descent and his achievement of inspiring love in Selene. His relations with Selene, it should be recalled, were claimed by the impostor long before he had conceived the idea of developing his own mysteries. All these weddings and actions had nothing to do with the Mysteries of Eleusis and what is brought forth as reflecting the Mysteries was drawn from details known to every-

[75] G. E. Mylonas, "Early Christian Fathers on the Eleusinian Mysteries," *Yearbook*, 1959, pp. 50-55.

body since they belonged to the public part of the Mysteries. They may even reflect Aristophanes' statements in the *Frogs*. Alexander was not initiated in the Mysteries, nor did he claim to have belonged to the divine cortege of initiates, to the group Herakles-Dioskouroi-Asklepios-Dionysos. Certainly if he could have, he would have claimed such association, which would have added to his genealogical teratologies. He could have had no knowledge of the secret telete and this we can deduce even from the details of his so-called mysteries. The work of Lucian therefore does not contribute, as it has been maintained,[76] to the theory of the existence of the "Sacred Marriage" at Eleusis.

Summarizing our survey of the more important statements regarding the Eleusinian Mysteries to be found in the writings of Clement, Hippolytus, Tertullian and Asterios, we may conclude that these statements do not reflect ideas, acts, or practices celebrated or performed at Eleusis and in the Mysteries of Demeter; they do not give us the content or any part of the substance of these Mysteries. Consequently the theories modern scholars have based on them are unfounded and are therefore untenable. They do not reflect actuality, they do not give us acts forming part of the mysteries; they are speculations proved to have missed the mark. Our general conclusion remains the same: *We cannot know, at least we still do not know, what was the full content and meaning of the Mysteries of Demeter held at Eleusis.* We know details of the ritual but not its meaning. The ancients kept their secret well. And Eleusis still lies under its heavy mantle of mystery.

> (Eleusis) where the dread Queen and Maid
> Cherish the mystic rites,
> Rites they to none betray,
> Ere on his lips is laid
> Secrecy's golden key
> By their own acolytes
> Priestly Eumolpids.

$$Χρυσέα$$
$$κλῂς ἐπὶ γλώσσᾳ βέβακε προσπόλων Εὐμολπιδᾶν.$$
(Sophokles, *Oid. Kol.*, 1052)

[76] Cf. for example Jane Harrison's *Prolegomena*, p. 550.

ADYTON: The most holy room of a temple to which entry was allowed to certain people or under specified conditions. Plural, adyta.

ANAKTORON: The holy of holies of the Temple of Demeter at Eleusis where the Hiera of the cult were kept. Only the Hierophant had the right to enter it.

ANATHYROSIS: The smooth marginal dressing or contact band of a joint surface of which the central portion is roughened and sunk to avoid contact. Being applied only to the top and two vertical edges of a vertical joint, it assumes the appearance of the rim of a door (thyra), hence the name. (Dinsmoor).

ANTA: The termination of a lateral wall of a structure which was architecturally treated and often served as respond to a column.

APOSTOLE: Triptolemos' mission to teach mankind how better to cultivate cereals.

ARCHON-BASILEUS: King-archon. Magistrate in Athens in charge of the religious and priestly functions of the state. Since his office inherited the priestly prerogatives of early kings, this magistrate was especially entrusted with the traditional ceremonies of the people of Athens.

ARCHON-EPONYMOS: The most important executive magistrate of Athens. His name served to date the year in muster rolls and decrees and he presided over courts, especially probate courts. He supervised such religious ceremonies as had been introduced in later years.

ARYBALLOS: A small globular oil-flask.

ἀφ᾽ ἑστίας: Boy or girl initiate representing the city and supposed to insure the favor of the Goddesses to the city.

BACCHOS: A thick wand made of myrtle branches tied at intervals with strands of wool. Carried by the initiate, it was emblematic of initiation into the Mysteries of Eleusis.

BOEDROMION: The third month in the Athenian calendar, in the course of which the Greater Mysteries were celebrated. It corresponds to September and the early part of October.

BOTHROS: A pit in which libations were poured.

{ 317 }

BUKRANIUM: Ox-skull carved in frontal view, serving usually as an architectural ornament. Plural, bukrania.

CELLA: The Roman name for the main room of the temple where the cult statue of the divinity was placed. In Greek the room is known as *naos* or *sekos*.

CHTHONIAN: Pertaining to a divinity of the lower world, usually dwelling in or beneath the earth.

DADOUCHOS: The torch-bearer. One of the important priests of the Eleusinian cult. He was next to the Hierophant.

DEIKNYMENA: The sacred objects revealed to the initiates.

DIATEICHISMA: The cross-wall that separated the Sanctuary of Demeter from the city and the akropolis of Eleusis.

DRAGMA: Handful of "civilized nourishment," wheat, etc. Plural, dragmata.

DROMENA: One of the parts of the Mysteries. The sacred pageant representing the myth of Demeter and Persephone formed part of the dromena.

ENCEINTE: An area enclosed by walls.

EPIMELETES: An official, a superintendent, appointed to take care and supervise the conduct of the procession and of the sacrifices.

EPOPTEIA: The highest decree of initiation. The initiates admitted to the highest decree were known as the epoptai. Singular, epoptes.

EUTHYNTERIA: The special top course of a foundation used as a leveling course.

HEROON: A shrine or an area set aside for the worship of a hero or a demigod.

HIERA: The most secret and sacred objects of the Eleusinian cult whose revelation completed initiation.

HIEROKERYX: The Herald of the Eleusinian cult.

HIERONYMY. The prohibition of stating the personal name of the Hierophant.

HIEROPHANT: The high priest of the Eleusinian cult.

IACCHOS: The personification of the enthusiasm and shouting of the pompe. He was pictured to be the leader of the pompe or procession of initiates from Athens to Eleusis. In Roman times he was confused with Bacchus and Dionysos.

IMPLUVIUM: A shallow trough sunk in the floor of the atrium of a

Roman house, made to receive the rain water falling from the central opening of the roof.

ISODOMIC: Regular masonry of squared stones laid in courses of equal height.

KATABASION: An underground crypt or chamber. A crypt below the altar in an Early Christian church.

KERNOS: The sacred vessel of the Eleusinian cult.

KISTE: A cylindrical box or cist in which were kept the Hiera of the Eleusinian cult.

KOSMETES: An official in charge of the youth in Athens; especially of the youth in the gymnasia.

KREPIS and KREPIDOMA: The foundation or platform on which stands a temple or a building of importance.

KYKEON: The special potion of meal and water seasoned with soft mint with which Demeter broke her fast. A similar potion partaken by the initiates in commemoration of the act of the Goddess.

LEGOMENA: Explanations and ritualistic formulae that were spoken in the course of initiation.

LOUTROPHOROS: A highly ornate vessel used to bring from a spring the water for the ante-nuptial bath.

MYSTAGOGOS: The sponsor of a mystes. The person who introduced the initiate and even performed some of the rites of preparation and initiation if he belonged to the sacerdotal families of the Eumolpids and the Kerykes.

MYSTAI: Persons who were being initiated into the Mysteries and whose lips were henceforth sealed as far as the secrets revealed to them were concerned. Singular, mystes.

NAOS: The main and sometimes the only room in the Greek temple. The hall of the Telesterion. Also called *sekos*.

OENOCHOE: Wine-jug.

OMPHALOS: The navel of the earth believed to be in or near the Delphic temple of Apollo.

OPAION: A structure projecting above the roof of a building to admit light and air.

ORTHOSTATE: The lowest course of the walls of a Greek temple. As a rule, it is twice or three times the height of the other wall courses.

PANSPERMIA: Totality of seeds.

PAREDROS: Assistant, or deputy director of a celebration. When used for Dionysos it means he who is enthroned beside Demeter.

PELANOS: Cake made of barley and wheat harvested from the sacred Rharian Plain. It was offered to the Goddesses in the main sacrifice that preceded initiation.

PELIKE: A small two-handled pitcher.

PENTETERIS: Special celebration of the Mysteries every fourth year.

PERIBOLOS: Walls surrounding the precinct of the Goddess to insure privacy.

PLEMOCHOE: A special vessel used in pouring libations for the dead.

POMPE: The procession of initiates and priests from Athens to Eleusis at the beginning of the celebration of the Greater Mysteries.

PROEDRIA: Special place of honor with presidential prerogatives.

PROPYLAEUM: The entrance or gate-building of the enclosure of a temple. When there is more than one gate-way, as at Eleusis, the plural form is used. (Propylaea).

PRORRHESIS: The proclamation made to the pilgrims at the very beginning of the celebration.

PROSTOON: Columniated portico placed in front of a hall or temple.

PROTHYRON: A shallow porch in front of a doorway.

PSEUDO-ISODOMIC: A wall of squared blocks having alternate low and high courses.

PTERON: The colonnade on the flank of a temple.

PYLIS: A small gate in the peribolos wall.

PYLON: Gateway.

SEKOS: The hall of the Telesterion. Same as *naos* and *cella*.

STAMNOS: Water jug.

STEREOBATE: The substructure of a building and especially of a temple.

STROPHION: A headband worn by the Dadouchos.

TELESTERION: The Temple of Demeter at Eleusis where was held the most sacred part of the celebration of the Greater Mysteries.

TELETE: The celebration of the Mysteries, from the verb τελέω, to make perfect.

TEMENOS: A sacred enclosure within which stood one or more temples and other structures of a religious nature and use.

TEMPLUM IN ANTIS: A small temple fronted by an open portico with two columns placed between the ends of the lateral walls or antae.

Allen, T. W., Halliday, W. R., Sikes, E. E. *The Homeric Hymns*, 2nd ed., 1936

Arbesmann, R. P. *Das Fästen bei den Griechen und Römern*, 1929

Blavette, V. "Fouilles d'Éleusis," *BCH*, 8, 1884; and "Légende du plan d'Éleusis," *BCH*, 9, 1885

Cavaignac, E. C. *Le trésor sacré d' Éleusis*, 1908

Delatte, A. *Le Cycéon breuvage rituel des mystères d'Éleusis*, 1955

Davis, P. *Some Eleusinian Building Inscriptions*, 1931

*Deubner, L. *Attische Feste*, 1959

Deubner, O. "Zu den grossen Propyläen von Eleusis," *AM*, 62, 1937

Dieterich, K. *Eine Mithrasliturgie*, 1903

Dittenberger, W. K. F. *Sylloge Inscriptionum Graecarum*, 2nd ed., 1915; 4th ed., 1960

*Evelyn-White, H. G. *Hesiod, the Homeric Hymns and Homerica*, Loeb ed., 1954

*Farnell, L. R. *The Cults of the Greek States*, III, 1907

Foerster, R. *Der Raub und die Ruckkehr der Persephone*, 1874

*Foucart, P. *Les Mystères d'Éleusis*, 1914

Frazer, J. G. *Pausanias' Description of Greece*, 1913

Goudis, D. N. Tὰ μυστήρια τῆς Ἐλευσῖνος, 1935

Graindor, P. *Athènes sous Hadrien*, 1934

Grossman, Betty. *The Eleusinian Gods and Heroes in Greek Art*, unpublished Doctoral Dissertation, Washington University

Guthrie, W. K. C. *Orpheus and Greek Religion*, 1935

Harrison, J. E. *Prolegomena to the Study of Greek Religion*, 2nd ed., 1908

Heberdy, R. "Das Weiherelief des Lakrateides aus Eleusis," *Festschrift Benndorf*, 1898

Hörmann, H. *Die inneren Propyläen von Eleusis*, 1932

Judeich, W. *Topographie von Athen*, 2nd ed., 1931

Kern, O. "Das Kultbild der Göttinnen von Eleusis," *AM*, 17, 1892

———. *Religion der Griechen*, 1926

*Kern, O. *Die griechischen Mysterien der classischen Zeit*, 1927

Körte, A. "Zu den eleusinischen Mysterien," *ArchRW*, 18, 1915

Kontoleon, N. "Megaron," *Mélanges offerts à Octave et Melpo Merlier*

Kourouniotes, K. "Συμβολὴ εἰς τὸ τυπικὸν τῆς ἐν Ἐλευσῖνι λατρείας," *Ephem*, 1898

————. "Τὸ ἐν Λυκοσούρᾳ Μέγαρον τῆς Δεσποίνης," *Ephem*, 1912

————. "Ἐλευσινιακά," *Deltion*, 8, 1923

————. "Εἰς τὸ Ἀνάκτορον τῆς Ἐλευσῖνος," *Deltion*, 10, 1926

*————. "Ἀνασκαφαὶ Ἐλευσῖνος," *Deltion*, 13-16, 1930-1935, Parartema

*————. Ἐλευσίς, Ὁδηγὸς τῶν Ἀνασκαφῶν καὶ τοῦ Μουσείου, 1934

————. *Eleusiniaka*, 1, 1937

*————. "Das eleusinische Heiligtum von den Anfängen bis zur vorperikleischen, Zeit," *ArchRW*, 32, 1935

Kourouniotes, K., Mylonas, G. E. "Excavations at Eleusis," *AJA*, 37, 1933

*Kourouniotes, K., Travlos, J. N. "Τελεστήριον καὶ ναὸς τῆς Δήμητρος," *Deltion*, 15 (1933-1935)

*————. "Συμβολὴ εἰς τὴν οἰκοδομικὴν ἱστορίαν τοῦ Ἐλευσινιακοῦ Τελεστηρίου," *Deltion*, 16, 1933-1935

Lenormant, F. *Monographie de la voie sacrée éleusinienne*, 1864

Lobeck, C. A. *Aglaophamus sive de Theologiae mysticae Graecorum causis*, 1829

Loisy, A. F. *Les mystères paiens et le mystère Chrétien*, 1914

Mommsen, A. *Feste der Stadt Athen*, 1898

Mylonas, G. E. "Eleusis in the Bronze Age," *AJA*, 36, 1932

————. "Ὁ ἐνεπίγραφος ἑτερόστομος ἀμφορεὺς τῆς Ἐλευσῖνος καὶ ἡ Ἑλλαδικὴ γραφή," *Ephem*, 1936

————. "Eleusiniaka," *AJA*, 40, 1936

————. Προϊστορικὴ Ἐλευσίς, 1937

————. *The Hymn to Demeter and Her Sanctuary at Eleusis*, 1942

————. "Early Christian Fathers on the Eleusinian Mysteries," *Athens Yearbook*, 1959

Nilsson, P. M. "Die Eleusinischen Gottheiten," *ArchRW*, 32, 1935

*Nilsson, P. M. *Greek Popular Religion*, 1940
――――. *Geschichte der griechischen Religion*, 1, 1941-1950
*Noack, F. *Eleusis, die baugeschichtliche Entwicklung des Heiligtumes*, 1927
*Orlandos, A. "'Ο ἐν Ἐλευσῖνι ναὸς τῆς Προπυλαίας Ἀρτέμιδος," *Eleusiniaka*, 1
Persson, A. "Der Ursprung der eleusinischen Mysterien," *Arch RW*, 21, 1922
Pfuhl, E. *De Atheniensium pompis sacris*, 1900
Philios, D. "Ἐλευσινιακὰ ἀνάγλυφα καὶ κεφαλὴ ἐξ Ἐλευσῖνος," *Ephem*, 1886
――――. "Τοιχογραφίαι ἀρχαίου οἰκοδομήματος ἐν Ἐλευσῖνι," *Ephem*, 1888; "Ἐπιγραφαὶ ἐξ Ἐλευσῖνος," *Ephem*, 1892
――――. "Ἐπιγραφαὶ ἐξ Ἐλευσῖνος," *BCH*, 19, 1895
――――. "Τό ἐν Ἐλευσῖνι Τελεστήριον," *AM*, 21, 1896
――――. "Eleusiniaka," *JIAN*, 7, 1904
――――. "'Ο Πίναξ τῆς Νι(ι)ννίου," *Ephem*, 1906
*――――. "Ἐλευσίς, μυστήρια, ἐρείπια καὶ μουσεῖον αὐτῆς," 1906
*Picard, Ch. "Sur la patrie et les pérégrinations de Déméter," *REG*, 40, 1927
――――. "La prédiction de Déméter aux Éleusiniens," *R.Phil*, 4, 1930
*――――. "Les luttes primitives d'Athénes et d'Éleusis," *RHist*, 166, 1931
Pringsheim, G. H. *Archäologische Beiträge zur Geschichte des Eleusinischen Kults*, 1905
Reinach, S. *Cultes, mythes et religions*, 1905-1923
Rohde, E. *Psyche*, 1925
*Roussel, P. "L'initiation préalable et le symbole Éleusinien," *BCH*, 54, 1930
*Rubensohn, O. *Die Mysterienheiligtumer in Eleusis und Samothrake*, 1892
――――. "Kerchnos," *AM*, 23, 1898
――――. "Eleusinische Beiträge," *AM*, 24, 1899
*――――. "Das Weihehaus von Eleusis und sein Allerheiligstes," *Jahrbuch*, 70, 1955
Ruhland, Max. *Die Eleusinischen Göttinnen*, 1901

Skias, A. "Παναρχαία Ἐλευσινιακὴ Νεκρόπολις," *Ephem*, 1898 and 1912

———. "Ἐπιγραφαὶ Ἐλευσῖνος," Ephem, 1900

———. "Ἐλευσινιακαὶ κεραμογραφίαι," *Ephem*, 1901

Strube, C. *Studien über den Bilderkreis von Eleusis*, 1870

Svoronos, J. N. "Ἑρμηνεία τῶν μνημείων τοῦ Ἐλευσινιακοῦ μυστικοῦ κύκλου," and "Ἑρμηνεία τοῦ ἐξ Ἐλευσῖνος πίνακος," *JIAN*, 4, 1901

———. "Ἐλευσινιακά," *JIAN*, 8, 1905

Threpsiades, J. C. "Decree in Honor of Euthydemos of Eleusis," *Hesperia*, 8, 1939

*Travlos, J. N. "The Topography of Eleusis," *Hesperia*, 18, 1949

*———. Τὸ Ἀνάκτορον τῆς Ἐλευσῖνος, *Ephem*, 1951

———. Πολεοδομικὴ ἐξέλιξις τῶν Ἀθηνῶν, 1960

Toepffer, I. *Attische Genealogie*, 1889

Wehrli, F. R. "Die Mysterien von Eleusis," *ArchRW*, 31, 1914

Wilamowitz, K. von M. *Der Glaube der Hellenen*, II, 1932

Willoughby, H. R. *Pagan Regeneration*, 1929

Ziehen, L. and Prott, J. *Leges Graecorum sacrae*, 1906

ONLY *the most significant references are included for subjects to which very frequent reference is made, for example, Athens, Eleusis, Demeter, Persephone, Kore, Temple of Demeter.*

abacus, of columns of Lesser Propylaea, 158

abduction, of Persephone, 102, 258; in the pageant, 261-262

Achmet Aga, proprietor of Eleusis, 10

admission, to Mysteries, 77, 155, 236, 244, 247, 248, 282

Adrastos, in Eleusis, 123, 147n19

adyton, of temples, 69, 317

Aegean, sea, 3, 23

Aelian, on Anaktoron, 86

"Agelastos Petra," *see* "Mirthless Stone"

Aghios Kosmas, houses of, 35n31

Aghyrmos, 247

Aglauros, 234

Agora, excavations, 247; inscriptions, 225n3; sculpture, 189n9, 199, 203n47

Agorakritos, statue attributed to, 193-n21, 195

Agra or Agrai, site of Lesser Mysteries, 215, 240; precinct at, 220

Aidoneus, 4, 6

Aigeus, King of Athens, 27

Aigina, cult objects transferred to, 90

Aischines, on Eleusinian functionaries, 235n57; on festival of "kana," 300-n40

Aischylos, divulging secrets, 227; and vestments, 87, 209, 230n27

aithousa, of Megaron B, 35

akademy, propyleum at, 156; temple at, 277

Akarnanian, youth punished, 225

Akropolis of Athens, 25, 26, 236, 246, 247, 278; figurines from, 66; Periklean buildings, 113, 127; sacked by Persians, 89, 90, 106

Alaric, destroys Sanctuary, 8, 186

Albanian families, established at Eleusis, 9, 10

Alexander the Great, destroys Thebes, 257; death of, 152; in sculpture, 199

Alexandria, 288, 301, 302; Christians of, 312; Eleusis in, 300; mysteries of, 304; Synthema devised at, 302

Alexandrian, Goddess, 207

Alkibiades, accused, 224, 239n79; restores pompe, 259

altars, 79, 83, 143, 205; Archaic (Z13), 70, 71, 72, 73, 170; of Artemis, 169; of Demeter, 5, 39, 47, 57, 58; of Demeter and Kore, 64, 68, 90, 125; eschara, 104, 169, 170; of Demeter in Lykosoura, 217; of Dionysos in Athens, 227; in house of Kerykes, 172; in outer court, 168-170; in Sacred House, 59; in south court, 137; of classical times, 137; of Triptolemos, 185; Peisistratean, 90, 91

Amaseia, 311

American School of Classical Studies, 13

amphiktyons, uphold claims of Athens, 21

amphiktyony, of the north, 19

amphora, as urn, 61; for pot-burials, 74, 75; by "Chimaira painter," 76, 208; by "Polyphemos painter," 75, 208; Geometric, 204; inscribed Mycenaean, 50, 51

Anaktoron, 51, 205, 317; burned by Persians, 89; discussed, 83-88; entered by Hierophant, 230; function, 84; Hiera kept in, 69, 84, 87, 88; Kimonian, 111, 112, 113; Kretan repositories and, 16, 17; omphalos in, 217, 218, 219; opaion over, 112, 114, 115, 117, 119; Peisistratean, 82, 83, 111; Periklean, 114, 120, 121; Solonian, 69, 70; works of art in, 189

anassa, 88

anathyrosis, 81, 124, 317

anax, 85, 88

ancestral worship, 62, 63

Andania, mysteries of, 41, 191, 245, 253, 298, 301

Andokides, accused, 225, 272, 306; on exegetai, 235n55; on kerykes, 234-n50; on showing Hiera, 299; on Solon's law, 63, 64n21

Androklos, 41

Andron, 27

anthemia from Peisistratean Telesterion, 80; from house of kerykes, 172

ILLUSTRATIONS

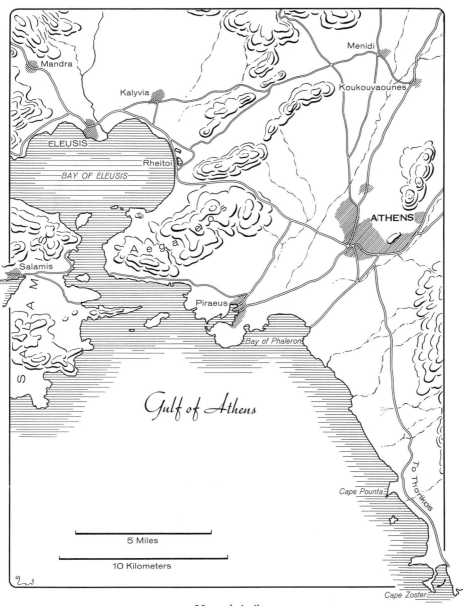

Mandra

Menidi

Kalyvia

Koukouvaounes

ELEUSIS

Rheitoi

BAY OF ELEUSIS

A e g a

ATHENS

Salamis

S A L A M I S

Piraeus

Bay of Phaleron

Gulf of Athens

To Thorikos

Cape Pounta

5 Miles

10 Kilometers

Cape Zoster

1. Map of Attika

K7

3. Airview of the outer court and its structures, the Greater and the Lesser Propylaea, and the Ploutonion

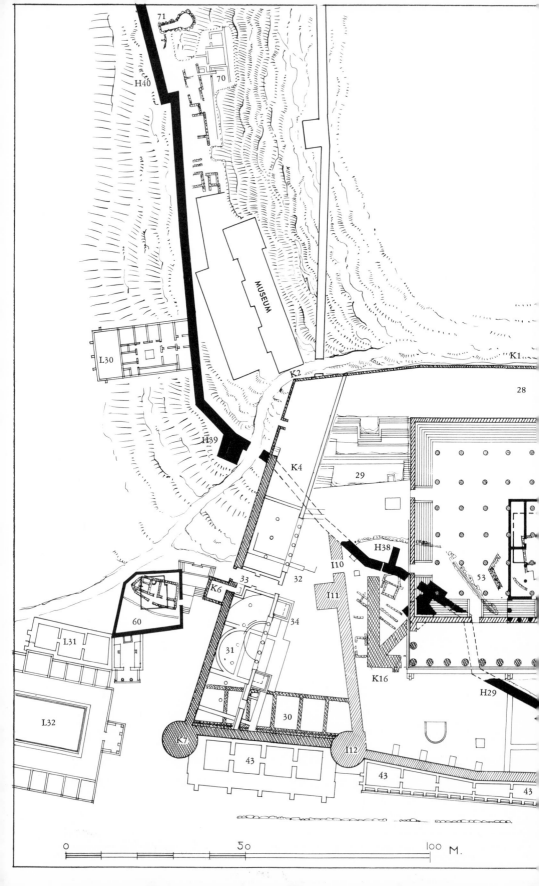

71

H40

70

MUSEUM

L30

K1

K2

28

H39

K4

29

I10

H38

53

I11

33   32

K6

34

K16

60

H29

L31

31

30

L32

K7

I12

43

43

43

0   50   100 M.

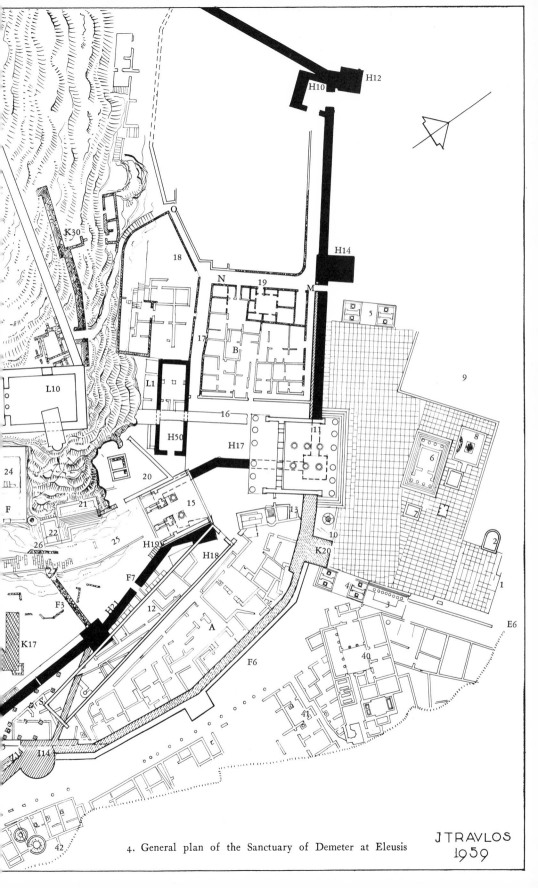

4. General plan of the Sanctuary of Demeter at Eleusis

JTRAVLOS
1959

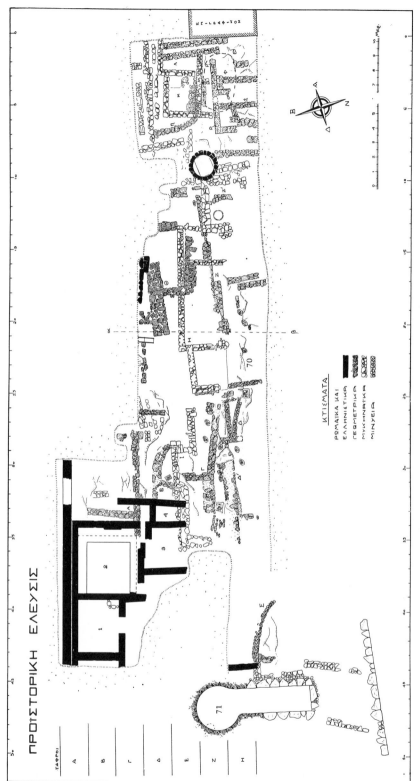

ΠΡΟΙΣΤΟΡΙΚΗ ΕΛΕΥΣΙΣ

ΤΑΦΡΟΙ

KTIΣMATA

ΡΩΜΑΙΚΑ ΚΑΙ
ΕΛΛΗΝΙΣΤΙΚΑ
ΓΕΩΜΕΤΡΙΚΑ
ΜΥΚΗΝΑΙΚΑ
ΜΙΝΥΕΙΑ

5. Plan of the prehistoric village on the South Slope (By J. N. Travlos)

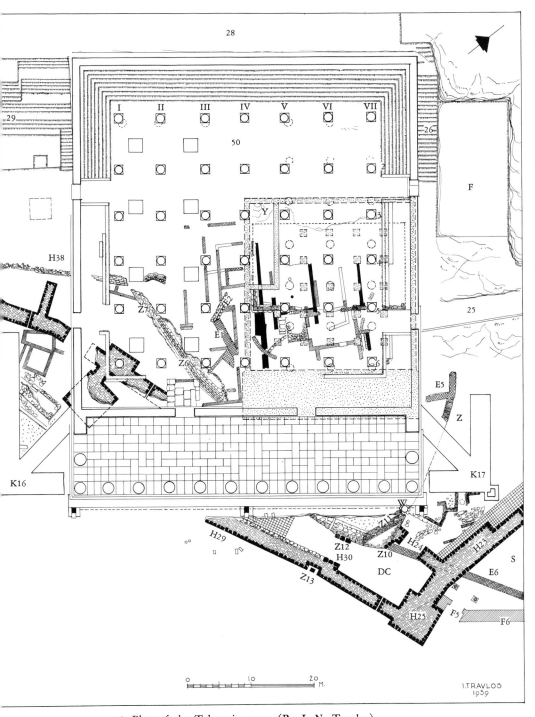

6. Plan of the Telesterion area (By J. N. Travlos)

7. a. Built grave of the closing years of the Middle Helladic period;
b. Terracotta larnax of the 5th century B.C.; c. Pot burial

8. Mycenaean chamber tomb with Geometric burial

9. Typical cremation burial of Geometric times (for the urn cf. Fig. 86b)

10. Pot-burial Γ 10 of Late Geometric times

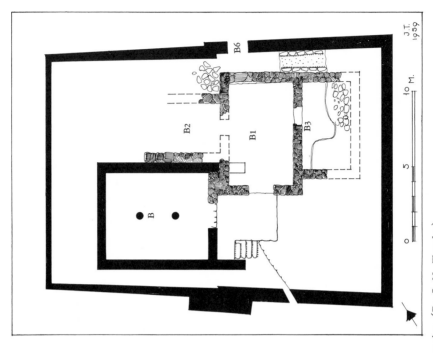

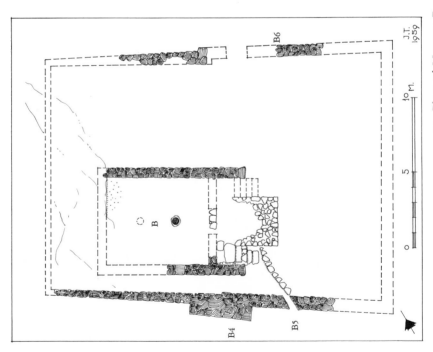

11. Plans of Megaron B and of extension (By J. N. Travlos)

12. General view of remains below the floor of the southeast section of the Periklean Telesterion

13. Early remains below the Archaic Telesterion

14. Retaining terrace walls. a. Geometric. b. Early Archaic

15. Remains of South Geometric retaining wall (E1) and stairway (E2)

16. Foundation of south retaining wall of the Archaic terrace

17. Area around Peisistratean inner gate

19. Stepped podium of the
Early Archaic period (Z14)

18. r. Niche in Archaic terrace wall; W. Area of
"Kallichoron" well; c. Foundations of
Philonian Stoa and mason's mark

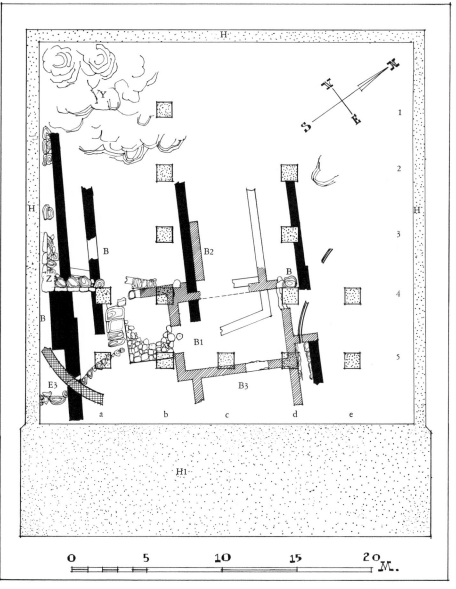

20. Plan of structures below the Peisistratean Telesterion (H)
(After drawing by J. N. Travlos)

B, solid black and hatched, Mycenaean. E₃, cross-hatched, Geometric. Z, stone contours, Archaic. H, dotted, Peisistratean. Dotted squares, Peisistratean column foundations.

21. Ram's head from the
Peisistratean Telesterion

22. Corner of Peisistratean tower H14

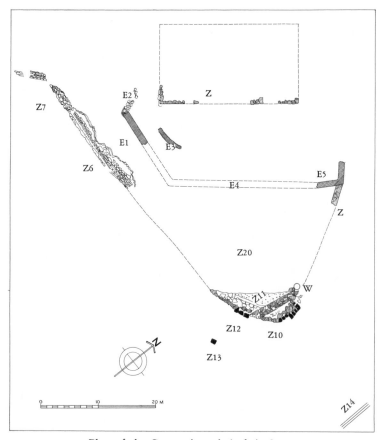

23. Plan of the Geometric and Archaic Sanctuary

24. Remains in the area of the "hollow road"

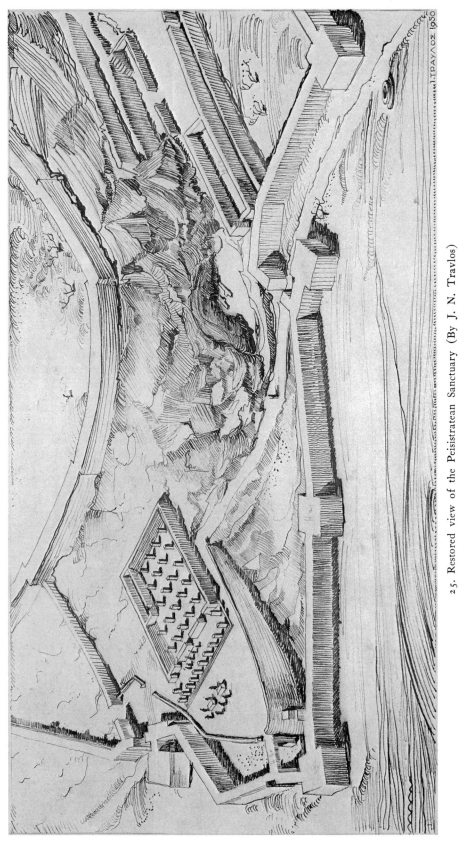

25. Restored view of the Peisistratean Sanctuary (By J. N. Travlos)

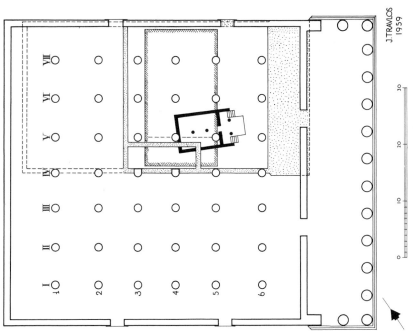

ELEUSIS TEMPLE OF DEMETER AND KORE = TELESTERION

A TIME OF SOLON

B TIME OF PEISISTRATOS

C TIME OF KIMON

D TIME OF PERICLES (PLAN OF IKTINOS)

E FROM THE TIME OF PERICLES TO THE ROMAN PERIOD

J.T. 1959

26. Plans of the Telesteria of the Historic era
(By J. N. Travlos)

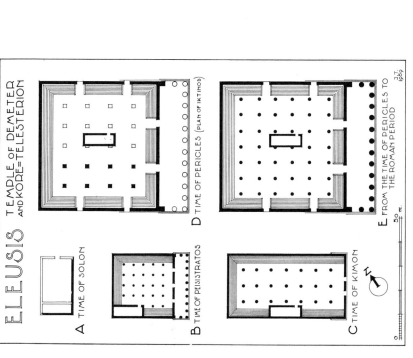

J. TRAVLOS 1959

27. Plan showing the relative position of the Anaktoron
in the Telesteria (By J. N. Travlos)

28. Kimonian reconstruction of the "Persian Breach"

30. Amphora by the "Chimaera painter" (Height 0.53m.)

29. The proto-attik amphora of Eleusis, by the "Polyphemos painter" (Height 1.42m.)

31. The "Asty Gates"

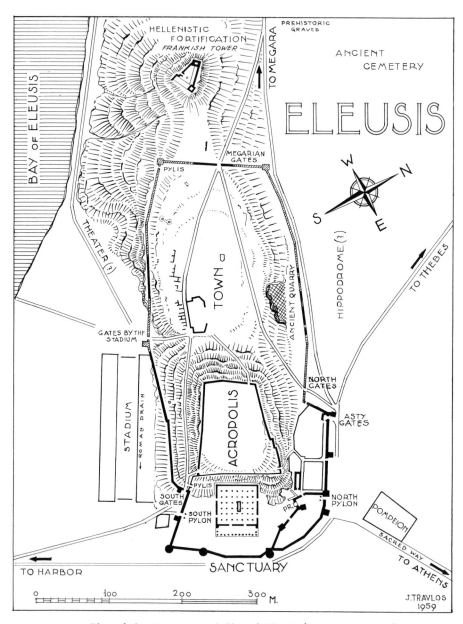

32. Plan of the Sanctuary and City of Eleusis (By J. N. Travlos)

33. The "Kallichoron" well of Pausanias

34. Fleeing maiden from the pediment
of the Sacred House

35. Kimonian Gate F5

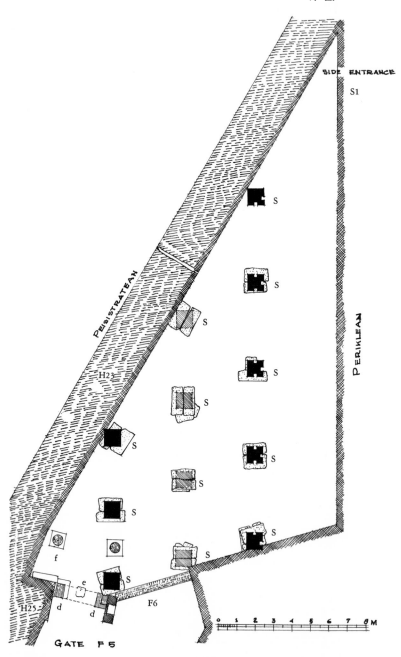

H 21

SIDE ENTRANCE

S1

PEISISTRATEAN

PERIKLEAN

H23

S

S

S

S

S

S

S

S

S

f

e

S

H25

d

d

F6

GATE F5

0 1 2 3 4 5 6 7 8 M

36. Plan of the Kimonian Gate F5 and of the Periklean storage building (after Noack)

37. West section of the Telesterion viewed from south to north

38. West section of the Telesterion viewed from north to south

39. Periklean peribolos wall I14 to I12

40. Fourth century peribolos wall with terminal round tower K7

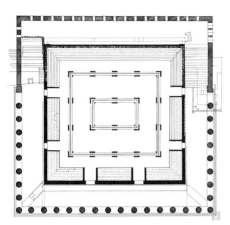

41a. Noack's plan of the
Iktinian Telesterion

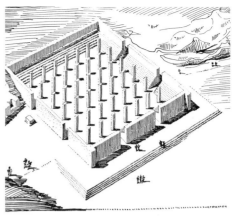

41b. Periklean Telesterion with its platform
(Kourouniotes' and Travlos' restoration)

42. Detail of round tower K7

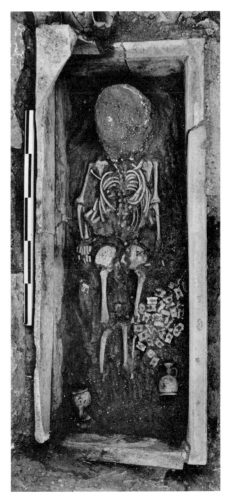

43. Larnax burial θ26
from west cemetery

44. General view of the Periklean Telesterion. In the foreground the Stoa of Philon

45. South end of the Inner Sacred Way

46. Fourth century tower K6 and south Pylon

47. Rock-cut stepped platform in the south court

48. Rock-cut stairway along northwest corner of the Periklean Telesterion

49. Rock-cut stepped platform No. 21

50. The Ploutonion. In the foreground the Lesser Propylaea

51. North chamber of the Ploutonion

52. Stairway outside the north chamber
of the Ploutonion

53. Remains of the Hellenistic city and the "Frankish tower" in the distance

54. The Lesser Propylaea (right foreground) with the Greater Propylaea
and the Outer Court beyond it

55. Capital from the prothyron of the Lesser Propylaea

56. Caryatid from the Lesser Propylaea

57. Architrave-frieze of the Lesser Propylaea

58. General view of the Eleusinian hill from the Outer Court (in the foreground)

59. Outer Court with stairway to Greater Propylaea

60. Re-assembled pediment of the Triumphal Arch

61. The Temple of Artemis Propylaia and corner of the Greater Propylaea
(Courtesy of Professor A. K. Orlandos)

62. The *eschara*

63. Demeter and Persephone. Relief
in the Museum of Eleusis

64. Building inscription in
the Museum of Eleusis

65. Head of Eubouleus. National Museum of Athens

66. Statuette of a sacrificial pig

68. The Grand Relief of Eleusis

67. Stele of Demeter and Hekate

69. The Rheitoi inscription

70. Stele of Persephone (?) as Hydranos

71. The Lakratides Relief

72. Demeter on the "Mirthless Stone" approached by votaries

73. Demeter (?) with Kore (?) on her lap

74. Votive relief of the Mission of Triptolemos

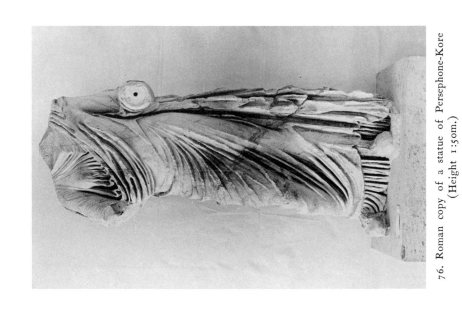

76. Roman copy of a statue of Persephone-Kore
(Height 1:50m.)

75. Statue of Demeter attributed to Agorakritos

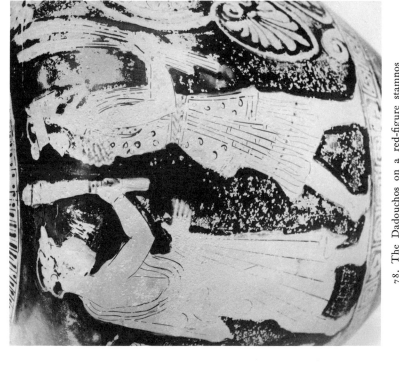

78. The Dadouchos on a red-figure stamnos
in the Museum of Eleusis

77. Archaistic statue of maiden (Height 0.75m.)

79. Statue of Antinoos
(Height 1.67m.)

80. Statuette of a boy-initiate
(Height 0.24m.)

81. Representation on the Pourtales vase in the British Museum

82. Marble sarcophagus with the Kalydonian Boar-hunt

83. Compositions on the Lovatelli urn

84. Relief on the Torre Nova sarcophagus

85. Representation on the Pantikapaion Hydria in the Hermitage

86. Geometric vases from the cemeteries

87. Eleusinian kernoi

88. The Niinnion tablet
Upper row: 5, 6, 7, 8, 9
Lower row: 10, 11, 12, 13